Frederick William Faber

The Foot of the Cross or the Sorrows of Mary

Frederick William Faber

The Foot of the Cross or the Sorrows of Mary

ISBN/EAN: 9783337201630

Printed in Europe, USA, Canada, Australia, Japan

Cover: Foto ©Lupo / pixelio.de

More available books at **www.hansebooks.com**

THE

FOOT OF THE CROSS:

OR,

The Sorrows of Mary.

BY

FREDERICK WILLIAM FABER, D.D.

PRIEST OF THE ORATORY OF ST. PHILIP NERI.

"Tanto dolore compassa est Virgo, ut inexplicabile sit linguæ angelicæ; et solus Jesus dicere potuit, qui solus potuit maternos penetrare dolores."
—*St. Bernardino of Siena.*

NEW EDITION.

BURNS AND OATES.

LONDON:	NEW YORK:
GRANVILLE MANSIONS,	CATHOLIC PUBLICATION SOCIETY CO.
28 ORCHARD STREET, W.	9 BARCLAY STREET.

1886

TO

THE LADY GEORGIANA FULLERTON,

This Volume

IS INSCRIBED,

IN AFFECTIONATE REMEMBRANCE

OF

A SEASON OF DARKNESS,

WHICH GOD CONSECRATED FOR HIMSELF

BY A MORE THAN COMMON SORROW.

PREFACE.

THIS Treatise was sketched for the first time at St. Wilfrid's in the summer of 1847, more than ten years ago. It has however been several times revised, and more than once entirely recast. It was not, however, finally settled in its present shape until the spring of 1855; for not till then was the Author satisfied with the consistency of our Lady's position throughout, nor with its adaptation to the requirements of scholastic theology. The Author has had the completed Treatise by him for some time, as the stage of preparation, in which his materials were for a work on the Passion, rendered it necessary for him to ascertain, how much of that ground would be occupied by the Dolours, and in what manner; and it appeared better to compose the present Treatise, and even finish it for the press, before advancing his book on the Passion into another stage of its preparation, in order that the ultimate harmony between the two might be the more complete. But as the time was not come for the publication of the Dolours in its predetermined place in the series of books which the Author has planned, it was laid by until its turn should arrive.

It is now twelve years since the Author became a tertiary of the ancient Order of the Servites, and so bound to advance, as much as he might be able to do so, the Devotion to the

Seven Dolours; and he has always confessed to himself the obligation. When the London Oratory was founded in 1849, the Rosary of the Seven Dolours was adopted as one of its public characteristic practices, and other measures were taken with success to propagate the devotion. There seems some warrant for believing that graces and blessings have accompanied this humble apostolate of that practice so dear to our Blessed Mother.

The Treatise is now submitted with much diffidence to those who love our Lady's honour, and the spread of all devotion to her, with a hope that they may feel less disappointment in reading it than the Author has done in writing it; and may not be haunted, as he has been throughout, with an ideal which he could not reach, and a vexation that, when he had said all he could in the best way he could, it should always seem so little to be said of Mary, that it almost appeared as if it had better not have been said at all. The thought of the love that prompted the endeavour is, however, some compensation for the imperfection of its success.

THE LONDON ORATORY,
FEAST OF ST. THOMAS OF CANTERBURY,
1857.

CONTENTS.

CHAPTER I.
THE MARTYRDOM OF MARY.

SEC.	PAGE
I.—The Immensity of Our Lady's Dolours	6
II.—Why God permitted Our Lady's Dolours	19
III.—The Fountains of Our Lady's Dolours	28
IV.—The Characteristics of Our Lady's Dolours	41
V.—How Our Lady could Rejoice in her Dolours	52
VI.—The Way in which the Church puts Our Lady's Dolours before us	56
VII.—The Spirit of Devotion to Our Lady's Dolours	59

CHAPTER II.
THE FIRST DOLOUR.

THE PROPHECY OF ST. SIMEON. . . . 69

CHAPTER III.
THE SECOND DOLOUR.

THE FLIGHT INTO EGYPT 104

CHAPTER IV.
THE THIRD DOLOUR.

THE THREE DAYS' LOSS 152

CHAPTER V.

THE FOURTH DOLOUR.

MEETING JESUS WITH THE CROSS 198

CHAPTER VI.

THE FIFTH DOLOUR.

THE CRUCIFIXION 245

CHAPTER VII.

THE SIXTH DOLOUR.

THE TAKING DOWN FROM THE CROSS 293

CHAPTER VIII.

THE SEVENTH DOLOUR.

THE BURIAL OF JESUS 338

CHAPTER IX.

THE COMPASSION OF MARY.

SEC.
- I.—The Divine Purpose of Mary's Compassion . . . 379
- II.—The Nature of her Compassion 392
- III.—The Actual Effects of her Compassion 400
- IV.—Our Compassion with her Compassion 407
- V.—The Passion and Compassion Compared 413
- VI.—The Seeming Excess of the Compassion 415
- VII.—The Measures of Mary's Compassion 417

THE
FOOT OF THE CROSS.

CHAPTER I.

THE MARTYRDOM OF MARY.

THE beauty of Jesus is inexhaustible. Like the Vision of God in heaven, it is ever diversified, yet always the same, always cherished as an old and familiar joy, yet ever surprising and refreshing the spirit as being, in truth, perpetually new. He is beautiful always, beautiful everywhere, in the disfigurement of the Passion as well as in the splendour of the Resurrection, amid the horrors of the Scourging as well as amid the indescribable attractions of Bethlehem. But above all things our Blessed Lord is beautiful in His Mother. If we love Him we must love her. We must know her in order to know Him. As there is no true devotion to His Sacred Humanity which is not mindful of His Divinity, so there is no adequate love of the Son which disjoins Him from His Mother, and lays her aside as a mere instrument, whom God chose as He might choose an inanimate thing, without regard to its sanctity or moral fitness. Now it is our daily task to love Jesus more and more. Year follows year; the old course of feasts comes round; the well-known divisions of the Christian year overtake us, make their impression upon us, and go their way. How we have multiplied

Christmases, and Holy Weeks, and Whitsuntides, and there has been something or other in each of them which makes them lie like dates in our mind! We have spent some of them in one place, and some in another, some under one set of circumstances, and some under another. Some of them, all thanks to God! have been distinguished by remarkable openings of heart in our interior life, such as to change or to intensify our devotion, and materially influence our secret relations with God. The foundations of many buildings, which did not rise above ground till long afterwards, have been laid almost unconsciously in those times. Yet, whatever may have been the changes which these feasts have brought or seen, they have always found us busy at one and the same work, trying to love Jesus more and more: and through all these changes, and in all this perseverance at our one work, unerring experience has told us that we never advance more rapidly in love of the Son than when we travel by the Mother, and that what we have built most solidly in Jesus has been built with Mary. There is no time lost in seeking Him if we go at once to Mary; for He is always there; always at home. The darkness in His mysteries becomes light when we hold it to her light, which is His light as well. She is the short road to Him. She has the "grant entry" to Him. She is His Esther, and speedy and full are the answers to the petitions which her hand presents.

But Mary is a world which we cannot take in all at one glance. We must devote ourselves to particular mysteries. We must set aside certain regions of this world of grace, and concentrate ourselves upon them. We must survey them and map them accurately before we pass on to other regions, and then we shall learn much which a general view would have omitted to notice, and store our souls with spiritual riches, riches both of knowledge and of love, which will draw us evermore into closer union with our dearest Lord. As God's blessed will still persists in keeping us alive, and for

His own gracious purposes detaining us amid all this cold weariness and these dejecting possibilities of sin, let us at least determine to occupy ourselves with nothing but God; for we have long since learned that there is truly no other occupation which is worth our while. He has a thousand Edens still, even in the bleak expanse of this salt steppe of a world, where we may work, to the sound of running waters, not without colloquies with Him in the cool time of the day; and we may wander from Eden to Eden, either as the weakness or the strength of our love impels us. For the present let us shut ourselves up in the garden of Mary's sorrows. It is one of God's choicest Edens, and we cannot work there otherwise than under the shadow of His presence, nor without the love of Jesus taking a marvellous possession of our souls. For love of Jesus is in the very viewless air of the place, in the smell of the upturned soil, in the fragrance of the flowers, in the rustling of the leaves, in the songs of the birds, in the shining of the sun, in the quiet tunes of the waterfalls as they dash down its rocky places. There for awhile, for our Lord's love, we will enclose ourselves as in a cloistered place, and let the world, in which we are of no great importance, and which is even of less importance to us than we are to it, miss us for a season from our post.

The law of the Incarnation is a law of suffering. Our Blessed Lord was the man of sorrows, and by suffering He redeemed the world. His Passion was not a mystery detached from the rest of His life, but only the fitting and congruous end of it. Calvary was not unlike Bethlehem and Nazareth. It exceeded them in degree; it did not differ from them in kind. The whole of the Three-and-Thirty Years was spent in consistent suffering, though it was of various kinds, and not of uniform intensity. This same law of suffering, which belongs to Jesus, touches all who come nigh Him, and, in proportion to their holiness, envelops them, and claims them wholly for itself. The Holy Innocents were, in the counsels of God, simply our Lord's contemporaries, but that is similitude enough to plunge them in a sea of suffering, and for His sake their fresh lives must bleed away in their distracted mothers' arms, to be followed by eternal crowns and palms: a happy merchandise, a huge fortune swiftly made, and then so marvellously secured! The same law wound itself round each of the apostles upon whom the indescribably blessed choice of the Incarnate Word had fallen. It was a cross to Peter and his brother, a sword to Paul, hard stones to James, the flaying-knife to Bartholomew, and the boiling oil and the long years of wearisome delay to John. But in whatever shape it came outwardly, inwardly it was always suffering. It went with them into all lands. It overshadowed them in all vicissitudes. It walked with them along the Roman roads, as if it was their guardian angel; it strode by the side of their uneasy galleys on the stormy waters of the Mediterranean. They were apostles. They must be like their Lord. They must enter into the cloud, and the darkness of the eclipse must fall upon them on the top of some Calvary or other from Rome to Bactria, from Spain to Hindostan. The same law has environed the martyrs of all ages. Their passions have been living shadows of the great Passion, and the blood they shed mingled its kindred stream with the Precious Blood of their Redeemer, the King of Martyrs. So with the saints. Whether they have been bishops or doctors, virgins or matrons, seculars or religious, unusual love and unusual grace have always reached them in the shape of unusual trial and unusual suffering. They too must be drawn into the cloud, and they will come out of it with their faces shining, because they have seen, and seen closely, the Face of the Crucified. It is so in its measure with all the elect. They must stand at least within the fringes of the dark cloud, or it must overshadow them in transit, perhaps more than once, in order to secure the salvation of their souls by giving them at least an adequate likeness to their Lord. What then must we think of His Mother, who came nighest to Him of all?

It can plainly be no wonder if she shall suffer more than any one but Himself. The immensity of her sorrows will neither be a distress nor a surprise to us, but rather the obvious conclusion from all we know of the grand mystery of the Incarnation. The amount of her sufferings will be the index of the magnificence of His love for her. The depth of her pains will come the nearest of all things to fathom the abyss of her love for Him. Her far-rolling sea of sorrow will measure the grandeur of her holiness. The loftiness of her divine Maternity will raise her dolours close up to His gracious Passion. Her sinlessness will almost seem to enclose it within the same life-giving law of expiation. Her union with Him will render her Compassion inseparable from His Passion, even while for a thousand reasons it is so manifestly distinguishable from it. The Woman clothed with the Sun will be wrapped round and round with the bright darkness of that same terrible destiny which He vouchsafed first to appoint and then to accept as the great law of His Incarnation. We must be prepared to find Mary's dolours beyond the reach of our imagination, above the possibility of our description. We can only gaze upon them with such instruments as faith and love supply, and note the beauty and the strangeness of many phenomena which we can only imperfectly comprehend. Especially can we thus increase our devotion to the Passion, many unknown regions of which are momentarily lighted up for us by the contact of her dolours, just as in the occultation of Jupiter, the luminous tear-like planet, as it touches the dark portion of the moon, scatters a momentary line of light along the unseen edge, like a revelation, and then by its disappearance proves the reality of that which we cannot see.

But, before we ask St. John the Evangelist to hold us by the hand, and go down with us into the depths of that broken heart which he, the saint of the Sacred Heart, knew

better than others, we must take a general view of our
Blessed Lady's dolours, just as we familiarise ourselves with
the general outlines of the geography of a country before
we endeavour to master its details. There are seven points
on which it is necessary for us to have some information
before we can study with advantage the separate mysteries
of her surpassing sorrow. We must know, as far at least
as lies in our power, the immensity of her dolours, why God
permitted them, what were the fountains of them, and what
their characteristics, how it was that she could rejoice in
them, in what way the Church puts them before us, and
what should be the spirit of our devotion to them. These
are questions which need answering, and the answers to
them, however imperfect, will serve as a sort of introduction
to the subject.

SECTION I.

THE IMMENSITY OF OUR LADY'S DOLOURS.

When we think how we can best describe our Lady's
dolours, it gradually dawns upon us that they are in fact
indescribable. We see but the outside show of them, and
there are no adequate figures by which even that can be
represented. He who looks over the wide Atlantic sees
a waste of waters with a white horizon on every side; but
that waste of waters tells nothing either of the multitudinous
manifold life which it contains within its bosom, nor of the
fairy-like ocean-gardens of vivid painted weeds, its woods of
purple, deep thickets of most golden green, grottoes of fantastic rock, with tufted palm-like yellow trees overhanging,
and the blue water flowing all round, park-like vistas of
glossy, spotted, arborescent herbs, or leagues on leagues of
rose-coloured forests teeming with strange, beautiful, heretofore unimaginable life. So is it with the sea of sorrows
which rolls over the secret depths of the Immaculate Heart

of the Mother of God. What we see is amazing, yet it hardly indicates what is below. How then shall we say what her woes are like? Holy men have tried to do so, and they have done it by calling her the co-redemptress of the world, and speaking of her sorrows as they blended with the Precious Blood, and the two made but one sacrifice for the sins of the world. There is a deep truth, and a most substantial one, hidden under these great words, and yet they may easily be understood in a sense in which they would not be true. They are the expressions of an excellent devotion, striving to assist the feebleness of our understandings to a true conception of Mary's grandeurs. They are accuracies, not exaggerations. Yet they need cautious wording and careful explanation. We shall consider them in the ninth chapter; and in the rest of the treatise we shall travel to our end by some other road, not only because we dare not trust ourselves to such a method of procedure, but also because it is against our habits and predilections, and in matters of devotion what does not come natural is not persuasive. We will prefer therefore to approximate to our subject, inevitably falling short, rather than to overshoot it, making things indistinct by too strong a light, and dissatisfying by a feeling of unreality, like a sunset in the hands of an unskilful painter. We shall come at last to the same end in a manner which is not only most fitted to our own infirmity, but also most calculated to win the confidence of our readers.

The first thing, then, which strikes us about our Lady's dolours is their immensity, not in its literal meaning, but in the sense in which we commonly use it with reference to created things. It is to her sorrows that the Church applies those words of Jeremias,* O all ye that pass by the way, attend, and see if there be any sorrow like to my sorrow. To what shall I compare thee, and to what shall I liken thee, O daughter of Jerusalem? To what shall I equal thee that

* Lament. i. and ii.

I may comfort thee, O virgin daughter of Sion? for great as the sea is thy broken-heartedness: who shall heal thee? Mary's love is spoken of as that which many waters could not quench. In like manner the saints and doctors of the Church have spoken of the greatness of her sorrows. St. Anselm* says, Whatever cruelty was exercised upon the bodies of the martyrs was light, or rather it was as nothing, compared to the cruelty of Mary's passion. St. Bernardine of Siena † says that so great was the dolour of the Blessed Virgin that if it was subdivided and parcelled out among all creatures capable of suffering, they would perish instantly. An angel ‡ revealed to St. Bridget that if our Lord had not miraculously supported His Mother it would not have been possible for her to live through her martyrdom. It would be easy to multiply similar passages, both from the revelations of the saints and the writings of the doctors of the Church.

But the immensity of Mary's dolours is especially shown in this, that they exceeded all martyrdoms. Not only was there never any martyr, however prolonged and complicated his tortures may have been, who equalled her in suffering; but the united agonies of all the martyrs, variety and intensity all duly allowed for, did not approach to the anguish of her martyrdom. No thoughtful man will ever speak lightly of the mystery of bodily pain. Possibly in that respect his own experience may have shamed him into wisdom. It was in a great measure through bodily pain that the world was redeemed; and is it not mainly by the same process that we ourselves are being sanctified at this hour? It is the unerring justice of God which places on the heads of the martyrs that peculiar crown which belongs to those who, in the heroism of physical endurance, have laid down their lives for Christ.

---

* De excell. Virg. cap. 5.
† Ap Novatum i. 359. Also Sinischalchi, Preface to his Dolori di Maria, p. xx.
‡ In sermone angelico ap Revelat. S. Birgittæ, c. 17.

But even in respect of corporal anguish Mary exceeded the martyrs. Her whole being was drenched with bitterness. The swords in her soul reached to every nerve and fibre in her frame, and we can hardly doubt but that her sinless body, with its exquisite perfections, was delicately framed for suffering beyond all others but that of her Son. Moreover, in the case of the martyrs, they had long looked at their flesh as their enemy and their hindrance on the heavenward road. They had punished it, mortified it, cruelly kept it under, until they had come to regard it with a kind of holy hatred. Hers was sinless. It was the marvellous mine, the purest, sublimest matter creation could supply out of which our Lord's Sacred Flesh and Precious Blood had been obtained, and she could know nothing of that exulting revenge with which heroic sanctity triumphs in the sufferings of the flesh. But what is the grand support of the martyrs in their tortures? It is that their minds are full of light and radiance. It is that their inward eye is bent on Jesus, by whose beauty and glory they are fortified. It is this which puts out the fires, or makes them pleasant as the flapping of the warm wind in spring. It is this which makes the scourges fall so soft and smooth, and causes the lash to cheer like wine. It is this which makes the sharpness of the steel so dull to the divided flesh and wounded fibres. What is within them is stronger than that which is without them. It is not that their agonies are not real, but that they are tempered, counteracted, almost metamorphosed, by the succours which their soul supplies, from the influx of grace and love wherewith their generous Master is at that moment filling them to overflowing. But where is Mary to look with her soul's eye for consolation? Nay, her soul's eye must look where her body's eye is fixed already. It is bent on Jesus; and it is that very sight which is her torture. She sees His Human Nature; and she is the mother, the mother beyond all other mothers, loving as never mother loved before, as all mothers together could not love, if they might compact their myriad loves into one intensest nameless act. He is her Son, and such a Son, and in so marvellous a way her Son. He is her treasure and her all. What a fund of misery, keen, quick, deadly, unequalled, was there in that sight! And yet there was far more than that. There was His Divine Nature.

We talk of mothers making idols of their sons, that is, worshipping them, turning them from creatures into creators, regarding them as truly their last end and true beatitude, so giving their hearts to them as they have no right to give them to any one but God. This Mary could not do, and yet in another sense might well do. For Jesus could be no idol, and yet must of necessity be worshipped as the Eternal God. None saw this as Mary did. No angel worshipped Him with such sublimely abject adoration as she did. No saint, not even the dear Magdalen, ever hung over His feet with such mortal yearning, with such human fondness. Yes! He is God—she saw that through the darkness of the eclipse. But then the blood, the spittings, the earth-stains, the unseemly scars, the livid, many-coloured bruises, what did all that mean on a person only and eternally divine? It is vain to think of giving a name to such misery as then flooded her soul. Jesus, the joy of the martyrs, is the executioner of His mother. Twice over, to say the least, if not a third time also, did He crucify her, once by His Human Nature, once by His Divine, if indeed Body and Soul did not make two crucifixions from the Human Nature only. No martyrdom was ever like to this. No given number of martyrdoms approach to a comparison with it. It is a sum of sorrow which material units, ever so many added together, ever so often multiplied, do not go to form. It is a question of kind as well as of degree; and hers was a kind of sorrow which has only certain affinities to any other kinds of sorrow, and is simply without a name, except the name which the simple children of the Church call it by, the Dolours of Mary.

Her dolours may also be called immense, because of the proportions which they bore to other things in her; for even immensity must have proportions in its way. If she was to sorrow perfectly, if after Jesus, and because of Jesus, she was to have a pre-eminence of sorrow, then her sorrows must be proportioned to her greatness. But she was the Mother of God! Who will take the altitude of that greatness? St. Thomas tried to do so, and said that omnipotence itself could not contrive a greater greatness. It had done its utmost, though it has no utmost, when it had imagined and effected the dignity of the Divine Motherhood. What are we to a saint, or a saint to the highest angel, or the highest angel to Mary? Perhaps we are nearer—it is to be suspected that we are much nearer—to Michael or Raphael, than they are to Mary; yet it is weary even for a strong mind to think how far off we are from those tremendous intelligences and uncomprehended sanctities. Yet a sorrow proportioned to our capacities, and even indulgently measured to our grace, can be something so terrific that it makes us dizzy to think of what God might will about us. And then what can those spirits bear, and yet perish not, who have left the world wrongly, and fallen out of time when there was no root of eternity within them? Their strength is laden now in their hopeless home, yet not overladen, and who thinks of their burden without forthwith hiding his thoughts in God, lest something should happen to him, he knows not what? Yet Mary's soul was as immortal, as indestructible as their spirits, and stronger far; and her body was miraculously supported by the same omnipotence which confers an imperishable resurrection. Nay, it was perhaps the same Blessed Sacrament unconsumed within her, and in all of us the seed of a glorious resurrection, which was the miracle that kept her standing and alive at the foot of the bleeding Cross. What then must that sorrow have been which was proportioned to her greatness, to the greatness of the Mother of God, to her vast strength to bear, to her manifold capability of suffering? If we pause and think, we shall see how little our thinking comes to.

But her dolours must have been proportioned also to her sanctity. The trials of the saints have always an analogy with their holiness, and match it in degree as well as adapt themselves to it in its kind. If Mary's sorrow was the work of God, and was to do work for Him, if it was meritorious, if it closely resembled our Lord's, if it hung to His, subordinately, yet inseparably, if it was populous with supernatural actions, if it multiplied her graces, then must it have been suitable to the excellences of her soul, and proportioned to her sanctity. But that arithmetic of Mary's merits has long been a bewildering question, bewildering not because a shadow of doubt hangs over it, but for the want of ciphers to write it down in, of factors whereby to work the gigantic multiplication. The holiness of the Mother of God was not absolutely illimitable; and this is the lowest thing which can be said about it. If then we cast the most cursory glance over the number of her graces, their kinds, and their degrees, if, starting at the Immaculate Conception, we make a sort of reckoning up to the Incarnation, using angels' figures because men's have failed us long ago, and then if we think, however briefly, of the way in which at the moment of the Incarnation our figures fell over into the infinite, or something very like it, and then if we contemplate, stupidly and wildly as we must do, the velocity of indefinable grace during three-and-thirty years, all thickly strewn with infinite mysteries, we may form some idea, not of the amount of sanctity ready to bear its proportionate amount of sorrow at the foot of the Cross, but of the impossibility of our forming any clear idea of such a sanctity at all. So that we go away with a most overwhelming impression, but it is an impression like a faith, of the enormous weight of suffering which such a sanctity required, in order to engross it, to match it, to accelerate it, to complete it, to crown it, and to augment it by another infinity.

Neither can we doubt that her sorrows were proportioned to her enlightenment. Knowledge always puts an edge on grief. Sensibility does but give it additional acuteness. For the most part, when we suffer we hardly know half our actual misfortune, because we hardly understand more than half of it. Neither are we generally in full possession of ourselves. Some part of us is deadened and dulled by the blow which has been dealt us, and all that portion of our soul is a refuge to us from the sensitiveness and vigilance of the rest. A child weeps when his mother dies; but alas! how many a long year it takes to teach both boy and man what a mother's loss really means! Now our Lady's whole being was flooded with light. Not only did a reason and intelligence of the most consummate perfection illuminate every faculty, and secure the utmost excellence in the exercise of it; but she lived within herself in a very atmosphere of supernatural air and light. In her dolours this light was a torture to her. We may well suppose that no one, except our Blessed Lord Himself, ever fully understood the Passion, or grasped all its horrors in their terrible and repulsive completeness. Yet Mary's knowledge of it is the only one which came at all near to His, and simply because of the excess of heavenly light which shone unsettingly upon her sinless soul. We have but narrow ideas of the light which God can pour into the spacious intelligences of the angels, much less into the vast amplitude and serene capacity of His Blessed Mother. Hence it is that we find the theology of the Beatific Vision so singularly difficult. What blindness is to the blind, and deafness to the deaf, that is ignorance to us. We cannot comprehend its opposite. We make guesses, and draw the most erroneous pictures. Our way lies through darkness, and the twilight is the utmost our weak sight can bear. Light is painful to us, and puzzles us and troubles our thoughts, and makes us precipitate. Even with the saints, sudden light let in upon them acts as with us, and partially blinds them, until they learn how to suffer the keen ecstatic operations of grace. It brings to mind what a devout writer on the Passion has said of our Lord, following probably some revelation, that after He had been violently struck by the gauntleted hand of the soldier, His eyes were so affected that He could not bear the light, so that the sunshine caused exquisite suffering, and He went about through the streets from shame to shame, from violence to violence, like one dazed, and that can only imperfectly see his way. Ignorance is so completely our atmosphere, that we can conceive less of an excess of spiritual light, an intellectual effulgence, than of anything else. So here again the extent of our Lady's sorrows escapes us, as we have no means of measuring the supernatural enlightenment to which they were proportioned, or which perhaps rendered them co-extensive with itself.

Their multitude is equally beyond our powers of measurement. Every look at Jesus drove the swords deeper into her soul. Every sound of His dear voice, while it lifted her far up on the wings of maternal transport, brought with it its own bitterness, which pierced all the deeper and the keener for the joy that went along with it. Every action of His came to her with a multitude of pains, in which past and future blended in one terrible prevision which was always actual to her blessed soul. Every supernatural act which rose up within her heart, and such acts were for ever rising there, was a new dolour; for either it taught her something new of Jesus, or it was a response to some fresh love of His, or it was a growth of new love in her, or it drew her into closer union with Him, or it illuminated her mind, or it ravished her affections, or it intensified her worship; and in all these things the dearer and the more precious our Blessed Lord became to her, the more unutterable were the heartrending woes of the cruel and ignominious Passion. Thus, full as her life was of great events, rapidly succeeding each other, the multitude of her sorrows was being swollen every hour by the mere hidden life of grace in her heart. They came together like the streams of people in a huge city, swelling the crowd from every side, and swaying it to and fro. They were independent of external events, whose necessary sequence, with the time and room they occupy, keeps the intolerable fulness of human life within limits. It was more like a perpetual creation. They created themselves, only it was not out of nothing; it was out of her own exceeding holiness, and still more out of the exceeding beauty of her Son. If the number of her woes is beyond our power of counting, what must their pressure have been when they concentrated themselves as one weight upon one point of her affections, and then ever and anon distractedly dispersed themselves all over her soul with an amazing universality of suffering which it is not easy to picture to ourselves? We need not fear for her. She who was as tranquil as though she had been divine in the moment of the Incarnation can forfeit her peace for nothing else; but oh, how bitter must her peace have been. In pace amaritudo mea amarissima!

There was also another very true sense in which the sorrows of Mary were immense, in that they were beyond the power of human endurance. They went beyond the measure of the natural strength of life. It is the unanimous verdict of the devout writers on our Blessed Lady, supported by the revelations of the saints, and indeed founded upon those revelations, that she was miraculously kept alive under the pressure of her intolerable sufferings. In this, as in so many other things, she participated in the gifts of our Blessed Lord during His Passion. But this is true of our Lady, not only during the horrors of Calvary, but throughout her whole life. Her prevision of all her sorrows, at least from the moment of Simeon's prophecy, was so vivid and real, that, without a peculiar succour from the omnipotence of God, it must have separated her soul and body. She could not have lived under so dense a shadow. She could not have breathed in so thick a darkness. She must have been suffocated in the deep waters in which her soul was continually sinking. It was impossible in so perfect a creature that her reason should be perturbed. It was impossible that peace should ever be dislodged from a heart in such transcendently close union with God. But her beautiful life might have been, nay, would have been, extinguished by excess of sorrow, unless God had worked a perpetual miracle to hinder this effect, just as through her whole life she was always on the point of dying from excess of love, and when His appointed moment came, and He withdrew His extraordinary succour, she did in fact die of simple love. What then must that sorrow have been which required a standing miracle not to force body and soul asunder; and this too in a sinless soul, where remorse could never come, where doubt never harassed the judgment, unless it were once during the Three Days' Loss, and where perpetual peace reigned amid the quietness and subordination of all the passions?

Our Lady's dolours also went in their reality beyond the measure of most human realities, and this both in reason and sense. In our sorrows there is generally a great deal of exaggeration. We fancy almost as much more as we have really to bear. If our suffering comes from others, we dress it up in circumstances of unkindness, which never had any existence. We impute motives which never crossed the mind to which we impute them. We throw a strong, unequal, and unfair light on little trivial occurrences, which are probably altogether disconnected from the matter. Or if it is some loss we are undergoing, we picture consequences far beyond the sober truth, and bearing about as much proportion to the real inconveniences implied in our loss as a boy with a lantern bears to the prodigious tall shadows he is all the while unconsciously casting on the opposite wall. The combined weakness and activity of our imaginations envelop our sorrow in a cloud of unreality, which is still further increased by a kind of foolish wilfulness, leading us to refuse comfort and turn a deaf ear to reason, to give way to culpable indolence and brooding, and to interrupt the continuity of our ordinary duties and responsibilities. Now in all this wilfulness and weakness there is a sort of pleasure, which is a great condescension to endurance. But with our Blessed Lady all was thoroughly true. Her sorrows went up into regions of sublimity, of which we can form only the vaguest conceptions. They went down into profound depths of the soul, which we cannot explore because they have no parallel in ourselves. They were heightened by the unappreciable perfection of her nature, by the exuberant abundance of her grace, by the exceeding beauty of Jesus, and above all by His Divinity. Each of these enhancements of her griefs carries them out of sight of our limited capacities. But to her, in the midst of the most serene self-collection, each was perfectly real, thoroughly comprehended in all its bearings, and heroically embraced with full intelligence of all that was either actual or involved in it. Her physical nature, free from all the ruin of disease, exempt from the disorganisation consequent on sin, was full of the keenest vitality, of the most delicate susceptibilities, of the most tender and lively sensitiveness, and endowed with a most fine and amazing capability of suffering. Hence there was nothing, either in reason or sense, to deaden a single blow. Use did not make her sorrows more tolerable. Continuity did not confuse their distinctness. Not one of them was local; they were felt all through, with a swift circulation and a fiery sharpness which exempted no part of her body or soul from its piercing anguish, or gave so much as a transient dispensation to this or that particular faculty. Tranquil herself with that unutterable tranquillity of hers, there was no repose in her sorrows. They never left her. They never slept. They gave her no truce. Day and night was their uproar heard round the walls of the city of her soul. Day and night their flaming shafts fell in showers all over her most sacred shrines. There was not one, a jot of whose malice was lost upon her. She missed none of the bitterness. She knew their full value, and had none of those

B

surprises which sometimes force us suddenly across great trials we hardly know how. There was no succession in them, because they all stuck in her, like Sebastian's arrows, and their poisoned barbs were all rankling there at once. It is terrific, this reality of Mary's sorrows. It is a feature of them which must not be forgotten when we cease to speak of it, else we shall understand but very imperfectly what has yet to follow. Truly this is an immense reality, such as could not be found anywhere out of Jesus and Mary, another participation in the depths of the Passion.

But these sorrows of hers had some sort of share in the redemption of the world; and this gives them a peculiar immensity of their own. This, however, is a matter to be examined hereafter, and at length. It is sufficient then to say now that, by the ordinance of God, Mary was mixed up with the Passion, that her dolours were added to our Lord's sufferings, not without a purpose, but, as is the case with all divine things, with a most real and mysterious purpose, and that, as the Mother and the Son can in nowise be separated at any other point in the Thirty-Three Years, least of all can they be separated on Calvary, where God has joined them so markedly, and almost unexpectedly.

Of the diversified romance and artistic beauty of Mary's dolours we need not speak. Such things belong of right to all divine works. Her compassion was part of the great epic of creation, a pathos and a plaintiveness not to be disjoined from the sublimities and terrors and sacred panics of the Passion of the Incarnate Word. But it is not touching poetry of which we are in search. Rather it is plain piety, and a downright increase of love of Mary, and of devotion to her Son. If there be one department of practical religion from which we could desire that a sentence of perpetual banishment were passed upon mere sentiment and feeling it would be the department of Mary. Mary is a great reality of God, and sentiment is prone to rob us of our reality by turning substance into fancy, solidity into prettiness, and so overclothing the outside that we almost come to doubt whether there be an inside at all. Let then the exceeding beauty of Mary's martyrdom find us out if it will, and catch us up into the air, and surprise us into sweet tears, and calm the trouble of our sympathies; but do not let us seek it, or go out of our doctrinal, devotional way for it. Yet if artistic things can in any way increase our genuine love of God, let even them be welcome.

SECTION II.

WHY GOD PERMITTED OUR LADY'S DOLOURS.

But may we now ask why God permitted these dolours of Mary? Is it reverent to institute such an inquiry? All things are reverent which are done in love. We do not inquire because we are in doubt, or as if we were calling God to account, or as though we had a right to know; but we inquire in order that we may gain fresh knowledge to mint into fresh love. Perhaps there is no one work of God of which we are capable of knowing all the reasons, or of understanding them if He vouchsafed to tell them. Things, which God does, come out of infinite depths. But we find that the more we know the more we love, and therefore we inquire into many things, where love alone gives us the right of questioning, and the courage also. Why did God permit the dolours of His Mother, whom He loved so unspeakably, who was sinless and had nothing in herself to expiate by penance, and whose tears were in no way needful to the Precious Blood, which was of its sole self the redemption of the world? Such reasons as we see on the surface of the matter are these. It was because of His love for her. What can love give, which is better than self? But, with Him, self was suffering. Even in the matter of earthly greatness high destinies are destinies of glorious pain and more than common trial. And how human and earthly, even when most heavenly, is all in the Three-and-Thirty Years! The same law which lies round Him must also lie round her. She could not have a more passionate wish than this in her tranquil soul. But the law is a law of suffering, of sacrifice, of expiation, of ignominy, of abjection almost touching on annihilation. She would have been a mere instrument rather than a Mother had she been disjoined from all this, had she lain like a quiet low-lying landscape with the sun on it, away from the storm-enveloped glory of those heights of Calvary, more terrible by far than the ledges of ancient Sinai. Is it not even now, even to those far off from Him compared with the nearness of His Mother, is it not the fashion of His love to show itself in crosses? He left heaven because pain was such a paradise for Him, and it was an exclusively terrestrial paradise; and if He loved it so, He may well expect that those who love Him shall love it also. Great graces are the mountain chains thrown up by the subterranean heavings of pain. Martyrdoms have crowns belonging to them of right. Was Mary to be uncrowned? Would not the excess of His love for her be likewise an excess of suffering? But why waste many words, when it is enough to appeal to our own Christian instincts? What would an unsuffering Mary be like? The idea implies nothing less than the disappearance of the Madonna from the Church. An impassible Incarnation would have brought in its train an unsuffering Mother; but the passible Babe of Bethlehem has swathed His Mother in the same bands of suffering which compass Himself. The keenness of her martyrdom is the perfection of His filial piety.

The augmentation of her merits is another reason of her dolours; and nowhere has the force of merit such velocity as in suffering. Her being the Mother of God will not raise her high in heaven, apart from the sanctifying grace preceding and following the dignity of the Divine Maternity. The greatness of her dignity is an argument with us for the greatness of her grace, because in the purposes of God the two things are inseparable; and thus the dignity which we see is an index to us of the grace which we do not see. Her exaltation must depend upon her merits, and her merits must be acquired by lifelong suffering. O who shall tell the crowds of nameless raptures this day in heaven, and within her soul, in which our Blessed Mother recognises the distinct rewards of each separate suffering, the special crown of each supernatural act? And in all these, discerning it even through the amazing excess of the recompense, she beholds a congruity, a suitableness, to the sorrows rewarded, nay even a sort of natural growth of them, though in a supernatural way. For grace is not a different thing from glory. It is only glory in exile, while glory is but grace at home. Grace is the solid treasure; glory is only its exultation and success. So that huge Compassion of Mary's has come to be glory by the ordinary and lawful processes of the kingdom of heaven. Sixty-three years of ecstatic joy would never, under the present dispensation of things, have raised that Maternal Throne in such extraordinary vicinity to God. The queen of heaven must of necessity be trained as a queen, that she might queen it the more lawfully and the more supremely when the day of her accession came. The buoyancy of the Assumption was due to the bitterness of the Compassion.

There is always a look of cruelty in high destinies. Fortune drags its favourites through drawn swords. Mary's high destiny is not without this look of cruelty; and that which seems so cruel is the Divine Nature of her Son. It is the result of the infinite perfection of God that He must necessarily seek Himself, and be His own end. It is thus that He is the last end of all creatures, and that there is no true end in the world but Himself. Hence it is part of His magnificence, part of His deep love, that all things were made for Him, and that His glory is paramount over all things else. His greatest mercy to His creatures is to allow them to contribute to His glory, and to permit them to do it intelligently and voluntarily. Rightly considered, the creature can have no blessedness so great as that of increasing the glory of his Creator. It is the only true satisfaction both of his understanding and his will, the only thing which can be to him an everlasting rest. Here then is another reason for the divine permission of our Lady's dolours. They were permitted in order that God might receive from her more glory than from any other creature whatsoever, or from all creatures taken together, always excepting the created nature of our Blessed Lord. They were permitted that she might have the surpassing privilege of being equal to the whole creation in herself, nay, absolutely and transcendently surpassing it, in the praise and worship, the glory and adoration, which she paid to the Creator. Terrible as the heights were which she had to climb, far removed beyond all sympathy and intelligence of the saints, deep as were the torrents of blood and tears through whose rocky channels she had to make her way, exacting as were the mighty graces which claimed so wonderful a correspondence, there was not a gift that Jesus ever gave her which she prized so highly as her stern Compassion. O not for worlds would she have been excused one least exaggerating circumstance of her sorrow! In the very excess of the most intolerable of her afflictions, she enjoyed in the spirit of deep worship the inexorable sovereignty of God. It was God who hung upon the Cross. Her Son was God. It was the Crucified, pale and faint and feeble and bleeding, whose glory was more illimitable than the world-girdling ocean, and was feeding itself with unimaginable complacence on the streams of supernatural beauty and consummate holiness, which the deeply piercing swords of her grief were drawing from the caverns of her immaculate heart. She as it were supplied for all that the saints owed Him for His Passion, but could never pay. At the foot of the Cross she was the world's worship; for what else in the world was worshipping Him in His abasement at that hour? And all this cruelty of God's avaricious glory, this insatiableness of His thirst for creatures, was to her the perfection of delight, the supremest exercise of her royalty, while it was on the part of her Divine Son by far the most inconceivable outpouring of His love, which she had received since the midnight of the Incarnation. The Church would be a different thing from what it is if the sea of Mary's worship in her dolours were not part of its beauty, its treasures, and its powers before God. We can think less uneasily, less despondingly, of the unrequited Passion of our dearest Lord, when we remember the sorrow, like no other sorrow but His own, with which His Mother worshipped Him.

We too make our appearance in the matter. She must suffer for our sakes as well as for His. For is she not to be the mother of consolation, the comfort of the afflicted? And for this end she must go down into the depths of every sorrow which the human heart can feel. As far as a simple creature can do so, she must fathom them all, and experience them in her own self, without even excepting sorrow for sin, though it cannot be for sin of her own, but in fact for ours. She must know the weight of our burdens, and the kind of misery which each brings along with it. It must be a science to her to be sure of the measure of consolation which our weak hearts require in their various trials, and what soothes and alleviates our suffering in all its manifold, unequal, and dissimilar circumstances. Our Blessed Lord did not save us from our sins by a golden apparition in the heavens, by a transient vision of the Cross shown in the far-seen glory from the green dome of Tabor, or by an absolution once for all pronounced over the outspread west from seaward-looking Carmel. It was not His will that redemption should have the facility of creation, facility to Him at least, for to us the facilities are wonderful enough. He accomplished our salvation in long years, with infinite toilsome sufferings, out of abysses of shame, with the shedding of His blood, and with unutterable bitterness of soul. He earned it, merited it, struggled for it, and only mastered it by the prodigies of His Passion. All this need not have been so.

A word, a tear, a look, might have done it, nay an act of will, with or without an Incarnation. But it was not His good pleasure that it should be so. In His infinite wisdom He chose not to lean on His infinite power alone, but took another way. So is it with Mary. She is not at once created mother of the afflicted, as by a sudden patent of nobility. She does not become the consolation of mourners by a mere appointment emanating from the will of the Divine Majesty. It might have been so, but it is not so. Her office of our Mother is a long and painful conclusion worked out from her Divine Maternity. She has toiled for it, suffered for it, borne herculean burdens of sorrow in order to merit it, and has mastered it at last on Calvary. Not that she could strictly merit such an office, as Jesus merited the salvation of the world; nay, rather her motherly office to us was part of the salvation which He merited. Yet, nevertheless, according to a creature's capacity, she came nigh to meriting it, and met God's gratuitous advances to her on the way. How needful then was it for us that God should permit her dolours! What would the sea of human sorrows be without Mary's moonlight on it? The ocean, with the dark, heavy, overspread clouds lowering upon it, does not differ more widely from the silvery plain of green and whitely flashing waters, exulting in the sunlight, than the weary expanse of life's successive cares, without the softening and almost alluring light which falls upon it from Mary's love, differs from life as it now lies before us beneath her maternal throne. How many a tear has she not already wiped away from our eyes! How many bitter tears has she not made sweet in the shedding! And there is age, and the yearly narrowing circle of those we love, and sickness, and death, all yet to come, and to what amount may we not have to draw upon the treasure of consolations in her sinless heart? O it was well for us, and it was most entirely to her heart's content, that God permitted her dolours, that she might be so much the more really the mother of the afflicted;

for the heaviness of her sorrows is daily the lightening of ours; and how little it is that we can bear, and how great the load which she could bear, and how royally she bore it!

Our Blessed Lord was at once our atonement and our example. He redeemed the world solely by His Precious Blood. By His merits alone are we saved. His prerogatives as our Redeemer are simply unshared by any one. His Mother had to be redeemed as well as the rest of us, though in a different and far higher way, by prevention, not by restoration, by the unmated grace of the Immaculate Conception, not by regeneration from a fallen state. Yet it was His will that His Mother, her office, her consent, her graces, her sufferings, should be so mixed up with the scheme of redemption, that we cannot separate them from it. It was His ordinance that her Compassion should lie close by His Passion, and that His Passion without her Compassion would be a different Passion from what it actually was. Thus He seems to draw her almost within the same law of expiation which surrounded Himself, so that it should be true that there are many senses in which she may be said to have taken part in the redemption of the world. But if this is true of Christ as our atonement, where the union of the Divine Nature with the Human was needful to the infinite satisfaction of the work, much more is it true of Christ as our example. This was an office which she was more nearly competent, through His own grace, to share with Him; and one which the fact of her being simply a creature, and altogether human, would bring more touchingly home to us. Thus we may perhaps venture to suppose that God permitted the dolours of Mary, in order that she might be all the more excellently our example. Sorrow is more or less the characteristic of all human life; and it is one which, while it contains within itself especial capabilities of union with God, also deranges and perturbs our relations with Him more than anything else. It assaults our confidence in Him, and confidence is the only true worship. It engenders temptations against the faith, or finds something congenial in them when they come. It leads to a certain kind of peevishness and petulance with God, which comes from the very depths of our nature, from the same depths as love and adoration, and which, while it is secretly akin to both of these, often succeeds in destroying both, and usurping their vacant places. That this petulance is a true phenomenon of the creature's nature, is shown by the surprising manner in which God justifies the petulance of Job, and finds sin that needed expiation in the criticism of his friends upon him, while He, the Searcher of hearts, discerns in Job's bold querulousness nothing that damages the integrity of his patience, and much that is in harmony both with reverence and love. The endurance of sorrow is perhaps the highest and most arduous work we have to do, and it is for the most part God's ordinance that the amount of sorrow to be endured should increase with the amount of holiness enabling us to bear it. We must bear it naturally even while we are bearing it supernaturally. There is no sanctity in unfeelingness, or in the blunting of the soul, even when religious interests have blunted it by a superior engrossment and a higher abstraction. Spirituality no doubt hinders us from feeling many sorrows, and no one will say that such indifference is not in many ways a privilege. But it must not be confounded with an heroic endurance of sorrow. To be heroic in this matter, the heart must feel to the quick, and divine love must barb the more cruelly, and drive the deeper in, the shafts with which we are wounded. Now, in all this, Mary is our example, and a purely human example, an example moreover which has as a matter of fact produced such results of exceeding sanctity and supernatural gracefulness in the Church, that we may safely venture the conjecture that it was one of the reasons for which God permitted her surpassing martyrdom.

There is yet another reason which we may dare to suggest for the permission of her sorrows. As the Bible is a spoken revelation, so in a certain sense Mary is an emblematic revelation. God uses her as an instrument whereby to make many things plain which would otherwise have rested in obscurity. It is a line of thought familiar to theologians, which regards her as a kind of image of the Most Holy Trinity. As the Daughter of the Father, the Mother of the Son, and the Spouse of the Holy Ghost, she shadows forth in herself, faintly of course because she is a creature, but nevertheless truly, the revelations of the Three Divine Persons. She is as it were a still translucent lake, in whose bosom wonderful attributes of God, and far distant heavenly heights, are mirrored with faithful distinctness. We know more of God's mercy, of His condescension, of His intimacy with His creatures, of His characteristic ways, because of the light which He has made to shine on Mary, than we should else have known, and we have come also to understand better what we either knew or might have known in other ways. Thus God's perfections in Himself, His dealings with His creatures, and the fashion of His redeeming grace, the possibilities of holiness, the inventiveness of divine love, His training of the saints, His guidance of the Church, His inward walk with the souls that seek Him,—all these things are written upon Mary like hieroglyphical inscriptions, easily to be deciphered by the light of faith and the intelligent surmises of devotion. So, by her dolours, He has hung about her a complete revelation of the great mystery of suffering. He has illuminated in her that pregnant doctrine, that suffering is the only true conclusion to be drawn from love, where divine things are concerned. She had no sin of her own for which to suffer. She had no penalty to pay for the fall of Eve. She was not included in the law of sin. She was, in the order of heaven's purposes, foreseen before the decree permitting sin. She also had no world to redeem. All her dear blood, the sweet fountain and well-head of the Precious Blood, could not have washed away one venial sin, nor saved the soul of one new-born babe who had no actual sin at all to expiate. She was simply immersed in an unspeakable sea of love, and therefore the deluge of sorrow passed over her soul, and into it, by right, just as the great turbulent rivers run down unquestioned into the sea. Her sufferings close the mouth of complaint for ever. With sweet constraint and unanswerable persuasiveness they impose silence on all the suffering children of our Heavenly Father. The saints can doubt no longer that suffering is the one grand similitude of Christ. We too in our extreme lowness, whose patience is of so thin a texture that it was threadbare almost when it was new, learn, not to be silent only, but to bear with gentleness, and even wistfully to think the time may come when we shall actually love, that suffering which seems to be the golden coin in which Love repays our love.

SECTION III.

THE FOUNTAINS OF OUR LADY'S DOLOURS.

We may now proceed to our third inquiry, What were the fountains of our Lady's dolours? By fountains we do not exactly mean causes, but rather the peculiar sources of feeling in her heart, which gave to her sorrows their distinguishing bitterness. When a mother loses her only son, the loss is of itself bitterness enough; but a character and intensity are given to it by circumstances which awaken particular feelings within her breast. Either he was so beautiful that the loss seems all the more intolerable, or he was so full of moral or intellectual promise, or he was taken so young, or there was something which, humanly speaking, might have been so easily prevented in the actual cause of his death, or there was a special combination of family circumstances which just at that time made his death a greater blow than at any other date it would have been: these, and similar things which might be indefinitely multiplied, are centres of peculiar bitterness round which sorrow gathers, deepening, broadening, magnifying, embittering it, far beyond the measure of the real affliction. Yet all these things are to the mourner the most stern realities, and by no means imaginary or merely sentimental aggravations. In the case of our Blessed Lady nothing could go beyond the real affliction, because of Him whose sufferings were the cause of hers. On the contrary, human sorrow, even Mary's sorrow, could not equal the real cause of grief. Nevertheless there were centres also in her heart round which her sorrows gathered more thickly, and ached more cruelly, and throbbed more vehemently than elsewhere. It is these centres which we must now consider, these special fountains of perennial bitterness, premising that of course the perfections of Mary's heart are so far beyond our understanding, that there were doubtless many sources of keen suffering to her which we cannot appreciate, perhaps not even imagine, and that while we traverse the ground which is known to us we must not forget all the regions which lie beyond it still undiscovered, the exploring of which may perhaps be one of the many delightful occupations left for heaven.

The first of these fountains was in the thought that she could not die with Jesus. There is hardly any mother who would not under such circumstances have longed to die. Death is better than life to a broken heart; and where death is not a separation, but an unbroken companionship, only a companionship transferred from the desolate earth to the bosom of our Heavenly Father, to what stricken mother would it not have been a boon beyond all words? How incomparably such to Mary! Never was son so much to earthly mother as Jesus was to her, never was any son so good and beautiful and dear a son, never any so much a son. The rights of both father and mother centred in the one heart of the Virgin Mother; so that He was twice her Son, doubly her Son. Who can tell the attractions of His Sacred Humanity, or how the love of Him took root in that deep maternal heart? Then He was God beside, and for three-and-thirty years had been living in obedience to her, in a union of love so transporting that it would have taken her life a thousand times if He had not hindered it, and that, not by tempering the sweet vehemence of love, but by strengthening her heart with His omnipotence. He was going. His sun was sinking in a red sea of blood, among the wildest clouds of shame. She could never forget. Calvary would be in her heart to the last. It would be one of those remembrances which time could never soften, one of those horrors which grow more horrible in the distance when we can take them in, and not be confused by the presence of their excess. But even if it were not so, Jesus would be gone, and why should she live? What was there to live for? The sunshine was put out. It was more of an end than the end of the world could be. It was a darkness inconceivable, nay it might appear a downright impossibility: for how was the world to go on without Jesus? With the closing of His eyes, it might appear as if all benediction were withdrawn from the earth, and a cold freezing shade come over all its brightness. When His sweet accents were heard no more, surely all nature would keep an unbroken silence, unless those awful cries of the maddened people were to go on multiplying and reverberating through all space for ever. The earth was to have Peter; Mary was to have John. One was to be the apostle of the world, the other the apostle of the Mother. But Jesus was to go.

But it is not only why should she live, but how could she live? Was there a possibility of living without Jesus? None, dearest Mother, except by the help of His omnipotence! O how wonderful must have been her love to accept His will on Calvary, His will that they should part, His will that she should linger on through fifteen mortal years of unimaginable martyrdom! She asked once for water to be turned into wine, and He said His time was not yet come; nevertheless at her will the miracle was wrought, without her asking twice. She could hardly have forgotten that on Calvary. These fifteen years were His will, but what if she for a moment shows her will that it should not be so, will the Mother have to plead long with the dying Son? A word, a look, were possibly enough. How is it that she is still? Is it that she loves Him better now than at Cana of Galilee? And it is a higher love to stay and do His will, than to go with Him and enjoy His beauty. Is she holier now than she was then? For holiness, as it rises, loses more and more its individual will in the will of God. Both are doubtless true, and both facts are in no slight measure owing to her dolours. But is it not rather perhaps that she, like her Son, has gone down into the depths of suffering, and has become as it were enchanted with it, and as He thirsts for more suffering, in divinest discontent even with the excesses of Calvary, so she too thirsts to suffer more, and He gives to her what His Father grants not to Himself, another passion of a hundred and eighty waxing and waning moons. It must be remembered also that there was a peculiar grief to our Lady in not dying with Jesus, which we cannot appreciate, but only contemplate far off. Union with Jesus was so habitual to her, and union of so close and vital a nature, that it had become her life; and now in the most important act of all, she was not to be united with Him. She was to differ when she most longed to resemble Him. Nay, it was a want of union which was to involve actual separation. Who can estimate what this absence of union was to her? Yet her love had this prerogative, to suffer longer than our Lord, and to outlive Him by well-nigh half His life in suffering. Deep down in very deep sanctity indeed we find, that never scarcely was she more intimately united with Him, than when she let Him go without her.

Another fountain, which yielded additional bitterness to Mary's sorrows, was the knowledge that her dolours increased the sufferings of Jesus, nay, that they were actually among the worst agonies He had to endure. There was not one pain which she would not have given worlds to alleviate. There was not one fresh indignity offered to Him which did not pierce her soul, and make her bleed inwardly. As blows and blasphemies, insults, derision, and rude handlings were multiplied, it seemed at each new violence as if she could bear no more, as if the sea of sorrow needed but another drop to break in upon the fountains of her life, and wash them away in one terrific inundation. And yet she had to feel that the sight of her broken heart, ever before Him, was more dreadful to our Blessed Lord than the scourging, the crowning, the spitting, or the buffeting. She was made as it were executioner in chief of her own beloved Son. The more tenderly she loved Him, the more fondly she clung to Him, the more willingly she bore her griefs, so much the deeper the iron of them entered into the soul of Jesus. She knew all this; and yet her grief was not beneath her own control. Her very holiness increased it a thousandfold. It was in vain she strove to repress it. The very effort was anguish, and no calmness of face, no firmness of attitude, no tearlessness of eye, could have hidden from Jesus the secret abysses of her immaculate heart. Who shall tell the torture of all this to her unselfish devotion? O the seeming cruelty of that exceeding great love which had actually insisted on her being an integral and prominent part of His bitter Passion! How well He knew the plenitude of grace that was in her! How thoroughly He trusted the immensity of her holiness! Life had not been without joys to Him, not even without earthly joys. His Mother had been a whole world of sweetness to the Man of sorrows; and now, in His love of God, in His love of her, in His love of us, He turns all those sweet waters to an ocean of saltest bitterness for Himself, and keeps slaking His thirst from it incessantly all through the various mysteries of His tremendous Passion. He knew her love so well, and calculated its fortitude so truly, that He hesitated not to lay upon her a cross so nearly the weight of His own. But what all this was, in spite of the eager conformity of her willing heart, what intensity of misery, what unparalleled kind of woe it brought along with it, it is beyond our power to say. It is very deep sea close to shore, where Mary's dolours are concerned.

But is she then to be simply passive? If it is His will that she should be part of His Passion, may she not think that the fondness of her love will really be some alleviation of His pains? She has been too near the Incarnate Word not to comprehend that strange union of intensest pain with intensest joy, which was the normal state of His blessed Soul on earth; and deep down, deeper than the fountains of grief, might not her love be a wellspring of gladness in His heart? The heroic devotedness of the Mother must surely be a most pathetic contentment to the Son. Yet we venture to suppose that it was not so. The analogies of the Passion seem all to point the other way. He shut off from His lower nature the sensible beatitude of the unbroken Vision of God. He stripped Himself by an amazing detachment of all that could have consoled Him. The dereliction of His Father was an abyss into which He purposed to descend. He can hardly have allowed His Mother's love to have been a consolation and support to Him. He can hardly have kept to shine upon Him in His darkness the greatest earthly joy His Sacred Humanity had ever known. It would be out of keeping with the Passion, with that completeness of bleak desolation which He spread around Himself, the vastest, direst wilderness of soul that ever man had known, worse round Him, the sinless Saviour, than was the homeless earth that lay outstretched, with all its haunting shapes and shadows of terror, before the bloodstained, impenitently remorseful Cain! No! Mary might not think that in that hour her love could soothe His Sacred Heart. But were there no maternal offices which she might fill towards Him? Alas! only such office as the mother of the Machabees had filled of old. Slowly and incommodiously the blood from the thorns was trickling into His eyes; but she could not reach to wipe away the blood from Him, whose special office it is to wipe away tears from all eyes for ever. His lips are parched with thirst, white, bloodless, cracking; but she may not damp them for one moment with her moistened veil, though His blood shall henceforth daily damp the fires of purgatory for a thousand souls. His poor unpillowed head, that beautiful head, to her the most beautiful of created things—if He leans back the thorns are driven in, if He leans forward His whole body drags from the nails, may she not hold it in her Motherly hands, and let Him rest so for a little while until He dies? No! neither for Him nor for her is there to be any alleviation. O Mother! rob Him not of one jewel of His perfect Passion; for see how generously He is enlarging for thee every hour the bounds of thy great sea of sorrow! But this is a third fountain of her grief, that she cannot alleviate the Passion of her Son.

It was another fountain of peculiar sorrow to her that she was an eye-witness of the Passion. We learn from the revelations of holy persons that, though she was absent in body, she was present in spirit at the sufferings of Gethsemane, and even followed in her soul with mysterious and supernatural sympathy the various phases of our Saviour's agony. She was present bodily at the scourging, at the Ecce Homo, along the way of the Cross, and for the whole time on Calvary. It appears most probable that she was not in the houses of Annas and Caiphas, but that she was at the doors, and heard not only the insults, but even the blows which were given to Jesus, and that she suffered an especial torture in the separation from Him at those moments. Yet it was a fearful thing for a mother, particularly one of such exquisite sensibilities and profound love as Mary, to have to follow her only child through every step of that bloody drama. It would have been a terrific martyrdom, if she had spent those hours retired in the women's apartments of an oriental house, hearing the distant cries of the raging multitude, or listening to the mournful intelligence which would be brought her from time to time. Still she could better have collected herself there to suffer in quietness and peace. Others at least could have spent the time all the more undistractedly in prayer. But it was not so with her. Her Son was God. It was better to be nigh Him. The nigher God the better, always, for all of us; but for God's Mother most of all. Unbroken as was her union with the invisible God at all times and in all places, she would pray better when she saw Jesus. Besides, she had not the helpful distraction which Christian women have in their afflictions. She was not divided between the dear Child who was being taken from her and the all-holy God who was inflicting this blow upon her. Her grief and her religion did not fall two different ways. The suffering Child and the all-holy God were one and the same. This was the overpowering unity of her dolours. She must go forth therefore and follow the footsteps of Jesus, and wet her feet in the blood He has left behind Him. She must listen to the fierce singing of the scourges as they cleave the air, and count the stripes, and take into her heart the variety of deadly sickening sounds they made as they lit on this or that part of His Sacred Body. She must see the mock-king of Jews and Gentiles, as Pilate, half in worthless pity, and half in merciless derision, exposed Him to the crowd, and she alone adored His royal majesty almost out of the very annihilation of herself by the violence of grief. She must hear the dull hammering of the nails on Calvary, whose sounds, muffled by the soft flesh of His Hands and Feet, pierced her soul through and through. She must listen to the seven beautiful words upon the Cross, as if He Himself were singing His own dirge, with such melancholy sweetness as was enough to have drawn her living soul out of her weak, worn, and aching body. All this was terrible. Yet she was a true mother. Not for one instant would she have consented to have it otherwise. It was a portion of the royalty of her heart. Nevertheless it was an unspeakable aggravation of her suffering. It was true that the whole of it had lain before her in clearest prevision at least since the hour of Simeon's prophecy. But sense is something more than prevision, something different from it. The senses "betray the succours which reason gives." They interrupt that interior tranquillity in which the darkest visions may possess the soul, without disturbing it. Sight interferes with that self-collection, which is our attitude of strength in the endurance of interior pains. It throws the soul off its guard, or elicits from it a painful strain of inward fortitude in order to preserve its guard. Moreover, the senses have special things of their own in sights and sounds and touches of grief; and they pierce the flesh, causing it to tremble with chilly pains, torturing the nerves, freezing and firing the blood by turns, stabbing the brain like daggers, and nipping the convulsed heart as if it were within an iron vice. It was this eye-witnessing of the Passion which made Mary's martyrdom to be in her body as well as in her soul, and which was something more than the aching physical exhaustion in which excess of mental effort leaves the frame, because it laid each limb upon the rack, and made every pulse a beating instrument of pain.

Another fountain of sorrow is to be found in her clear view and appreciation of sin. We cannot doubt that, independent of her own sinlessness and of the magnificence of her reason, our Blessed Lord allowed her to participate in some degree in that supernatural perception of sin, of its exceeding malice and of God's adorable hatred of it, which distinguished Himself, and actually gave its character to the suffering of the Passion. It was the view of sin which crucified His soul in the garden of Gethsemane. It was the weight of sin which pressed Him down to the ground. It was the chalice of His Father's anger, which He so plaintively desired might pass from Him. We read of St. Catherine of Genoa fainting away, when it pleased God to show her in vision the real horror even of a venial sin. There could be no fainting with Mary. She was too strong, too perfect, too complete, for weaknesses like those. Her use of reason, which had begun at the moment of her Immaculate Conception, and had never been interrupted for one instant since, could not decorously be suspended by any trance or fainting-fit. But we must necessarily suppose that whatever supernatural gift of insight into sin was granted to St. Catherine of Genoa or any other saints, our Lady's gift of that sort must have unspeakably transcended theirs. Indeed, when we consider on the one hand the part which His deep view of sin played in our Blessed Saviour's Passion, and on the other the "communication of attributes," so to call it, which passed between His Passion and her Compassion, we cannot but suppose that our dear Lady was gifted with no inconsiderable portion of His amazing and overwhelming insight into sin. None estimated, as she did, the spotless innocence of the victim. None so truly appreciated the beauty and sublimity of His goodness. None so fathomed the ingratitude of those whom He had taught, and fed, and healed, and comforted, with such unselfish patience and such considerate affection. None felt more acutely the barbarous excesses of those cruel hours of Thursday night and Friday morning. When all these thoughts rushed into one, what a view it was which broke upon her of the amount, variety, intensity, malignity, of sin which there was in the Passion. But she saw more than that. She saw, hideous, appalling, mountainous vision! the sins of the whole world on the stooping shoulders of her blessed Son. But yet more—she saw up to the heights of His Divinity; she saw that it was truly God whom all this sin reached, assailed, defiled, and murdered; and then such a light, as from another universe of diviner things, broke in upon the sin of the Passion that none but Jesus and herself could have confronted and endured. O that we could better tell what this pain of sharp light was like! But it is far from us. Could we live if God showed us our real selves? We have need to be immortal before our hour of judgment comes. But the sins of the whole world, the concentrated sin of the Passion— Mary saw it all, and died a thousand inward deaths in the agony it made her bear.

It is not easy to say what was the highest point, or what

made the deepest wound in the Passion. The instruments of the Passion were not material only. There were invisible lances, and nails, and hammers, and thorns, and stripes. They were intellectual and moral, as well as physical. And in all these three departments the implements of torture were both numerous and diversified. Each of them went to the quick. None of them deserve to be considered subordinate or inferior. Each had its pre-eminence in its own way. All ran up higher than our eye can follow them. But it is not easy to say which of them, if any of them, reached higher heights in Him than others did. The Passion was an excess of excesses. Everything belonging to it was in excess. It is this in great measure which hinders it from being lowered into a mere epic of human suffering, even independently of the consideration of His Divinity. But there are some things which we can conceive of as being sharper than others, or wounding in more tender places. There is one of these, a participation in which will furnish us with a sixth fountain of Mary's sorrow. It is the foreseen ingratitude of the faithful for the Passion of our dearest Lord. The Mother of the Church, the queen of the apostles, sees it all in her heart. Such a scroll is unrolled before her eyes of carelessness about forgiven sin, of relapses into deadly sin, of astonishing prolific broods of venial sins, swarming in hordes all over the soul and laying waste that paradise of God, of cold-hearted negligences, of unbecoming imperfections, of immortified, consciously immortified lives, of distaste for spiritual things, of careless freedom with great sacraments that cost her Son so dear, of narrow, jealous, suspicious tempers, of the sickening, lukewarm ways of conceited human prudence, and of all that dismal infinite of pusillanimity, out of which here and there a saint stands up but half distinguishably, like a palm in the sand-fog of the wilderness. Neither was it altogether a vision of the future. Where was Peter? Was he weeping in some grotto outside the walls in the luxury of his new-found grace? Where was Andrew, who was to be the model of all lovers of the Cross? Where was James, in whose diocese his Master was at that moment crucified?* There was the passionate Magdalen, there was the beautiful heart of John, there was herself, to represent the world on Calvary! Alas! if from that day forth every baptized soul was to be a saint as high as an apostle, how fearful would the Passion have been, and how sadly unrequited too. But if this was not to be, surely those who love Jesus should love Him well. All the saved should be saints, saints before they reach heaven, saints that need not an exodus through the sea of fire beneath the earth, saints even while on earth. Half-hearted creatures hanging on to God by an occasional sacrament, clinging to the Church by a jubilee, balancing in silly indecision, like wayward stupid animals, between the shepherd and the hireling, giving their love of love to the world, and now and then their love of fear to God when He thunders, enjoying life and time and earth uncommonly, and making a clutch at eternity and heaven upon their death-beds—is the Crucified to be the own Father of such as these? O to the generous heroic heart of Mary this was a sight that was equal to a whole Passion in itself! She saw how the dear Heart beneath that white blood-seamed side upon the Cross was sickening over that very vision, and her heart yearned over it also with indescribable faintness and repugnance.

But what shall we say of the sight of those who should be lost? Think of the value of each drop of blood? But why talk of drops? She is slipping in it. It has trickled all over her hands as she clasped the Cross. It lies like a

---

* I have spoken of S. James, one of the Twelve Apostles, as bishop of Jerusalem after our Lord's Ascension. That opinion was once common, but not in ancient times, nor in our day. The Bollandists—Acta SS. Mai. i.—discussed its value and rejected it. Petavius held it, but Zaccaria disposed of the whole question, and proved, both by the words of the Gospels and the testimony of the ancients, that the first bishop of Jerusalem was not one of the Twelve Apostles. The question is not one of mere learning, for it refers directly to the Supremacy of S. Peter, who alone founded a local and Apostolic See.

red line between the foot of the Cross and the pillar of the scourging. The gnarled roots of the olives on Gethsemane are ruddy with it in more spots than one. Look up at the countless stars, strewing like luminous dust the purple concave of midnight. One stripe would have redeemed them all, if all had fallen a thousand times. And if there were six thousand stripes! What a calculation of the infinities of redemption! And all that blood and all those stripes given for each soul, each soul to have unshared for its own self all those infinite salvations; and yet to be lost eternally! Christ to pay that price, and then to be defrauded of its value! If one soul, for whom all that Passion had been thinkingly and intentionally undergone, and then with such solemnities as creation never saw before, and with such inconceivable priesthood, offered by God to God, —if one soul should perish everlastingly, should triumph by its guilt over its Saviour's love, should dry up the oceans of His Blood by the fiery heats of hell, what an anguish to the Sacred Heart of Jesus! It might have wrung from Him a worse cry than leaped out of the passionate broken heart of Jacob, when Joseph's many-coloured coat, with blood-stains on it, was held up before his eyes. But if not one soul only, but millions, and millions of millions should be lost, what then? Nay, if it should have to be a doubt, of which we might not be sure even while we believed it, whether as many adult believers are saved as are lost, what then? Well! He did not repent of the Cross, as He hung upon it. That is all we can say. But He had another crucifixion that was invisible, far worse than that one of wood, and iron, and red blood, and a mock title, which we see. It was the crucifixion of a Heart already crucified, because of the thought of the countless multitudes who would fall from Him and be lost and be no more members of Him, but turn from Him through the triumphant envy and rage of Satan with cruel sundering, with helpless irremediable dismemberment. They "brake not His bones;" but the bones of His Soul were all broken by this cruel inward Passion. And in this dark agony, in this special chalice apart, Mary also had her share: and if in that moment she could distinguish between what this thought made her suffer because she so loved Jesus, and what it made her suffer because she so loved souls, then did she see two separate, most frightful abysses, into which, half suffocated with anguish, she must enter, with shrinking yet unreluctant horror.

These were the seven fountains of Mary's dolours, beneath which, and underlying all of them, was the grand parent source of all, the incomparable divine beauty of our dearest Lord Himself. It was this which gave the vitality and keenness to every pain. It was this which aggravated everything, but could exaggerate nothing, because it could magnify nothing to a greater size than itself. Even she did not know all that beauty. It was incomprehensible, absolutely in itself incomprehensible. But what she did know is incomprehensible to us, it is so far above us and beyond us. Yet we can speak great words of our Saviour's beauty, and think thoughts of it far greater than any words, and when even thoughts fail, we can weep, weep tears of heavenly feeling. We can burn away with love, and die of His beauty; yet, though thus we shall reach Mary's home, we shall not attain to her comprehension of the exceeding loveliness of Jesus. There was an ocean of it in the lowest, most unfathomable caverns of her heart, which ever and anon broke upward in other seas that rolled above and made them bitter beyond endurance.

SECTION IV.

THE CHARACTERISTICS OF OUR LADY'S DOLOURS.

The characteristics of our Lady's dolours are, as might be expected, closely connected with the fountains out of which they spring, and these must now be the subject of inquiry. Although they will come out strongly and clearly as we consider the different dolours in succession, yet a general view of them is necessary in order to a true idea of her martyrdom as a whole. When we have once seen it as a unity, we shall the better understand the marvellous details which a nearer inspection will disclose to us. The first characteristic of her sorrows was that they were lifelong, or nearly so. It is generally agreed that our Blessed Lady did not know she was to be the Mother of God before the moment of the Incarnation. Until that time, therefore, she might have had such a gift of prophecy as to foresee confusedly that her life was to be one of great sorrow and heroic endurance, but her particular dolours could not have been distinctly before her. But when she actually bore within herself the Eternal Word made flesh, a great change must have come over her in this respect. She was in such unutterable union with God, and understood so deeply and truly the mystery of the Incarnation, and such a light was shed for her upon the depths of Hebrew prophecy, that it is impossible not to believe that the Passion of Jesus lay clearly before her, with all the Thirty-Three Years of poverty, hardship, and abasement, and consequently with it, at least in its main outlines, her own Compassion. This is the least we can think, but in truth we think much more. We cannot agree with those writers who make her dolours to begin with the prophecy of Simeon. No doubt God may have been pleased at that moment to bring the whole sorrowful future more distinctly before her, and to have painted the vision in more vivid colours. That Simeon's words were divine instruments for effecting a change within her soul is more than probable. But it seems hardly honourable to her to conceive that during the nine months of her intimate union with the Incarnate Word, she should not have understood His mission of suffering and blood, or the laws of expiation and redeeming grace, or the certainty that she also would have to drink deeply of the same cup with Him. At all events from the time of Simeon's prophecy, if not from the first moment of the Incarnation, her sorrows were lifelong. Like those of Jesus, they were ever before her. She had no bright intervals over which impending evil cast no sorrow. There was an inevitable uniformity of shade over her path. The darkest destinies of men are unequal, and in this inequality there is relief. The sorrow that clings closest sometimes relaxes its hold. The clouds now and then give way before strong sunshine, even though it be but for a while. The misfortune which occasionally dogs a man all through life at times seems to grow weary of its chase, and turns backward, as if it had forsaken its prey, or at least allowed him breathing-time. But Mary's subjection to sorrow was riveted upon her as if with iron. It never relaxed. It never grew milder. It gave her no respite. It was in her life, and only by laying down her life could she extricate herself from its inseparable companionship. The Passion was not a dark end to a bright life, or an obscure sunset after a checkered day of light and gloom, or an isolated tragedy in sixty-three years of common human vicissitudes. It was part of a whole, with consistent antecedents, a deepening certainly of the darkness, but a portion of the lifelong darkness which for years had known, in this respect at least, no light. We must bear this in mind throughout if we would understand her sorrows rightly. They were not so much separate events; they were the going on of a charmed life, round which heaven had wrapped a singular law of sorrow, only with a stronger light cast upon some of its abysses than upon others.

But her sorrows were not only lifelong; they were continually increasing. The more she became familiarised with the vision of them, the more also she realised them, and the more terrible they seemed. This growth of them does not appear incompatible with the immensity of her science, or do any dishonour to it. They gave up new features, new pains, new depths, new possibilities to her continual meditation, just as in a far lower degree they do still to ours. The more we occupy our minds with the mysteries of the Incarnation, the more do we learn about them. The horizon grows wider the higher we climb. When our eye gets used to the peculiar soft darkness, the more unfathomable do we perceive the depth of the abyss to be. What then must all this have been to her, whose penetrating steadfast gaze was so unlike our cursory distracted meditation, whose meditation was unbroken for years, and whose own heart was so deeply interested in the subject? Moreover, as they came nearer, they naturally became more terrible. They threw a deeper shadow. They inspired greater fear. The first breaths of the storm began to blow cold upon her heart. She clung to Jesus. He seemed more beautiful than ever. But there was no hope. The wide sea was around her, without a harbour. She had no home but the great deep. It was the will of God. Meanwhile Jesus waxed more beautiful day by day. The first twelve years ran out, leaving results of heavenly loveliness and love beyond our power of summing. Then the next eighteen, when every word, and every look, and every meek subjection were thick with mysteries of heaven. Her life had almost passed out of her into Him, so exceedingly had He become her light, and life, and love, and all. Then came the three years' ministry, and it seemed as if the Babe of Bethlehem, or the Boy of Nazareth, had been nothing to the Preacher of love, whose words and works and miracles appeared to charge the world with more of supernatural beauty than it could bear, so that men rose up madly to put out the light which hurt them by its strong shining. As this loveliness increased, her love increased, and with her love her agony: and all three were continually increasing with majesty and with velocity. The transcendent beauty of the three years' Ministry seemed to make it impossible for her to endure the Passion; and did it not seem to show as if by the beauty of His preaching alone, and by His human tears, and His vigils on the mountains, and His footsore journeys, and His hunger, and thirst, and sweet patience, and the persuasiveness of His miracles, and the wondrous enticing wisdom of His parables, the world might be redeemed, and Calvary be spared? It is a short word to say, but there are volumes in it: Jesus had become a habit to her: could He be torn from her, and she survive? And so one motive grew to another, and one thought quickened another, and one affection intensified another, and thus her dolours grew, quicker than the gourds grow in summer, and all the quicker as the time drew near.

It was also a characteristic of her sorrows that they were in her soul, rather than in her body. Not that her body was without its fearful and appropriate sufferings. We have seen that already. But they were nothing to the sorrows of her soul. The one bore no proportion to the other. Physical pain is hard to bear, so hard that when it comes to a certain point it seems unbearable. It lays hands upon our life, which shrinks away at the touch. No one can think lightly of bodily pain. Yet how light is it compared with mental suffering! Even to us the agonies of the soul are far more dreadful than the tortures of the body. Yet we are gross and material compared to our Blessed Lady, almost as if we were creatures of another species. The more refined and delicate the soul, the more excruciating is its agony. What then must have been the pains of a soul which was such an immaculate vessel of grace as hers was? We have no standards by which to measure what she felt. Her powers of suffering are beyond our comprehension. All we know is that they transcended all human experience, and that the two Hearts of Jesus and Mary were raised into a world of suffering of their own, where no other hearts of flesh can follow them. Her pains were martyrdom reversed; for the seat of the anguish was in the soul and flowed over, blistering and burning, on the sympathetic flesh, while with the martyrs the soul poured sweet balm into the wounded flesh, and the heaven within burned more brightly than the lighted fire or the wild beast's eye without. In this also she was distinguished in some respect even from Jesus. His Soul was crucified in Gethsemane, His Body upon Calvary. On her body not a wound was made; from her veins not a drop of blood was drawn. His Body and His Blood had come from hers, and it was enough that His should suffer for them both. This perfectly interior character of her dolours, so often independent of external circumstances, and requiring in order to its just appreciation a spiritual discernment, must not be lost sight of as one of their most distinguishing characteristics.

If we may make bold to think for a moment of what theology calls the Circuminsession of the Three Divine Persons, the way in which Each lies in the lap of the Others, it will carry us far beyond any prerogatives of Mary, putting a simply infinite distance between the Creator and the creature. Nevertheless the idea of that eminent unity will draw us out of our low thoughts more nearly to a just appreciation of the union between Jesus and His Mother. The Heart of each seemed to lie in the Heart of the other. This was especially true of Mary. His beauty drew her out of herself. She lived in His Heart rather than her own. His interests were hers. His dispositions became hers. She thought with Him, felt with Him, and, as far as might be, identified herself with Him. She lived only for Him. Her life was His instrument, to be done with what He willed. In this union sometimes she was the Mother, with her whole heart poured out upon her Son, rejoicing in all she was, in all she had, in all she could do or suffer, simply as so much material to sacrifice for Him. Sometimes it was almost as if she were the child and He the Father, she so leaned upon Him, and obeyed Him, and had not a thought which was not His, hardly a thought even for Him. It was for Him to think and to dispose; she would follow, minister, sympathise, agree, worship Him with her love. We read wonderful things of the saints, and of their union with God; but there never was any to compare with this union of Jesus and Mary. It stood alone in degree: it stood alone in kind. It was like itself, and it was like no other union, except that which it distantly, and yet so softly and so truly, shadowed, the Unity of the most Holy Trinity. Now she lived far more vitally in this outward life than in her inward life; or, to speak more justly, this outward life, this life in Jesus, was more inward, more really her own life, than the other; and it was one of the characteristics of her dolours that they were not so much in herself as in Him whom she loved far more than self. There are some human sorrows which have faint parallels to this. Shadows of it have crossed widowed mothers' hearts, when their first-born stood glorious on manhood's threshold, and death put out his light, and drew him under. But none have felt as Mary felt, for none have lived in such union with the object of their love, and none have had such an object, at once divine, and human, and their own, which they might so dare to love, with a love which they need not be at the pains to distinguish from absolute worship.

Another characteristic of our Lady's sorrows is the union of their great variety with the fact of their being interior, that is, of their being unitedly felt in one place, her heart. Indeed, this follows from the fact of their being interior, and is the cause of a very peculiar kind of suffering. When the instruments of torture went from one limb of the martyr to another, there was almost a relief in the vicissitude. We most of us know what the concentrated pressure of pain upon one nerve is like, especially when that pressure is kept tight for hours or days or even weeks. It is quite a different sort of agony from flying, shifting pains, or even from the fiery shooting pains which are so hard to bear. But when we transfer this uniform pressure from a limb or a nerve to the heart, the result of suffering must be incalculable. The variety of her sorrows was almost infinite. Both His Natures, human and divine, supplied countless diversities of grief, multiplied its motives, intensified its bitterness. The bodily pains of the Passion, the mental sufferings, the deep abasements, the cries, the faces, the very visible thoughts of the multitudes around, were so many different kinds of pain to her. And then the complete unity of her undivided affections added immensely to them all. She loved only One. The causes of her martyrdom were all centered in one. There was no other object in her heart to call off some portion of her grief, and distract it from its overwhelming fixity. How sweet are the child's cries to the fresh widow's heart! what an eloquent distraction, better than if an angel spoke! O that cry is like a great grace from heaven, strong-shouldered to bear so much of the dark burden! But Mary has no diversion to her woes. Innumerable as they were, they ran up into one supernatural, many-headed point, and pierced with all their might the very centre of her life, the beautiful sanctuary of her loving heart.

But this was not all. Not only was she without other objects, other duties, other loves, to distract her in her misery; but actually that which should naturally have alleviated her sorrows, only embittered and poisoned them. What should have been light was worse than Egyptian darkness. What ought to have given life was in her case enough to kill. The goodness of our Blessed Lord put a special barb of its own on every shaft that pierced her heart. It was His holiness that made His death so awful. His love of her, which in its own nature was more than a consolation to her, nay, was positively her life, was the grand cruelty of her Compassion. Had she loved Him less, or had He loved her less, her dolours would not have so far transcended all human parallel. The exquisiteness of each torture was precisely in her love. But His Divinity! the secret glory of His bright impassible Nature, might she not pillow her weary head thereon? O dearest of all the dogmas of the faith; how many an aching heart and outworn spirit and tempest-troubled soul, when all the world had gone to shipwreck round it, has laid down upon thy soft and welcome bed, and tasted peace when all was trouble above and beneath, within and without! To how many thousands has that doctrine been like an angelic visitant, bidding the storms cease, and smoothing even the bed of death! And shall it be nothing to her who has more to do with it than any other of God's creatures?

Nothing? O far from that; it shall be to her a new abyss, unknown hitherto, of human sorrow, in which she shall sink immeasurable depths, and yet find no end. It shall so swathe her in suffering that she shall lie to all appearance helpless on a vast sea of sorrow. Everything went by the rule of contraries in her martyrdom. The very things, which of themselves would lighten her load, were like murderous hands that held her under the dark waters with cruel force. And because she was too strong to suffocate, she suffered the more terribly. This also is not without parallel in human sorrow, though none such ever came nigh to hers.

But a sorrow without a sympathy is a rare phenomenon, even on this unkindly earth. Yet where shall she find sympathy with hers? There is but one in the whole world who can understand her, and it is He, who by His sufferings, is inflicting all this suffering upon her. She will give all her sympathy to Him rather than seek it from Him. She must bear in secret. St. Joseph knew her well, but he never knew her fully. Her heart is a mystery even to St. John, although he had been initiated into the secrets of the Sacred Heart. And that dear apostle himself needs her love to keep him upright beneath his Master's Cross. Even in the eighteen years it is not easy to think that Jesus and Mary talked much of their future sorrows, or sought sympathy in each other's love. To me it seems more probable that they never spoke of the matter at all. Besides which, her sympathy with Him was simply worship; it was love indeed, true fond maternal love, yet it was worship also, and unlike all common sympathy with grief. When she slowly walked away from the garden-tomb on Friday night, she re-entered a world where not one soul could understand her, not even the holy passionate Magdalen. It was darkness without one gleam of light, a wilderness of terrors, a life without one point of attraction, one resting-place for her broken heart. She shut her sorrows up within herself, enduring them in a hot-hearted silence, and there were none who could do more than guess the aching void that was beating like a wild pulse in that maternal heart.

These were the characteristics of her sorrows; and what is every word that has been said but a deepening shade to the dark, dark picture? What then shall we think of that last characteristic of her dolours, which so amazed St. Bernard, the moderation with which she bore them? Who is ever able to forget, when they meditate upon our Blessed Mother, the heavenly tranquillity of her "Behold the handmaid of the Lord," at the Annunciation? The same tranquillity is unbroken even when her heart is breaking beneath the Cross. Except in the case of very high sanctity, and even there the exception does not always hold, moderation in sorrow would imply something like coldness or insensibility. We should hardly love very tenderly any one, the even tenor of whose way deep affliction could not disturb. In the case of the saints the love of God acts as a counter-charm to the spells of sorrow. It at once distracts and compensates, and so makes endurance easier. But with Mary it was just in her love of God that the exceeding bitterness of her agony consisted. If then we figure to ourselves the bewildering complications of misery, the enormous weight of sorrow, the supernatural aggravations also of it, which she had to bear, and then the way in which with such resistless might it bore down upon her solitary heart, it is amazing to see it all break upon her tranquillity, as a billow breaks in idle foam upon some huge promontory, which quivers to its base as it flings the wild waters back, and yet remains unbroken. So it was with her. She was not insensible like the cold granite. On the contrary the tempest went through her, searching every corner of her capacious nature, filled to overflowing every possibility of suffering, and drenched with bitterness every faculty and affection. Yet not a ruffle passed on her tranquillity. Her peace within was as untroubled as the cavities of the ocean when the surface is wildly rocking in the storm. Nevertheless, this tranquillity was no protection to her against the intensity of suffering. It rather enabled her to suffer more. It allowed the grief to penetrate more unresistedly into every part of her. Yet there was no wildness, no loud sighs, no broken sobs, no outspoken words of complaint. Still less—the thought is one which would never have crossed the mind of an intelligent lover of Mary, if careless untheological pictures had not indecorously brought it before so many of us—still less were there any vehement attitudes of grief, any contortions of the venerable beauty of her face, any womanish wringing of the hands, any negligence of dishevelled hair, any prostrations on the ground as of one overcome with mortal anguish, least of all any fainting away, any need of a supporting arm around her, whether it were that of John or Magdalen, any suspension of that glorious reason which sleep even had not interrupted in its magnificent exercises since the very first moment of the Immaculate Conception. Let us in indignant love give to the flames these ignorant dishonourable representations, and drive out of ourselves the odious images which their skill and beauty may have left upon our minds. Mary "*stood*" beneath the Cross: that is the simple grandeur of the scriptural picture, which represented the actual truth, and whose artist was her own Spouse, the Holy Ghost. And it was the picture of that calm standing woman on which her fond child, St. Bernard, gazed in admiring love. This too is the attractiveness of our Lady's apparitions in the revelations of Mary of Agreda, compared with her portrait in the visions of Sister Emmerich. The instincts of the Spanish nun were more true than those even of the artistic soul of the ecstatic German. Never then must we put away from ourselves the thought of this moderation of Mary in her woes. There was nothing wild, nothing unsettled, nothing dramatic, nothing passionate, nothing demonstrative, nothing excessive; but she stood in calmest queenliest dignity, quiet, not as a sweet evening landscape, or a noontide summer sea, or a green wood at dawn, or a moonlit mountain-top, or as any other image in the poetry of nature, but quiet, in her measure and degree, as the Divine Nature of our Lord while the tumult of the Passion was trampling His Human Nature to death. Her tranquillity was the image of that tranquillity. It was one of many participations in Himself which Jesus gave to her in those dark hours.

SECTION V.

HOW OUR LADY COULD REJOICE IN HER DOLOURS.

Having thus considered the characteristics of our Lady's dolours, we must now pass to a peculiarity of them, which it is necessary always to bear in mind, namely, their union with the intensest joy. That her dolours were accompanied throughout with floods of heavenly joy, she herself revealed to St. Bridget. But indeed it could not be otherwise. Can we suppose it possible that a sinless rational creature can ever be otherwise than bathed in joy? Beatitude is the life of God, and it is out of that life that torrents of gladness inundate His whole creation. It is sin only that brings sorrow, and if the sins of others can make the sinless grieve, they can never interfere with that abiding gladness deep down, which union with God must of necessity produce. Moreover, there is no merit where there is no love. If our Lady's dolours had not risen out of her love and been animated by it, they would not have been meritorious. But in truth love was the very cause of them. Out of the excess of love came the excess of sorrow. Now it is undeniable that love cannot exist without delectation. Love is of itself essentially a joy; and in proportion to the eminence of our Mother's love must also be the eminence of her celestial joy. To sorrow and rejoice at once is possible even for us, whose inward life sin has distracted, and made irregular and uncompact. We have all of us done so, even though our sensitive nature is a battle-field where the struggles are quickly over, and one or other of the contending passions is left master of the field. But it is in Jesus and Mary that this perfect union of the uttermost of joy and sorrow has taken place, and been an abiding, lifelong, normal state. It is one of the most remarkable phenomena of the Incarnation, and has seemed, in our Lord's lower Nature, to be a sort of adumbration of His union of Two Natures in one Person. It is also one of His characteristics in which He has given His Mother largely to participate. In His Passion He restrained His Divinity, and would not let it sensibly penetrate His Human Nature with its light and glory. Nay, He even laid His hand upon that Beatific Vision, which was due to His Sacred Humanity, and which was uncloudedly before His Soul from the first moment of His Incarnation, and would not allow it to include within its sphere of gladness His sensitive nature, lest it should blunt His suffering and quench the fire of His great agony. So, in her measure, our Blessed Lady in the depths of her soul was filled with gladness because of her intimate union with God, and yet the gladness had a sphere of its own, and was not allowed to break out with its vast world of light, so at least as to banish all sorrow from the heart. As was said before, her joy, so far from alleviating her sufferings, probably made her suffer more. But once again we must remember it was not with her as with the martyrs. They sang among the fires and exulted among the panthers, because their soul was all whole and joyous, while their flesh was torn and their bones broken. But with her the soul was the chief sufferer; and joy and sorrow divided it against itself. This was nearer to a mystery. Indeed it was a true participation in the characteristics of Jesus, a cleaving asunder of the soul without disturbing its simplicity, a division without sedition, a wound which was a new life, a battle while all was harmony and peace. O Mother! we cannot tell how it was, only that so it was! Thou wert all joy, and being so near God, how couldst thou help but be so? Thou wert all sorrow, and what else couldst thou be in those dark abysses of the Passion! And thy sorrow had no power over thy joy; but thy joy had power over thy sorrow, and gave it a brisker acid, a more volatile and pervasive bitterness! Glad creature! sorrow crushed thee, and then a joy, like that of heaven, sat upon thy burden, and made it tenfold more hard to bear!

Yet we are hardly doing justice to her sorrows when we say that they had no influence upon her joys. Doubtless they increased them, and were to her the fountains of new joys which she had never had before, or of new degrees of old accustomed joys. It is not as if her joy and sorrow were two oceans in her soul, which had no mutual inlets, and did not commingle with each other, or ebb and flow in sympathy. So far from that, there is a sense in which we might say that her sorrow and her joy were almost identical: for her joys were sorrows, and her sorrows joys. They might be the one or the other, according to the double life that was in them. Truly in her sorrows were many reasons for joy, such as the grandest and happiest archangel of heaven has not in himself. If we look long at the darkness of Calvary, a beautiful light breaks out of its gloomiest centre. What is it all but a magnificent reparation of the Divine Honour. Not Michael, when flushed with triumphant sanctity he drove usurping Lucifer out of heaven, so rejoiced in the honour of God, as Mary did. She, who had been allowed to fathom sin so deeply, and who in the spirit of Gethsemane had tasted somewhat of the Father's anger, could exult in the satisfaction of His justice, as neither angel nor saint could do. She, who had lived thirty-three years with Jesus, and had caught from Him His passionate yearning for His Father's honour, could find depths of blissful congratulation in the restoring of that honour, which not all creatures together could discover. Sometimes there has been a minutest drop of that joy in our hearts, and we know what it was like, but could not tell even if we would. O for that land, where it will be an unchecked, eternal habit!

There was joy too through all the immense wisdom with

which God had endowed her, because of the divine wisdom which was apparent to her in the whole scheme of our redemption. There was not a cavern of shame, but it was illuminated by several of the divine perfections, shedding over it a perfect blaze of beautiful splendour. There was not a physical horror in the Passion, from which an unloving faith shrinks back in vulgar fastidiousness, but was clothed with a strange loveliness out of the treasures of the divine mind and will. The science of the Incarnation never came out, even to her, in such amazing, fascinating clearness as it did in her Compassion, with all its reasons, possibilities, adaptations, and conveniences. The sight she saw would have been enough to feed the worship of the nine choirs of angels for ever.

There was joy also in her foresight of the exaltation of Jesus. She saw Him already at the Right Hand of the Father, His Sacred Humanity, enthroned there as an object of highest worship for ever. To her eyes the bright clouds of Ascension Day were strangely interlaced with the darkness of the dun eclipse on Calvary. She saw the feet that were dropping blood, as if they were rising up in the sunny air, each with its glorified stigma gleaming like a roseate sun. She almost saw the angels in their glistening white, moving about amid the horses of those ruthless foreign centurions. The darkness of the depth set off the brightness of the exaltation, as if it were a background of storm throwing forward the bright things in front of it with vivid, lifelike light. There was joy also in her participation at the time in the interior joy of Jesus. For that failing Heart upon the Cross had a very ocean of gladness within itself, a gladness none on earth but His Mother knew, a gladness none else could share, because none else could understand it. If her share of it were parted among the numberless elect, we should each have more than we could bear. It was a joy also, of a peculiar kind, to see Him paying then and there for the glorious prerogatives He had given her. When the blood moistened her hand and stained its whiteness, she recognised and worshipped it as the price of her Immaculate Conception. Could she see that, and then not love Him ten thousand times more than she had loved Him hitherto? And with the rush of love must needs come a rush of joy as well.

It is impossible also not to rejoice in the operations of grace within our souls. Each augmentation of grace is a mission of a Divine Person, a contact with God, a more intimate and exquisite union with Him. If we were slower, graver, less occupied, and less precipitate in our spiritual life, we should feel this more than we do. How greatly then must she have rejoiced in the magnificent supernatural acts which her sorrows were causing her to elicit all the while! Such faith, such hope, such love, such fortitude, such conformity, such love of suffering, such spirit of sacrifice, such intelligent worship, such incomparable union! Millions of saints could have been made out of each of these royal magnificences, and yet have left a marvellous amount to spare. There was joy too, who can disbelieve it? in her thought that her Compassion should be so rich a boon to us, that it should win us so many graces, give us so many examples, excite so much devotion, lead us so much nearer Jesus, and fill us with a wiser spirit of more profound adoration. Here are seven joys, which came out of her very sorrows. They might be multiplied indefinitely; but these are enough for love, and more than enough for our comprehension in their fulness.

SECTION VI.

THE WAY IN WHICH THE CHURCH PUTS OUR LADY'S DOLOURS BEFORE US.

Such is a general description of the dolours of Mary. The Church puts them before us as part of the Gospel, as one of the facts of the Gospel, and as an object of special devotion. Marchese, in his Diario di Maria, mentions an old tradition, which would carry devotion to the sorrows of our Blessed Lady up to apostolic times. Some years after her death, while St. John the Evangelist was still grieving over his loss and longing to see her face again, it pleased our Blessed Lord to appear to him in a vision, accompanied by His Mother. The sorrows of Mary, together with her frequent visits to the holy places of the Passion, were naturally a constant subject of devout contemplation to the Evangelist, who had watched over the last fifteen years of her life; and, as if it were in response to these continual meditations, he heard her ask Jesus to grant some especial favour to those who should keep her dolours in remembrance. Our Lord replied that He would grant four particular graces to all those who should practise this devotion. The first was a perfect contrition for all their sins some time before death; the second was a particular protection in the hour of death; the third was to have the mysteries of the Passion deeply imprinted in their minds; and the fourth a particular power of impetration granted to Mary's prayers on their behalf. St. Bridget relates in the seventh book of her Revelations that she saw in a vision, in the Church of Santa Maria Maggiore at Rome, the immense price which was set in heaven upon the dolours of Mary. To the Blessed Benvenuta, the Dominicaness, it was granted to feel in her soul the sorrow which our Lady suffered during the Three Days' Loss. The Blessed Veronica of Binasco had several revelations regarding this devotion, in one of which, as related by the Bollandists, our Lord said that tears shed over His Mother's sorrows were more acceptable to Him than those which are shed over His own Passion. In like manner Gianius in his history of the Servites relates that, when Innocent IV. was raised to the apostolic chair, he felt some alarm regarding the new order of the Servites of Mary. There were several false and counterfeit religions which had troubled the Church about that time—the Poor of Lyons, the so-called Apostolic Men, the Flagellants, and the followers of William de Saint Amour—and the Pope was anxious to assure himself that the Servites, lately instituted near Florence, were not of the same character as these. He therefore commissioned St. Peter Martyr, the Dominican, to investigate the matter. Our Lady appeared to the inquisitor in a vision. He saw a lofty mountain, covered with flowers, and bathed in shining light, and on the summit of it sate the Mother of God as on a throne, while angels offered garlands of flowers before her. After this they presented to her seven lilies of exceeding whiteness, which she placed for a moment in her bosom, and then wreathed them like a diadem round her head. These seven lilies, as she explained the vision to Pietro, were the seven founders of the Servites, whom she had herself inspired to institute the new order in honour of the dolours which she suffered in the Passion and Death of Jesus. When St. Catherine of Bologna was one day weeping bitterly over our Lady's sorrows, she suddenly saw seven angels near her, weeping also, and joining their tears with hers. But it would not be difficult to compile a whole volume of visions and revelations regarding the dolours of Mary. The reader will find abundance of them in two books especially, both of which are of easy access—Marchese's *Diario di Maria*, and Sinischalchi's *Martirio del Cuore di Maria*; the first writer was an Oratorian, and the second a Jesuit.

This devotion has received the highest sanction of the Church, for it enters both into the Missal and the Breviary. Two distinct feasts are appointed in honour of these sorrows; one falls in September, and the other on the Friday in Passion Week. The Rosary of the Seven Dolours, as well as several other devotions, have been richly indulgenced. Among these may be mentioned the Hymn *Stabat Mater*, an hour at any time of the year spent in meditation on the dolours, an exercise in honour of her sorrowing heart, seven Aves with the *Sancta Mater istud agas*, another exercise for the last ten days of the carnival, and an hour or half-an-hour's prayer on Good Friday and other Fridays. Nothing therefore is wanting to the sanction of this devotion, nor has the Church spared any means to attract her children to it.

She has, however, especially selected seven of Mary's sorrows for our more peculiar devotion. She has imbedded them by means of antiphons in the Divine office, and she has made them the seven mysteries of the Rosary of the Dolours. They are—Simeon's prophecy, the Flight into Egypt, the Three Days' Loss, the Meeting Jesus with the Cross, the Crucifixion, the Taking down from the Cross, the Burial of Jesus. Thus, in one way of dividing them, three belong to our Lord's Infancy, and four to His Passion. Or, again, one covers His whole life, two His infancy, and four His Passion. Or, again, one puts before us all the Thirty-Three Years, two the Child Jesus, two Jesus Suffering, and two Jesus Dead. These seven are mysterious samples of her multitudinous other sorrows, and we shall find perhaps that they are types of all human sorrow whatsoever. The seven chapters, therefore, which follow, will consider one by one these seven dolours, observing the same simple and easy method in the investigation of all of them. Each dolour will present four points for our consideration—first, the circumstances of the mystery itself; secondly, its peculiarities; thirdly, our Lady's dispositions in it; and fourthly, its lessons to ourselves. A ninth chapter will be added on the Compassion of Mary, in order to explain the relation in which it stands to the Passion, whether it had any share in the redemption of the world, and what the true meaning is of those puzzling expressions, co-redemptress, and the like, which are sometimes found in approved writers on the grandeurs of Mary.

SECTION VII.

THE SPIRIT OF DEVOTION TO OUR LADY'S DOLOURS.

Before concluding this introductory chapter, however, it seems necessary to say something on the spirit of this beautiful and popular devotion. It produces in our minds an extreme tenderness towards our Blessed Lord, united with the profoundest reverence. Jesus demands from us our worship as God. He claims our undoubting faith in His goodness and in the abundance of His redeeming grace. He expects from us a rational conviction that our only trust is in Him, and that we should consequently discharge our duties to Him and obey His commandments, as our necessary and reasonable service. But He wants far more than this. He has something much nearer His Heart. He desires our tenderness. He wishes to see us with our hearts always in our hands for Him. He would fain win us to Himself, and unite us with Himself in the bonds of the most familiar and intimate affection. He would have us identify our interests with His, and concentrate our sympathies in Him. The thought of Him should fill our eyes with tears, and kindle our hearts with love. His name should be the sweetest music that we know; His words the laws of all our life. He wishes us, as it were, to forget the precise amount of our actual obligations to Him. Indeed, what is the use of remembering them, when we know that it is beyond our power to fulfil them? He would have us deal with Him promptly, generously, abundantly, with the instincts of love, and not as if the life of faith were a spirit of commerce, the balance of justice, the duty of gratitude, or the wise calculations of an intelligent self-interest. We should cling to Him as a child clings to its mother. We should hang about Him as a friend whose absence we cannot bear. We should keep Him fondly in our thoughts as men sometimes do with a sweet grief, which has become to them the soft and restful light of their whole lives. Now the way in which our Lady's dolours keep His Passion continually before us has a special virtue to produce this tenderness in us. We love Him, who is infinitely to be loved in all ways, in a peculiar manner when He is reflected in His Mother's heart; and although it is absolutely necessary for us perpetually to contemplate His Passion in all the nakedness of its harrowing circumstances and revolting shame, for else we shall never have a true idea of the sinfulness of sin, yet there is something in the Passion, seen through Mary, which makes us forget ourselves, and tranquilly engrosses us in the most melting tenderness and endearing sympathy towards our Blessed Lord. The emotions which are awakened by the Passion in itself are manifold and exciting, whereas the spirit of tenderness presides over Mary's sorrows with one exclusive, constraining presence.

But out of this tenderness comes also a great hatred of sin. If God were to let us choose which of the great and extraordinary gifts, that He has given to His Saints, should be conferred upon ourselves, we could not do better than ask for that piercing and overwhelming hatred of sin which some have had. It is a gift which lies at the root of all perfection, and is the supernatural vigour of all perseverance. It is at once the safest and the most operative of all singular graces. Devotion to our Lady's dolours is a great help both to acquiring the hatred of sin as a habit, and to meriting it as a grace. The desolation wrought by sin in the heart of the sinless Mother, and the reflection that her sorrows were not, like those of Jesus, the redemption of the world, fill us with horror, with pity, with indignation, with self-reproach. There is nothing to distract us from this thought, as there is in the sacrifice of our Lord, who was thus accomplishing His own great work, satisfying the justice of His Father, earning the exaltation of His Sacred Humanity, and becoming the Father Himself of a countless multitude of the elect. The Mother's heart bleeds, simply because she is His Mother, and it is our sins which are making it bleed so cruelly. We are ourselves part of the shadow of that eclipse which is passing so darkly over her spotless life. We can never help thinking of sin so long as we see those seven swords springing like a dreadful sheaf from the very inmost sanctuary of her broken heart.

Yet there is something also in the dolours, and even in this abhorrence of sin, to make us forget ourselves, without at all perilling our safe humility. We rise up from the contemplation of them with a yearning for the conversion of sinners. As if because they were the travail of the queen of the apostles, they fill our minds full of apostolic instincts. Whether this is a hidden grace which they communicate, or whether it follows naturally from the subject of meditation, it is certain that this is a favourite devotion with all missionary souls.* The fearfulness of losing Jesus, the unbearable anguish of ever so short a separation from Him, the darkness and the dreariness which come where He is not, these are notable figures in each of the seven processions of those mysterious woes. And how far from Jesus are sinners, misbelievers, heathens! How far out of sight of Calvary have they wandered! How many in number, and in so many ways how dear, are the wanderers! How unfathomable a misery is sin! And to us what a misery those merry voices and bright faces that care not for the misery, but go singing on their way to a dark eternity, as though they were wending gallantly to a bridal feast! Who can see so great a wretchedness and not long to cure it? Then, again, sin caused all that Passion, all these sorrows. Perhaps our heart in the heat of love forgets itself, and thinks for the moment that by hindering sin it can spare our dearest Lord some pain. Yet is this altogether a mistake, is it quite an unreality? Anyhow it will busy itself with reparation, and there is no reparation like the conversion of a sinner. And the lost sheep shall be laid at Mary's feet, and she shall gently raise them and lay them in the outstretched arms of the happy Shepherd; and we will sit down and weep for joy that we have been allowed to do something for Jesus and Mary; and we will ask no graces for ourselves, but only seek glory and love and praise for them.

He, who is growing in devotion to the Mother of God, is growing in all good things. His time cannot be better spent; his eternity cannot be more infallibly secured. But devotion is, on the whole, more a growth of love than of reverence, though never detached from reverence. And there is nothing about our Lady which stimulates our love more effectually than her dolours. In delight and fear we

---

* See the Author's Essay on Catholic Home Missions, p. 3.

shade our eyes when the bright light of her Immaculate Conception bursts upon us in its heavenly effulgence. We fathom with awe and wonder the depths of her Divine Maternity. The vastness of her science, the sublimities of her holiness, the singularity of her prerogatives, fill us with joyful admiration united with reverential fear. It is a jubilee to us that all these things belong to our own Mother, whose fondness for us knows no bounds. But somehow we get tired of always looking up into the bright face of heaven. The very silver linings of the clouds make our eyes ache, and they look down for rest and find it in the green grass of the earth. The moon is beautiful, gilding with rosy gold her own purple region of the sky, but her light is more beautiful to our homesick hearts when it is raining over field, and tree, and lapsing stream, and the great undulating ocean. For earth after all is a home, for which one may be sick. So, when theology has been teaching us our Mother's grandeurs in those lofty, unshared mysteries, our devotion, because of its very infirmity, is conscious to itself of a kind of strain. O how, after long meditation on the Immaculate Conception, love gushes out of every pore of our hearts when we think of that almost more than mortal queen, heartbroken, and with blood-stains on her hand, beneath the Cross! O Mother! we have been craving for more human thoughts of thee; we have wanted to feel thee nearer to us; we can weep for joy at the greatness of thy throne, but they are not such tears as we can shed with thee on Calvary: they do not rest us so. But when once more we see thy sweet sad face of maternal sorrow, the tears streaming down thy cheeks, the quietness of thy great woe, and the blue mantle we have known so long, it seems as if we had found thee after losing thee, and that thou wert another Mary from that glorious portent in the heavens, or at least a fitter mother for us on the low summit of Calvary than scaling those unapproachable mountain-heights of heaven! See how the children's affections break out with new love from undiscovered recesses in their hearts, and run round their newly widowed mother like a river, as if to supply her inexhaustibly with tears, and divide her off with a great broad frontier of love from the assault of any fresh calamity. The house of sorrow is always a house of love. This is what takes place in us regarding Mary's dolours. One of the thousand ends of the Incarnation was God's condescending to meet and gratify the weakness of humanity, for ever falling into idolatry because it was so hard to be always looking upwards, always gazing fixedly into inaccessible furnaces of light. So are Mary's dolours to her grandeurs. The new strength of faith and devotion, which we have gained in contemplating her celestial splendours, furnishes us with new capabilities of loving; and all our loves, the new and the old as well, rally round her in her agony at the foot of the Cross of Jesus. Love for her grows quickest there. It is our birthplace. We became her children there. She suffered all that because of us. Sinlessness is not common to our Mother and to us. But sorrow is. It is the one thing we share, the one common thing betwixt us. We will sit with her therefore and sorrow with her, and grow more full of love, not forgetting her grandeurs,—O surely never!—but pressing to our hearts with fondest predilection the memory of her exceeding martyrdom.

What is the wise life but that which is for evermore living over again the Thirty-Three Years of Jesus? What is all else but a waste of time, a cumbering of the world, a taking up room on earth which men have no right to? We should ever be in attendance upon some one or other of the mysteries of Jesus, steeping our thoughts in it, acting in the spirit of it. Our Blessed Lord's interior dispositions are the grand practical science of life, and the sole science which will carry away any of time's products into eternity. The way in which we should both learn and exercise this science is by pondering on the mysteries of Jesus, or indeed by faith personally assisting at them in the spirit of Mary. This imitation of Mary must be the lifelong attitude of Christians. She read off our Lord's Sacred Heart continually. She saw habitually, as in a glass before her, all His inward dispositions, whether they regarded His Father, herself, or us. There were times when He drew a veil over it; but, ordinarily speaking, that vision was abidingly before her. So say the Agredan revelations. But even if this were not so, who can doubt that Mary understood Jesus as no one else could do, and was in closer and more real union with Him than any saint could be? Hence no one doubts that her sympathy with Him in all His mysteries was of the most perfect description, and in keeping with her consummate holiness. We must, therefore, learn her heart. We must strive to enter into her dispositions. An interior life, taken from hers, faint and disfigured as the copy at best must be, is the only one which is secure from manifold delusion. Yet nowhere can we penetrate so deeply into her heart, or be so sure of our discoveries, as in the case of her sorrows. Moreover, the field for participation in the spirit of Jesus which they open to us is wider: for, immense as was His joy, nay, even perpetually beatific, His life was distinguished rather by sorrow than by joy. Sorrow was, so to speak, more intimate to Him than joy. Joy was the companion of the Thirty-Three Years: sorrow was their character, their instrument, their energy, their discovery of what they were to seek. Thus a participation in the spirit of Jesus through the spirit of Mary is the true spirit of this devotion to our Lady's dolours. Those, who have lived for some years amid their quiet shadows, can tell how they are almost a revelation in themselves.

But, when we speak of the spirit of this devotion, we must not omit to speak also of its power. We must not dwell exclusively on the spiritual effects it produces on ourselves, without reminding ourselves of its real power with God. In this respect one devotion may differ from another. One may be more acceptable to God, even where all are acceptable. He may promise prerogatives to one which He has not promised to another. Now there are few devotions to which our Blessed Lord has promised more than He has done to this. There is a perfect cloud of visions and revelations resting upon it, and in consequence, of examples of the saints also. Moreover, there are reasons for its being so in the nature of the devotion itself. We know what a powerful means of grace our Blessed Lady is, and our devotion to her must for the most part take its form either from her sorrows or her joys. Now, in her joys, as St. Sophronius says, our Lady is simply a debtor to her Son, whereas in her sorrows He is in some sense a debtor to her. St. Methodius, the martyr, teaches the same doctrine. Hence, if we may dare to use words which holy writers have used before, by her dolours she has laid our Blessed Lord under a kind of obligation, which gives her a right and power of impetration into which something of justice even enters. Yet when we think of the Sacred Heart of Jesus, of the immensity of His love for Mary, and of the great part of the Passion which it was to Him to see her suffer, we cannot for a moment doubt, without thinking of obligation, the extreme persuasiveness to Him of devotion to her dolours, a devotion which He Himself began, a devotion which was actually a solid part of His ever-blessed Passion. We draw Him towards us the moment we begin to think of His Mother's sorrows. He is beforehand, says St. Anselm, with those who meditate His Mother's woes. And do we not stand in need of power in Heaven? What a great work we have to do in our souls, and how little of it is already done! How slight is the impression we have made yet on our ruling passion, on our besetting sin! How superficial is our spirit of prayer, how childishly timid our spirit of penance, how transitory our moments of union with God! We want vigour, determination, consistency, solidity, and a more venturous aspiration. In short, our spiritual life wants power. And here is a devotion, so solid and efficacious, that it is eminently calculated to give us this power, as well by its masculine products in the soul, as by its actual influence over the Heart of our Blessed Lord. Who, that looks well at the saints, and sees what it has done for them, but will do his best to cultivate this devotion in himself?

In the affairs of this world steadiness comes with age. But who has not felt that it is not so in spiritual things? Alas! fervour is steadiness there, and that is too often but for awhile: when we have held on upon our way for some years, we grow tired. Familiarity brings with it the spirit of dispensation. Our habits become disjointed, as if the teeth of the wheels were worn down and would not bite. Our life gets uneven and untrue, like a machine out of order. So we find that the longer we persevere, the more we stand in need of steadiness. For behold! when we had trusted to the doctrine of habit, and dreamed that age would bring maturity in its own right, the very opposite has been the case. In easy ways and low attainments, and unworthy condescensions, and the facility of self-dispensing indulgence, in a word, in all things that are second-best, the power of habit is strong enough, indeed, altogether to be depended on. But in what is best, in effort, in climbing, in fighting, in enduring, in persisting, we seem to grow more uncertain, fitful, capricious, irregular, feeble, than we were before. A worse weakness than that of youth is coming back to us, worse because it has less hopefulness about it, worse because time was to have cured the old weakness and now it is time which is bringing this weakness on, worse because it makes us less anxious, for we have hardened ourselves to think that we attempted too much when we were young, and that prudence indicates a low level where the air is milder and better for our respiration. Then do not some of us feel that the world grows more attractive to us as we grow older? It should not be so; but so it is! This comes of lukewarmness. Age unlearns many things: but woe betide it when it unlearns vigour, when it unlearns hope! Rest is a great thing. It is the grand want of age. But we must not lie down before our time. Ah! how often has fervent youth made the world its bed in middle life; and when at last the world slipped from under it, whither did it fall? If we live only in the enervating ring of domestic love, much more in the vortex of the world, we must live with Jesus in the spirit of Mary, or we are lost. Let us learn this in increased devotion to her dolours. When we lie down to rest, we persuade ourselves it is but for a moment, and that we shall not go to sleep. But only let this most pathetic romance, which the destinies of humanity have ever brought before men, sound in our ears and knock at the doors of our hearts, and it will become in us a continually flowing fountain of supreme unworldliness. Torpor will become impossible. Oblivion of supernatural things will be unknown. We shall feel that rest would be pleasant for awhile: but we shall disdain the temptation. Mary will teach us to *stand* beneath the Cross.

CHAPTER II.

THE FIRST DOLOUR.

THE PROPHECY OF ST. SIMEON.

NOWHERE in the Old Testament do we seem to come so near to God as in the book of Job. Nowhere is He more awfully enshrouded in mystery, or more terrible in His counsels regarding the children of men; and yet nowhere is He more plainly or more tenderly our Father. It is because the mystery of suffering is depicted therein. Because it is all so human, it seems to lead us so far into the divine. Because it is the uttermost trial of the creature, he lies the more completely in the Creator's arms. The calamities of Job are to the Old Testament what the Passion of our Lord is to the New, and the one was an intentional foreshadowing of the other. When we come to speak of our Lady's dolours, we remember the touching picture of Job's friends, when they heard of his afflictions, and came to visit him. "When they had lifted up their eyes afar off, they knew him not, and crying out they wept, and rending their garments, they sprinkled dust upon their heads towards heaven. And they sate with him on the ground seven days and seven nights, and no man spoke to him a word; for they saw that his grief was very great." They knew that silence was the best consolation. There was nothing which could so touch the heart of the mourner as the fact that his friends appreciated the excess of his bereavement. When at last they spoke, then they irritated. The charm of their sweet silent presence was gone. Sympathy degenerated into an argument. An unconvincing argument could end only in reproach. They, more than Job himself, "wrapped up sentences in unskilful words." But still more wonderful than this silence of the friends of Job was the silence of Jesus on the Cross, deeply suffering a distinct inward martyrdom, because of the sorrows of His Mother. He spoke no word to her, but that one whereby He made her over to St. John. No maxim full of celestial wisdom, no tone of filial endearment, no acknowledgment that He saw and felt her sufferings, no blessing full of grace and fortitude, fell on her ear as He hung upon the Cross. In truth she needed none of them. She saw His Heart. She understood her Son. She was by this time marvellously accustomed to the ways of God. Silence was His devotion to her sorrows, just as silence was the magnificence of her suffering. Silence was in truth a wonderful thing with Jesus and Mary. Indeed it was almost the colloquy they had held together for Three-and-Thirty Years. But His silence was the silence of a full heart; and it is somewhat of that fulness which we must ask of Him, when we meditate on His Mother's sorrows. We cannot think rightly of them, unless He vouchsafes to help us to the truth. All we ask is one spark of what burned in Him during those silent hours; one spark would be enough to set our hearts on fire, and consume us with keenest love for the remainder of our mortal years. He must be our model in sympathy with Mary, as He is in all things else. Like all the rest of sanctity, it is He Himself who taught devotion to our Lady, both by precept and example.

Forty days had gone since the angels sang at midnight. Mary and Joseph had been deep down all the while in divine mysteries. The shepherds had worshipped the new-born Babe. The three kings had laid their mystic offerings at His feet, and the new star had melted away in the purple of the nocturnal skies. The world had gone upon its road as usual. Every morning there was political news in Rome, every morning philosophical discussions in the schools of

Athens. The caravans went in and out of the gates of the white Damascus, and the sun shone on the bend of the Orontes at Antioch. The imperial officials made up their books and lists at Bethlehem, and Joseph and Mary were items in the account of the provincial taxation. In the common course of things, and according to the law, on the first of January Jesus for the first time had shed His blood. How much had passed since the twenty-fifth of December. Since that day the Creator had been visible in His own creation, though it was almost underground, in a kind of grotto, or natural stable for kine. Now the second of February was come. Joseph and Mary, with the Child, leave the spot where those Forty Days have fled as swiftly as a heavenly vision. They wind round the skirt of the narrow hill whereon the city is built. The pruned vineyards on the steeps have scarcely yet begun to weep their vernal tears where the knife has wounded them. But the cornfields where Ruth gleaned are green, and the clear sunshine of early spring is on the gray rocks by Rachel's tomb. The roofs of the Holy City are in sight, with the glorious temple shining above all. To that temple, His own temple, the visible Infant God was now going.

Mary had spent twelve years of her sinless life in the courts of the temple. It was there that she had outwardly dedicated her virginity to God, which she had vowed in the first moment of her Immaculate Conception. It was there she meditated over the ancient scriptures, and learned the secrets of the Messias. She was coming back to it again, still virgin, yet, mystery of grace! a mother with a child. She came to be purified, who was purer than the untrodden snow on Lebanon. She came to present her Child to God, and do for the Creator, what no creature but herself could do, give Him a gift fully equal to Himself. When the second temple was built, the ancients of the people lifted up their voices and wept, because its glory was not equal to the glory of the first; but the first temple had never seen such a day as that which was now dawning on the temple of

Herod. The glory of the Holy of Holies was but a symbol of the real glory which Mary was now bearing thitherward in her arms. But she had two offerings with her. She bore one, and Joseph the other. She bore her Child, and he the pair of turtle-doves, or two young pigeons, for her purification. Many saw them pass. But there was nothing singular in them, nothing especially attractive to the eyes of the beholders. So it always is, where God is. Now that He is visible, He is in truth, except to faith and love, just as invisible as He ever was.

Others too were drawing towards the temple for the morning sacrifices. There was the aged Simeon. The blossoms of the grave were clustered thickly on his head. He had outlived his own day, with its men and things, its sympathies and associations. He was not mixed up with the spirit of the times. He was above its politics. He kept apart from the conflicts of its disputatious Pharisees and Sadducees. The world seemed to him to be growing more and more intolerably wicked, and less and less a place for him, less and less a home at all possible for weary souls. But there was one thing he had longed to see. He was willing his rest should be put off, if only he might see that sight on earth, The Christ! God had promised him that so it should be. "He had received an answer from the Holy Ghost, that he should not see death before he had seen the Christ of the Lord." He was coming that day to the morning sacrifice, whether with clear views, or any spiritual presentiments, or an unwonted fire in his heart, who can tell? There was another also that morning in the temple, a widow of fourscore years and four, the daughter of Phanuel, of the tribe of Aser, from the olive-spotted plain of Acre and the mild inlets of the western sea. The spirit of prophecy dwelt within her. She needed not to come to the temple; for she never departed from it, "by prayers and fasting serving night and day." And now Mary and Joseph have entered with the Child. What preparations has not God vouchsafed to make for that solemnity in the temple on the second of

February! How many graces have gone to sanctify the aged Simeon! What long years of austerity and what great heights of prayer are known to the soul of Anna! There has been more work in the soul of Joseph than went to the creation of the world. Mary is the very chosen trophy of the divine magnificence. Volumes of commentary have been written on her gifts, her graces, and her interior beauty, and yet how little do we know! Then there is the Incarnate Word, whom the silent angels of the temple are worshipping in tremulous awe, as He crosses the threshold of His earthly house. Was there any lighting up in the Infant's eye, as He took possession of His temple? Did the lights go out in the Holy of Holies, now that the Holiest of all was outside the veil, throned in a mortal Mother's arms?

Mary made her offerings, and "performed all things according to the law of the Lord." For the spirit of Jesus was a spirit of obedience; and although the brightness of angelic innocence was dull beside the whiteness of her purity, she obeyed the law of God in the ceremony of her purification, the more readily as it was in fact a concealment of her graces. But she bore also in her arms her true turtle-dove, to do for Him likewise "according to the custom of the law." She placed Him in the arms of the aged priest Simeon, as she has done since in vision to so many of the saints: and the full light broke on Simeon's soul. Weak with age he threw his arms around his God. He bore the whole weight of his Creator, and yet stood upright. The sight of that infant Face was nothing less than the glory of heaven. The Holy Ghost had kept His promise. Simeon had seen, nay was at that moment handling, "the Lord's Christ." O blessed priest! worn down with age, wearied with thy long years of waiting for the "consolation of Israel," kept alive in days which were out of harmony with thy spirit, even as St. John the Evangelist was after thee, surely He who made thee, He who is so soon to judge thee, He whom thou art folding so fondly in thine arms, must have sent the strength of His omnipotence into thy heart, else thou wouldst never have been able to bear the flood of strong gladness which at that moment broke in upon thy spirit! Look at Him again. See those red lips so soon to speak thy sentence of eternal life. Light thy heart at the fire of those little eyes. It is the Christ! O how much prophecy is fulfilled! The history of the world is finding its accomplishment. The crown is being put upon creation. The long secular yearnings of patriarchs, and kings, and prophets,—they were all after the beauty of that Infant Face. Thou hast seen the Christ. Everything is in that word. The sight was heaven. Earth has nothing more to do with thee. It had best roll itself away from under thy feet as quickly as possible, and let thee drop into the infinite Bosom of thy Father, the beauty of whose Son may kill thee by the gentlest and most beautiful of deaths.

It is hard for him to part with that sweet burden from his arms. In that extreme old age the vents of song have been opened in his soul, and in the silence of the temple he sings his Nunc dimittis, even as Zachary sang his Benedictus, and Mary her Magnificat. Age after age shall take up the strain. All the poetry of Christian weariness is in it. It gives a voice to the heavenly detachment and unworldliness of countless saints. It is the heart's evening light, after the working hours of the day, to millions and millions of believers. The very last compline that the Church shall sing, before the midnight when the doom begins and the Lord breaks out upon the darkness from the refulgent east, shall overflow with the melodious sweetness of Simeon's pathetic song. Joseph was wrapt even then in an ecstasy of holy admiration. Even Mary "wondered" at the words, so deep, so beautiful, so true; for she knew, as no others knew, how marvellously her Babe was of a truth the light of all the world. And when in her humility she knelt for the blessing of the aged priest, had he Jesus in his arms still when he blessed her, and did he wave the Child above her in the sign of the cross, like a Christian Benediction, or had she Jesus in her arms, holding Him at His own creature's feet, to get a blessing? Either way how wonderful the mystery! But what a strange blessing for thee, happy sinless Mother! There is other poetry in Simeon than those strains of light which flashed from him but awhile ago. There is other music now for Mary's ear, the terrible music of dark prophecy which the Holy Ghost utters from His sanctuary in the old priest's heart; and we would fain think that Simeon held Jesus in his arms when he uttered it, by the very way in which he begins. "Behold this Child is set for the fall, and for the resurrection of many in Israel, and for a sign which shall be contradicted. And thy own soul a sword shall pierce, that out of many hearts thoughts may be revealed."

Simeon was silent. But over Mary's soul there came an inexplicable change. Perhaps she learned now what she had not known before. But more probably it only came to her then in another way. Yet it was a change, an operation of grace, a new sanctification, an immense work of God. A clear and detailed vision of all her sorrows, especially of the whole Passion, was with its minutest circumstances instantaneously impressed upon her soul; and her immaculate heart was deluged with a sea of sorrow, which was supernatural both in its kind and its intensity. It seemed as if the vision came from the very face of Jesus, as if His eyes looked it into her and engraved it there. She saw His own Heart all unveiled, with all its inward dispositions. It was as if the Incarnation had come upon her again, and in a different way. She was raised to fresh heights of holiness. She entered upon another vast region of her appanage as the Mother of God. She was the same Mary, and yet a different one, who but awhile ago had entered the temple. But there was no surprise with this portentous change. No starting, no weak tremor, no fluttering of the spirit. Her unshaken peace grew more peaceful, because of the world of bitterness that had gone down into it. The Light of the World had flashed up on high in Simeon's arms, in Simeon's song, and there followed darkness, deeper, thicker, more palpable, than that of Egypt. Suddenly out of the sunshine of Bethlehem, she found herself in the heart of the eclipse on Calvary; and she was calm as before, with unastonished dignity, with the tranquillity of unutterable love, with the strength of divinest union, and with the sword right through her broken heart, which should remain there for eight-and-forty years, and then when Jesus should draw it out of the wound, she would bleed to death with love.

She heard Anna come into the temple, and acknowledge Jesus as her God. She heard the words the aged prophetess spoke about Him to those there who "looked for the redemption of Israel." She was careful that the least things which the law ordained should be obediently fulfilled; and then, with Joseph and the Child, she wended her way back to the green hollow of Galilee, to the steep sloping streets of the sequestered Nazareth, with the sword, that sharp sword of the Holy Ghost, within her heart. Since she left her home in December how much has passed! But the sunset looks on Nazareth, gilding its white cottages, as though all things had gone on the same from the beginning. O how cruel unchanging nature looks to a heart that has been changed in its own despite!

Such is the mystery of our Lady's first dolour. Let us now pass to the consideration of its peculiarities. The time at which it came, the action in which it found her engaged, are remarkable. She had just given to God a gift equal to Himself. There never had been such an offering made to Him since creation began. There never can be such another, only repetitions of the same. She had thus surpassed all angelic worship; and she well knew that in giving Jesus back to God, she was giving Him away from herself. Her reward was immediate; it was an unutterable lifelong sorrow. Such is the way of God. This first dolour discloses to us one of the most universal supernatural principles which characterise His dealings with His saints. Earthly sorrows are the roots of heavenly joys. A cross is a crown begun. Suffering is dearer to the Saints than happiness; for the similitude of Christ has passed upon them. They have His tastes, His inclinations. They thirst for suffering, because there is something in it which is favourable to union with God. It puts out the deceitful lights of the world; and darkness is the light by which we can most spiritually discern God. Moreover, the immensity of the sorrow, and the instantaneous manner in which it followed upon her oblation, illustrates the surpassing holiness of our Blessed Mother. God proportioned her cross to her powers of bearing it. Nor was there any reason for delay. She needed no preparation, no gradual process of inferior graces, no ascending scale of lesser crosses. A whole world of sorrow might fall at once upon her. She was ready for it, more immovable than the hills which stood around Jerusalem. O who would ever have dreamed that human fortitude could have been so like divine omnipotence?

Henceforth every action became a suffering, every source of joy a fountain of bitterness. There was no hiding-place in her soul whither the bitterness did not penetrate. Every look at Jesus, every movement that He made, every word He uttered,—all stirred, quickened, diffused, the bitterness that was in her. The very lapse of time itself was bitterness, for she saw Gethsemane and Calvary coming down the stream towards her. Postures and attitudes, in which she saw her beloved Son, no matter how natural they were, or, as we should speak, accidental, had some startling likeness in them to something which was to happen in the Passion. He was a constant study to her for the Passion, a model which she had always before her. When a carpenter's tool pressed against the palm of His hand, she saw the wound of the nail there. The white brow of boyhood often seemed as if it had a coronal of rosy spots around where the thorns should be. The prickly pears, that made garden-hedges for the villages of Nazareth, always reminded her of the crown of thorns. The Passion had become an inevitable vision to her. It was always before her eyes. She could not look away. She could not see either to the right or the left of that apparition, which like a blood-red sunset occupied the whole field of sight. Never was there such a strange alchymy of life. Everything about it was commuted into bitterness. The brightest joys made the most rigorous bitters; and the process went on the most successfully when the sun was shining brightest, and the mother's heart expanded to its genial light and heat. We could not bear so much as five minutes of the suffering she then endured; and hers was lifelong. She belonged to sorrow. It had drawn her life under its dark waters. Her life was hidden in the Heart of Jesus, amid gloomy forms, appalling shadows, dread insights into horrible gulfs of sin, thunders and lightnings of divine wrath, frenzies of lawless demons, excesses of human cruelty, and a very living show of instruments of the Passion.

But common life was still to go on, common duties had still to be performed. No truce was given her, no dispensation. It is not often that extreme poverty can grant a dispensation even to the extremest grief. And in her life the hardships of poverty were carried to the uttermost. Whenever she had aught to spare, it went straightway to the poor. Joseph and herself had to earn their livelihood, and Jesus must share the task when He is old enough. Now let us think of this. When grief has come and fastened its burden upon our backs, when the white-faced dead is lying in a silent room upstairs, we have tried to move about the house as usual, and to give our orders, and to take an interest, or to seem to do so, in a variety of things, and to appear calm. And did it succeed? Was it not just the most heart-breaking thing of all? O yes! we should have rested. The planet should have stopped whirling eastward for awhile, and all the world's duties stood still in a dead calm, till we had lain down and wept, and then got up again to go about our work. Yet we never had more than the touch of God's little finger upon us, while both His hands, heavier than a thousand worlds, held Mary down in the dust. Nevertheless no duty saw her absent. No common thing missed at her hands the same degree of zeal and attentiveness which the greatest could require. She seemed busy everywhere, engrossed in everything, with a mind all free and at her own disposal. She went and drew water from the well. She cleaned the house, and prepared the food, and spun the flax. Everything was at its right time and in its proper place. But the sword was there, in the very quick of her heart. It stirred at each step, till it made every nerve shrink, and her whole being thrill with agony. And this did not last a week, until her dead was buried, and the green grass of the grave-mound waved above it, and time went by shaking healing off its wings on the soul which sorrow had parched and dried. O no! her dead was never buried. There He was, living before her, and it was His very life that to her was continual death. What a life,—to work, to be active, to be collected, to be unselfish, under such an overwhelming burden! Her grief was all interior. She was obliged to deny it the satisfaction of an outlet. She would have seemed beside herself, and would have been treated accordingly had she allowed it to appear. Her very thoughts were poisoned with wormwood; but she must not speak. Who would have understood her, if she had spoken? She must not weep, or only in secret and at dead of night; for why should she weep without visible cause for it? She had food, she had raiment, she had Joseph for a husband, Jesus for a son. Summer came and filled the hollow valley with greenness and with plenty. Away from the great roads, peace and tranquillity were round Nazareth. Why should she mourn? Never has the earth seen a grief like this, never a grief like it in magnitude, never a grief of like kind with this.

Time brought no relief. The vision was always there with a terrible fidelity. And it was the same vision too. There was not even the cheerless comfort of a vicissitude of sorrow. It belonged to the greatness of her mind that she could call before her at any moment all the impressions which had ever been made upon her, that they should continually be present to her inward eye in multitudes, and that there should be in her as little succession of ideas as comports with the imperfection of a created mind. Thus the past was one present to her, and the future was a second present, and the present was a third present. The greatness of her science was simply converted into an incalculable power of suffering. The clearness of her perceptions was as knives in flesh and soul. There was something dreadful in the immutability of the vision. Moreover there was something infinite in the vision. For custom did not familiarise it to her; on the contrary it became fresher, its edges grew sharper, it went in deeper. There was a perpetual novelty about its monotonous images. Depths of significance kept opening out in it, like the interlacings and unfoldings of an unwieldy thunder-cloud; and each of these depths pushed the boundaries of her possibility of suffering far further than they were before. Who can think of any alleviation she could have had? Can the imagination suggest any! None! None! The beauty of Jesus, we know, was hourly driving Simeon's sword in. It was a hammer that rose and fell with almost every pulse that beat in His veins. The Light of the World was for ever passing in and out of the house; but, strange to say! He cast terrific shadows upon her, her whom He enlightened most of all; and the more she exulted, the more intolerably she suffered. And so her days went by, in the village of Nazareth, and among the Bazaars of Heliopolis.

It was occupation enough for her to attend to her sorrows. It was a cruel distraction to have to go through her ordinary actions, and the round of daily domestic duties. Is it not our experience that almost all distractions are cruel, even when they are kindly meant? We had rather weep than be consoled. We shall come round sooner if those who love us will only let us muse on our sorrow for awhile. But Mary had other sorrows to look to than her own, sorrows, that not only caused hers, but absorbed them again, and made them so forgetful as to be hardly conscious of themselves, the sorrows of Jesus. Yet this was no alleviation to her lifelong woe. On the contrary it was an aggravation. It barbed every one of them afresh with a double barb. Thus each sorrow was double. It echoed in two hearts. And the reverberation made both hearts ache. What she suffered in the heart of Jesus was far worse than what she suffered in her own. And all this mysterious process went on in secrecy and concealment for years and years. She sought no sympathy; she made no lamentation. She was as quiet as heaven when its songs are silent.

A life, with a heart broken almost from the first! This it was to be the Mother of God. This came of her being so bound up with Jesus. A heart-broken life! And what is life? What does the word represent? O such a breadth of diversified experiences, such multitudinous flocks of thoughts, such crowds of complicated actions, such weariful endurance, such tiresome coming round of the four seasons, such a swift slowness of time, everything so long in coming, and then coming before its time! And to her powers of soul life was so much broader, so much deeper, so much longer, so much more vital! And her life was a heart-broken life. What is a broken heart? Hearts do not often break. But we can tell what an aching heart is, or a wounded heart. Nay, we have lived on, when our heart got crushed once. It was only a momentary crush. The wheel of life went over it. Then it was over. Yet the surviving it seemed a miracle. But what is a broken heart? And then a life with a heart broken all the while, almost from the first! O Mary! thou wert the Mother of God, and therefore thou knowest!

But if we look attentively at this first dolour, we shall see that it contains five distinct dolours, five separate wounds in itself. First of all, in the offering she had made to God, she had offered Jesus of her own free-will to death. Strange fruit of the greatness of a mother's love! Yet it was out of love that she had made the offering, out of the holiest, purest, most disinterested love of God. For He who was her son was also God, and He who was God was the victim likewise. But could she have foreseen all that was involved in this? O yes! everything. Nothing had escaped her. Nothing could be more intelligent, nothing more mature, than the offering she had made. And when long years of oppressive sorrow had come to lay their added weights upon her broken heart, the very thought of retreating would have seemed worse than Calvary; for it would have been an infidelity to Him whom she so lovingly adored. But she had given Him away; she had given Him to death. For nine months she had possessed Him. Never was creature so rich, never creature so supremely blessed. Even then almost her first thought had been to bear Him over the hill-country of Juda to Elizabeth and John. All the while she had been longing to see His Face, and behold the light in His eyes, to hear the tone of His infantine voice, to throw her arms around Him and press Him, her treasure, the world's treasure, the Father's treasure, to her bosom. She was His human Mother, and her heart was human, exquisitely human. She woke from her ecstasy, and He was lying on her robe upon the ground on Christmas night, stretching out His little hands to her, as if her arms were His home, as they were. She had only had Him forty days. Her maternal love had not begun to satisfy itself, though it had been feeding all the while on His perfections. Nay, it was further from being satisfied than when she first saw Him. Forty days, not a thousand hours; and now she was giving Him away, giving Him to death, and the sword of Simeon had gone deep into her heart to show her what a gulf henceforth lay between herself and Him. She could have no more quiet possession of Him. She could not forbid His Passion. He belonged to sinners, He belonged to the anger of His Father. He was a victim whom she was to guard until the hour of sacrifice was come. What an office for a mother to hold. This is what came of being the Mother of God.

But if she had thus made Him over to the cruelty of

His divine office, she could the less bear the contradictions of others to His honour, His happiness, or His doctrine. Simeon had spoken of contradictions. What! would not the whole world be at His feet? Even if He was to die, because by the divine ordinance without shedding of blood there is no remission of sin, surely till then men will hang upon His lips, will follow Him wherever He goes, to feed on His celestial words. Sinners will everywhere be converted. The days of the saints will come back again to the chosen people and the promised land. And when He has died upon the Cross, the whole world will hasten to confess His royalty, and will throng into the Church which He has founded. No! it was not to be so. She knew it was not to be so. But what was there to contradict about Him? He was beauty, He was truth, He was love, He was gentleness itself. Who could be rude to Him? Who could contradict truth, eternal truth? But she saw how it was all to be. He showed it to her in Himself, when He unveiled to her the secrets of His soul. There was not a dark look ever cast on His venerable face, there was not a cold word, or a wilful misunderstanding, or a petulant retort, or an unbeseeming liberty, or an irreverent taunt, or a dire imprecation, or a chilling blasphemy, from that hour to the day of doom, which did not go into her heart with excruciating distress. The howling cries of those multitudes at Jerusalem, ravening for His Blood, echoed day and night within her maternal heart. This then was to be the first fruits of that magnificent oblation, in order to make which grace had to raise her almost to heights, certainly to neighbourhoods, divine! Men would not appreciate her offering. They would not understand it. They would scout it, mock it, contradict it, be cruel to it. No one yet has ever understood it, either in heaven or earth, save the Eternal Father to whom she made it. He alone knew the worth of what she gave, the worth of Jesus, of the Incarnate Word. Do we know it? Impossible, for if we did, our lives would not be what they are. There is a knowledge which brings practice along with it; it is the knowledge by which sanctity knows, not the mere knowledge of the understanding.

Alas! poor Mother! Her heart is all wounds, one opening into another, lifelong wounds, which, like the stigmata of the Saints, bleed, but never ulcerate. At least those who contradict Him shall learn at last to see the greatness of their error. They shall come back to Him like wanderers. They shall one day become themselves triumphs of His redeeming grace. Out of Him flow grace, and sweetness, and attraction, and healing. His beauty, confessed at last, shall wind itself around them as a spell. Thus the grief of all this contradiction may be endurable. But no! the sword of Simeon, like the sword of the Cherubim that guards the entrance of the earthly paradise, "flames and turns every way." Positus in ruinam multorum, set for the fall of many, for their utter fall, their ruin, their irreparable ruin! Is Jesus to lose for ever some of His own creatures? Nay, is He to drive them from Himself by the very brightness of His light, by the very heavenliness of His beauty? Are there to be souls, for whom it would have been better had He never come? O cruel thought, the cruellest of all! For the more Mary mused upon the Passion, and the longer she had it all before her eyes, all the more avariciously she coveted souls, the more she hungered and thirsted after the harvest of the Passion, and became the Mother of sinners, because she was the Mother of the Saviour, the Mother who gave Him away to death when she had possessed Him but for forty days in Bethlehem. The countless multitudes of those who were to be saved were the nearest approach to an alleviation of her inconsolable sorrow. But even upon this semblance of a consolation she was not to lean. O it was a fearful thought to think of her beautiful Child, that He was to be in some sense a destroyer. Not altogether a Saviour, but a law of life which was to be a sentence of death to some, nay, to many. Things had become very grave now between God and His world. Jesus would be a touchstone. Men must take their sides now, more definitely, more intelligently. God was weary of their sins, weary of waiting for their return. The very greatness of this last long-prophesied mercy made the rejection of it the more fatal and irretrievable. The salvation of men would now be in some respects more like that of the angels. Their probation was becoming more divine, and therefore more decisive. To reject Jesus was to be lost eternally, and yet the "Rejected of men" was one of the very names which Scripture gave Him. If anything could have been hard to Mary's faith, it would have been that Jesus was to be the ruin of many souls; and faith's heroic acceptance of this worshipful truth only made the edge of it keener, and the point sharper, to go down into her heart.

It is part of our imperfection that one impression upon our mind dulls another. We cannot attend to many things at once. Even sorrows, when they come thickly, in some measure neutralise each other. Great sorrows absorb us, and then little ones fall upon us, and we hardly feel them more than the drops of a thunder shower. We are conscious of them: but the suffering they cause is hardly distinct. But it was not so in our Lady, with the perfections of her unfallen nature. Her self-collection was complete, and embraced everything. There was no confusion in her mind from want of balance. It received, appreciated, and thoughtfully handed on to her exquisite sensibilities of pain, every slightest aggravation of any one of her multiplied sorrows. So it was now. The curse incurred by her native land because of the rejection of Jesus, was a distinct and bitter grief. All the glories of its past history, from the Exodus to the Macchabees, rose up before her mind. Her heart swelled over the vicissitudes, now sad, now glorious, of her people. She thought of the Tombs of the saints and prophets scattered among the hills. Her eye traversed the battlefields, where the sword of man had so often avenged the majesty of God. It was the land of promise, very various, very beautiful. It had, what no other land had upon it, the golden light of God's mysterious choice. It was the holy east advancing to the water's edge, and confronting that grand west which it was first to convert, and then civilise, and last of all to glorify. It was not a mere feeling of patriotism which stirred within her. That land had been the earthly home of heavenly truth, when the rest of the world lay in the cold shadow of spiritual darkness. It was more like a sanctuary, than a region of the earth's geography. There was hardly a mountain which had not seen some miracle, hardly a hollow to which some promise was not attached. The banks of its river, the shores of its inland sea, were overhung with clouds of sacred poetry. A very network of prophecy lay over the whole land, over all the localities of the separate tribes. Their virtues and their faults had to do with the geography of the regions allotted for their dwelling. The peculiar scenery of the country was the imagery of the Scriptures; and it was soon to be something more, because of the teaching of her Son. Then there was Jerusalem. Even the great God had loved that city, almost as if He were a man, with a human affection. He had cherished it in His heart, as fondly and as wistfully as any Hebrew who mused upon it beneath the willows by the waters of Babylon. Jesus Himself wept over it, as if His heart would break, from the top of Olivet. Poor city! fair city! it was the trophy of so many mercies, of so much divine tenderness, of so many victories of divine love. It was the tabernacle of the visible glory of the Most High. The sweet savour of sacrifice rose from it evermore. And now the adorable Blood of Jesus was to lay it all desolate, and the Roman fire, and then the ruin of ages were to lick up almost the vestiges of its holy places! What made Jesus weep, what made Him feel like a mother, who would fain shelter her young beneath her wings, must needs have been to Mary the intensest misery. And Simeon's sword had not forgotten even this! Sweet Mother! Thy Son and thyself must ruin Juda, the chosen, the long-endured, the delightful of the world. Fain as thou art to be nothing but the glad channel of God's love to earth, thou must be content to be an instrument of His wrath as well. Thou too, Mother of mercy! art not thou thyself, even to this day, set for the fall of many, both in the old Israel and in the new? Sweet is the will of God, even when it is terrible in its counsels over the children of men.

This was not altogether such a picture of Jesus, and of the consequences of His coming, as a mother's heart would have desired, if nature had been bidden to paint it. The sun should have been without clouds. The shadows that darken the landscape were too many and too heavy. Around the Infant Jesus what should there be but light and joy, unmingled mercy, unbroken peace, all night and the relics of night passed away, and gloriously melted down to gold in the sunrise! He came with the sole intention of love, and lo! the immediate consequence of His coming is contradiction, ending with the everlasting ruin of many souls, and the laying waste of His earthly country, and the dispersion of His chosen people. But the blood of the Holy Innocents would have been a lesson to Mary, if she had needed teaching, of what those are to expect, and in what mysterious dark laws they are involved who come very near to Jesus. Now at least if His coming shall not exclusively accumulate praise and worship for the single attribute of the divine clemency, the justice of God shall find its glory therein. All things at any rate shall be for the great, the greater, the greatest glory of God. Yes! they shall in truth; but not altogether as might have been expected. The mission of Jesus was an infinite possibility of glory for God. But what was infinite in it rested at the possibility. God was not to have one tithe of the glory which was due to Him for the sending of His Son. The wills of men should contrive to frustrate it at every turn. To such an extent should their malice succeed, that there should actually be an appearance of failure over the whole scheme of redemption. It should be possible, in time to come, for theologians to speak as if the redemption of Mary in the Immaculate

Conception were the grand, almost sufficient work of redeeming grace. The very sweetness and humility and forgivingness of Jesus should act as stumbling-blocks in the way of His Father's glory. Nay, the very things, which, because they were so divine, should have fructified most to the glory of God, shall furnish occasions and opportunities for greater outrage against the Divine Majesty, than sinners could have had without the Incarnation. Alas! how darkness is gathering round the very cradle of the child! Christmas is deepening into Passion-tide with unnatural, unseasonable combination. Poor Mother! here are five wounds in one. Thou hast offered Him to death: His appearance will be the signal for numberless contradictions to start up against Him: He is set for the downright ruin of many: because of Him, the land and the people will be cursed: He will enable men to desecrate God's glory more than all generations have done before. Poor Mother! which way wilt thou look? Jesus Himself has the crown of thorns round His Infant Heart, which will one day be seen upon His brow; and is it less cruel on the heart than on the head? As to sinners, there is to be no such universal salvation of them, as might come near to a compensation for all this grief. As to God, there is far from free course to His glory, much glory doubtless, but then also unheard-of impiety, the ways and means thereto being furnished by His own exceeding paternal love.

Such were the peculiarities of the first dolour. Not much need be said about her dispositions in it. Partly, they have been in great measure anticipated in what has been said, and partly they are, many of them, so far above our comprehension, so indistinguishable in the dazzling brightness of the inward beauty of "the King's daughter," that we know not what to say. A book might be written on Mary's interior beauty; and in these days it greatly needs writing. Meanwhile we will delay awhile on three graces which our Lady exercised in an heroic degree in this first dolour. The first was her practical acknowledgment of the sovereignty of God. There can be no doubt that this is the fundamental idea of all worship. There is no making terms with God. The obligations are all on one side. The completeness of our subjection is the perfection of our liberty. God is master. There can be no questioning of justice or of goodness, where He is concerned. The essence of sanctity lies in the enthusiastic acknowledgment of this sovereignty. Our prerogative is in our responsibility. It is by this that we come to have royal hearts towards God. It is comparatively easy to say this, when the sun shines, and even to fancy that we believe it. But when darkness closes in, and sorrows give us no respite, and the doors of heaven seem barred to prayer, and human injustice makes us its victim, and human unkindness tramples on us when we are fallen, and human love betrays us, and God's face is turned the other way, then it is hard, with whole-hearted sincerity and royal equanimity, to confess the absolute, irresponsible, majestic sovereignty of God, with no desire to tear the veil from off its mysterious reasons, with no shadow of desire to turn ever so little the other way the Will that seems riding us down so fiercely. We hold all from God. Who does not know that? All good comes from Him. All good must go to Him. His glory is the sole significance of all good. His will is law, and the sole law. All laws that are eternal are only so, because He is eternal from whom they flow. They are manifestations of Him, not His obligations. It cannot be otherwise; for the nature of things, as we speak, what is it but the character of God? All this is very clear when the sun shines on it. Happy they whose natures are such that all through life there is a fixed sunbeam on this grand truth of God's sovereignty. But listen to the cries of anguish from Job, which make the rocks of Edom ring again, till the whole world hears. By the side of his magnificent patience, whose clamorous submission God has bidden to pass into a proverb of sanctity, place the silent endurance of the Mother of God, her heart quelled, beautified, made glorious, well-nigh beatified by the exulting sense of God's supreme sovereignty. There can be no magnificence among creatures equal to the perfection of obedience. God-made-man was so enamoured of the loveliness of obedience, that He clung to it for thirty years, and left Himself barely three wherein to save the world, and, in order even to do that, only changed the outward form of His obedience. And this old wicked world, why is it rocking to and fro, and getting weary of itself, but for the want of that spirit of subjection in which alone terrestrial beatitude consists?

Furthermore, in this dolour our Blessed Lady entered perfectly into all the dispositions of God about Jesus, herself, and us. We are often told in spiritual books that we ought to enter into the dispositions of God about us or conform ourselves to the interior dispositions of Jesus. Since the seventeenth century such language has become universal among spiritual writers, expressing an old truth in a new way, a way adapted to the change which has come over the modern mind. Let us try to affix a definite meaning to this language. Everybody has a certain way of looking at things, especially things which concern himself. He has a point of view peculiar to himself. This is the reason men can so seldom agree perfectly about the commonest things, hardly indeed about matters of fact; and this shows how intimate to a man is this private point of view, how much of himself is implicated in it, how it helps to fix and stereotype his character. Now this point of view arises from a variety of causes, a man's own disposition, the dispositions of his parents, his early associations, the circumstances and localities of his youth, and above all, his education. Nearly every family and household have mental peculiarities of their own, which others recognise and appreciate far more distinctly than themselves. The same is true of religious communities, of large cities, and finally of nations themselves. In this peculiarity we shall for the most part find that the weaknesses and unworthinesses of our character entrench themselves. There is a necessity of littleness in all peculiar spirit, whether it be family spirit, party spirit, community spirit, or national spirit. In the case of the individual there is a necessity of selfishness. It is from our own point of view that we are able to take magnified views of self: it is that which supports our vanity, and makes it seem reasonable and true; it is that which is the standard whereby we judge others; it is that out of which all misunderstandings come. It is plain therefore that, in the work of the spiritual life, this stronghold has, if not to be destroyed, and destruction is a rare work in holiness, at least to be taken, sacked, and garrisoned afresh. How is this to be done?

Let us turn from ourselves to God. God also has His point of view. In Him it is essentially true. He has His view of the world, of the vicissitudes of the Church, of certain maxims of life, of vocations, of duties, of sins. He intends each of us for a particular work, and gives us the number and the kind of graces requisite to fit us for that work. He gives us light up to a given point and no further, grace in certain quantity and not beyond, and of one sort, not of another. He has dispositions about us, both with reference to our natural characters, and to our supernatural correspondence to His grace. He has certain dispositions with regard to our sanctity. This is the foundation upon which all spiritual direction rests. It is of immense importance to us to know what God's particular dispositions are about ourselves; and these are chiefly discernible in the operations of grace in our souls. But we ourselves cannot see these operations, nor pass any safe judgment upon them, at least in the long run, because of the disturbing force of self-love. Hence we put ourselves under the guidance of others, of men who have a particular gift in them because of their priestly character, and whose prayers for light God will answer very specially, in reward of our obedience and in aid of their responsibilities.

When we come to know God's dispositions about us,—and many of them, the most important, we may know at once, because they are general, and follow from His being God,—

then the next step is to enter into them, that is, to banish from our minds our own corresponding dispositions, and put His in their place. This is not done all at once, but by degrees. Gradually, first in one thing, then in another, we come to take God's views of things. We look at them from His point of view, either forgetful or disdainful of our own. It is His interests, or the supernatural principles He has infused into us, or the disclosures He has made to us of His will, which regulate this point of view, and not our own likings and dislikings, our natural tastes or acquired character. This emancipates us from the littleness of family, from the littleness of community, from the littleness of country, but above all from the littleness of self. The work implies nothing less than a complete inward revolution. It makes the new man. It is the similitude of Jesus. It is the mystical death of self. But there are seasons of fearful struggle to go through, before we reach the goal. It is a long, an arduous transformation, with many digressions, many wilful retrograde movements, many dull times of stupefied cowardice. There are excesses of acute suffering to be endured, for the whole operation goes on in the very quick of our nature.

In Mary this deifying operation was complete. This was owing to her immense graces, and also to the perpetual nearness of Jesus. The prophecy of St. Simeon, though it did not lay bare to her for the first time, brought formally before her for her acceptance, manifold dispositions of God regarding Jesus, herself, and us sinners. As she had been formally called upon to give her consent to the Incarnation, so now she was definitely called upon to enter into these dispositions of God, and make them her own, to appropriate them to herself by an heroic sanctity. We have already seen that these dispositions were by no means such as the mother's heart would naturally have desired. They involved terrible sacrifices. They raised her to heights where mere humanity could hardly respire. They plunged her in oceans of supernatural sorrow. Indeed in the sorrow of this first dolour there is something which we might almost venture to call unnatural, because, not only of the relation in which it placed the Mother to the Son, but also of the free-will of the Mother in the matter. Into these dispositions, and with the most perfect intelligence of them which a creature could have, she entered heroically. A ship could not sail into harbour with more calm dignity or more irresistible grace than she glided out of nature, earth, and self, into the deep bosom of her Heavenly Father.

The third disposition we shall notice is her generosity in the acceptance of this dolour. With us, generosity in spiritual things is often to be measured by the degree of struggle and reluctance through which the virtue forced its way. But it was not so with our Blessed Lady. It was with her supernatural generosity, as it is with our natural generosity. Its gracefulness was in the absence of effort. It was born without the pains of birth, out of the abundance of her heart. It leaped forth spontaneously. It waited to make no calculations. It fought no battle. What had it to fight with in a nature so subjected to grace in its inmost recesses, as hers was? From the greatness of her grace what was supernatural came as obviously to her as what is natural comes to us: and it is in this instantaneous, almost unconscious alacrity, that the attractiveness of generosity consists in us. Suffering and reluctance are two different ideas. She suffered intensely; but there was no rebellion in her lower nature. There was no conflict in her will. There could have been, but there was not. It was inconsistent with the grandeur of her union with God. What took place in our Lord in the garden of Gethsemane had no parallel in His Mother. She had no chalice of sin to drink, no chalice of the Father's anger: but a cup of simple bitterness which Jesus Himself was for ever holding to her lips. Could she have struggled against Him ever so little? Could the slightest ripple pass over her conformity to His will, when He Himself was her cupbearer? In the Agony in the Garden, we have to suppose our Lord's Divine

Nature mysteriously cloistered off, so far as regarded many of its principal effects, from the human nature to which it was united. Nay, more than this, we have to suppose a miraculous desertion of the lower part of His human nature even by the higher human faculties, in order to arrive at that stupendous conflict in His all-holy Soul, that momentary and apparent, yet intensely mysterious, insurgency of His lower will against His higher. But surely this is a specialty to Him. It is part of the world's salvation. It is a sublimity in Him of which she is not capable, without being lowered. It has to do with sin and with the angry justice of the Father. It was the revolt of His purity against the loathsomeness of the manifold iniquity in which He was to clothe Himself. It was the culminating point of the magnificence of His sacrifice. In Mary it would simply be the transient failure of her consummate holiness, without the necessity, or the dignity of redemption. We cannot therefore admit it for one moment. It would have broken her tranquillity. It would have loosened the compactness of her perfect nature. It would have exaggerated the womanly element in the exalted Mother of God. It would have brought her down to a lower level. It would have made her more like one of the saints. For one moment her will was visible in the mystery of the Annunciation, and then it sank down into the deep will of God, and was never seen again. Far out at sea, in the wide calm a wave will rise up from the heaving plain of waters, crest itself with silver, catch the light, and fall back again all noiselessly into the huge deep, and leave no traces, no wake behind. So was it with our Lady's will. God called it up in the Annunciation. It shone for the moment, and withdrew itself again into His, and was seen no more. She who often saw God, she who was so united with Him as never saint or angel was, she who had more grace than all the world beside, she who was more glorious than the blessed in their glory, who have no will apart from the will of God—could it be otherwise with her? No! the generosity of our Blessed Mother was in the spontaneous alacrity and untroubled calm of her conformity to the sweet Will of God. She, who had given without struggle all that God had asked of her in the Incarnation, gave also without struggle all that followed from that first consent.

But let us now consider the lessons which this first dolour teaches to ourselves. It was a lifelong unhappiness. Unhappiness is not without mystery even in a fallen world. By rights there should be no unhappiness at all. For is not the whole world full of God everywhere, and can there be unhappiness in the neighbourhood of God? How much goodness and kindness is there in every one around us, if we only take a kindly view of them ourselves! Sin is easily forgiven to those who are in earnest. Grace is prodigally bestowed. There is an almost incredible amount of actual enjoyment, and pain and suffering themselves are quickly turned to sanctity. Yet for all this the unhappiness of the world is real. Almost every heart on earth is a sanctuary of secret sorrow. With some the grief is fresh. With others it is old. With immense numbers the unhappiness is literally lifelong, one out of which there is no possible escape except through the single door of death. With some it arises with having chosen an unfit lot in life from the first. With others it is from the unkindness, misconduct, or misunderstanding of those they love. In some cases men have to suffer for their religion, and its consequences are made by the cruelty of others to last to the end of their days. Not unfrequently it comes from men's characters, or from their sins, or from some consequences of these. Now and then it is the burden of a broken heart, a heart which has been overweighted, and so has snapped, and thus lost its elasticity and the power of throwing off its sorrows. To much suffering time brings no healing. The broken heart lies bleeding in the hand of its Heavenly Father. He will look to it. No one else can. It is astonishing how shallow all human consolation is. The waters glitter so in the sun, we do not see the sandy bottom only just below the surface.

We believe it deep, till we have once been to draw water there, and then we learned all about it, for we drew as much sand as water.

Now what is to be done with this lifelong sorrow? Let our Lady teach us out of the depths of her first dolour. Her sorrows were lifelong. This was the characteristic the first dolour impressed upon them. She suffered without seeking consolation. She suffered without needing to lean on human sympathy. She suffered in silence. She suffered in joy. Let us put this aside, not as inimitable; the time will come when we shall be able to imitate even these things; but let us put it aside as beyond us now. But she had no suffering which was dissociated from the Passion of Jesus. We can make our sorrows in a measure like hers by continually uniting them to the sorrows of our dearest Lord. If our sorrow comes from sin, of course it cannot be like Mary's sorrows; but it can be just as easily, just as acceptably, united with the Passion of our Lord. He will not despise the offerings. The fact of our griefs being a consequence of sin need not even increase the measure of our grieving. Happy they, and true sons, whom our Father punishes in this life! Like Mary, we must be loving, sweet, and patient with those who cause us any unhappiness, and laying our head, with unrestrained and unashamed tears, on our Lord's Bosom, let us think quietly of God and heaven. It is not a slight consolation for lifelong mourners to know that our Blessed Lady was a lifelong mourner too. Let us be of good cheer. Let us look our great sorrow in the face, and say to it, "You have made up your mind not to part with me till I go down to the grave: be then a second guardian-angel to me: be a shadow of God, hindering the heat and glare of the world from drying up the fountains of prayer within my heart." All of us, even if we have not a lifelong sorrow, have a guardian-angel of this description. Our sorrows may not be one, but many. They may come on guard, like sentinels, one following the other, as each watch of this earthly night is done. Unhappiness is like a secret subterranean world. We are perpetually walking over it without knowing it; and so seeming unkind and thoughtless one to another, when in our hearts we are not really so. What a consolation then it is to us to reflect, that the lives both of Jesus and Mary were lives of one incessant, secret unhappiness! With confidence therefore may we seek the Mother of sorrows, and ask her to be the Mother of our sorrow. Jesus has a special love for the unhappy. The longest day has its evening, the hardest work its ending, and the sharpest pain its contented and everlasting rest.

Another lesson which we learn from this first sorrow of Mary is, that the highest use of God's gifts is to give them back to Him again. Nothing is in reality our own, except our sin. God is jealous of anything like a proprietary feeling, even in the gifts of nature; but in respect of the gifts of grace this jealousy is increased a thousandfold. We must make Him the depositary of His own gifts, because we do not know how to use them rightly. We must be like children who bid their father keep the little treasures which he himself has given. So with the gifts of God. They are more ours, when in His keeping, than in our own. Everything which increases our feeling of dependence upon Him is sweet, and safe, and true, and right, and the best thing. Besides which, God is the end for which all things were given. Nothing good is meant to stay with us. It would not keep good. It would spoil. Every creature is a channel through which things find their way back to God, as surely as blood finds its way back to the heart, through endless turnings, and has done its work, not in delaying anywhere, which would be disease, but in passing on, and in passing swiftly, kindling and making alive as it went along. Moreover our humility is always in peril, if we detain a gift of God, even if it were for no longer than to look it in the face, and love it, and then think of it with complacency when it is gone. We must refer everything to God. It is the secret of being holy. Grace comes, and temptations give way, and great things are done, and love is all in a jubilee, and then self begins to sing an undersong, but we are making such a noise with praising God that we do not hear, and she is wounded, and holds her tongue, and we know nothing of it. Could we not keep up that beautiful noise for ever? O yes! for graces are always coming; like the people in the streets, there is no end to them, sometimes a thinning, never a break. So we could be always praising God, always sending back to Him, when we have humbly kissed them, the gifts and graces He has sent us. Besides which, God and His gifts are two very different things. Sometimes He feigns as if He would over-reach us, in order to try our love. He sends us some very heavenly gift, and then watches to see if we will take it for Himself, and rest in it, not as if it were our own, yet not as if it were His, but as if it were Himself. But the soul that loves truly can never fall into this mistake. It no more thinks of lying down on one of God's best gifts to rest itself, than we should dream of lying on the green yielding billows of the sea to sleep. It must reach God, nothing short of God. It keeps giving back His gifts, as if in constant protest that, needful as they are, they are not Himself, and cannot stand in His stead.

Another lesson to be learned is, that in this world sorrow is the recompense of sanctity. It is to the elect on earth, what the Beatific Vision is to the saints in heaven. It is God's presence, His manifestation of Himself, His unfailing reward. We must not be amazed therefore, if new efforts to serve God bring new sorrows in their train. By the supernatural principles of the spiritual life, they ought to do so. If we are able to bear them, these sorrows will come at once. Their delay is only the index of God's estimation of our weakness. Yet we need not fear that they will be disproportioned to our strength. God's blows are not dealt out at random. Our crosses are poised to a nicety by divine wisdom, and then divine love planes them, in order to make them at once smoother and lighter. But we can have no real comfort in devotion, if we are without trials. We have no proof that God accepts us, no security against delusion.

We know that the stars are in their old places in the sky; but in different states of the atmosphere they seem much farther off than at other times, or again much nearer, like teardrops of light on the very point of falling to the earth. So is it with God. Joy makes Him seem far off, while sorrow brings Him near, almost down into our bosom. When sorrows come, we feel instinctively their connection with the graces which have gone before, just as temptations so often have an odour about them of past victories. They come up, one after another, dealing their several blows upon our poor hearts, with such a modest heavenly significancy upon their faces, that it is easy to recognise angels beneath the thin disguise. As we touch them, even while the thrill goes through us, we feel that we are almost handling with our hands our own final perseverance, such solid evidence are they of our adoption, so full of substantial graces in their presence, and leaving such a legacy of blessings when they go. A heart without sorrows is like a world without a revelation. It has nothing but a twilight of God about it.

Furthermore our sorrow must be our own. We must not expect any one else to understand it. It is one of the conditions of true sorrow, that it should be misunderstood. Sorrow is the most individual thing in the whole world. We must not expect therefore to meet with sympathy at all adequate to what we are suffering. It will be a great thing if it be suitable, even though it is imperfect. It is a very desolate thing to have leaned on sympathy, and found that it would not bear our weight, with such a burden of sorrow upon our backs. It is very difficult to erect ourselves again. The heart sinks upon itself in dismay. It has used its last remaining strength to reach the place where it would rest itself, and now what is left for it, but a faintness which opens all the wounds afresh, and a dismal conviction that the grief is less tolerable than it was before? It is best therefore to keep our sorrows as secret as we can. Unfitting sympathy irritates us, and makes us sin. Inadequate sympathy lets the lame limb fall harshly to the ground. The denial of sympathy excites almost a querulous despair. God knows everything. There are volumes of comfort in that. God means everything. There is light for every darkness out of that simple truth. Our hearts are full of angels when they are full of sorrows. Let us make them our company, and go on our road, smiling all the day, scattering such sweetness round us as mourners only are allowed to scatter, and God will understand us, when we go to Him. Who can comfort like those who also mourn ?

We must expect also that it will be in some measure with us, as it was with Mary; our sorrows will be fed even by our joys. God sends us joys before sorrows, to prepare our hearts; but the joys themselves contain prophecies of the coming sorrows. And what are those sacred fears, those strange presentiments, those vague expectations, of approaching evil, by which joys are so often accompanied, but the shadows which they bring along with them ? It is out of the brightness of life that its darkness mostly comes. In all manner of strange ways joys turn to sorrows, sometimes suddenly, sometimes gradually. Sometimes what was expected as joy, comes in the shape of sorrow. Sometimes the very enjoyment of the joy turns it into sadness, as if an enchanter's wand had been waved over it. Sometimes it is gladness to the last, but when it goes, it leaves grief behind, a grief it was all the while concealing under its cloak, and we never suspected it. So again when a sorrow has become calm, and the freshness of its sting seems worn off by time, by endurance, or by the distraction of our duties, a joy comes to us, makes us smile as it enters our souls, but, when there, goes at once to the fountain of sorrow, wakes up the slumbering waters, digs the source deeper, and shakes the earth around to make the spring flow more abundantly. There are few who have not experienced this kindling and enlivening of grief by the advent of gladness. But in truth in a world where we can sin, in a strife where we so often lose sight of God, in a dwelling which is rather an exile than a home, all joys are akin to sorrows, nay are almost sorrows in holyday attire. Joy is life looking like what it is not. Sorrow is life with an honest face. It is life looking like what it is. Nevertheless there is the truest, the heavenliest of all joys in sorrow, because it detaches us from the world, and draws us with such quiet, persuasive, irresistible authority of God. The sunrise of grace within the soul is full of cloud, and doubt, and uncertain presages, even amid the flashings of beautiful light which are painting the troubled sky everywhere. But when the orb has mounted to the top of its noonday tower, all clouds will have melted away into the blue, no one knows how. For to turn joys into sorrows is the sweet safe task of earth, to turn sorrows into joys is the true work of heaven, and of that height of grace which is heaven on earth already.

There is still another lesson to be learned. We must all enter into this dolour in some way or other in life. The characteristic of Mary's sorrow is that Jesus caused it. But this is not peculiar to her affliction. He will be a cause of blessed sorrow to every one of us. There are very many happy earthly things, which we must sacrifice for Him; or if we have not the heart to do so, He will have the kind cruelty to take them from us. Persecution is a word of many meanings, a thing of countless shapes. It must come infallibly to every one who loves our dearest Lord. It may come through the hard tongues of the worldly, or in the suspicions and jealousies and judgments of those we love. In the peace of family love and domestic union it often comes from hands which make it hard to be endured; and, because of religion, there is keen misery where the casual visitor sees nothing but the edification of mutual love. Who was ever let alone to serve Jesus as he wished? It is idle to expect it. The husband's love rises against it in the wife. The mother will tear her children from the Saviour's arms. The father looks with suspicion on the claims of God, and jealousy of the Creator will make him harsh to a child who has never given him an hour of trouble in life beside, and to whom he never has been harsh before. The brother will forego the manliness of fraternal affection, and bring the bitterness of the world's judgments into the sacred circle of home, if Jesus dares to lay a finger on his sister. O poor, poor world! And it is always the good who are the worst in this respect. Let this be laid to heart, and pondered. Outside of us, beside this inevitable persecution, our Lord will bring trials and crosses round us, at once to preserve our grace and to augment it. The more we love Him the thicker they will be. Nay, our love of Him often gets us into trouble we hardly know how. It almost leads us into faults, into imprudences to be repented of. Suddenly, especially when we are fervent, the ground gives way under our feet, and we sink into a pit, and in the retrospect, our fall seems inexcusable, and yet how did it all come to pass? How also is it within the soul? Are there not such things as the pains of love? Are they not more common than its joys? Then there is the worse pain of not feeling our love, of seeming to lose our love, of its for ever slipping away from us. There are also interior trials, by which self-love is put to a painful death, and a cleansing of our inmost souls by fire, which is exceeding agony. Then there are the distresses into which the love of Jesus entraps us. It persuades us to give up this world, to put out all the lights wherewith earth had made our hearts gay, to break ties, to eschew loves, to commit ourselves to hard dull lives, and then it leaves us. God hides His countenance from us. All view of the other world is shut off from us. Just as it is at sundown, no sooner has the last rim sunk below the horizon, than, as if evoked by a spell, from river-side, from woody hollow, from pastures where the kine are feeding, from meadows with the haycocks standing, there rises up a cold white blinding mist: so is it in the soul, no sooner is God's Face gone, than past sins, ghastly things, break up from the graves in which absolution laid them, and present imperfections, and unknown temptations, and chilling impossibilities of perseverance, all rise up together, and involve the soul in the coldest, gloomiest desolation, through which no star can pierce, and it is much if a sickly whiteness tells us that there is a moon somewhere. Who does not know these things? It is no use shuddering. They are not on us now; but they will come back again, be sure, when their hour arrives. Thus Jesus is in us a cause of sorrow, in us He is a sign to be contradicted, in us is He set for the rise and fall of many.

These are the lessons which the first dolour teaches us, and they are lifelong lessons, as its sorrow was. Let us now go home to Nazareth with Mary. Angels accompany her steps, full of astonishment and reverence at her grief. Perhaps it is their first lesson in the profound science of the Passion. So she went her way through the streets of Sion, and over the hills, and through the glens by the watercourses, until she came to the green basin of Nazareth, the Mother bearing her Child! And they were all in all to each other. And who shall tell what mute language they spoke, as the Child's Heart beat against the Mother's heart in sorrow and in love? And each was dearer to the other than before, and we also perhaps were dearer to them than an hour ago: for the shadow of Calvary had already fallen, both on the Mother and the Son; and they loved the shadow; and it was we who cast it.

CHAPTER III.

THE SECOND DOLOUR.

THE FLIGHT INTO EGYPT.

THE Flight into Egypt has always been a fountain of poetry and art in the Church at large, while it has been a source of tears and of rich contemplation to religious souls. It is not only that the mystery is so exceedingly beautiful in itself; but the Gentiles have loved to regard it as, after the Epiphany, the beginning of our Lord's dealings with them. He flies from His own people to take refuge in a heathen land. He consecrates by His presence that very land which had been the great historical enemy of the chosen people, and which was, as it were, the express type of all heathen darkness. Amid those benighted Gentiles He finds a peaceful home, where no persecutions trouble the even tenor of His childish life. The idols fall from their niches, as He moves. A power goes out into the rich Nile-valley, nay, overflows it, and runs far into the yellow sands of the desert, sanctifying and setting apart the whole region as a future Church, as a blossoming wilderness, as a barren mystical paradise populous with saints. The fathers of the desert are to pass into a Christian proverb throughout the magnificent west, a phenomenon which men will never be weary of admiring, a living discipline, an enduring academy, in which all future generations of catholic saints are to be brought up and to take their degrees. Thus the Gentile west has loved to accumulate traditions about the Flight into Egypt, the Sojourn there, and the Return.

If there is not peace in sequestered Nazareth, where shall we find it ? Can the eye of jealous power, quickened by the acute discernment of selfish fear, find out the Holy Child amid the many children of that retired village ? The evil one will see to that, we may be sure. Peace is not the inheritance, either of Jesus or Mary. It is true that He is the prince of peace, but not of such peace as earth dreams of. Mary has but lately reached her home. Her heart is broken. She needs rest. It shall come to her in the time of rest, but otherwise than might have been expected. In the dead of night the Lord appeared in sleep to Joseph, the keeper of heaven's best treasures on earth, and bade him rise, and take the Child and His Mother, and fly into Egypt. The three kings had gone back to the east without letting Herod know, whether they had found the new-born king, and who He was. Herod had bidden them return to him; but Scripture does not tell us that they had promised to do so : or if they had, the commandment of God, which came to them in a dream, superseded the promise they had made. Tyranny was not, however, to be so baulked; and lest it should miss its aim, involved all Bethlehem in blood by the massacre of the Innocents. O Mary ! see what a stern sister thou hast been to those poor mothers of Bethlehem, who saw thee on Christmas Eve wandering homeless through their streets, they perhaps fondling their little ones at their doors ! What a concourse of wailing sounds rose to heaven from that narrow hill-top, while the gutters of the steep streets ran down with blood ! It was the law of the Incarnation, the law that was round the gentle Jesus, which was beginning to work. Dearest Lord ! His great love of us had already broken His Mother's heart. It was now desolating the happy hearths of Bethlehem, and staining its inhospitable door-posts with blood. And all to keep Himself for Calvary, where He was to shed with a thousandfold more cruel suffering His Precious Blood for us !

The night was dark and tranquil over the little town of Nazareth, when Joseph went forth. No commandment of

God ever found such promptitude in highest saint or readiest angel, as this one had found in Mary. She heard Joseph's words, and she smiled on him in silence as he spoke. There was no perturbation, no hurry, although there was all a mother's fear. She took up her treasure, as He slept, and went forth with Joseph into the cold star-light; for poverty has few preparations to make. She was leaving home again. Terror and hardship, the wilderness and heathendom were before her; and she confronted all with the calm anguish of an already broken heart. Here and there the night-wind stirred in the leafless fig-trees, making their bare branches nod against the bright sky, and now and then a watch-dog bayed, not because it heard them, but from the mere nocturnal restlessness of animals. But as Jesus had come like God, so He went like God, unnoticed and unmissed. No one is ever less missed on earth, than He on whom it all depends.

The path they took was not the one which human prudence would have pointed out to them. They returned upon the Jerusalem road they had so lately trodden. But avoiding the Holy City, they passed near Bethlehem, as if His neighbourhood should give a blessing to those unconscious babes that were still nestling warmly in their mothers' arms. Thus they fell into the road which leads into the wilderness, and Joseph going before, like the shadow of the Eternal Father, they crossed the frontier of the promised land, far on until they were lost to the eye, like specks on the desert sand. Two creatures had carried the Creator into the wilderness, and were taking care of Him there amid the stony sands of the unwatered gullies. Sunrise and sunset, the glittering noon and the purple midnight, the round moon and the coloured haze, came to them in the desert for many a day. Still they travelled on. They had cold to bear by night, and a sun from which there was no escape by day. They had scanty food, and frequent thirst. They knew whom they were carrying, and looked not for miracles to lighten the load they bore.

THE FLIGHT INTO EGYPT.

Old tradition said that one night they rested in a robber's cave. They were received there with rough but kind hospitality by the wife of the captain of the band. Perhaps it was her sorrow that made her kind; for it is often so with women. Her sorrow was a great one. She had a fair child, the life of her soul, the one gentle spotless thing amid all the lawlessness and savage life around. Alas! it was too fair to look at; for it was white with leprosy. But she loved it the more, and pressed it the more fondly to her bosom, as mothers are wont to do. It was more than ever her life and light now, because of its misfortune. Mary and Jesus, the robber's wife and the leprous child, together in the cave at nightfall! How fitting a place for the Redeemer! How sweet a type of the Church which He has founded! Mary asked for water that she might wash our Blessed Lord, and the robber's wife brought it to her, and Jesus was washed therein. Kindness, when it opens the heart, opens the eyes of the mind likewise. The robber's wife perceived something remarkable about her guests. Whether it was that there was a light round the head of Jesus, or that the Holy Spirit spoke in the tones of Mary, or that the mere vicinity of so much holiness strangely affected her, we know not; but, in much love and with some sort of faith, the mother's heart divined :—earth knows that maternal divination well. She took away the water Mary had used in washing Jesus, and washed her little leprous Dimas in it, and straightway his flesh became rosy and beautiful, as mother's eye could long to see it. Long years passed. The child outgrew its mother's arms. It did feats of boyish daring on the sands of the wilderness. At last Dimas was old enough to join the band; and though it seems he had to the last somewhat of his mother's heart about him, he led a life of violence and crime, and at length Jerusalem saw him brought within her gates a captive. When he hung upon the cross, burning with fever, parched with agony, he was bad enough to speak words of scorn to the harmless Sufferer by his side. The Sufferer was silent, and Dimas looked at Him. He saw something heavenly, something unlike a criminal, about Him, such perhaps as his mother had seen in the cave three-and-thirty years ago. It was the Child in the water of whose bath his leprosy had been healed. Poor Dimas! thou hast a worse leprosy now, that will need blood instead of water! Faith was swift in its work. Perhaps his heart was like his mother's, and faith a half natural growth in it. He takes in the scene of the Crucifixion, the taunt, the outrages, the blasphemies, the silence, the prayer for their pardon, the wishful look cast upon himself by the dying Jesus. It is enough. Then and there he must profess his faith! for the Mother's prayers are rising from beneath, and the sinner is being enveloped in a very cloud of mercy. Lord! remember me, when Thou comest into Thy kingdom! See! how quickly he had outrun even some of the apostles. He was fastened to the cross to die, and he knew it was no earthly kingdom in which he could be remembered. This day shalt thou be with Me in Paradise. Paradise for thy cave's hospitality, poor young robber! And Jesus died, and the spear opened His heart, and the red stream sprang like a fresh fountain over the limbs of the dying robber, and though his mother from the cave was not there, his new Mother was beneath the cross, and she sent him after her Firstborn into paradise, the first of that countless family of sons who through that dear Blood should enter into glory.

Ages ago the Jewish people, after their deliverance from Egypt, had wandered over that desert. Its grey sands, its ruddy rocks, its stone-strewn plains, its regions of scant verdure, its sea-coast, and its wells of pastoral renown, had been the scenes of such wonders as the world had not beheld before. Never had the Creator interfered so visibly, or for so long a time together, in favour of His creatures. The whole camp, with its cloud and fire, its cruciform march, with Ephraim, Benjamin, and Manasses, bearing the relics of Joseph, its moving church beautified with the spoils of Egypt, was a standing miracle. In Sinai God had thundered from the heights, pouring through that wandering Hebrew people over the whole world the glorious light and transcending faith of the unity of God, a doctrine that came to the world most fitly from the austere grandeur of a wilderness. There had those commandments of heavenly morality been given, under which we are living at the present day, and which shall be men's rule of life until the doom, the Judge's rule in fixing the doom of each. In our Christian childhood we have wandered with the Jews over that silent wilderness, learning the fear of God. In their pilgrimage we have seen a type of our own. In their vicissitudes we seemed almost to take part ourselves. The very names of the wells and halting-places sound like old songs in our ears, songs so early learned that they can never be forgotten. Here now was the very Creator Himself, in the reality of human childhood, wandering over that historic wilderness, reversing the Exodus, going to make Egypt His home, driven out of the delectable land of the old Canaanites by the very people, whom He had led thither by a pillar of light, whose battles He had fought, whose victories He had gained, and whose tribes He had established, each in its characteristic and suitable allotment. There was Mary with her Magnificat, instead of Miriam and her glorious sea-side song; and another Joseph, greater and dearer far than that saintly patriarch of old, who had saved the lives of men by husbanding the bread of Egypt, whereas this new Joseph was to guard in the same Egypt the living Bread of everlasting life. And that very wilderness both the Josephs had crossed.

How wonderful must have been the thoughts of Jesus and Mary as they wandered over those scenes of God's past mercies, past judgments, past grandeurs! We may reverently follow them in our meditations, but it would be hardly reverent to write our guesses down. It was a journey of hardship and fatigue. At last they reached the shores of the Red Sea, and saw the waters that lay between Egypt and themselves. We can hardly conceive that they did not as it were re-consecrate by their presence the exact scene of the Exodus, wherever it was. Thence it would be most likely that they would follow the coast, and round the gulf by Suez, and so pass on to Heliopolis, now truly, for some years to come, to be the City of the Sun. Tradition speaks of trees that bowed down their leafy heads, inclining their branchless stems, to shade with their fanlike plumes the Mother and the Child. It speaks also of the uncouth images of the heathen gods which tumbled, like Dagon, from their pedestals, when the True God went by. There, on the banks of that old river where Moses wrought his miracles, amid crowds of benighted idolaters, and in all the straitnesses of poverty, the Hebrew strangers dwelt, for seven years, for five years, or for two years and a half, as different authorities maintain. Joseph pursued his trade of carpenter, and Mary doubtless contributed to the support of the modest household, while Jesus unfolded His infantine beauties day after day, more delicate and lovely a thousand times in His human loveliness, than the fairest snowy lotus that was ever cradled on the bosom of the Nile.

During those years that Egyptian city was the centre of the world. The garden of Eden was as nothing to it in beauty or in gifts. Thither were the angels gathered in multitudes to wonder and adore. Thither, though men knew it not, went all the world's prayers, its sighs, its secret expectations. Thither also went the voices of pain and sorrow in Heliopolis itself, into God's ear, and that a human ear, in the next street or in the self-same house. Supernatural actions of consummate sanctity, and of infinite value, were pouring forth day and night from the Human Soul of Jesus in more abundant volume than the Nile-flood at its highest, meriting graces which should carry fertility over the whole wilderness of a fallen world. Beautiful also was the heart of Mary during those years. Her holiness was rising perpetually, her union with God, the closeness of which was already far beyond what any technical term in mystical theology can express, grew closer and closer; so that the Mother seemed to be well-nigh identified with the Son, in spite of that whole infinity which always lay between the Creator and the creature. Her sorrows grew as well. There was still the lifelong sorrow of the first dolour at her heart; and to this were superadded the many new sorrows which this second dolour, this Flight into Egypt, had of necessity brought with it. Did dark Egypt know of the great light which was shining on the banks of its famous river? Did the priests, in spite of themselves, offer sacrifice to the sun with less faith, now that *He* was close at hand, smelling the sacrificial odours, and in hearing of the wild worship, who invented the sun, called it out of nothing, gifted it with all its occult influences, set it up as a hearth at which the golden ether should kindle itself into heat and light, and made it the centre of such vast outlying regions of life and such magnificent far-stretching phenomena, right away beyond still undiscovered planets, and all out of His own unimaginable wisdom? Did no misgivings come across the more thoughtful in the multitude, when they joined in the undignified rites of their debasing animal worship, now that the Eternal had assumed a created nature, and was to be seen and heard in their land? Some truth, some sweet gracious trouble in many souls, must surely have stolen like an infection from the nearness of Jesus and Mary. For are they ever near, and some benediction does not follow? But all these things, all the secrets of this Egyptian life, are hidden in divine concealment.

So the appointed years ran out; and when Herod was dead, an angel of the Lord appeared to Joseph in sleep, saying, Arise, and take the Child and His Mother, and go into the land of Israel. For they are dead that sought the life of the Child. Joseph arose with the same promptitude as of old. There was no delay. No one at Heliopolis would care to detain them. They were too obscure. They were free to come and go as they pleased. The stars of night were still standing tremulously like thin shafts of light in the breast of the Nile, when they began their homeward wanderings. Once more they saw the waters of the Red Sea. Once more the weary night-wind of the wilderness sighed round them as they sank to rest upon the sands. Once more the hills and the vineyard walls of Southern Juda greeted their eyes, the welcome land which God had chosen. But the cross was not to be removed all at once. The temple at Jerusalem was their natural attraction. But Joseph knew the value of that treasure he was set to guard; and when he heard that Archelaus reigned in the room of his father, he was afraid to go there. In his fear he doubtless sought light in prayer, and again a supernatural warning came to him in his sleep, and he was bidden to retire into the quarters of Galilee. So the long journey was made longer, until at length the old home at Nazareth received the three.

Such was the mystery of the second dolour. It extended over an uncertain length of time, for we must not confine the dolour to the Flight only. Epiphanius thought that our Lord was two years old when He fled, and remained in Egypt two. Nicephorus fixed the duration of the sojourn at three years. Barradius calls it five or six, Ammonius of Alexandria seven. Maldonatus fixes it at not more than seven, nor less than four. Baronius gathers from a variety of considerations that our Lord fled in His first year, and returned in His ninth, thus giving at least seven full years to Egypt; to this Suarez also inclines, though he says that nothing positive can be decided about it. Seven years is also the most commonly accepted time amongst the faithful. This dolour presents three different objects of devotion to us: the Flight with all its fears, its hardships, and fatigues, the Sojourn with its sense of exile and its companionship with the idolaters, and the Return, with those peculiarities which followed from the increased age and size of Jesus. Some writers dwell on one or other of these in preference to the rest. Pious contemplation may shift from one to another according to its mood. But to comprehend the dolour in its unity, we must consider it as a drama in three acts, the

Flight, the Sojourn, and the Return, by which, as we shall see presently, it is made a double dolour.

We may now therefore pass from the narrative of the mystery to a consideration of the peculiarities of this dolour.

The first thing to be noticed is, that as Simeon was the instrument of the first dolour, so Joseph was the instrument of this. There was much in this to the loving heart of Mary. There is a certain appearance of cruelty in sending sorrow through those we love. Shakspeare says that the first bringer of unwelcome news has but a losing office. Thus it was at once a sorrow to Joseph to convey fresh sadness to Mary, and to her to receive it from him. The world has often been glorified by heroic examples of conjugal affection. Many have been recorded in history as notable phenomena, which were too precious for the wisdom and the solace of mankind to be forgotten. In the deeper depths of private life it is a pure fire which is burning evermore. But never did marriage throw its divine sanctions round a conjugal love so pure, so true, so intense, as that which existed between Joseph and Mary. Never was there such oneness, such identity, such living out of self and in each other, as was in them. It was the very perfection of natural love. Next to her natural love for Jesus, earth has never seen such another love as that between Joseph and herself, unless it were also Joseph's love for the Holy Child. But added to this natural love there was so much that was supernatural: and supernatural love is not only deeper, but more tender, than natural love. It brings out the capabilities and depths of the human heart far more than natural affection can do. Joseph was to Mary the shadow of the Eternal Father, the representative of her Heavenly Spouse, the Holy Ghost. In him she saw with awful clearness and most reverential tenderness two Persons of the Most Holy Trinity. When she saw Jesus in his arms, it was a mystery to her too deep for words. Tears only could express it. Then the exceeding sanctity of Joseph was continually before her, and she was privy to operations of grace within his soul, which probably surpassed those of any other saint. For they were the graces of him who was the master of God's household. While then it was an exercise of obedience to him as her appointed master, it was also no slight aggravation of Mary's sorrow, that this time it should come to her through Joseph.

There was a further aggravation in the fact that her suffering seemed to come less directly from God and more from the wickedness of men, than was the case in the first dolour. There it was prophecy, God's disclosure of the future, and His infusion of a vivid vision of it to be her perpetual companion. But now the hand of sinful man was actually upon her. She was in contact with the violence, of which Jesus was to be the victim. Here was the first touch of Calvary; and it chilled her to the heart. In our own limited sphere of endurance, we must surely all have felt that there is an additional difficulty in receiving a cross, when it comes to us, not directly from God, but through the hands of our fellow-creatures. But not only is it an additional difficulty, it often seems to be the peculiar difficulty. We fancy, doubtless not unfrequently deceiving ourselves, that we could have borne it patiently and cheerfully, if it had come at once from Him. But there is something which dishonours the cross in its transmission through the hands of others. Thus it is a trial, not to our patience only, but also to our humility. There is nothing humbling in having the weight of God's omnipotence simply laid upon us by Himself, with the intervention only of inanimate secondary causes. There is nothing humiliating in the death of a dear child, or the taking away of a beloved sister, or in the breaking up of a household by death, or in the desolation of home by some terrific accident. Humility is not exactly or immediately the virtue which divine catastrophes elicit from the soul. But when God punishes us through the injustice of men, through the base jealousies of others, through the unworthy suspicions of unbelieving friends, through the ingratitude of those we have benefited, or through unrequited love of any sort, then the bravest natures will shrink back, and decline the cross if they can. It is true that reason tells them God is really the fountain of sorrow. It comes from Him, even though it flows through others. But nothing except an unusual humility will make this dictate of reason a practical conviction. Even with inanimate causes there is something of this reluctance in submission to sorrow. If a mother hears of the death of her son, her soul is full of bitterness, yet, if she be a real Christian, full of resignation too. But fuller tidings come. It was a mere accident. The slightest change in the circumstances, and he would have been saved. If it had not happened when it did and where it did, it could not have happened at all. Take away a little inculpable negligence, or imagine the least little common foresight, and her son might this hour have been in her arms in the flush of youth. His death was so exceptional, that circumstances rarely combine as they combined then. They seem to have combined, like a fate, on purpose to destroy him. Ah! and is not this veil thin enough for a Christian eye to discern our Heavenly Father through it? Does it not give a softening sweetness to the death, that it was brought about with such a manifest gentle purpose? Look at that Christian mother, and see. Her resignation has almost disappeared. Hard faith is all that is left to sustain her in her sorrow. The tears have gushed out afresh. She has broken silence, and grieved out loud. She has wrung her hands, and given up her work, and sits by the wayside weeping. She has told the story so often, that it has grown into her mind. Each time she told it the slightest tint of exaggeration entered in, until now the death of her son had become to her own self a painful mystery, an unaccountable injustice, a blow which will not allow itself to be borne, but is manifestly unendurable. So bitter, so trebly bitter, does the actions of creatures render the fountains of our sorrow.

But there is something more than this in our impatience at the intervention of creatures in our misfortunes. It is a deep-lying trust in the justice of God, which is far down in our souls, and the foundation of all that is most manly in our lives. It seems to be our nature to bear blows from Him; nay, there is something comforting in the sense of His nearness to us which the act of punishment discloses. Our whole being believes in the infallibility of His love, and so is quiet even when it is not content. No idea of cruelty hangs round our conception of God, even though we know that He has created hell. But every created face has a look of cruelty in it. There is something in every eye which warns us not to trust it infinitely; greatly perhaps we may trust it, but not to the uttermost. It is the feeling of being at the mercy of this cruelty, which makes us shrink from sorrows that come as if directly from the hands of creatures. Our sense of security is gone. We do not know how far things will go. Strange to say! it seems as if we knew all, when we are in the grasp of the inscrutable God, but that, when creatures have got their hands upon us, there are dreadful things in the background, undiscovered worlds of wrong, subterranean pitfalls, dismal possibilities of injustice, magnified like shadows, and to appearance inexhaustible. There is the same difference between our feelings in misfortunes coming straight from God, and misfortunes that come through men, that there is between the feeling of an unpopular criminal hearing the wild yells of the multitude that seek his blood through the thick walls of his prison, which he knows to be impregnable, and his terror when he is exposed to the people in the street, with their fierce eyes glaring on him, and a feeble guard that must give way at the first onset. In the one case he has to confront the considerate tranquillity of justice, in the other to face the indefinite barbarity of savages. Even David, whose heart was after God's own heart, felt this deeply. When God gives him his choice of punishments, after he had numbered the people, he answers, I am in a great strait: but it is better that I should fall into the hands of the Lord, for His mercies are many, than into the hands of men. And so he chose the pestilence. Who is there that does not feel that the immutable God is more easy to persuade than the hearts of flesh in our fellow-sinners! He will change His purpose sooner than a man. When God stands between us and the unkind world, we feel secure, and grieve quietly, our head leaning on His feet even while we sit desolate upon the ground. But when the merciless world itself is down upon us, no shorn sheep on the wide treeless wold, with the icy north wind sweeping over it, is in more pitiable plight than we. This is what Mary felt. The partition was wearing away. The wall was sinking that had stood between the world's actual rudeness and her broken heart. Her martyrdom grows more grievous, as it grows less placid, notwithstanding that the current of her inward tranquillity flows unquickened still.

So much for the manner in which this dolour came to her. But St. Joseph's share in it is by no means exhausted there. He is a new ingredient throughout all the years, over which this sorrow extends. He was old, and his years had need of rest. He dwelt for ever in an atmosphere of calmness, which seemed to suit his graces best, and in which they developed freely, like the magnificent foliage we read of in almost windless islands. His life has been a life of outward tranquillity, as well as inward. Haste, precipitation, and unsettlement were foreign to him. He combined virginal meekness with the most fervent love. He was simple like Jacob, meditative like Isaac, living a deep life of faith, far beneath the surface of the soul's storms, like Abraham. He was like, at least the thought comes natural, like the gentle gifted Adam, full of soft sanctities and placid familiarity with God, before he fell. He seemed rather a flower to blossom somewhere just outside the earth, or to be caught up and planted inside that old hidden Eden of man's innocence. O how Mary's heart was poured out in love and admiration upon this trophy of God's sweetest, gentlest graces! But she was to drag him out into the storm. She was to throw him into life's rude, rough, swift, jostling, inconsiderate crowd, and see his meek spirit bruised, wounded, and outworn with the struggle. At his age how unbecoming the cold and heat, the wind and wet of that houseless wilderness! How his eyes shrank from the wild fiery faces of the Arabs and the dark expression of those keen Egyptians, and how strangely his voice sounded as it mixed with theirs! Mary felt in her heart every one of these things, and many more, many worse, of which we know nothing, but may surmise much. It was only the sight of Jesus, only the thought of the Child's peril, which enabled her to bear it. And then, like a transplanted flower in a new climate, Joseph gave out such new light, such fresh fragrance, such altered blossoms, such different fruits. His soul was more beautiful than ever, and with the brightness of its beauty grew the intensity of Mary's love, and, with that love, each trial, each grief, each incommodity of his winning old age was a keener sorrow and a deeper grief than it was before.

But she was positively encircled with objects of sorrow. From Joseph she looked to Jesus. Her nearness to Him became a supernatural habit full of consequences to her soul. It brought with it swift growths of sanctity. It adorned her with extraordinary perfections. It was a perpetual process of what the hard style of mystical theology calls deific transformation. We can form no just idea of what it was. But there are moments when we get a transient glimpse in our own souls of what the habitual nearness of the Blessed Sacrament has done for us. We perceive that it has not only done something to each virtue and grace God may have given us; but that it has changed us, that it has done a work in our nature, that it has impregnated us with feelings and instincts which are not of this world, and that it has called up or created new faculties to which we cannot give a name or divine their functions. The way in which a priest says office, or the strange swiftness of his Mass, is a puzzle to those who are outside the Church. They are quite unable to understand the reality of the view of God which a Catholic gets from the Blessed Sacrament, and how that to him slowness, and manner, and effect, whether they be to tell on others or admonish self, are in fact a simple forgetfulness of God, and the manifest *unfrightenedness* of a creature who has for the moment forgotten Him, and His terrible nearness on the altar. From this experience we may obtain an indistinct conception of what the nearness of Jesus had done in Mary. How much more sensitive therefore did she become about His sufferings! The change, which His presence wrought in herself, would be daily adding new susceptibilities to her sorrow. She saw trials to Him in little things, which yesterday perhaps she had scarcely discerned. For if her love grew, her enlightenment must have grown also: in divine things light and love are co-equal and inseparable. Just as in our small measure our tenderness and perception about the offended majesty of God grow with our advance in holiness and our more refined sensibilities of conscience, so in an astonishing degree Mary's capabilities of wounded feeling about Jesus were daily being augmented.

But this was not all. There was a change in Him, as well as in her; and it also, like the other, went as another spring to feed the stream of her sorrows. He was not a stationary vision, just as we all know how the Blessed Sacrament is not a stationary presence, but one which lives, acts, grows, puts out attractions, makes manifestations, and is as immutably changeful as the worship of heaven which never wearies even the vast intelligence of angels. Thus the Holy Child was constantly giving out fresh light and beauty. He was an inexhaustible treasure of supernatural loveliness. It always seemed as if at once she knew Him so well, and yet was but just beginning to know Him at all. There was a mixture of custom and surprise in her love of Him, which was like no earthly affection. For, while she felt instinctively as if she could prophesy how He would act in given circumstances, she was quite sure there would be some divine novelty in the action when it came, which would take her unawares. Thus the delight of wonder for ever mingled with the delight of habit. Her powers of observation, and the completeness of her intelligence, must also have been quickened by the velocity and expansion of her love. Nothing escaped her. Nothing was without its significance. If there were unfathomable depths, at least she was becoming more and more expert in fathoming them. Jesus was a revelation, and therefore called out science as well as faith. Even to us, to learn our Blessed Lord is a different thing from believing in Him. Such a lesson it is,—with Himself as the professor to teach it, divided into a million sciences, eternity the university to learn it in, where the best of us will never finish the course, never take our degrees! Mary was learning it, as even the angels in heaven cannot learn it. So infinite was the worth of the grace our Lord was disclosing, so infinite the value of His manifold daily actions, so infinite the satisfaction of each of His least sufferings, that in this one dolour Mary had what with so many infinities may well be called three eternities in which to learn His loveliness and raise her own love to the mark of her learning. There was first the wilderness, and then Egypt, and then the wilderness again. And all these accumulated lights, sensibilities, beauties, graces, attractions, increments of love, were but so many fresh edges put on Simeon's sword. The result of each, the result of all, the product of their combination, was simply an immensity of sorrow.

There are two ways of doing battle with grief. One is in the privacy of our own homes, in the secrecy of our suffering hearts, with the undistracted presence of God round about us. But under the most favourable circumstances it is no easy task. The common round of indoors duties is heavy and irksome; and somehow, though if sorrow had chosen its own accidents it would not have made itself more endurable, the cross seems always as if it never fitted, as if there were peculiar aggravations in our own case to justify at least some measure of impatience. But the fight is much harder when we have to go forth to meet the enemy, not only before the faces and among the voices of men in an unsparing publicity, but to receive our sorrow at their hands, and to feel the pressure of their unkindliness upon us. In this case it is not that external work is an unwelcome distraction to our sorrow; it is not merely that grief gives us a feeling of right to be dispensed from the actual conflict of work: but our very external work is our sorrow. We go out to sorrow. We pass from the shelter of home on purpose to meet our grief. We do our best to let suffering take us at a disadvantage, and off our guard, amid a multiplicity of things to do, and having to look many ways at once. Neither is this our own choice. It is simple necessity. Of the two battles with sorrow, this is far the hardest to fight, and the unlikeliest to win. In passing from the first dolour to the second, our Lady's sorrow shifted from the easier battle to the harder one, if battle is a right word to use of such a supreme tranquillity as hers. Her new sorrow called for actual outward obedience, not the mere assent of an inward generosity. She had suffered in the sanctuary of her own soul before; now personal toil, external privation, rough work enter into her sorrow. They, who appreciate rightly the shyness of extreme sanctity, will have some idea of what this change, in itself, and considered apart from other aggravating circumstances, inflicted upon the delicate nature of our Blessed Mother.

It not unfrequently happens that persons beginning in holiness feel, almost in spite of themselves, a kind of disesteem for the outward observances of religion. They may be too well instructed to fall into any erroneous opinion on the subject; but, for all that, the feeling is upon them, and will show itself for awhile in many little ways. Habits of interior piety are comparatively new to them, and, with the fresh feeling of how little outward devotion is worth without the inward, they exaggerate the importance of interior things, and look at them in too exclusive a light. There is something so delicious, there is no other word for it, in the first experiences of communing with our Blessed Lord down in our own hearts, that faith, for want of practice, does not see Him, as it will one day, in the commonest ordinances and most formal ceremonies of the Church. But, as the soul grows in holiness, a reverse process goes on. Vocal prayer reassumes its proper importance. Sacraments are seen to be interior things. The calendar of the Church leaves a deeper impress on our devotion. Beads, scapulars, indulgences, and confraternities work ascetically in our souls,—a deep work, an interior work. At last, to high sanctity outward things are simply the brimming vases in which Jesus has turned the water into wine, and out of which He is pouring it continually into the soul. To a saint a single rubric has life enough in it to throw him into an ecstasy, or to transform him by a solitary touch into a higher kind of saint than he is now.* To an inexperienced beginner there is nothing perhaps in St. Teresa less intelligible than her devotion to holy water. They can understand her doctrine of the prayer of quiet more readily than her continual reference to holy water, and the great things she says of it. From all this it comes to pass that there was one peculiarity of this dolour of our Lady, into which none can enter fully but a saint, indeed even a saint not fully; for we must remember that it is of Mary we are speaking. This was the deprivation of spiritual advantages in the wilderness and in Egypt. There was no temple, probably no synagogue. There were no sacrifices, but such as were abominations and horrors to her soul. There was not the nameless atmosphere of the true religion round about her; but on the contrary the repulsive darkness and the depressing associations of the most abandoned misbelief and degrading worship of the inferior animals. To her this was a fearful desolation. Her height of sanctity did not lead her to dispense with the commonest assistances of grace, but on the contrary to cling to them with a more intelligent appreciation. It did not teach her to stand and walk merely resting or guiding herself by outward ordinances, but rather to lean her whole weight upon them more than ever. She felt less able to dispense with little things, because she was so richly endowed with great things. She had reached to that wide

---

* We may instance the conduct of St. Andrew Avellino in Holy Week.

view of saintly minds, and to her it was wider and more distinct, that in spiritual things one grace never supersedes another, never does the work of another, never stands in the stead of another. Less intelligent piety mistakes succeeding for superseding, and so loses in reverence, while it misses what is divine. As the loftiest contemplation works its way back again through the accumulated paraphernalia of meditation almost to the indistinct simplicity of the kneeling child's first prayer, so is it wonderful in all things else to see how the saints in their sublimities are for ever returning to the wise littleness and childlike commonplaces of their first beginnings. The puzzles of spirituality are only the symptoms of imperfection. We are fording the river to reach Canaan. The water is shallow when we first begin; it deepens as we advance; but it gets shallow again near to the other side, and shelves quite gently up to the heavenly shore. Hence it was doubtless a keen suffering to Mary to be deprived of the outward ordinances of her religion. Her spirit pined for the courts of the temple, with its crowds of worshippers, for the old feasts as they came round, for the stirring and the soothing show of the ceremonial of the law, and for the sound of the old Hebrew Scriptures from the reader's desk within the synagogue. The presence of Jesus, instead of being to her in lieu of these things and superseding them, would only make her crave for all those sacred things, which He, long years before He was her Babe, had Himself devised, and ordered from out of Sinai. We shall not do justice to this peculiar grief of hers; but we must remember it. We shall not do justice to it, because we have no such acute sensibilities, no such excessive hunger for the things of God, no such visible presence of Jesus to turn that hunger into downright famine.

It happened once to a traveller, who had been long among the sights and sounds of Asiatic life, in whose ears the musical wailing of the muezzin's voice from the gallery of the minaret, over the nightly city or amid the bustle of the day, had almost effaced the remembrance of Christian bells, that from the Black Sea he passed up the Danube, and landed nowhere till he reached the frontier of Transylvania. He landed in a straggling village, and heard the bells jangling with a sound of strange familiarity, and very barbarous singing, and he saw a cleric with a Crucifix glittering in the sun, and some rude banners, and girls in white with tapers, and a pleasant rabble of Christian-faced boys with boughs of hawthorn, or some white-flowering tree, in their hands, and then a priest in poorest cope and under humblest canopy, bearing Jesus with him, to bless the village streets on Corpus Christi. And there came a light and a feeling, and an agitation, and a most keen, most sweet pain, in the traveller's heart, which gave him a surmise far off from the real truth, but still a surmise, of what Mary felt in Egypt. Such to him was the first sight of holy things at the gate of Christendom, when he passed out of the influence of the strange imagery of the Mahometan law. He only saw what he had lost; she realised what she was losing.

But it was not only her own religious feelings, which were wounded by the false and loathsome worship round her. She mourned for the souls it was destroying, souls that knew no wiser wisdom, and so their ignorance at least was innocent, but in whom it was deadening the moral sense, vitiating the conscience, making its judgment false and corrupting its integrity. It was a system of wild enchantment, which held that ancient people as in a net, entangling them in its iniquities so that they could not escape. It was a vast, complete, national organisation. They were going down upon the silent sweep of its stream into everlasting darkness, as irresistingly as a log goes down the Nile. O how much glorious understanding gleamed out of the dark faces of many of them! What hidden sweetness, what possibilities of gentleness and goodness, almost trembled in the voices of many! And she all the while holding Jesus in her arms on the river-side, the Saviour of the world, the fondest lover of souls, who would have drunk the whole river of souls dry, if they would have let Him! Why should He not preach to them at once, He whose mind knew no growth but the knowing by acquisition what He knew otherwise before? Why should He not let His light shine on them at once? Was there not something cruel in the delay, something perplexing, like the slowness of the Church in converting the heathen? And it was not only all those Egyptian souls which lay on her heart, like an oppression in a dream; but there was the glory of God also. One word from Jesus would repair it all; but that word was not spoken. It was not hard for her to bear precisely because it was so strange a will of God. She had too often adored the four thousand Decembers, in which Jesus had not come, not to comprehend the mystery of the delays of God. But it was hard to bear, because of the destiny of that land which swarmed with souls, the multitudes which the Nile mud was feeding and fattening for so insecure an end.

Great things look little by the side of things which are inordinately greater than themselves. So it is with many of the items in Mary's sorrows. Things, each one of which would make a very Romance of misfortune in the commoner lots of men, gathered in almost imperceptible numbers round those tall griefs of our Blessed Mother, which pierce the storm-clouds and go up out of our sight. Yet they must not be forgotten. We must let them accumulate even as they accumulated in the actual mystery. There are many sufferings in exile on which we need not dwell here. They are sufferings which make the heart very sick, and a burden which grows heavier as each year that lapses adds its weight to those that have gone before. There is no getting used to exile. It becomes less of a habit daily. The iron is always in the soul. It is always hot, always burning. It makes terrible wounds, whose lips cannot reach over, and will not heal. Poverty is hard to bear everywhere, but it is hardest of all in a foreign land, where we have no right, scarcely the right to sympathy. The land bears us, because we put our feet on it and tread there. But this is all it does. It bears us as a camel bears its load, because it is more trouble to throw it off than to carry it. It is only because the soil is more merciful than men, that a foreign land does not fling the alien and the mendicant impatiently from its corn-bearing fields. There was something also inexpressibly dismal in Mary's utter loneliness amid her own sex. She was far more lonely in the crowds of Heliopolis, than the penitent Thais or Mary of Egypt could have been in the savagest sequestration of the voiceless Thebaid. And she too so frail, so helpless, so unknown, such a girlish mother, such a delicate flower that the rude wind ought hardly to blow upon. It is fearful to think of. But God was with her. Yes! but look at Him, less than His young mother, more helpless even than herself. And Joseph, his very meekness was against him, and so old, so infirm, so uncomplaining, what protection was he against the pressure of those wild-faced Egyptians? The prophet wept over the vineyard of Sion, because its hedge was broken down. But what Edens were these that were left unsheltered in Egypt, and so unsheltered!

But we must pass on to greater things. There seems nothing contrary to our Blessed Lady's perfections to suppose that in this dolour the fear, which belongs to human nature, and which even our Lord felt in His most holy Soul, was allowed to exercise sway over her. If such were not the case, we should then have to put her before ourselves as a creature apart, not belonging to the angelic family on the one hand, nor to the human family on the other, but as a glory of God, not singular only, as in her office and her sanctity she truly is, but removed also from the sphere of humanity. We should have to imagine that her gifts did for her, what His divine Nature even did not do for our Lord, that they should make her cease to be woman while it left Him true Man. She would then be no example to us, and the idea of sorrow in her would be so strange and unsphered a thing, that it would seem fictitious and unreal, a merely symbolical doctrine, or a beautiful allegory of the Incarnation. There can therefore be little doubt but that fear was one of the chief sufferings of this Flight into Egypt. There is perhaps hardly a passion which exercises a more tyrannical sway over the soul than fear, or any mental impression more closely connected with physical pain. It comes over us like a spirit from without, leaping upon us from some unsuspected cavern we know not where or how. We cannot prepare for its coming, for we know not when to expect it. We cannot resist it when it comes; for its touch is possession, and its mere advent is already victory. It brings a shadow over skies where there are no clouds, and turns the very sunshine into beams of frost. It breathes through us like a wind, searching everywhere, and chilling our most vital faculties. It goes near to paralysing our powers of action, so that we are like men who can see and hear, without being able either to speak or move. If it were not eminently a transient passion, ever flowing by the law of its own restlessness, we should lose first of all the freedom of our will, and then the light of our reason. Meanwhile its presence in the soul is accompanied, one while by a disquietude which is worse than suffering, and the continuance of which it seems to us would be incompatible with life, and then another while by a sharpness of anguish which is always on the very point of being literally unendurable. It is not pain, it is torture. How seldom have we ever found the reality of an evil so insufferable, as the terrified expectation which preceded it. Earth does not grow a sorrow, human justice has not devised a punishment, of which this is not true.

Now we have to imagine the operation of this passion among the indescribable sensibilities of our Lady's soul, and at the same time in the midst of her incomparable holiness. There is ever the union with God unbroken; there is ever the tranquillity, which comes of that union, undisturbed. The sanctuary is assailed, but it is not desecrated. Fear dwells within the precincts, but the cloister is not forced. She knew full well that Calvary was to come, and she knew how far off it was. Hence she could have no doubt that her Child was not now to perish by the hand of Herod. Yet fear, without obscuring her mental vision, might destroy her feeling of security. For thoughts in fear may be just and judicious in themselves, but they dwell alone; they are barren; they have no conclusions. Is not this just what the book of Wisdom says of fear,* that it is "nothing else but a yielding up of the succours from thought, and while there is less expectation from within, the greater doth it count the ignorance of that cause which bringeth the torment." Besides, our Lord may have veiled His Heart from her then. True, He was not to die; but what other abysses of misery might not be yawning invisibly at her very feet? There are many things short of death, which are worse than death. Possible sufferings are inexhaustible, even within the limited lot of man. She might be separated from Him. Herod might give Him to another to nurse, under his own eye. What Egyptian darkness would be like that! The eclipse on Calvary would be comfort and sunshine, in the face of such a woful separation as that. Her foresight did not cover everything with its wide field of vision, or if it did, she might not be sure that it did. There might be depths which she had to come upon unawares, like the Three Days' Loss. Might she not be coming on some now?

What were the extremities to which a sanctity like hers could suffer panic? Would she start at the forms of robbers, as they distantly scoured the wilderness? When the uneasy night-wind awoke suddenly in the muttering palm-tops, or in the tresses of the pensile acacia, like indistinguishable human whispers, was she afraid? Did the dark eyes of the Egyptians frighten her, when their gaze was fixed inquiringly upon the Child? Did fears spur her footsteps, deceive her eyesight, play cruelly with her suspicious hearing? Did she every now and then clasp her Babe with a more tremulous firmness, and inwardly vow she would never part with Him without laying down her life? Did the ears of her informed spirit ring with the lamentations of Bethlehem's

* Cap. xvii.

mother's, or the heartrending trebles of the little ones fly after her on the winds of the desert ? Thou knowest, Mother! We must not dare to say. But who can doubt that fear inflicted upon her the most awful sufferings, making both the wilderness and Egypt a Gethsemane of years ? Truly it was the shadow of an Egyptian darkness that fell upon her; and although with her we cannot take to the letter what Scripture says of that old Egyptian darkness, yet there is much in it which will help us to that vague and indefinable view of what our Lady suffered, which alone it is desirable or reverent to take. "During that night, in which nothing could be done, and which came upon them from the lowest and deepest hell, they were sometimes molested with the fear of monsters; sometimes fainted away, their soul failing them: for a sudden and unlooked-for fear was come upon them. Moreover, if any of them had fallen down, he was kept shut up in prison without irons. For if any one were a husbandman or a shepherd, or a labourer in the field, and was suddenly overtaken, he endured a necessity from which he could not fly. For they were all bound together with one chain of darkness. Whether it were a whistling wind, or the melodious voices of birds, among the spreading branches of trees, or a fall of water running down with violence, or the mighty noise of stones tumbling down, or the running that could not be seen of beasts playing together, or the roaring voice of wild beasts, or a rebounding echo from the highest mountains,—these things made them to swoon for fear. For the whole world was enlightened with a clear light, and none were hindered in their labours; but over them was spread a heavy night, an image of that darkness which was to come upon them. But they were to themselves more grievous than the darkness." *

But the most grievous part of this dolour remains to be told, and there is no one who can tell it as it should be told. We should understand it, if we had a revelation of Mary's heart; but even then we could not translate it into words.

* Wisd. cap. xvii. 13-20.

It was a mixture of sharpest pain, wounded feeling, distress so great as to seem unexpected, horror that yearned to disbelieve what it saw, a cruel crushing together of all the loves of her immaculate heart. It arose from the vision of men's hatred of Jesus, made visible in this dolour. Beautiful Child! wonderfully sheathing the keen grandeurs of the Godhead in that scabbard of true infant's flesh! Was there ever anything so winning, ever anything so hateless, as that blessed Child? Why should men turn against Him thus? Why should the eyes of kings pierce the shrouds of His innocuous obscurity, like wild lynxes, and why thirst for the little shallow stream of His blood, as if He were a tempting prey for savage natures? Harmless, helpless, silent, pleading, beautiful! and men drive Him from their haunts as if He were a monster, heartless, tyrannical, blood-stained, with all the repulsion of great iniquity and dark secret crime about Him! And she knew how beautiful He was, and therefore how unutterable was the sacrilege of that cruel exile, of that murderous pursuit, which only ended in exile, because God would not let it go further, and baulked ferocity of its victim. She knew too that He was God, the Creator come among His creatures; and although He has not interfered with them yet, has not even spoken to them, but has only looked at them with His sweet Face, they are tormented with restlessness, feel Him a burden, though she who carried Him all over the desert can testify that He is lighter than a feather, or at least seems so to her maternal love, and finally make Him fly before them even before He can walk. This was the welcome God has been waiting for, now these four thousand years! Merciful heavens! is not Divine Love a thing simply incredible?

All the loves in her heart were crushed. Jesus was hated. Had men simply avoided Him and got out of His way, it would have been an intolerable sorrow. Had they gone by Him with indifference as if He was no concern of theirs, but just a living man, as their senses told them, who increased by one the population of the world, and was otherwise poor and commonplace, even that would have been acutest grief. For men to ignore, to misapprehend, to disappreciate Jesus, would have been a lifelong thorn in her heart, which nothing could have extracted. But He was hated. And there He was flitting like a speck over the wilderness out of sight of the people, whom He loved the most of all those He came to save. She loved Him with many loves, because by many rights, and under many titles. She was wounded separately and bitterly in every one of these loves. She was His creature and His mother. She loved Him with the intensest natural affection as having borne Him. Her love was marvellously grown with His growing beauty and her increasing experience of Him. She loved Him with supernatural love because of His holiness, and her own which was attracted by His. She loved Him as the Saviour and Redeemer of the world. She loved with perfect adoration His Divine Nature, and the Person of the Eternal Word. Beyond this, where could love go? Whither could it reach? But she loved also, and with an enthusiasm which was like a second life to her, the glory of God, His exaltation by His creatures, and the honour of the Divine Majesty. She loved the Most Holy Trinity with all the loves the saints have ever known, with complacency, congratulation, desire, condolence, imitation, esteem. Now Jesus was the very end at which all these glories of God aimed, the very monument on which they were all hung, the very fountain out of which they all came, the very food by which alone they were all to be satisfied, the very price which was equal to their value, the very means, the only means, by which Mary could love them as she desired. There was not one thing about which God is tender, which was not outraged and wounded in this attempt upon the life of Jesus, in this hatred of His Son whom He had sent. And fearfully, like stigmata upon the saints, upon Mary's ardent love passed the many wounds of the Eternal Object of her love.

This was not all. She loved men. Their own wives and

mothers never loved them as she did. No missionary ever burned for souls, as she burned. She had all their interests at heart, and the interests of every one of them. She would have died to save the lowest of them, if the limited sacrifice of a mere creature could have merited their salvation. She would have suffered tortures to hinder any of them from a single sin, for their own sake as well as God's. But what need of more words? She was going to give them Jesus. She had made up her mind to it. Nay, virtually she had done it. O how men wounded her now in this love of hers, unrequited, disdained, as it were thrown back upon her. She shuddered at the abysses of darkness, the capabilities of separation from God, which this hatred of Jesus disclosed; and a sort of sacred horror passed upon her, when she perceived in it such a terrible manifestation of the power and malice of the evil spirits. They did not yet know that Jesus was God, but their instincts drew them round His grace and holiness by a sort of attraction which they did not understand, but which nevertheless rendered them furious. And men, men whose nature the Word had assumed, men for whom Jesus was to die, men whose mother she was to be, even the chosen tribes of Israel, were almost possessed by these evil spirits, were following their leading, doing their bidding, without knowing how terrible were the things that they were doing. O can we not conceive how out of the most broken of all broken hearts the Mother of mercy would forestall that sweet omnipotent prayer of her Child, Father, forgive them, for they know not what they do?

Now this second dolour, as has been already said, was not a transient mystery. It was not a complete action done and over at once. It spread itself over a long time. It endured for years. For all those years Mary had to suffer all these sorrows. Besides the seven years' sojourn in Egypt, which opened the wound wider in the exiled heart day by day, this dolour was a double dolour. It had an echo for it; for the Return was a sort of echo to the Flight. There was the same weary way to travel, the same fatigues, the same privations, and many of the same dangers. The fear however was less, or rather it had sunk into anxiety about the great object, the Child's life; though it had still many lesser objects by the way. There were however some aggravating circumstances in the Return, by which it is distinguished from the Flight. The age of Jesus presented a peculiar difficulty to their poverty. He was in His eighth year, too young to walk, too old and heavy for His Mother's arms. Either it would entail upon them the cost of some beast of burden, which would also materially increase the toils of St. Joseph in the wilderness, or they must have borne their precious Burden by turns, when He had allowed the natural consequences of weariness, or the soreness caused by the burning sand and prickly sand-plants, to work their will upon Him, and make it impossible for Him to walk further. The increased age of St. Joseph was also a feature in the Return, which Mary never for a single hour forgot. Labour had bent him, and years, years especially of recent disquietude, had left their furrows on his holy face. He was easily tired; for his strength was soon spent; and Jesus helps less with their cross those that are near Him, than those who are further off. The age of Jesus also brought to Mary, as usual, fresh reasons for loving Him, and ceaseless augmentations of the old love, and all this heightened the pangs she was enduring. Moreover, she and He were now upon the road to Calvary, their faces turned right towards it. Can that thought ever have left her through the whole Return? And on the frontiers of the Holy Land fear met them again, and turned them away from Sion, and sent them back to the seclusion of Nazareth. Scripture says, There is no peace for the wicked. Alas! when we look at the world we are tempted to cry out, that it is rather for the good that there is no peace.

From these peculiarities of the second dolour we may now pass to the dispositions with which our Blessed Lady endured it. Much may be gathered from what has been already said. But there are three points to which our attention should be especially directed. The first is, her unselfish absorption in the sufferings of others. It is as if her heart was put out into the hearts of others in order to feel, to love, to suffer, to be tortured. As we pass in review the incidents of this dolour, it never comes to us for a moment to think how cold she often was, how hungry, how wind-burnt, how sleepless, how footsore, how harassed in mind, how great her bodily fatigue, as if these were the elements of her own sorrow. They were sufferings which we, her sons, do not forget, and as sufferings they were part of her endurance. But as subjects upon which she dwelt, or which she bewailed, or which she even much adverted to, we should feel that we were dishonouring her, if we put them in the reckoning. Her sorrowful sympathies were all abroad. They were lavished on Joseph, or they were centered in Jesus. They covered the whole majesty of God with their humblest condolence, or they went out like a deluge over the entire earth, bathing all the souls of men in every generation with her mournful pity and efficacious compassion. They were everywhere but in her own miseries. They were for every one, except herself. There seemed to be no effort about it. It was her way. It came natural to her, because she behaved with grace as if it really was a nature to her. As the moon reflects the light of the sun without the least trouble to itself, and beautifies the earth without any exertion, so Mary reflects God, and gives light, and shines, without effort, almost unconsciously as if it was simply her business to be luminous and beautiful, and that there was no wonder in it at all.

Another disposition in this dolour was her keen sensitiveness about the interests of God defrauded by sin. This is the new sense developed in the soul by sanctity; and the more we grow in holiness, the more keen does this sense become. The range of its vision is wider, while at the same time its perceptions are more accurate and minute. Its ardour increases with the increase of grace, and by a natural consequence its powers of making us suffer increase likewise. In the case of very great saints it becomes completely a passion, and at last possesses itself of the whole life. There can however be hardly a comparison between this sensitiveness as developed in the highest saints, and the same feeling as it existed in the Mother of God. She was drawn inside a divine ring, and lived a divine life. She had a sort of unity with the Divine Majesty, a spiritual unity, which gave her a right to share in the concerns of God, a right to be interested only in His interests, a sort of actual participation in the sensibilities of His glory, such as can belong to no other creature whatsoever. She is one of the household, and therefore feels differently from one outside, however dear a friend, however near a neighbour. Her prayer is not mere intercession; there is in it a permitted jurisdiction over the Sacred Heart and the Will of God, which renders it a different thing from the intercession of the Saints. All the elect work together with Jesus in multiplying the fruit of His Passion; but there is allowed to her an indefinable co-operation in the redemption of the world, to which the co-operation of the saints bears the same relation as their sympathy with our Lord's Passion bears to our Lady's Compassion. If the sufferings of St. Paul in his flesh * " filled up those things that are wanting of the sufferings of Christ, for His Body, which is the Church," what must be said of Mary's dolours? These considerations, if they cannot help our spiritual obtuseness to an adequate conception of our Lady's sensitiveness for the glory of God, will at least enable us, when we are astonished at the sublimity of this instinct in the saints, to remember that hers was so much higher as to be out of sight of theirs.

Even to us, down in the deep valleys where the merciful inquisitiveness of grace has found us out, there is something inexpressibly mournful in the way in which God is excluded from His own creation. We are considering now the mystery of the Creator's flight from His creatures. Is there not also something quite as dreadful in the flight of the creatures from their Creator, which we see going on all day?

* Coloss. i. 24.

When faith has opened our eyes, what a scene the world presents! Everywhere God with His omnipresent love is pursuing His creatures, His guilty creatures; but it is to save them, not to punish them. There is not a recess of the world, not a retirement of poverty, not a haunt of sin, not an unlikely or unbeseeming place for so vast a Majesty, where He is not following His creatures, and trying almost to force His great gifts upon them. Swifter than the lightning, stronger than the ocean, more universal than the air, is His glorious many-sided compassion poured out over the world which He has made. Everywhere are men flying from this generous, this merciful, this tender pursuit. It seems as if the grand object of their lives was to avoid God, as if time were a respite from the necessity of God's presence in eternity, which it is unfair of Him to interfere with, as if space were a convenience expressly provided for creatures to get out of the way of their Creator. Little boys even are flying from Him with all their might and main, as if they understood the matter just as well as grown-up men, and had made up their minds as determinedly about it. God speaks, entreats, pleads, cries aloud; but still they run. He doubles His sunbeams upon them, to win their hearts by the excess of His fatherly indulgence; but they run. He throws shadows and darkness over them, to make them sober and wise; but they run. He *will* have them. Great graces go forth to their souls, like swift stones from a sling, and they fall. But they are up again in a moment, and continue their flight. Or if He gets up with them, because they are too much hurt to rise on the instant, they only let Him wipe the blood and earth from their wound, and kiss them sweetly on the forehead, and they are off again. He will not be baffled. He will hide Himself in the water of a sacrament, and make loving prey of infants, before they have reached the use of reason. It is well; but then He must slay them also, if He will keep them; for almost before they can walk, they will run away from Him. And what is this picture compared to the vision, which was always before our Blessed Mother's eyes?

But let us make the world stand still, and see how it looks. If our common love of God, which is so poor, is irritated by the sight, what must Mary have suffered? For what is irritation to our weakness, to her would be the most deep and transcending sorrow. God comes to His creation. It does not stir. It cannot. It lies in the hollow beneath Him, and has no escape. He comes in the beauty of a mercy, which is almost incredible, because it is so beautiful. But seemingly it does not attract the world. He draws nigh. Creation must do something now. It freezes itself up before His eye. He may have other worlds, more fertile, more accessible to Him than this. In the spiritual tropics, where the angels dwell, He may perhaps be welcome. But not here. This is the North Pole of His universe. He shed His life's blood upon it, and it would not thaw. It is unmanageable, unnavigable, uninhabitable for Him. He can do nothing at all with it, but let His sun make resplendent coloured lights in the icebergs, or bid the moon shine with a wanner loveliness than elsewhere, or fill the long-night sky with the streamers of the Aurora, which even the Esquimaux, burrowing in his hut, will not go out to see. The only difference is that the material pole understands its business, which is to make ice in all imaginable shapes; whereas we men are so used to our own coldness, that we do not know how cold we are, and imagine ourselves to be the temperate zone of God's creation.

If God gets into His world, matters are not much mended. It is dismal to think, would that it were also incredible, how much of the world is tied up from Him, so as to render almost a miracle necessary in order to insinuate grace into the soul. Look at whole regions of fair beginnings, of good wishes, holy desires, struggling earnestness, positive yearnings, and see how tyrannically the provisions of life deal with all these interests of God. Here are souls tied up from God by family arrangements. They have to live away from the means of grace, or they are thrown among bad examples, or they are forced into uncongenial dissipation, or they are put into the alternative of either judging their parents or blunting their perceptions of God, or they are entangled in unsuitable marriages, or they are forced into the ambitious temptations of worldly positions, or their religious vocations are rough-ridden. God is not to have His own way with them, and will not have it. He on His side will not work miracles, and souls are lost. How much again is tied up by money arrangements. The religion of orphans is endangered by executors who have not the faith. Fortunes are left under conditions, which, without heroic grace, preclude conversion. Place of abode is dictated by straitened circumstances, and it so happens that spiritual disabilities come along with it. Questions of education are unfavourably decided on pecuniary grounds, as also are the choices of profession. Want of money is a bar to the liberty of many souls, who, as far as we can judge, would use that liberty for God. Even local arrangements tie up souls from God. There is a sort of necessity of living for part of the year where regular sacraments are not to be had, or where men must mix very much with people of another creed, or must lay themselves out for political influence, or where young people must break off habits of works of mercy only imperfectly formed in the great city, which after all is a truer sanctuary of God than the green, innocent country. How many also, without fault of their own, or fault of any one, are tied up from God by the temporal consequences of some misfortune. Homes are broken up. Souls are imprisoned in unsuitable occupations, and in unfavourable places; and a host of religious inconveniences follow, from which there is literally no escape. It may be said that, after all, the excellence of religion is interior. But to how many is this interior spirit given? Surely it is not one of God's ordinary graces. And how few really interior persons are there, who are not visibly deteriorated, when their public supplies of grace are impoverished! Others again are tied up from God by some irretrievable steps which they themselves have taken, culpably or inculpably. It is as if an eternal fixity had insinuated itself into some temporal decision. And now souls are helpless. They cannot be all for God, if they would, unless He communicates to them some of the extraordinary graces of the mystical saints. We have often need here to remember for our comfort, that, if steps are irretrievable, nothing in the spiritual life is irremediable. Who could believe the opposite doctrine, and then live? It is fearful the power which men have to tie their fellow-men up from God. What an exercise it is for a hot temper, with a keen sense of injustice, and an honest heartiness of love for God and souls, to have to work for souls under the pressure of the great public system, organisations, and institutions, of a country which has not the faith! To watch a soul perilously balancing on the brink of the grand eternal question, and to see plainly that the most ordinary fairness or the cheapest kindness would save it, and not be able to command either,—it is a work of knives in one's flesh, smarting unbearably. We have no right to demand the fairness; indeed the fairness is perhaps only visible from our own point of view. We are more likely to get justice, if we ask for it under the title of privilege and by the name of kindness. For the sake of Christ's poor let us insist upon God's multiplying and prolonging our patience! Thus, all the world over,—in all classes, especially the upper classes, creation is tied up as it were from God, and His goodness has not fair play with it, unless He will break His own laws, and throw Himself simply on His omnipotence. There is a tyranny of circumstances, which does not seem far short of a necessity of sin. It needs a definition of the faith to assure us that such a necessity is happily an impossibility. We feel all this. It cuts us to the quick. Now it depresses, now it provokes, accordingly as it acts on the inequalities of our little grace. Multiply it till the sum is beyond figures, magnify it till its bulk fills space and hangs out beyond, and then we shall have our Lady's sensitiveness about the honour of God's majesty.

There is still another disposition in our Lady to which our

attention must be called. Her charity for sinners was proportioned to her horror of sin. While on the one hand she mourned over the slighted love of God and the scant harvest of His glory, she had no feeling of bitterness against sinners. She was not angry with their guilt, but unhappy for their sakes, because of the consequences of their guilt. It was not in her heart to condemn them, only to pity them. To her eyes sin came out clear and hideous when seen against the honour of God, but, when seen in the sinner, the horror melted away in the flood of compassion. Her zeal was not anxious to avenge the outrage on the Divine Majesty by startling judgments and condign penalties. It sought rather to repair the outrage by the conversion of the sinner. She thought herself best consulting the interests of God's justice by wishing well to His mercy. There is in truth a sort of reverence due to sinners, when we look at them, not as in their sins, but simply as having sinned, and being the objects of a divine yearning. It is the manifestation of this feeling in apostolic men, which lures sinners to them, and so leads to their conversion. The devotedness of our Blessed Lord to sinners transfers a peculiar feeling to the hearts of His servants. And when the offenders come to repent, the mark of divine predilection in the great grace they are receiving is a thing more to admire and revere and love, than the sin is a thing to hate in connection with the sinner. In all reformatory institutions it is the want of a supernatural respect for sinners, which is the cause of failure, the abundance of it which is the cause of success. When our Lord strove to convert, it was always by kind looks, by loving words, by an indulgence which appeared to border upon laxity. He did not convert by rebuking. He rebuked Herod and the Pharisees, just because He did not vouchsafe to try to convert them. Because He let them alone, therefore He spoke sharply to them. Such were the feelings of our Blessed Lady in the view of sin, which this dolour brought before her. She was not angry with men. She loved them, and was in her heart so pitiful to them that she seemed rather to think their lot a hard one than a guilty one. Her love for them rose with the measure of their sins, just as the fulness of our Lord's time seems to have been the fulness of the world's iniquity. However much their sins widened, her love was always wider. There is scarcely anything in which the instincts of sanctity are more peculiar, than the view which a holy heart takes of sinners. It testifies more unerringly than anything else to secret communion with Jesus, to deep tender union with God, and to the right apprehension, as well as the happy infection, of the Sacred Heart. It is always the contemplative saints who have loved sinners best, even more than the active saints who were wearing out their lives to convert them. Is this the reason why the contemplative element is an essential ingredient in a complete apostle ?

But this dolour contains also many lessons for ourselves. In fact the Residence in Egypt is a complete picture of the way in which God, our Blessed Lord, the Blessed Sacrament, the faith, and the saints, are in the world. There is the life of common things made wonderful by an interior spirit. There is the company of Mary and Joseph. There are the three evangelical sisters, labour, poverty, and detachment. There is the mysterious hiddenness, with apparently nothing to hide under. There is the exile, and an Egyptian exile. There is the love of God in supreme sovereignty. And finally there is our Lord in the world as a little Child; and so is the invisible God, despite the blaze of His perfections, in His own creation; and so is our Lord also still, in His Church and Holy See, despite of all its triumphs; and so is the Blessed Sacrament, notwithstanding all the luminous theology which has been written about it; and so is the faith, in the jostling interests and grandeurs of modern civilisation, despite of its old historic conquests and its present daily propagation; and so are the saints, down in the hollows of life where publicity cannot find them out, despite the miracles they work. They are all in the world as little children. We too are part of the picture. There is the mighty Nile, "lapsing through old hushed Egypt like a dream." There are the pyramids, the monuments of pagan greatness. There are the sandy wilds, the rich loamy fields, which the inundation annually renews, the palm-groves, and the many coloured life of the oriental bazaar, and Jesus, Mary, Joseph, somewhere. The allegory is complete. Such is the world, such is our native land to us. God is hidden in it. All is awkward and foreign to us, though it is native; for grace has made aliens of us after a strange fashion. Patiently we wait to do God's word, counting the years. One will come which will be the last. It will bear us home and drop us at His feet; and as we have been all for God in our exile, so God will be all to us in our eternal home. Blessed be His mercy! it was unloving to say that; for is He not all to us already?

But, besides the lesson which the allegory itself contains, there are others which we must lay to heart. We must learn first of all to sympathise with Jesus, especially in the sufferings which we ourselves have caused Him. Religion is a personal love of God, the sincerity of which is attested by our obedience. It is the love which is the soul, the value, the significance of it all. To be truly religious our souls must live in a peculiar atmosphere of their own, a charmed atmosphere which the world cannot breathe in, and therefore cannot break through. We must be unable to breathe out of an atmosphere of prayer. The soul must have a world of hopes and fears of its own, its own set of tastes and sympathies, instincts and forebodings of its own, its own gravitations and repulsions. It will not do merely to believe a number of doctrines, or to keep certain commandments. These things are essential; but they do not make up the whole. They are the flesh and the blood, but the soul is love. Now the chief way in which we create this charmed atmosphere around ourselves is by devotion to the mysteries of our Blessed Lord. Mary sanctified herself in this dolour by sympathy with Jesus. The venerable Joanna of Jesus and Mary, a Franciscaness, when she was meditating on our

Lord's Flight into Egypt, suddenly heard a great noise, like the running and clashing of armed men, pursuing some one, and presently she saw a beautiful little boy, panting with fatigue, and running up to her at the top of his speed, crying, O Joanna! help Me, and hide Me. I am Jesus of Nazareth, flying from sinners, who wish to kill Me, and who persecute Me as Herod did; I beseech you save Me! The grand thing at which we must aim is to bring it to pass, that our Lord's mysteries, His Passion and Childhood especially, should be continually in our thoughts. They should not be in the least like some past history, about which we may feel poetical, or sentimental, or have favourite views. But they should be as if they were living, contemporaneous, going on perpetually before our eyes, and in which we ourselves are actors. This is the difference between the mysteries of the Incarnate Word in the New Testament, and the glorious manifestations of God in the Old Testament. These last are our lessons: the first are our life. They do not simply remain written there, and shine. They live, they put forth attractions, they give power, they hold grace, they transform. The vitality of the Incarnation has gone into them. Here is the secret reason of the preference of the Old Testament over the New, which is so congenial to the temper of heresy. They who have no Blessed Sacrament, and have dethroned Mary, have lost the meaning of the Incarnation. The Gospels are beautiful history to them, and little else. But the Exodus is far more romantic, more stirring, more glorious, and so is the Conquest of Canaan, and the Reign of David, and the lofty patriotism of the Prophets. Hence the enthusiasm, which Catholics feel for the Gospel incidents, heretics feel in the Old Testament History. But with the former it is more than enthusiasm. It is the life of their religion, the breath of their sanctity, the endless Presence and Vision of their Beloved. So by assiduous meditation, by sorrowing love or by rejoicing love, must we wear our way into the mysteries of Jesus, assimilating them to ourselves, living in them, feeling with them, until their mere character of history has added to itself the reality of a worship, and His Heart as it were beats in ours, as another, better, and supernatural life.

A further lesson, which this dolour teaches us, is that suffering, when it is God's will, is better than external spiritual advantages. The Blessed Veronica of Binasco, an Augustinianess, was permitted in spirit to accompany Jesus and Mary in their Flight into Egypt, and when it was over, our Lord said to her, "My daughter, thou hast seen through what fatigues we have reached this country. Learn from this, that no one receives graces, except he suffers." This we can better understand; but when suffering is pitted against the means of grace, when its presence involves the loss of our external spiritual advantages, it might have seemed otherwise. To submit joyously to suffering under these circumstances involves something more than ordinary submission. To believe that, because it is our Lord's will, suffering is therefore better for us than even the continuation of those advantages, requires a large exercise of faith. The question of being religious, is the question of our eternal salvation. Experience has amply disclosed to us how much depends on regularity in our spiritual exercises. A day for God, what else is it but the legitimate conclusion from a morning with God? Many a man leans his whole life on his daily mass, and it bears him well through to the end. Is there a more helpless being on earth than the soul, long used to frequent communion, and then suddenly and for a length of time deprived of it? Besides, how many people do we see who are the better for suffering? Does it not harden many? Guilloré says sickness unsanctifies more than it sanctifies. This is a hard saying. Let us make abatements from it. There is enough truth left to make us exceedingly melancholy. Cardinal de Berulle, speaking of interior sufferings and trials of spirit, said he had known many eminent souls in them, and he had only seen one who had not retrograded under their influence. He was not a man who exaggerated. And yet, in spite of all these terrible sayings and experiences, we are to welcome suffering from God as better than hours of prayer, or the daily sacrifices, or heavenly sacraments. We may look back wistfully upon those things, but not unconformedly. It is a hard lesson to learn. Who does not remember the first time he had to learn it? How disquieting it seemed! Common things looked unintelligible. Conscience had to rearrange itself on a great number of questions. Never was more spiritual direction wanted than now, when least of it was to be had. Say our suffering was illness. How much did pain dispense us from, and what pain was great enough to dispense us from anything? There were more trials, more demands upon us, because of our suffering, and apparently less means of grace to keep up the interior supply. A great many things which had seemed fair and strong in health, were now tried in us, stretched and let go again, and proved in a variety of ways. Not a few of them broke down altogether. It was a hard time. Sorrows always rush upon a sorrowful man, like cowardly beasts who dare not attack their prey till it is wounded. So we had more to bear then, when we had less strength to bear it. It was a vexatious lesson, learned in dread and insecurity, fruitful of annoyance and tears. But for the time it was learned; and, if the remembrance now is all blotted and blurred by the tiresome venial sins which disfigure it all over, nevertheless self-distrust was deepened; we got near to God; we had grown in the inner man; we were more real, because we were more interior; and we were conscious of additional power, because grace was more at home in us.

Our Lady's conduct in this dolour teaches us the additional lesson that we must aim most at compassion for others, when we are suffering most ourselves. This is the way to gain the peculiar graces of suffering. Grace and nature are almost always at cross purposes. Because Moses had the hastiest of tempers, he became the meekest of men. So sorrow naturally shuts us up in ourselves, and concentrates us upon itself, while grace forces us to become more considerate because we are suffering, and to go out of ourselves, and to pour out upon others, as a libation before God, all that tenderness and pity which nature would make us lavish upon ourselves. There is something in diverting ourselves from ourselves when we are in grief, which has a peculiar effect of enlarging the heart, and swelling the dimensions of the whole character, and something also so particularly pleasing to God that, when it is done from a supernatural motive and in imitation of our Lord, He seems to recompense it instantly by the most magnificent graces. To sit by the bedside of a poor invalid, when we are ourselves inwardly prostrated by illness, and our pulses are throbbing, and our head beats all over, and through pain our words a little wander, as if we were inattentive, or again to listen by the hour to the little complaints of a heart ill at ease, while we ourselves are secretly groaning under a still heavier load,—or to throw out joy and light, by tone, by look, by manner, by smile, over a circle dependent upon us, when uneasy cares are secretly gnawing at our hearts, and comfortless expectations, and perturbing foresights, and suspicions are haunting us like ghosts,—these are the grand ventures in the commerce of grace. These bring the galleons from the heavenly Indies safe into port with untold wealth and foreign rarities. One hour of such work as that is often worth a month of prayer, and who does not know the enormous value of a month of prayer? Moreover it is the want of this forcible unselfishness, which makes sorrow generally so much less sanctifying than Christian principles would lead us to expect. We almost look upon suffering as a sort of dispensation from charity. We deem it to be a time, when we may lawfully love ourselves. By the very touch of affliction God draws us, as we suppose, for a while out of the calls upon our brotherly affection, which surround us on every side. We are to receive now, rather than to give. But in reality there is no time when we may lawfully love ourselves; for, as St. Paul says, "Christ pleased not Himself." If there be a moment in which it might be lawful to feel no love for others, it would be the act of dying, because in that moment all our love is due to God. Self has no place anywhere in love. When love touches self, it either becomes a duty, or is an unworthiness. It is true also that sorrow draws us into solitude, but not an uncharitable, selfish solitude. It guides us gently away from the world as a theatre of worldliness, but not from the world as a field of mutual and self-sacrificing love. When the saints keep their sorrows secret, it is no doubt mainly because love is fond of secrets, which none but its object and itself shall know, and divine love is the shyest, and the most secret-loving, of all loves. The saints fear lest God should not prize what others know, because of His dear jealousy, and lest the sympathy of others should take off that heavenly bloom which a sorrow keeps only so long as it is untold. But, beside this, we may be sure that unselfishness was another reason for their secrecy. They would not spread sorrow in the world. There was too much of it already. They would not swell the contagion. If suffering was harder to bear untold than told, were they not ambitious to love suffering? Anyhow, if they could help it, their particular griefs should never unwreathe a single smile from any face on earth. The tired pedestrian sighs when he sees a steep and rugged hill to climb, and he is already fit to faint from weariness: so is it with the poor mourner, bent beneath his burden, when he is shown Jesus and Mary in their woes, and is told that as they sorrowed, so must he. But how else can it be? Our sorrows must be measured by our sympathy with others. Our active, cheerful, quiet, unobtrusive ministries to others must be the invariable index of the keenness of our martyrdom.

We learn also from the Flight into Egypt that we must not question the ways of God, either in our own sufferings, or in the gifts of those we love. God might have spared Mary in many ways. Almost every circumstance of this dolour seems unnecessarily aggravated. Even without miracle how many alleviations might have been contrived. But, beyond that, would it have surprised us if omnipotence had stepped in to work miracles in such a case as this? There is something not uncommon about religious people which it is very difficult to define, but which looks like irreverence. Of course it is not so. But persons, who have habits of prayer, and do not with sufficient exactness and recollection extend those habits into the actions of the rest of the day, and so saturate them with the spirit of prayer, unintentionally acquire a sort of familiarity with God, which is not altogether respectful to Him. They think that, if they pray more to God than others, they must necessarily know more of God than others. This however is by no means the case. Prayer is not the *whole* of spirituality, neither is it *in itself* the most solid part of devotion. It wants ulterior processes to make it solid. There are some good men, in whom prayer is really the least solid part of their spirituality. There are exercises more interior than prayer, in which the soul learns more of God, and learns it faster. Not that these things can exist without prayer, or will survive its discontinuance. Only they are not prayer. Then these men, whose almost exclusive spiritual practice is prayer, put themselves upon intimate terms with God, and, especially if their prayer is the prayer of sentiment, acquire a habit of thinking of God and themselves, not of God alone,—of God in them, rather than of God in Himself. The results of this betray themselves in times of sorrow, and particularly of interior trials. The submission of such men is not instantaneous. They would fain talk to God about it, and if they cannot persuade Him, at least let Him persuade them. To this extent He must flatter them. They will accept the cross directly God and they conjointly agree to put it on self, but not if it is His act, done without consulting them. Or at least they will satisfy nature by dignifiedly complaining to God of what He has done, and insisting somewhat freely and untimorously on the additional graces by which He is to compensate them for this new burden. In fact they question the ways of God, and so lose the childlike spirit of sanctity. Men may not *assail* God, even with the impetuosity of their prayers: their business is to adore. Otherwise the gracefulness of submission is gone. The right to more intimate union with God is forfeited. The waters of grace in their soul become shallow, and their spirit of prayer thin, peevish, vexed, and wailing. All this is because in their prayer they have had the habit of being something before God, instead of being nothing. It is melancholy to see how apt spiritual persons are to be impertinent to God. Perhaps the fewness of the saints is attributable to this.

But there is comfort even here. God knows our weakness. We think no one can enter into it as we do. But He knows it infinitely better. He practises the most incredible forbearance towards us. He makes the most unimaginable allowances. Woe unto us if we should venture to make excuses for ourselves, if it were but the thousandth part of the excuses He makes for us! But we have yet another lesson to learn. We spend the most of our lives in the Holy Land, in quietness and at home. Either we are in the Holy City, with the courts of the temple conveniently at hand, or in the unworldly sequestration of Nazareth, or by the blue water flapping on the shore of the calm Gennesareth. But sometimes we have to go down into Egypt to buy the wholesome corn of tribulation, the best sustenance of our souls. Sometimes we have to fly thither from before the face of men, or the machinations of the devils. Now, the lesson is, that, whatever and wherever we are, we always have Jesus with us. No time is inconvenient for Him, no place unlikely. There is no darkness but He is the light, no light but its best light is He. Alas! that a truth so sweet to be remembered, should so easily be forgotten! Yet who does not forget it? Who is not always forgetting it? Could Mary forget Him when she bore Him in her arms? Why should we? Why distract ourselves from such a companion? How be so near Him yet so seldom advert to Him? There are many heavy weights, which the thought of Him would make lighter. There is a self-willed liberty, which displeases self, and leaves dejection after it, which would be sweetly taken captive, if His arms were felt twining round our necks. There are chills in the heart, which we should not feel if He were nestling warmly against it. There is a loneliness which beckons temptation to come and people its wilderness, which the company of Jesus would turn into blameless talk, and song, and gladness. It is easy to leave Jesus, if we let Him run by our side over the sands, and forget His presence; but, if we carry Him in our arms, as love and Mary do, it requires much evil courage to lay our Burden down upon the sand, and wilfully walk away. He is ever with us; and He is with us ever as a child, partly that the burden may be lighter, partly that love may come more easily, partly because His littleness better suits our own. There is but one true symbol of the Christian soul. We must never paint it otherwise before our mind's eye. In the dark, and in the bright, by dear Jordan or by dark Nile, it is truly, and for ever, a Madonna and Child.

Such is the second dolour, the Flight into Egypt. Who has not been devoted to it from his childhood upwards? With how many early pious imaginings has it not been interwoven? It has been a type of life to us. It was a poetry with prayer in it, a prayer whose reality was enhanced by its poetry. Ah! it wakes old years, and old tears as well; for it seems to wake those who have been long dead. Childish memories, early beginnings of which God has taken care, flowers that have borne fruits in grace, a divine love, sometimes obscured, but never lost, and distinct steps taken in the knowledge of Jesus,—all these things, with the soft light of an unremorseful childhood over them, come sweetly out of this beautiful mystery of Jesus and Mary. Times come back when it looks, in the distance, as if He and we had been but one then, and His Mother and our own blend indistinctly into one shape, and speak with one kind of voice. And there is the sunset in the wilderness, the great orb flashing on the rim of the desert horizon, its light reflected in Joseph's eyes; and then there is Jesus sleeping on His Mother's lap, and the round moon above, and the glittering well, and the whispering palm, and night breathing heavily over the yellow sands. But the dead do not come back again. There were figures in the picture once, which are missing now. The years rob us as they pass. One by one, men and things are missing, God alone is never missing.

CHAPTER IV.

THE THIRD DOLOUR.

THE THREE DAYS' LOSS.

THE Mother without the Child! This is indeed a change to pass upon our Lady's sorrows. Bethlehem had its sorrows, and Nazareth had still more, and on Calvary the tide rose highest. But in all these places the Mother was with her Child. There was light therefore even in the darkness. In this third dolour, the Three Days' Loss, it was not so. When we wish to depict our Blessed Mother with reference to her own graces, such as the Immaculate Conception, we paint her without her Child, looking heavenwards, as if to show that she was a creature upon whom heaven was falling in fast showers of grace from the Creator. When we wish to see her as she stands to us, as the Mother through whose hands the Son pleases to make His graces pass, we represent her also without her Child, her eyes cast downwards towards the earth, and her hands dropping light and freshness on the world. But there are two childless pictures of her in Scripture, which have nothing to do with either of these. The one is her third dolour, when in sorrowful amazement she is searching Jerusalem to discover Jesus; and the other is her seventh dolour, when she is returning at nightfall from the garden-tomb, to the great city, leaving her buried Love behind in His chamber of the rock. Thus are the likenesses of the Passion more and more mingling with the Infancy. They mingle especially in this third dolour, which, both on the side of Jesus and of Mary, is one of the greatest mysteries of the Three-and-Thirty Years. We however are merely concerned with it as it regards Mary's sorrow.

The quiet life of Nazareth was only interrupted by the duties of religion, which brought back fresh blessings to the Holy House, and augmented its tranquillity. According to the law the Jews were obliged to go up to Jerusalem to worship God, three times in a year, unless they were legitimately hindered. The first time was at the Pasch, or feast of unleavened bread, instituted in remembrance of the Exodus from Egypt, and corresponding to our Easter. This was the greatest of them all. The second time was the feast of weeks, which was Pentecost, or our Whitsuntide. The third was the feast of tabernacles, or the feast of light-heartedness and gratitude, to be observed when "they had gathered in the fruits of the barn-floor and the wine-press." To all these feasts Joseph went up yearly. The women were not bound by this law, and some contemplatives have said that, while Joseph went up to Jerusalem three times a year, Mary went up with Jesus once a year, at the Pasch, or feast of unleavened bread. Five years had now passed since the return from Egypt, and Jesus was twelve years old. In that year, as the Gospel narrative tells us, He went up to Jerusalem at the Pasch, with Mary and Joseph, and according to the tradition He went on foot. In the minds of all three there could be but one thought. It is probable that St. Joseph knew of the mysteries of the Passion, as well as our Blessed Lady; and Jane Mary of the Cross tells us that it was revealed to her, that before he died, he was allowed to feel all the pains of the Passion in such measure as was fitting, just as we read of other saints, some of whom have been permitted to participate in some one mystery of it, and some of them to go through all. Thus, as His last Pasch was always before our Lord, so was it never forgotten either by Mary or by Joseph. It would be especially and vividly before them, as they went up yearly to Jerusalem. As they journeyed upon their way, over the hills or through the glens, upon the white road that lay like a thread over the green uplands, Calvary with its three crosses rose ever against the sky as the real goal to which they were tending. But all things were not always clear to our Lady. As our Lord at seasons veiled the operations of His Sacred Heart from her sight, so sometimes the future was not present to her, nor the whole mystery of the present understood. She hung upon Jesus for everything; and it was her joy that everything was His, and nothing was her own. For what is the creature but the emptiness which the Creator fills? So, according to His will, our Blessed Mother little deemed that, while His Calvary was still years off, hers was close at hand.

How her love for Jesus grew in that journey to Jerusalem! The thought of His bitter Passion in her heart united itself with the sight of the Boy of twelve before her outward eyes, and love rose in a flood. Each moment He seemed to her so infinitely more precious than He had done the moment before, that she thought she was only just beginning to love Him rightly, and yet the next moment distanced that love also. She knew well, she had known it all along, that she never could love Him as He deserved to be loved. A thousand Maries, which seems to our minds like something more than all possible creations, could not have loved Him worthily. There was something also in the Creator being a Boy, which was more than the Creator being a Child. The speechlessness, the helplessness of infancy, the visible palpable contradiction between that state and His eternal perfections, stamped it more completely as a mystery. The Human Nature was tranquil, was passive, and the Divine Nature hidden under it. The actions which were seen, were the mere mechanical actions of human life. They were its spontaneous vegetation. The operations of the perfect reason, perfect with all its ungrowing and unutterable perfections from the first moment of Conception, were invisible. It was plain it was a mystery, and somehow things are less mysterious when they openly announce themselves as mysteries. But in the Boyhood there was more of the human will apparent. There were perhaps disclosures of a particular human character. The mind gave a cognisable expression to the countenance. There was a gait in walking, a way of using the hands, and many other things which make boyhood more definite, more individual, than childhood. By a mother's heart none of these things are either unnoticed or unvalued. They are the aliments of maternal love, just when the incipient independence of boyhood is a trial after the sweet dependences of infancy. But we must remember what all these things were in Jesus, in order to estimate fairly what they were to our Lady. Who can doubt that there was a spiritual beauty shining in all He did, a celestial gracefulness, breathing over everything, which would take captive every hour by new surprises the Mother's heart? But, above all, these things brought out wonderfully the Divine Nature. It seems a contradiction to say so; but, if we reflect, we must see that the more the human will was manifested, the more development, the more action, there was about the lower nature,—the more also by virtue of the Hypostatic Union must the glory of the Divine Person have disclosed itself. When the mystery lay still, in the hush of childhood, it was worshipped as in a sanctuary, but when it moved, and spoke, and worked, and willed, in the countless daily acts and movements of life, it came forth as it were from its sanctuary, and exhibited itself to men. It flashed out of His eyes; it spoke from His lips; its music escaped through His tone; it betrayed itself in His walk; it made His fingers drop "with the choicest myrrh:" His whole outward life was light and fragrance, as His childhood passed away, and the day of His boyhood broke, and the shadows retired. All day long He was acting, and His actions had on them the stamp, or the scent, of the human will of a Divine Person, and therefore they flowed "like the fountain of gardens, the well of living waters, which run with a strong stream from Libanus." Would it be wonderful then, if Mary reached the gates of Jerusalem in that twelfth year, less able than ever to do without Jesus, feeling that it was more and more impossible that her heart should live away from His?

They reached Jerusalem before the beginning of the seven days of unleavened bread; and during that time they made their devotions in the temple, visited the poor and the sick, and performed the other customary works of mercy. It would be impossible to reckon up the supernatural wonders, which arose before the throne of the Most Holy Trinity from those earthly Three during the week of unleavened bread. Who would venture to compare any saint with St. Joseph? In what amazing union with God, in what flames of heroic love, in what Mary-like depths of self-abasement, did not that shadow of the Eternal Father dwell, ever honouring by the shadow that he cast that stupendous majesty and awful adorable Person, whose representative he was. Generations of Hebrew saints had ascended those temple steps, and had made sweeter offerings of prayer and praise than all the aromatical spices that for centuries had been burned before Him. Yet what was their collective worship to one of Mary's prayers, to one of her hymns of praise, to one recital of her Magnificat? But when Mary and Joseph knelt together in the temple, all created sanctity, such as had shone in angels and saints, was left behind, outstripped, and gone out of sight. Many a good old man in those times would think of David's days, and of the tide of worship that flowed and never ebbed in his glorious Psalms, and he would almost weep to think how degenerate were modern times compared with those, and modern worshippers by the side of those grand prophets and singers of ancient Israel. They little dreamed of the incomparable glory of those hearts of Joseph and Mary. But how the mystery deepens, when between Joseph and Mary kneels down the Everlasting God, He with the unspeakable Name, now just twelve years old, human years counted by circling seasons and the filling and emptying of moons! Would the songs go on in heaven, when the Incarnate Word prayed on earth ? Would not all the angels fold their wings around them, timorously hushed, while the prayer of the Coequal God rose up before the throne, casting far away into invisible shades the poor permissions of creature's worship ? And Mary and Joseph ceased to pray to the Throne in heaven, or to the presence behind the Veil, but in prostrate ecstasy they adored the Eternal who was between them, and confessed in mute thanksgiving the dread Divinity of the Boy whose words were almost stealing their souls out of their earthly tabernacles. Was ever temple consecrated with such a consecration ? Was it not strange that earth should go on rolling through space the same as ever, and the sun rise and shine and say nothing, and the moon get up behind the hills and silver the whole landscape and float down again to the opposite horizon, without so much as a smile of consciousness ? Was it not more strange that Jerusalem went about its work, and did not instinctively feel that something had happened to it more wonderful than David's triumphs or the dazzling court of Solomon ? A son of David, "greater than Solomon," older than the day of Abraham, was among the crowds, one who could destroy the temple, and build it up again in three days, a Boy of twelve, fair to look upon, but to Jerusalem only as one of many boys whom many mothers had brought to the feast within its ancient walls and in its historic sanctuary.

But the week of unleavened bread came to a close. Multitudes, as usual, had thronged the Holy City, like a modern Roman Easter. Every tribe had sent its worshippers. They had come, who dwelt in the southernmost villages of Simeon, or in the lot of Reuben, beyond the mountains of Abarim, or from Manasses beyond the river, or from the shores of Aser, or from where Lebanon looks down on Nephtali. According to custom, the multitudes were told off in separate throngs, leaving Jerusalem at different times, the men together, and the women together. They left in the afternoon, the men by one gate, the women by another, to reunite at the halting-place of the first night. By this means confusion was avoided. The city was emptied without scenes which would hardly be appropriate to so solemn a season, and would be especially undesirable after the religious occupations of the past week. The roads also would not be crowded all at once, but that huge multitude would thaw quietly away in order and tranquillity. Thus it was that Mary and Joseph were separated during the first day's journey, which was in reality but the journey of an afternoon. An opportunity was also thus presented to our Blessed Lord to separate from them unperceived. So when the women, to whose caravan Mary belonged, were mustered at their proper gate, Jesus was not there. But children might go either with the father or the mother. He was therefore doubtless with Joseph. Mary missed Him; but it was sweet to think how He was all the while filling Joseph's heart with tides of joy and love. She must learn to be unselfish with Him betimes; for the day would come when He would be taken from her. Alas! it was come, another day that she had not suspected, and He was gone. She went upon her journey; and, as the revelations of the saints tell us, what indeed God's ordinary ways would lead us to expect, the Holy Ghost flooded her soul with unusual sweetness, the common preliminary to unusual trial. Her thoughts were gently diverted from the absence of Jesus. She was absorbed in God, and trod the ground and kept the path and answered questions only mechanically. Her soul was being annealed again in the furnaces of divine love to enable her to pass through the ordeal that was coming.

The shades of evening had fallen on the earth, before the two bands of men and women met at the accustomed halting-place. Joseph was waiting for Mary, but Jesus was not with him. Mary's heart sank within her before she spoke. Joseph knew nothing. His unworthiness would have felt surprise if Jesus had accompanied him rather than His Mother. He had supposed He was with Mary, and had not been disquieted. The bustle of the halt, the cries of the crowd, the preparations for the evening meal, the unloading and watering of the beasts of burden, all died out of their ears. They were suddenly alone, alone amidst the multitude, more lonely than two hearts had ever been, since the sun set on Adam and Eve, flushing the mountains of paradise which to them were as cloisters they might cross no more. Joseph was crushed to the very earth. The light went out in Mary's soul, and a more terrific spiritual desolation followed than any of the saints had ever known. What could it mean? Jesus was gone. It was a harder idea for her to realise than the mystery of the Incarnation had been. If the rolling universe had stopped, it would have been less of a surprise. If the trumpets of doom had blown, her heart would not have quailed as now. They would ask among their kinsfolk and acquaintance, if He was with them; as many of them loved the Boy exceedingly, with yearnings of heart which they who felt them could not comprehend. They would ask, but Mary knew it would be all in vain. She knew Him too well not to be certain, that if He had been in the company, He would long since have joined her. No such ordinary occurrence would have been allowed to break the union between her heart and His. She felt that the depth of her misery was not going to be so shallow as this. An abyss had opened, and a cold wind was rushing out of it which froze every sanctuary within her soul. They made their search. It was only to receive one negative after another, varied by the different amounts of sympathy which accompanied each. Their inquiry ended, and deep night had come. The sun had set on one side of the globe and had risen on the other, but the thousands of leagues of darkness did not hide, nor the thousands of leagues of light reveal, two hearts in such consummate misery as Joseph's and her own. There were many sorrows on earth that night, but there were none like hers. There have been many nights since then, with their beautiful raven darkness braided with stars, and many incredible sorrows, with nothing like a star set in their dismal blackness; but there have been no sorrows like hers. The stars would not have shone, if they had had hearts within them. The darkness should have wept blood instead of dew to be in keeping with the forlorn anguish of that memorable night. When all Egypt rang suddenly at midnight with the terrible wail for the firstborn, and the troubled river hurried away from the intolerable sickening sounds of human woe, the countless cries that wove themselves into one amazing voice, as if the great earth itself had spoken in pain, from the Cataracts to the Delta, were not freighted with such a load of misery as lay that hour on Mary's single heart.

In the darkness, alone, silent, Mary and Joseph were treading the road again to the Holy City. Their feet were sore and weary. What matter? Their hearts were sorer and more weary. The darkness in Mary's spirit was deeper than the darkness on the hills. Even if the paschal moon were not shining, they would see the white glimmer of the road; but no road out of this sorrow glimmered in her heart. Had it all been, not a dream certainly, but a transitory thing? Was she to see Jesus no more? Had He withdrawn His wonted illumination from her heart for ever, for ever veiled now that beautiful Heart of His where for the last twelve years the curtains had been looped up, and she had seen all its mysteries, read all its secrets, lived almost perpetually in its life? Was she unworthy of Him? She knew she was. Had He therefore left her? It was not like Him. But she did not see things as before, and it might be so. Had He gone back to His Father leaving unredeemed the world which did not want Him? No! that was impossible. He had not paid the price of her Immaculate Conception yet. Tyrants seldom slumber. Had Archelaus watched his opportunity, and seized Him? Herod might have left his son that charge as a legacy of state-craft. Had she perhaps mistaken the date of Calvary, and was it to come now? Was the Boy hanging on a cross that moment in the darkness on some mount outside the gates? O the bewildering agony of this unusual darkness! She had seen all the Passion before in her spirit. How did it go? Was she not there?

She cannot remember. She can recover nothing. Within, there is nothing but darkness, covering everything. Is He actually dead without her, His Blood shed, and she not there? Agony! Has He gone to death, purposely without telling her, out of kindness? Oh, no! so cruel a kindness would have been contrary to the union of their hearts. But this, this very separation, without a word, and then this interior darkness in which He has wrapped her soul,—how do these comport with that union of their hearts? Ah! then there is not certainty to go upon, except the certainty that He is God. This very sorrow shows her that she is not to argue from what has gone before. The past, it seems, did not necessarily prophesy the future. Not to understand it, that is such suffering. Sudden darkness after excessive light is like a blow. Her soul wants to see. But it is hooded. A baffling blindness has come on. She has nothing left her now, but that which never was dislodged from the depths of her soul, the gift of peace. O how the waters of bitterness rose silently out of the endless caverns of that peace, the subterranean bitterness which—who does not know that has once felt it?—leaves its taste for life.

Perhaps He had gone into the wilderness to join that marvel of eremitical sanctity, the boy John, the son of Zacharias, hereafter to be called the Baptist. He was making his noviciate of years, in that tender age, among the wild beasts, lonely, hunger-smitten, the prey of heat and cold, of wind and wet, preparing for his mission, which was to forerun the preaching of Jesus. Has her Boy gone to join him, gone to share in that noviciate? She would have known it was not so, if she could have seen as usual. But it was the misery of her inward darkness that she no longer seemed to understand Jesus. It was the only light she wanted. All the world beside might have been dark to her, and she could have borne the burden lightly. But not to understand Jesus was a variety of martyrdom she had never dreamed of. Yet do not most mothers taste it somewhat as their children, now in new trials and unproved spheres, and so needing most the old unity with the mother's heart, outgrow their childlike confidence, and live down in their own hearts, and have mysteries written on their brows? There are hearts to whom this is sharp. But they are far off from the woe of Mary when the Boy of Nazareth first began to look unlike the Babe of Bethlehem. Perhaps He had gone to Bethlehem, on a visit to His own sanctuary. But could He have any work there, connected with the redemption of the world? And if He had only gone because He loved to go, was that like Him? Mary was perplexed. A while since she would have answered No! with the utmost confidence. Now she was not so sure, and even her humility made her less sure than her darkness by itself would have done. All this was so unlike Him! He might do anything now. Whatever He did would of course be holy. But He might do anything, so far as her understanding Him went. But if He had gone only out of devout pleasure, His pleasure would have been so much greater, if they had been with Him. Besides that, would He have gone for pleasure without telling them, when He knew how awful the pain of missing Him would be to them? Mary could not be sure He would not; for why did He do what He had done? Why give this pain at all? Has He emancipated Himself? But He is only twelve! Again, if He had done so, would He not have spoken? She cannot tell. She can tell nothing. She knows nothing. Only He is God. Her bruised heart must kneel and bleed, and bleed and kneel. She is crucified in the darkness, as He will one day be. He has abandoned her, as His Father will one day abandon Him. Go on, weary, forlorn, forsaken mother! the daybreak is catching the towers of Sion: thither drag this inexplicable load of grief, thou wonderful daughter of the Most High!

Meanwhile where is our Blessed Lord? In Jerusalem. Of what He has been doing we know somewhat. Scripture tells us the strangest part; the revelations of the saints disclose what we might have divined as likely. He prayed long prayers in the temple. He has gone to the meetings of the doctors and elders; and there He finds how they strive to face the oracles of ancient prophecy, and make out a glorious, warlike, triumphant, statesman Messias, who shall effect a political deliverance for His oppressed people. Here He beholds the grand obstacle to the reception of His doctrine and to the mystery of the Incarnation. This must be removed. Those at least who have ears to hear must be allowed to hear the truth. It is His Heavenly Father's work. So He modestly puts Himself forward, as if to ask questions. His sweetness wins all hearts. The gravest doctors hang upon His words. He puts His objections gently, suggests wonderful meanings to deep prophecies, leads them to see that their own view is not tenable, and elicits from them the spiritual truth as if it was the lesson He Himself was receiving, not a new wisdom He was Himself infusing into them. How many hearts did He thus prepare for Himself, of how many apostolic vocations may He not have indirectly laid the foundations then! When Peter converted thousands at a sermon, when he offered a thousand souls to each of the Three Divine Persons, the first time he preached, how much of the work may have been done already by the doctrine which had flowed from the questions of the Boy of Nazareth. During these three days, as we learn from some of the saints, our Lord had begged His bread from door to door, so that He might practise even greater poverty than that which straitened Him at Nazareth. Out of this He had given alms to the poor. He had also visited the sick, performed menial offices for them, spoken kinds words to them and drawn them to God. At night He had slept on the bare ground under the walls of the houses. Earth at least could hardly refuse Him a bed, who had called it out of nothing. Thus the Creator of all things, left for the time without His Mother's care, shifted for Himself in His own world, as a beggar-boy at the age of twelve. O upon how many shades of life did not our Blessed Master scatter the consecration of His own endurance!

We cannot doubt but that Mary and Joseph, when they

entered Jerusalem in the morning, went first to the temple to seek God's blessing on that load of sorrow which weighed them to the ground. Nor were they without hope of finding Jesus there. Throughout the day they threaded the streets of Jerusalem wearily. Mary scanned the passers-by as she had never done before; but Jesus was nowhere to be seen. Everywhere they made inquiries. Some listened patiently but coldly, others peevishly and as if it were a trouble; others, again, were kind and feeling, but they had no consolation to give. One woman asked her to describe her Boy, and how faithfully did Mary do it! But no! the woman had seen a boy, but no such boy as that. She could never have forgotten such an one, if she had ever had the good luck to see Him. Others too raised hopes, which were as soon to sink again. On the top of Mary's sorrow came now a world of good advice, which made the load no lighter. Why did she not seek Him here? Why did she not seek Him there? Kind souls! she had sought Him everywhere. She had sought Him as mothers will seek missing children; and many spots are not overlooked in such a search as that. Then some one had given an alms to a boy, who was not unlike the description, and whose loveliness and manner had left an impression behind. But she could say nothing further. However it was a gleam of light to Mary. There were clearly not two boys in the world who would answer to her description. Then another woman, when she opened her house in the morning, had seen a boy lying on the ground under the eaves. She only saw Him for a moment, but He was fair-haired and beautiful. Another had seen a boy, not unlike the description, breaking a loaf between two beggars in the street; but he had not watched which way He went. He had then been in Jerusalem yesterday, if He was not there to-day. But another had seen Him that morning by the side of a sick person. Here was more light. Mary could be shown where the sick person lived. She saw her and spoke with her. She heard the poor sufferer describe the winning ways of the boy-nurse, His voice, His eyes, His holy word which had brought the tears into her eyes, and the strange presence of God which He had left behind Him in her soul. Mary's heart burned. She drank in every word. It was Jesus. It could be none else. But where had He come from? whither was He gone? The invalid could not say. She knew nothing. He had come and gone. While He was with her, she was so engrossed with Him, she had not thought of asking Him any questions. And the sun sloped westward, and went down, and the shades fell and the quiet of night came upon busy Jerusalem; but Jesus was not found. It had been a weary day. Neither Mary nor Joseph had broken their fast all day. They were hunger-smitten for the Child. A broken heart wants sleep and food less than others. The night outside was dark, but the night of Mary's soul was darker.

Whether it was after three full days, during which Mary was left as it were entombed in this hideous darkness, or whether it was on the third morning, so it was that Mary and Joseph went up to the temple to lay their sorrows again before the Lord. They went in by the eastern gate. Now close to this gate there was a spacious room, a sort of academy, in which the interpreters of the law sat, and answered questions, and resolved doubts, and moderated in disputations. St. Paul speaks of this place in his defence before Felix, when he says that he was not found disputing in the temple. It was there also at Gamaliel's feet that the great apostle of the Gentiles learned the traditions of the law. By the opening into this academy Joseph and Mary had to pass. It was not a likely place for them to enter. But the Mother's ear has caught a sound, in which it was impossible that she should be mistaken. It is the voice of Jesus. They enter. The doctors are looking on Him with a mixture of awe and pleasure. There has never been such a doctor in that academy before. Joseph and Mary also wondered. She had never heard quite that tone of voice before. She had never seen that light in His eye before. Her soul worshipped in His presence. But she had rights over that Boy, who was astonishing the wise elders of the nation. She would fain have knelt before Him, but she knew that was not the place, nor the time. But she came forward, and said to Him, Son, why hast Thou done so to us? Behold Thy father and I have sought Thee sorrowing. He could see that, without her saying it. He could see the ravages which grief had made in her countenance. He could hear it in her voice, weak and trembling. He could see it in the feebleness which was letting the flush of joy almost overpower her. But He had no need so to see, and hear it. He had never been away from her. He had been lying in her heart the whole while. He had been meting out to her just those supplies both of physical strength and of heavenly grace, which were needed to enable her to endure. His own heart had been crucified with hers. But the mystery was not over. He said to them, How is it that you sought Me? Did you not know that I must be about My Father's business? He has taken out Simeon's sword, and thrust in His own. Why had Mary sought Him? O think of Bethlehem, the wilderness, Egypt, and Nazareth! Why had she sought Him? Poor Mother! could she have done otherwise than seek Him? How could she have lived without Him? There were a thousand reasons why she should have sought Him. Does He deny her rights? Is He about to take them from her, and just too in the joy of finding Him? Rights? They were His own gift. He could take them back if He pleased. But His Flesh, His Blood, His beating Heart, were not these in some sense hers? No! Rather hers were His. But the right to love Him, can even the Creator take that away from the creature? No! that right is inalienable. Creation must be uncreated before that right can be forfeited. If He is going to part with her now at that very eastern gate of the temple, which was a type of herself, nevertheless she will love Him as before, and not only as before, but a thousand times more. That look, that tone, when He was among the doctors—they have gone deep into her soul. To her, they were absolute revelations of God.

Is the darkness gone? Far from it! For the moment He has thickened it by His words. "They understood not the word that He had spoken unto them." But He is not going to leave her. He has been about His Heavenly Father's business in Jerusalem. Now the same business takes Him back to Nazareth. And He, so much more lovely, and she, so much more holy, and Joseph, nigher to God than ever, and more like the shadow of the Eternal Father since the late eclipse, went back upon their way to Nazareth, where for eighteen unbroken years, with the annual visits to Jerusalem, Mary shall enjoy His sanctifying presence, and by His toil in the shop it shall appear that His Heavenly Father's and His earthly father's business were but one. Those broad eighteen years,—to Mary it was like seeing the beautiful free ocean after climbing the dark mountains. "And He went down with them, and came to Nazareth, and was subject to them; and His Mother kept all these words in her heart."

In describing the mystery of this third dolour, much has been already said of its peculiarities. Nevertheless we must now dwell upon its characteristics at greater length. In the first place it was the greatest of all her dolours. This arose partly from its involving a separation from Jesus, and partly from a union of other circumstances, to be considered presently. We read in the life of the Blessed Benvenuta of Bojano, a Dominicaness, that, while she was suffering from the illness which for many years would not allow her to lie down, but forced her to remain sitting in a chair, she began to contemplate the grief of our Lady during the Three Days' Loss. She desired to participate in that affliction inasmuch as she had herself been accustomed to sorrow all her life, and had sought for it, and desired ill-health, and fled from every joy. She prayed earnestly therefore, both to our Lord and His Mother, to grant her the grace to feel in herself our Lady's sorrow. And behold! a holy and venerable Lady appeared to her, with a beautiful and graceful Child, who began to walk about the room, keeping close to His Mother.

His aspect and conversation inspired her with sublime happiness. But when she sought to touch Him, He withdrew from her, and both He and His Mother suddenly disappeared. On this a vehement sorrow took possession of her soul, which continually increased, and afflicted her so deeply that she found no consolation in anything; and it appeared as if her soul and body would be torn asunder. She was compelled therefore to call on our Lady to help her; for she could no longer endure it. At the end of Three Days, our Lady appeared to her, with her Son in her arms, and said, You asked for a taste of that sorrow which I suffered in the loss of Jesus; and it is but a taste which you have had. But do not ask such things again, because your weakness could not live under such an agony of grief!* The seventh dolour, the Burial of Jesus, alone approaches to this third dolour in severity. But for many reasons it was much less severe. Both of them involved separation from Jesus; but in the case of the Burial, she knew that He could suffer no more. She understood the mystery. She triumphed in the accomplishment of the great work of the world's redemption. She could count the hours to the moment of the Resurrection. In this third dolour she had lost Jesus, and she knew not why, nor where He was, nor what He might be suffering. She was plunged into a dense spiritual darkness, and God seemed altogether to have abandoned her. Hence the torture of her heart never rose to a more intolerable height than during these Three Days, not even amidst the horrors of the Passion.

The loss of Jesus would have been under any circumstances a most fearful sorrow; and one which it is impossible for us, with our little grace and less love, to appreciate at all adequately. We must have Mary's heart to feel Mary's grief. But the peculiar circumstance of the Three Days' Loss, which rendered the loss of Jesus so dreadful, was the darkness in which her soul was cast as into a pit. She, who heretofore had been all light, was now all darkness.

* Marchese. Diario. Ottobre 30.

She did not know what God was doing with her. She had to act, and could not understand the circumstances under which she was acting. It was not only the contrast with the past, which made the present so hard to bear. The night that had come down upon her was in itself intolerable anguish. She had ever leaned on Jesus. She never knew till now how much she had leaned upon Him. And He had withdrawn Himself. She did not see into the future; the past was all blurred together and gave no light; the present was full of perplexity, accompanied by intense anguish of heart and bitterness of spirit. Sister Mary of Agreda says that the very angels withheld their colloquies from her lest they should give her light about the loss of Jesus. There can of course be no doubt that this darkness of Mary was a divine operation. We must look for parallels to it in those indescribable interior trials which some of the greatest saints have passed through, always remembering that if they were sent to the saints as cleansings of the spirit, to her Immaculate Heart this trial could only be as it were another marvellous sanctification superadded to those which had gone before. For in her spirit there was nothing to cleanse. The work, the parallel to which in the saints took long years to do, might be accomplished in our Lady's soul in three days, not only because of her perfections which would enable grace to work more rapidly, and without the shadow of an obstacle, but also because the divine operations in the soul seem scarcely to need the lapse of time. Who does not know how in dreams, in accidents, in moments of great suffering, time appears almost miraculously compressed? Long years of previous life pass in distinct, orderly, and cognisable array before the soul, which seems intelligently to comment on each of them, and yet the whole process has occupied only the space of a lightning-flash. In the same way we have apparitions of souls from purgatory, complaining of the long years in which their friends have left them in the flames without mass or suffrage, when the sun of the day on which they died is not yet set. We are taught to believe that the particular judgment, which awaits us at the end of life, will occupy but a moment of time. Again, one action will sometimes appear to do the work of years, even in respect of the formation of habits. This is especially the case with heroic actions, such as Abraham's sacrifice. The same thing may occur in the profession of a religious. There may be something akin to it in the special grace of the different sacraments. Are there any of us who do not remember experiencing some marvellously swift processes of grace, which seemed hardly to require succession of time, so instantaneous were they, and yet a veritable procession and sequence of different steps ? So in the perfect soul of Mary, already elevated by grace and union to so sublime a height, this divine darkness of three days may have wrought the most astonishing effects, which we cannot describe, seeing that her height, even before that, was far above out of our sight. This darkness is a peculiarity of the third dolour, in which no other of our Blessed Lady's sufferings shares in the slightest degree.

It is not possible for us to say with any certainty when this darkness ceased. But we should be inclined not to refer to it the fact that Mary did not understand the words of Jesus in the academy of the temple. This we should regard as rather a separate peculiarity of this third dolour, referable to other causes, and an evidence of the hold which this sorrow had taken upon her nature. The darkness may indeed have passed off gradually, beginning with the first sight of Jesus. We would venture however to conjecture that it passed away entirely the moment she had found Him, while some of its consequences remained. It may be also that the weakness and weariness which had been hardly felt, because the darkness and the sorrow absorbed all feeling, now told upon her, and would even be brought out by this sudden revulsion from grief to joy, just as we read of some of the saints when long ecstasies have passed away. Various reasons have been assigned by theologians for our Lady's not understanding the words of Jesus. Rupert thinks she did understand them, but out of humility acted and looked as if she did not. But this is not satisfactory, from the difficulty of harmonising it with the direct words of the Gospel. Our own Stapleton attributes it to the excess of her joy at finding Jesus, which so acted upon her mind that she could not understand His words, just as from an opposite cause, namely the excess of sorrow, the apostles later on could not understand what our Lord said about His own death. But there is hardly a parity between our Blessed Mother and the apostles; and it would be a hard inference to receive, except upon authority, inasmuch as it would represent our Lady's tranquillity as shaken, and her self-possessed use of reason for awhile perturbed, and perturbed too when He was speaking whose voice could lay the winds and calm the seas. Denys the Carthusian limits her ignorance. He says she knew that Jesus spoke not of Joseph but of His Eternal Father, that He alluded to the work for which He had come into the world, and that, according to the human nature He had assumed, He must ever be intent upon that one work, but that the circumstances of time, place, and manner had not yet been revealed to her. This supposition, while it is more honourable to our Blessed Lady than that of Stapleton, proceeds upon the notion that the Thirty-Three Years, and the Passion, dawned upon her gradually in successive revelations. We have throughout assumed that she knew all, or almost all, from the beginning, which last hypothesis is more consonant with the visions and revelations of the contemplative saints.

Suarez makes two suggestions. He holds that Mary understood Jesus to speak of His Heavenly Father, but that she did not know exactly what the particular things were, relating to the divine science, on account of which He had left Joseph and herself. Or again, she was not quite sure whether our Lord meant to imply that He intended to hasten the time of His manifestation to the world, which otherwise would not be before His thirtieth year. So that, he adds, there was no "privative ignorance" in her, but only the absence of knowledge of some particulars not necessary to the perfection of her science. But were this the case, we should be more inclined to refer it to the continuance of that divine darkness, with which God had visited her. St. Aelred, with others, insists upon the words being taken by the figure synecdoche, and so applying only to St. Joseph, and not to our Lady, just as the Evangelist says both the thieves blasphemed, upon the cross, whereas in reality, according to some commentators, only one did so. Thus, according to St. Aelred, our Lady understood the words, and laid them up in her heart that she might teach them to the apostles afterwards. But it may be replied that it is not certain only one of the thieves blasphemed. On the contrary, it is the more common opinion that they both did. Moreover St. Aelred's interpretation seems to be taking a liberty with the words of the Gospel, which would hardly be warrantable without much more authority from tradition. Others think the words "*they* understood not" apply to the audience in the academy, and not at all to our Lady and St. Joseph. But this does not recommend itself. The sense of the faithful has always found both difficulty and mystery in the passage, which it would not have done if that interpretation had been obvious or natural. Novatus thinks that, by a special permission of God, Mary did not understand at once the words which Jesus had spoken, but that she came to the understanding of them by pondering them in her heart. He finds this interpretation most suitable to the words in the Gospel, and he discovers a parallel to the process in her mind, in the way in which the saints, who have had the gift of prophecy, often foresaw the future, not by direct prophetic light, but by comparing one light with another, and so drawing fresh inferences from the comparison. Yet it does not exactly appear what end is gained by this supposition. No one would deny that our Lady had all the gifts which the saints have had; but why should we gratuitously suppose that any of the imperfections, which accompanied the exercise of these gifts in the saints, should have adhered to her, beyond those which belonged to her of necessity as a creature?

Let us venture to add another to the number of conjectures, which theologians have made upon the subject. It may be supposed that every increase of sanctity in our Blessed Lady was accompanied by a proportionate increase in her science. In a perfect and unfallen nature like hers it is not easy to conceive of the two processes being separate. In the case of one who has sinned, hardness of heart may be removed in degrees quite disproportioned with the removal of darkness of mind. Light and love, though always correlatives, are not such in sinners in the perfect way in which they are so to the innocent. Thus we presume that the mystical darkness, which God sent as a spiritual trial to overspread Mary's soul, gave rise to such heroic acts of love and union, that it raised her to enormous heights of holiness above those lofty mountain-tops on which she had stood before. We presume that there was more difference of a supernatural kind between the Mary who left the temple gate at the end of the week of unleavened bread and the Mary who entered it the morning she found Jesus, than there ever was between a saint in his saintly youth and the same saint in his far more saintly old age. There could be no revolutions in Mary, because there was nothing to destroy, nothing to overturn. All that could be done was to superadd. But the superadditions might be so immense, or so swiftly accumulated, or so instantaneously conferred as to produce a change which in any case but hers we should call a revolution. This is surely what theologians mean, when they speak of her first sanctification, her second sanctification, her third sanctification, and so on. They do not mean to deny that she was always meriting and thus always growing in grace; but that the Immaculate Conception, the Incarnation, the Descent of the Holy Ghost, or her Death, were, so to speak, creative epochs in her sanctification, which did not follow the laws of common growth. We would regard the interior darkness of the Three Days' Loss as an epoch of this description.

But how does this bear upon her not understanding the words of Jesus? We must mount for awhile to the highest regions of mystical theology. There is a science so high that it confines upon ignorance. It is where the human borders on the divine. It is at an unspeakable height, only not unapproachable because some few saints, and the seraphim, have reached it. Our Lady perhaps reached a higher height. There are limits to the possibilities of creatures. Our Lady reached the uttermost of those limits, and looked out on the Divine Abyss, which lay beyond. There the darkness is excess of light, and the science ignorance, not only because language has no vessels to hold its definitions, thought no moulds to contain its ideas, but also because the eyes of the soul are closed and God is reached. What the spirit sees is, that it does not know, that it cannot know, that it is submerged, that its light is a marvellous indistinct distinctness, that knowledge has lost itself in love, and love is living hiddenly in fruition. The same words will convey different ideas to different minds. If we say the moon goes round the earth, the countryman understands us, but the scientific man understands it differently because he understands it more widely. An angel might understand it differently still. So the words which our Blessed Lord spake in the temple were not understood by the doctors, because they did not know who His father was, or what was His business, or why His father should not seek Him because He had stayed away to do His father's work. St. Joseph did not understand them, because though he doubtless knew that Jesus spoke of His Eternal Father, and of the redemption of the world which was His Father's business, he did not know what part of that work Jesus meant, nor why it was a reason He should have left them without notice. Mary did not understand them, because each word rose to her from some unimaginable abyss of divine wisdom, carrying the work of the Incarnation far into the everlasting counsels of the Divine Mind, immensely enlarging her range of view, yet without giving her any distinct images, drawing her more closely within the folds of the Divine Wisdom till she almost touched what she saw, and so ceased to see, and elevating her to that uttermost point of knowledge where a divine ignorance is the consummation of the creature's science. It was the very words themselves which hindered her understanding, because they carried her into a region where understanding has died out into something better, in consequence of the vicinity of God. It was the preceding darkness, which had carried up the life of her soul to the point where this divine ignorance was possible. Such, with all submission, is the conjecture we would venture to make in explanation of this difficulty. Our Blessed Mother knows how much ignorance and foolishness it may contain; but she will not disdain a guess, whose motive is love and whose end is her greater honour.

There is another peculiarity of this dolour, which is in perfect keeping with the mysterious features of it already mentioned. The first dolour was inflicted on her by Simeon, and the second by Joseph, this one by Jesus Himself without any intervention of creatures at all. It is very important to remember this in meditating on the third dolour. From one point of view this made it easier to bear, but from another point of view it was harder. There was more to reconcile her to the endurance, while there was also more to suffer in the pain itself. What God condescends to do Himself is not only better done than the creature can do it; but it is done very differently. It is not only more efficacious in producing its results, but its results are of another kind, and bear a different impress on them. Even His words, when He speaks them to the soul Himself, are substantial, and creative, and effect what they utter, and effect it by the simple utterance. Thus there is something extremely awful in the immediate action of the Creator on the creature's soul. It is a divine touch, pressing on us without any medium, not even sheathing itself in the very flesh belonging to the soul it touches; it is a keen spiritual operation, like no other. Hence the direct action of God on the souls of the saints is ineffably more sanctifying, than the persecutions of creatures, or the pain of austerities, or the pressure of God's own external providence. It has also the same characteristic which belongs to the highest class of miracles, in being instantaneous in its effects. When therefore the intention of God's immediate action is to cause suffering, it must attain its end in a manner which we tremble to think of. It is fearful to contemplate a created thing, which has been called out of nothingness by omnipotence, for no other end than to inflict torture. Such is the fire of hell, and the mysterious action of that fire on disembodied souls in hell. Who can think of it without shuddering? No beneficent office does it fill. There are no indirect results into which its being wanders, and as it were rests. It was created to torture. It is no element turned to another end. It has an end. It keeps to it. Through eternity it will never flag. Multiply, deepen, broaden, condense the mass it has to act upon, and it is ready to work upon that mass, undiverted, unstretched, unweakened. It knows what it has to do, and it does it with terrific truth, with unblamable success. Yet this fire is but a secondary cause. What must the touch of God Himself be, a touch too which is lovingly bent on inflicting pain? O there were many martyrdoms in one in the Three Days' Loss! We are not worthy to tell or to conceive them. Let creatures stand aside, or rather let them lie prostrate near, while God does what He wills with His Mother's soul. Yet creation has something to do with it; for the natural Mother was crucified in her own heart by the Son whom she had borne. Both His Natures had fastened on her to make her suffer. The fairness of His Face, the light in His Eyes, the attractions of His Human Heart, racked her with anguish as she thought upon her loss; while as God, He was visiting her with those appalling interior trials, which we have seen formed the chief part of the third dolour. It is useless to talk of seas of suffering here; infinities would better express our inability to speak of them at all.

When Mary grows into her right place in our minds, there are many things which have a different meaning in her from what they would have in one of the saints. The idea of Mary which the Gospels, as interpreted by Catholic theology, convey to our minds is not merely an intellectual view. Although it is in one sense a theological conclusion, yet it is something much more than that. It is a product of faith and of love, worn in by habits of prayer. Thus, over and above the knowledge of the Gospel mysteries, there is in the soul of the pious believer an appreciation, an apprehension, an instinctive, almost intuitive realisation of Jesus and Mary, which has its own certainties, its own associations, its own perceptions, its own analogies. It is true that the individual mind gives some colour and consistence to these things; yet when in the popularity of various writings, in the spirit of devotions, in the contemplations of the saints, and in other ways, such ideas attain a kind of universality, they become the sense of the faithful, and express the true Catholic idea. The cultivation of right instincts about our Blessed Lord and His Mother is obviously a matter of great importance, because of its necessary connection with sanctity, and of the influence which it exercises over our worship of the Blessed Sacrament, over various other devotions, and over the spirit in which we observe the great feasts of the Church. Now when we have a clear and consistent idea of Mary in our minds, certain things we hear or read will startle us and strike us as unlikely. If they do not rest upon the authority of the faith, but are simply the view of some preacher, or the teaching of a book, or the contemplation of some single saint, we put them away as unsuitable, because we have more confidence, and rightly, in that view of our Lady which has become part of our spiritual life, than in the preacher, the book, or the single saint. We do not condemn them, perhaps do not even like to differ from them; we simply put them away. But if what startles us comes to us on the authority of the Church, then either we must reform the idea in our minds, or we must expect to find

M

some deep and unusual significance in that which surprises us. Now there are one or two such things in this third dolour; and these must be enumerated among its peculiarities.

First of all it strikes us as unlike our Blessed Lady that she should have allowed her sorrow to wring from her any outward demonstration of grief. She not only showed her sorrow in her outward deportment, but she told Jesus that Joseph and herself had sought Him sorrowing. She told it Him almost reproachfully. Now the saints have borne the greatest sorrows in complete, heroic, and supernatural silence. It has always been their characteristic to do so. They have wished none but God to know their sorrows. Was our Lady inferior to any of the saints in this gift of silence? On the contrary, her silence was one of the most remarkable of her graces. Tradition says that the three hardly ever spoke in the Holy House at Nazareth. The sweet heavenly colloquies, which we should have pictured to ourselves, as a main part of the life of the Holy Family, are in our own imagination. They do not exist. A deeper silence than that of a Carmelite desert reigned there, or a Carthusian house where the alpine winds moan in the corridors and shake the casements, and all else is silent as the tomb. The words of Jesus were very few. That was the reason Mary laid them up in her heart, because, like treasures, they were rare as well as precious. When we reflect, we shall see it could hardly be otherwise. God is very silent. So far as Mary is concerned, the Gospel narrative fully bears out the tradition. It is amazing how few words of hers are recorded there. Moving or still, she appears there like a beautiful statue, whose beauty is its only language. So striking is this, that some contemplatives have supposed that in her humility she commanded the Evangelists to suppress everything about her, which was not absolutely necessary to the doctrine about our Blessed Lord. St. John, who was most with her, says, and doubtless in obedience to her own will, next to nothing about her; and St. Mark does not mention her but once, and then indirectly only. We can have no doubt that no saint ever practised silence as she did. Her silence to St. Joseph is a wonderful proof of this. But how should she be otherwise than silent? A creature, who had lived so long with the Creator, would not speak much. Her heart would be full. Her soul would be hushed. She had been with Him for twelve long years, long years so far as the formation of habits is concerned, though they had passed to her like a saint's ecstasy, full of painful love. She had borne Him in her arms. She had watched Him sleep. She had given Him food. She had looked into His eyes. He had perpetually unveiled His Heart to her. Thus she had learned His ways. All manner of Divine similitudes had been transferred to her soul. We know how silent God is. Between the Creator and the creature, in such relations as He and Mary were to each other, silence would be more of a language than words. What could words do? What could they say? They could not carry the weight of the Mother's thoughts, much less the Son's. It must have been an effort to speak, a condescension, a coming down from the mountain, on her part as well as His. And why come down? St. Joseph did not need it. He too dwelt high up among those mountains of silence, too high for any voice to reach, almost too high for earth's faintest echoes to sound there. He did not need teaching as the multitude did, from the green mound, or on the plain, or by the shore of the inland sea. Even the days of His Ministry, which was the "time to speak," as the Hidden Life was the "time to keep silence," our Lord was very silent. How remarkably this is hinted at the close of St. John's Gospel, the disciple of the Sacred Heart! The text itself sounds as if it would be less of an exaggeration if it spoke of words instead of works. "But there are also many other things which Jesus did; which, if they were written every one, the world itself, I think, would not be able to contain the books that should be written." Was he speaking of the Thirty-Three Years, or was he ending his Gospel, as he had begun it, with the eternal doings of the Word?

But is it not then all the more surprising that our Lady should have indulged in this outward, almost reproachful demonstration of her grief? It is indeed most mysterious. We know, from the book of Job, in what boldness of complaint, in what seeming petulance of familiarity and love, God allows His creatures. He seems even to take a pleasure, and to find a worship, in the truthful utterance which comes up from the very depths of the nature He Himself has fashioned. This is the mourner's consolation, when he thinks of God. But nothing of all this will apply to Mary. Was it an heroic act of humility, by which she expressed Joseph's sorrow and coupled herself with him? It may have been. It would be like her. But there is such an intense truthfulness in the Gospel words, that we do not like to relax the strictness of their meaning by such interpretations as this, unless compelled by obvious necessity. We have but few of her words. We would rather those few should have meanings in them about herself. Was it meant to convey to us the exquisite suffering of this dolour, without implying any need or satisfaction of her own in making the complaint? The Gospel sometimes does so; and once when our Lord prayed, and a Voice came from heaven, He said to His disciples that it was for their sakes that He had prayed His Father to glorify Him. But this interpretation labours under the same difficulty as the last. There was indeed humility in our Lady's words. But it was in coupling the great but far inferior sorrow of Joseph with her own. The words do indeed reveal to us the severity of her affliction, but it is by their own truthfulness, and in their literal acceptation. It was the excess of her anguish which wrung from her, not in the excitement of a sudden revulsion of feeling, but with all tranquillity and unbroken self-possession, those marvellous words. Neither was there any imperfection in this. The idea of imperfection only comes in with the idea of disproportion. We complain, because of our weakness. Our sorrow is out of proportion with our strength, and so without shadow of blame we utter a complaint, and our complaint is a faultless imperfection. The saints suffer, and do not complain; because their inward strength is proportioned to their sorrow, and their silence is a perfection. But there is a step beyond this. Speech, in the creature's extremity, is its necessary resort to the Creator. Complaint to creatures is complaint; but complaint to God is adoration. The sorrows of the saints have never been co-extensive with the possibilities of their natures. We presume Mary's sufferings in this dolour to have been so. It went not only beyond the power, but beyond the right, of silence. It drove her nature to its outermost limit of endurance, magnificent and worshipful as that nature was. It exacted of her that which was proportioned to it, the ultimate resort of the creature, the perfect unbosoming of itself to the Creator. Our Lord's perfection in His Human Nature culminated in a word. His silence was indeed a most adorable perfection; but it was a higher height, when He broke out into that cry, My God, My God, why hast Thou forsaken Me? Then it was that His Passion had reached to the whole breadth of His Humanity, and had covered it. Thus it was that our dearest Mother had her Passion at the end of the Infancy, and her Compassion, together with His Passion, at the end of the Ministry. The darkness of this third dolour was the Gethsemane: the loss of Jesus was the crucifixion of her soul; her complaint was her cry upon the Cross, just when the torment of the Cross was ending. It was with her now, as it was to be with Him hereafter.

There is yet another thing which strikes us as unlike our Lady in this third dolour. It is her venturing to question our Blessed Lord as to the reasons of His conduct. In the midst of her love of Jesus, the thought always uppermost in her mind, the memory that never went to sleep, the faith which was her life, the fact which was her worship, was His Divinity. Indeed the greatness of her love arose from this very thing. It seems most probable that our Lord had actually shown her His Divine Nature. But at all events she saw it always by faith. It was the prominent thing which she saw in Him incessantly. Hence it would seem impossible for her to question Him. Her humility and her intelligence would alike forbid it. She had asked a question for one moment, just before consenting to the Incarnation. But it was of an angel, not of God; and moreover those days were passed. How is it then that she thus seems to call upon Him, and in public also, to explain and justify Himself for what He had done? In all the Gospels her words are without any parallel. They stand out by themselves, inviting notice, and yet full of mystery. Her spirit was not troubled by the interior darkness of her soul. It never had been troubled by it. Trouble is not the word. Besides, the darkness had gone at the first sight of Jesus. It was not in the flush of joy, which at that instant was crowding in at all the inlets of her soul, that she spoke, not knowing what she said, like Peter upon Tabor when he talked of building three tabernacles. Neither joy nor sorrow ever made the balance of her tranquillity even to quiver. There was never any conflict in her. Struggle would have desecrated her Immaculate Heart. It was not exactly that she wanted to know. Her science was so vast, that it was absolutely without desire of increase, so far at least as it was merely science, and not the beatifying accompaniment of an ever-augmenting love. Her science was such as was befitting her altitude as the Mother of God. She knew, not only all that was due to her, not only all that was convenient for her, but all which could perfect her perfections within the limits of a creature. Everything in her had its limits. Everything was vast, but it was also limited. Her beauty was in her limitations. She remained a creature. Hence her science was perfect, having nothing imperfect about it but the inevitable imperfection of whatsoever is created. God only is illimitable, God only omniscient, God only perfect with absolute, independent, intrinsical perfection. Why then did she question Jesus thus? We must reverently venture upon a conjecture. It was by an impulse of the Holy Spirit, by an attraction from Jesus Himself, by a will of His which she read in His Sacred Heart. She had just been raised to a fresh height of sanctity. She had been drawn closer to God. The time of boldness follows great graces, just as the time of great graces follows great trials. Heavenliness of mind takes the form of an adoring familiarity, when it is in actual contact with God. We see this in the saints. But what will the corresponding phenomenon be in the sanctity of Mary? Jesus invited her to claim Him, to assert her rights over Him, to exercise her authority upon Him. And all this publicly before the doctors. Thus would He make solemn proclamation of her being His Mother, and do her honour before all, while they who heard little knew the import of that royal proclamation. Just as it required vast grace in St. Joseph to enable his humility to govern and command his God, so now did it require immense grace in Mary thus to assert her rights over Jesus. But she did it in the same calm simplicity with which she had consented to the Incarnation; and that moment she stood once more on another mountain, higher than that which a moment since had been the pedestal of her wonderful grace. The glory of obedience, the triumph of humility, the magnificence of worship, all these were in the bold question of the Blessed Mother.

It should be mentioned also as a peculiarity of this dolour, that it was one of the chief sufferings of our Blessed Lord. Perhaps more than the chief. In the seventeenth century there was a nun of the order of the Visitation at Turin, who lived in a state of the most unusual union with our Blessed Lord. Her name was Jeanne-Bénigne Gojos. She had a special devotion to the Sacred Humanity, and the peculiar form of her spirituality was the offering up of all her actions to the Eternal Father in union with those of Jesus. It had been revealed to her that this was the particular devotion of Mary and Joseph on earth, an "amorous invention," so she called it, by which they themselves had gained enormous graces. In passing over in her mind the various mysteries of our Lord's Thirty-Three Years, she felt herself supernaturally attracted to unite her soul with Him in the mystery of the Three Days' Loss. This became her interior occupation, until at last it pleased our Lord to reveal to her some of the secrets of His Sacred Heart about it. He told her that it had cost Him more suffering than all the other pains of His life. For then in His Mother's grief, caused by the separation, He beheld all that grief included, which was to be her martyrdom on Calvary, and that as there her body and soul would have been sundered by an agony of grief, unless He had kept them together by His omnipotence, so during the Three Days' Loss His almighty love had kept both Mary and Joseph united to Him, and that the cruelty of the pain was so great that without this secret assistance they could neither of them have survived. He added moreover that their sorrow was simply incomprehensible, and that none could understand it but Himself.* Let us meditate on this, without daring to add to it.

The heights of mystical theology, into which this dolour has led us, must not however make us omit some other considerations, which come more nearly to our own level. There is no need to seek for a climax in divine things. Little things are not dwarfed by the side of great ones, when the presence of God is seen in both. We may therefore remark this peculiarity of the Three Days' Loss. If we may say so, it enabled Mary better to understand the wretchedness of those who are in sin. She was to be the mother of mercy and the refuge of sinners. She was to love them as never mother loved faultless child. She was to be a sanctuary so fortified by love, that hardly omnipotence itself should tear from it the victims due to justice. It was not then enough for her to have a marvellous vision of sin. She must know how they felt who unhappily had sinned. But how was this to be? What had sin to do with her? It had at once to make her childless, and to give her multitudes of children. Its shadow had fallen from the first upon the joy of her heart, the living joy outside her that moved about the house

* Vie, p. 453.

of Nazareth, and the joy within her which was her life. Otherwise, within her, sin had nothing to do. It never passed there. The decree in which it was foreseen did not concern her. She was decreed before. She can see the malice of sin well enough, when she looks on Jesus, and knows that it will slay Him. But how is she to divine the feelings of poor sinners, and still keep her own soul inviolate? It is by means of this third dolour. Sin is the loss of Jesus. She knows now the misery of that. Sin is the loss of Jesus when we have once possessed Him. She knows that also; for there was the sting. The uncertainty to which she was a prey, while the supernatural darkness rested on her soul, and which made her doubt if her own unworthiness had repelled Jesus from her, gave her an approach at least to the dismay of one who has forfeited grace, and lost our Lord by his own fault. At least it enabled her to know the *kind* of pain. But to lose Jesus after having once possessed Him, and not to feel the loss, nay to be positively indifferent to it, to acknowledge it, and yet not care for it,—this after what she had felt, most piteously disclosed to her the worst unhappiness, the direst need of the luckless sinner! Henceforth, if she measures sin by Calvary she will measure her love of sinners by the dolour of the Three Days' Loss; and have we not said already that it was the greatest of them all?

But there was still another peculiarity in this dolour. It did what beforehand could never have been expected. It brought forth in Mary's heart a new love of Jesus, the love of what we have lost and mourned, and then got back again. Affection has no greater consecration than this. It is a flower which grows very commonly on human sorrows, but it is surpassingly beautiful in all its varieties. Mothers have bent over the beds of their dying children, as though their hearts would burst. They would not stay God's hand, even if they could. Their will is with His. But their hearts! O this very conformity of their will sends all the sorrow rushing to the heart. The flower withers. They see it withering before their eyes hour by hour. Human skill has certified now to the absence of hope. It should have said rather to the absence of trust in itself. It is useless to speak of no hope to a mother. It is a language she does not understand. The bitterness of death is in her soul; but she hopes. She has made her sacrifice to God; but still she hopes. Nobody else hopes, but she hopes. Hope holds her heart together, but only just holds it. But a change comes over the face of her child. It seems to be sinking. She would almost recall her sacrifice; but she does not. She is God's daughter, as well as her child's mother. She sees it sink back, and its eyes close, and its little weight indents the pillow somewhat deeper. Is it death? In the mother's heart it was; and hope went, and the world gave way under her feet, and it was not the floor of earth that held her up, but the arm of her Heavenly Father. But to the child, it is not death. It is sleep. It is hope. A few days, and weak, silent, very white, the child is lying in her lap, smiling feebly into her eyes; it could speak, but it is not allowed. The silence of that smile is such music to the mother's heart. But does she love her child as she did before? O no! it is a new love. She is twice its mother now, because her Heavenly Father has given it to her twice. Some of us have been children twice over to our mothers, and Mary has now to be twice a mother to us, for the earthly one is gone. Poor earthly mother! What art thou compared with Mary? What is thy child compared with Jesus? We then have no experience by which to reach the new love of that Blessed Mother for the Son, whom the Eternal Father had now given twice unto her. We have put up our little ladders, the comparisons of our sweetest loves, but we cannot mount to the top. Truly, if Mary had many crosses in this dolour, she also came out of it with many crowns, and a new way of loving Jesus was the best of all.

Such were the peculiarities of the Three Days' Loss. May our dearest Mother pardon our attempt to fathom the depths of that sorrow, which our Lord Himself has pronounced to be unfathomable! She promised that they who "elucidate her shall possess eternal life." The loving endeavour will not therefore be altogether without reward. But we must turn now from the peculiarities of the mystery to the dispositions in which she suffered. The grand disposition which lasted throughout the dolour, was a mixture of yearning with detachment, which it is not possible for us to understand. It could only happen once in creation, and to one creature, the elected Mother of God. She yearned for Jesus, because she was His Mother. She yearned for His sensible presence, for His visible beauty. She yearned for them the more intensely, because her thoughts were not habituated to separate the Eternal from the Child. Why should she stay her devotion, or unsimplify her worship, by disuniting in thought what God had united, and united by such rivets as those of the Hypostatic Union? But while she yearned with such ardour, she did so with perfect conformity to the will of God. She practised the hard virtue of detachment in the most heroic degree ever known; and she was detached broken-heartedly, not coldly. But for God Himself, for the Divine Nature of Jesus, she yearned without any detachment whatever. Detachment is from creatures, and detachment from the created gifts of God is a higher virtue still. But detachment from God is a horror, belonging only to impenitence and hell. Next to Mary and Joseph, perhaps also we should name the Baptist, St. Peter probably loved our Blessed Lord more than any other creature, even the burning seraphim, and next to him St. John, the disciple whom Jesus loved. But there was something in the love of the apostles, deep, ardent, glorious as it was, which was not altogether perfect. Some dross of earth adhered to it. It was "expedient that He should go away." It was necessary for their complete sanctification that His dear sensible presence should be subtracted from them. Now the operations of grace cleanse away imperfections, not merely by expelling them from the soul, but by filling up their room with some great gift or peculiar presence of God. This gift which they leave, and by which they effect a cleansing of the soul, is quite separable from the cleansing operation; even though, as a matter of fact, they always go together in the saints. Our Lady had nothing to cleanse. She had no merely natural tenderness for Jesus, which was not already absorbed in the supernatural, and canonised by it. Nothing earthly, nothing unworthy, clung to her love of Him. But the subtraction of His sensible presence might give her the same gift it gave the apostles, without the cleansing virtue which she did not need; and it might give it to her in an eminent degree above their gift because in proportion to her eminence. Thus, as in the third dolour she had found a new love of Jesus, the grace of it might be to raise her whole love of our Lord immensely higher, more nearly equal to His worth, to which at best it must remain infinitely unequal. But so it is with many of our Lady's graces. They strike across the trackless desert of the infinite. They can never reach the other side; for it has none. Yet somehow they gain a nearer vicinity to God.

We have already noticed another of her dispositions, namely, her extreme humility in the temple. Indeed every moment of the three days was drawing forth from her the most astonishing acts of humility. Her tranquillity in the midst of that perturbing darkness, which came down like deep night upon her soul, and yet perturbed her not, was the effect of her intense humility. The doubt as to whether Jesus had not left her because of her unworthiness was also the offspring of that lowliness, which by thinking exaggerated evil of itself comes nigh to divine truthfulness. But above all was her humility tried and triumphant, in the public assertion of her rights over Jesus, whom she was longing to fall down and worship as the Second Person of the Most Holy Trinity, an act which Mary of Agreda tells us she did do as soon as she had got outside the gates of Jerusalem and beyond the sight of men. Her silence also when His answer came, which was in reality no answer to her question, but sounded like reproof, the more strange from the mouth of a Boy of twelve, was the continuance of the same marvellous humility. All this is like our dearest Mother. All this is what we expect, and recognise. The picture grows familiar again. We breathe more freely, than when awhile ago we were straining up those high hills, which were not meant for such as we are. Mary still astonishes us. There are sweet surprises in her commonest graces, because their beauty is at once so heroic and so gentle. It is far beyond us, but it does not look so. It tempts us on. It seems attainable. At least it draws us towards itself, and it is the best road for us to be on. How strange it is that finding God always humbles, even while it ravishes, even while it elevates. Humility is the perfume of God. It is the fragrance which He leaves behind, who cannot be humbled Himself, because He is God. It is the odour, the stain, the token, the Creator leaves upon the creature when He has pressed upon it for a moment. It must be a law of the world of grace, because we find it in Mary, in the saints, and in the faintest, most nearly indistinguishable way in ourselves. Perhaps it is something inseparable from God. We trace the Most High, the Incommunicable, by it in the Old Testament. We trace Jesus by it in the New. The glory of humility is in the Human Nature of our Lord, on which the mysterious pressure of the Divine Nature rested for evermore. It is this inevitable perfume that God leaves behind Him, which hinders His altogether hiding His traces from us. It is "the myrrh and stacte and cassia from His ivory houses." Mary has found Him now, and she has laid down to rest in the lowliest, most flowery valley of humility, and the fragrance of God has perfumed her garments, her "gilded clothing surrounded with variety."

Another of our Blessed Lady's dispositions in this dolour was the resignation by which she simplified as it were with one endurance such multiform and manifold sorrows as were involved in it. Altogether there is no disposition of the soul, no gift, no grace, for bearing misfortune, which is at

all to be compared with simplicity. It brings along with it
singleness of heart and eye. It is not amazed. It is not
precipitate. It does not distract itself with many things.
It has a sort of unconscious discretion about it, which is
very serviceable in times of grief. Self-oblivion is at once
the hardest and the most needful lesson, which we have to
learn in trouble, and simplicity is half way to it already.
Moreover it strengthens our faith by keeping our eye with a
gentle, hardly constrained fixedness on God. It is in its
own nature too self-possessed to be taken unawares by those
subtle temptations, which assail us in sorrow, and which,
under the pretext of prudence or of greater good, lead us
artfully away from God to rest on creatures. Simplicity
makes a ring of light round about it, even in darkness, like
the moon shining through a mist. If there be not enough
light to walk by, there is at least enough to guarantee us
against surprises. Such was our dear Mother's simplicity.
It had a fearful complication of sorrows to cope with.
There was first of all the intense suffering, which is itself a
bewildering distraction. It seems to divide our nature into
many pieces, and to live and ache in each one of them.
Then there was added to this the bodily pain arising from
inward grief, and also from fatigue, hunger, and want of
rest. To sit down and die would have been easy, had it
been right. But she had to work, to think, to plan, to consider, to be stirring; and activity was almost insupportable
in such a conjuncture as this. But God chose that very
moment to overwhelm her supernaturally with interior trials.
She was in darkness. A sudden change seemed to have
come over the life of her soul. She was battling, not with
one evil but with many, not with an evil which she knew
where to find or how to confront, but with uncertainties, surmises, suspicions, torturing suspense, unaccustomed nescience,
and a baffling darkness which met her thoughts whenever
they went forth, and turned them back again. All this was
on her at one and the same time. Yet, throughout, her will
was calmer than a summer lake. It lay in the lap of God's

THE THREE DAYS' LOSS. 191

will, as the lake lies in the bosom of its green valley. It never stirred. Not a first movement, not an indeliberate breath from self, rippled ever so indistinctly the silver level of the waters. This came of her simplicity. It wrought many wonders in her Three-and-Sixty Years. But, except at the moment of the Incarnation, it never wrought a wonder like to the loving stillness of her heart during the Three Days' Loss. It looked, of course it could be but a look, as if the loss of the Son had made her sink down more deeply in the Bosom of the Father.

Although this dolour for the most part keeps up among the high hills, which do not belong to us, it is nevertheless so full of lessons for ourselves, that it is difficult to select from them. It teaches us, first of all, that the loss of Jesus, however brief, is the greatest of all evils. It was this which was almost unbearable even to our Lady, and Jesus is not more needful to us than to her, because to all creatures He is absolutely needful; only to us He is a more pressing necessity, because of our weakness and our sin. The greatness of Mary's sorrow is to us a visible measure of the magnitude of the evil. Yet alas! how little we feel it! How happy can men be, who yet have lost Jesus, often unconscious almost of their loss, more often indifferent to it when they know it! We should have thought the loss of Jesus was in itself so fearful an evil, that nothing could have aggravated it; and yet our want of perception of the greatness of our loss is a token of still deeper misery. It is sad indeed when the voice of the world is more musical in our ears than the voice of our Lord. It is just the very wretchedness, the very hatefulness of the world, that it has no Jesus. He does not belong to it. He refused to pray for it. He pronounced its friendship to be on our part a simple declaration of war upon Himself. It makes our hearts sink to look out upon the world, and to know that it has no part in Him. It is like gazing upon a cheerless and disconsolate view of barren moors or dreary swamps. No sunshine can gild it. It is dismal on the brightest day.

Nay, it is ugliest when the sun shines upon it. So is it with the world, because it has no Jesus. So does it become with us in proportion as we are friends with the world, or even at peace with the world. He and it are incompatible. Are we not afraid? Pleasure, gaiety, fashion, expense,—dare, we, even in our thoughts, put these things into the Heart of Jesus? Would He smile when worldly things were said? Would He wish to please people round Him, who are taking no pains whatever to please His Father? Would He seek to be popular in society, to stand well with those who have not at heart the only one interest which He has at His, to keep out of sight His principles, not simply through silence and reserve, but lest they should ruffle others and interfere with that smoothness of social intercourse which takes the place of charity.

Alas! sin is bad; excess of pleasure is bad; giving God the second place is bad; worshipping the rich is bad; hardening our Christian feelings to become accustomed to worldly frivolities and very slightly uncharitable conversation is bad. But these at least are evils which wear no masks. We know what we are about. We give up Jesus with the full understanding of the sacrifice we are making. We are taking our side, choosing our lot, and we know it. But, wishing to please!—this is the danger to a spiritual person. Total separation from Christ, is already implied in the very idea. What is it we wish to please? The world, which is the enemy of Jesus. Whom do we wish to please? Those who are not caring to please God, and in whom Jesus takes no pleasure. Wherein do we wish to please? In things, conversations, and pursuits which have no reference to God, no savour of Christ, no tendency towards religion. When do we wish to please? At times when we are doing least for Christ, when prayer and faith and hope and love and abiding sorrow for sin would be the most unseasonable. Where do we wish to please? In haunts where there is less evidence of God than elsewhere, where every circumstance, every appurtenance, flashes the world's image back upon us as from a lustre. Yet we see no evil. We want smoothness, polish, inoffensiveness, discreet keeping back of God. He said that He and Mammon would not dwell together. But to some extent we will force Him so to dwell. He shall at least keep the peace with the world, and learn to revolve alongside of it in His own sphere, without encroaching, without jarring. Dreadful! Is there not hell already in the mere attempt? Yet how little men suspect it. It is like something noxious getting into the air, and not at first affecting the lungs. But the lights burn dim, then one by one they go out, and we are left in the darkness, unable to escape, because lethargy and suffocation have already begun with ourselves. In other words, high principles gently lower themselves, or are kept for state occasions, such as Lent, or a priest's company. Then we begin to be keenly alive to the annoyance which comes to us from the conversation of uncompromising Christians, and we pronounce them indiscreet, and by that ceremony they are disposed of to our great comfort, and we praise them more than ever, because by that reserve we have got rid of what fidgeted us in them, and we lull to rest the remaining uneasiness of conscience by this greater promptitude of a praise which we have first made valueless by counterweighting it. Then it dawns upon us that it is a duty to keep well with the world even for God's sake. Then keeping well edges on to being friends with the world. Then there begin to be symptoms of two distinct lives going to be lived by us; but we do not see these symptoms ourselves. Then uncomfortable feelings rise in us, taking away our relish for certain persons, certain things, certain books, certain conversations. We rouse ourselves, and take a view, an intellectual view, of the rightness of being smooth and not offending, and getting on well with the world. The view comforts us, and we are all right again. Then God's blessings, His spiritual blessings, very gradually and almost imperceptibly, begin to evaporate from us, from ourselves, our children, our homes, our hearts, and everything round us. But the sun of prosperity shines so clearly, we do not see the mist of the evaporation rising up from the earth, and withdrawing itself into heaven. Perhaps we shall never awake to the truth again. Trying to please is a slumberous thing. So we drift on, never suspecting how far the current is carrying us away from God. We may die without knowing it. We shall know it after that, the instant afterwards.

Thus we may lose Jesus in three ways. We may abruptly break from Him by sin. We may quietly and gracefully withdraw from Him, confessing the attractions of the world to be greater than His. We may retire from Him slowly and by imperceptible degrees, always with our face towards Him, as we withdraw from royalty, and all because He is not a fixed principle with us, and the desire to please is so. But if we have lost Him in any one of these three ways, sin, worldliness, and the love of pleasing, and He rouses us by His grace, what are we to do? This third dolour teaches us. It must be a dolour to us. We must search for Him whom we have lost. He may not allow us to find Him all at once. He probably will not. But we must put off everything else in order to prosecute our search. Other things must be subordinate to it. They must wait, or they must give way. But we must not be precipitate in our search. We must not run, we must walk. We shall miss Him if we run. We must not do violent things, not even to ourselves, although we richly deserve them. It is not a time for taking up new penances. The loss of Jesus is penance enough, now that we have found it out. We must be gentle, and sorrow will give us gentleness. Hence our search must be also a sorrowful one, as Mary's was. We must seek Jesus with tears, with tears but not with cries, with a broken heart but a quiet heart also. We must seek Him also in the right place, in Jerusalem, in the temple, that is, in the Church, and in sacraments, and in prayer. He is never among our kinsfolk; He never hides in the blameless softness of a kind home. This is a hard saying, but this dolour says it. All these are the conditions of a successful search.

It was so Mary sought Him; it was so she found Him. We must be of good cheer. Everything has its remedy. Even worldliness is curable, and it is by far the nearest to incurable of any of our diseases. If our whole life has been but a desire to please, if every thought, word, action, look, and omission has got that poison at the bottom of it, we must not be cast down. To change the habit is too difficult. We will change the object. It shall be Jesus instead of the world. Who ever knew people more thoroughly all for God, than some who were once notably all for the world, nay, it would seem, the more notably heretofore for the world, the more thoroughly now for Him?

We must however, so also this dolour teaches us, be on our guard against a temptation which is likely to assail us in our search. We soon lose the feeling of guilt in the feeling of beginning to be good again. It is part of the shallowness of our nature. We shall not have gone far on our road in search of Jesus, before we shall be drawn to attribute the loss of Him, not so much to our own fault, as to some mysterious supernatural trial which God is sending us, and the coming of which is itself an index of our goodness. We feel our hearts sorrowfully burning after our Lord. They cannot surely be the same hearts which we thought but a while ago were living contentedly without Him. The change of feeling has not been sudden or marked, therefore it cannot be new. So we argue. Alas! the truth is, our own changeableness is so great that it is incredible even to ourselves except at the moment of the turn, when we see it with our eyes. Let us not take any grand views of supernatural chastisements. They are rare, and they are not for such as we are. Simply we have sinned, and we are being punished for it. It is our punishment to have to search for Him, who once dwelt with us, and only left us reluctantly. Let us be sure that everything about us is very commonplace. We have lost Jesus, not in a mystical darkness of soul, but in the weakness of a worldly heart; we shall find Him not in a vision or in any masterful interior operation of grace, but in the resumption of our old prayers, in the frequentation of the old sacraments. It is here the Evil One deludes many. They look out for a more striking appearance of our Lord than they had before. So they come up to Him, do not know Him, and go past Him. It is not often men turn back upon a search. But if these souls do not do so, cannot every one see that they have a wilderness before them in which they may die, but which they will assuredly never cross? Mary might have thought her loss of Jesus a supernatural trial, and she would have thought truly. But she thought it was her own fault, and so she reached a far higher truthfulness.

It is true there is a loss of Jesus which is not altogether our fault, which is half trial as well as half punishment. It is not so much a loss of Him as a veiling of His Face. We only think we have lost Him because we do not see Him. This happens to us again and again in our spiritual life; and if we watch attentively, we shall be sure to detect the action of some law in these disappearances. We shall come to know the circumstances under which they happen, which regulate their duration, and which accompany His re-appearance. For He does nothing except in order, weight, and measure,— more so if it were possible, in the world of souls than in the world of matter. God has His own way with each one of us, and it is of consequence we should know His way with ourselves. But, with all, His way is a system. It has its laws and its periods, and is just as regular in its deflections, and as punctual in its catastrophes, as it is in its peace, its sequence, its uniformity. There is perhaps no infallible way of knowing when this disappearance of Jesus is our own fault. Perhaps it is always in some measure our own fault. If it were only a trial, it would cease to be a very efficacious one, were we sure it was but a trial, and no fault of ours. Even then we must not be passive, even then we must sorrow, even then we must search. We must not wait for Him to come back to us; we must go and find out where He is. But, till we find Him, do not let us seek for consolation, either from our guides or from ourselves, least of all from the sympathy of creatures or the comforts of earth; He is our only true consolation. It would be the saddest of things if we were consoled by anything but the finding of Him! All this the third dolour teaches us; for it mirrors on its surface, without being disturbed by the deep things under it, all the relations of the soul with its Saviour and its Lord.

There is something almost selfish in the feelings with which we turn away from the death-bed when the grim work is over. There is a sense of calm and of repose, which for the moment seems as if it were an enjoyment of our own. But it is not so, or not more so than to our nature is unavoidable. It was anguish to see one we loved suffer so terribly, to watch him struggling with the dark enemy, and to be unable to assist him except by prayers we were too distracted to pray, only that the mourner's unselfish will is itself prayer with God. So much hung upon the struggle, such interests were on the balance; we were sick to think of them, but sicker still to see them, now uppermost, and now undermost, in that tremendous hour. Now all is over; as far as we can see, well over, happily over, eternally right. His body is harmless, his soul is accepted. There is nothing to annoy our love of him, because there is nothing to afflict and harass him. It is a beautiful change to him, a soothing change to us. Our hearts are full to overflowing with that expansion, which belongs to true repose. Such is our feeling, as we watch Jesus and Mary, on the threshold of the house of Nazareth, together again, the two hearts like one, on the shore of that broad and tranquil sea of eighteen years, during which they shall separate no more. Mary's heart is still broken. It must be broken always. But it beats inside another Heart, which will not leave her again for years and years, and there is a quiet pensive evening brightness about her sorrow, most unlike the darkness and the wandering and the weariness of the Three Days' Loss. She has got Jesus back again. It is peace to us as well as to her. Truly she is to be envied now for her joys even amidst the number of her sorrows.

CHAPTER V.

THE FOURTH DOLOUR.

MEETING JESUS WITH THE CROSS.

WE have passed into a new world since the last dolour. Bethlehem and Nazareth are left behind. We have bidden farewell to the scenes of the Sacred Infancy, the Boyhood and the Hidden Life. The Three Years' Ministry has passed. It is twenty-one years since the Three Days' Loss. The Immaculate Heart of Mary has traversed a world of mysteries since then, always in supernatural joy, but always with her lifelong sorrow lying on her soul. Henceforth we remain in Jerusalem, which is the scene of her four last dolours, as it has been also of two of the three preceding. We have come to the morning of Good Friday, to her meeting Jesus with the Cross, which is reckoned as her fourth dolour.

But in order to understand the mystery rightly, we must make a retrospect of the last twenty-one years. Mary is continually changing, though it is only in one direction. Her life is an endless heavenward ascension. She is always increasing in holiness, because she is always increasing in love. She is always increasing in love, because Jesus is always increasing in beauty. Thus each dolour found her at once less prepared and better prepared: less prepared, because she loved Jesus more, and it was in Him that she suffered,—more prepared because stronger sanctity can carry heavier crosses. We saw before how the augmentations of her love, from the Return from Egypt to her entry into the gates of Jerusalem when they went up to our Lord's twelfth pasch, had increased her capabilities of suffering. So now the marvel of sanctity, whom we left with her recovered Jesus in the house of Nazareth, is very different from that heart which we are now to accompany along the Way of the Cross. This fourth dolour was not in itself equal to the third, but it fell upon greater capabilities of suffering.

The beauty of the earthly paradise, which God planted with His own hand, and whither He came at the hour of the evening breeze to converse with His unfallen creatures, was a poor shadow of the loveliness of the Holy House during the eighteen years of the Hidden Life. We cannot guess at all the mysteries which were enacted within that celestial cloister. The words were few, yet in eighteen years they were what we, in our human way, should call countless. The very silence even was a fountain of grace. There were tens of thousands of beautiful actions, each one of which had such infinite worth that it might have redeemed the world. During those eighteen years an immeasurable universe was glorifying God all day and night. The beauty of the trackless heavens swayed by their majestic laws, vast unpeopled orbs with their processes of inanimate matter or their seemingly interminable epochs of irrational life, earth with all its inhabitants, the worshippers of the true God amid whatever darkness in all its regions, the chosen flowers of the bygone generations in Abraham's bosom in the limbus of the fathers, the little children a multitudinous throng of spirits, in their own receptacle beneath the surface of the earth, the souls worshipping amid the fires of purgatory,—all were swelling as in one concourse of creation the glory of the Most High. The wide creation of angels, above all, peopling the immeasurable capacities of space, sent up to God evermore, the God whom they beheld clearly with the eyes of their intelligence, a worship of the most exquisite perfection. But the entire creation was as nothing to the Holy House of Nazareth. One hour of that life outweighed ages of all the rest, and not only outweighed it on a comparison, but outweighed it by a simple infinity. There was the centre of all creation, spiritual or material, in nearly the most sequestered village of that obscure Galilea. Why should the centre be there? Who does not see that God's centres in all things baffle the calculation of the sciences of men?

There was a sense too in which Mary seemed to be the centre of this central point of all creation. For if Jesus was the centre to Joseph and herself, and the countless ranks of wondering and adoring angels round, it appeared as if she was the centre of Jesus, which was higher still. He had come to redeem a whole world, and had allotted Himself but Three-and-Thirty Years for the gigantic work. Twelve had been given to Mary. Some Shepherds had knelt before Him, three Eastern kings had kissed His feet, Simeon had held Him in his arms. Anne had blessed Him, some Egyptian infidels had wondered at Him, the townsfolk of Nazareth thought Him no common Child. Otherwise the world knew nothing of Him. He was one among many Galilean children. He had given Himself to Mary. The twelve years ran out, and ended in the strangest mystery of grief. It seemed as if it were a sort of initiation for Mary into some exalted regions of nameless sanctity. From that mystery there starts a period of eighteen years during which our Blessed Lord appears to devote Himself exclusively to Mary and Joseph. It is as if He were her novice-master, and she in a long noviciate, to be professed on Calvary. It could not be waste of time. It could not be out of proportion with the work of His Public Ministry, or with the suffering of His Passion. It was in harmony with His wisdom, which was infinite. Just as the Three Years' Ministry was the Jews' time, and the Passion our time, the Eighteen Years were Mary's time.

Would it not be a hopeless task to make any calculations, for the sake of approaching to that sum of love, which these years produced in Mary's heart? The spiritual beauty or the Human Soul of Jesus, the contagion of His heavenly example, the attraction of all His actions, the efficacy of

His superhuman words, the sight of His unveiled Heart, the visions, granted from time to time, of His Divine Nature and of the Person of the Word, were all so many fountains of substantial grace flowing at all hours into Mary's soul. Without special assistance she could not have lived in such vicinity to Him. She could not have survived such a super-angelic process of sanctification. Her life could not have lived with her love. If there was anything like a respite, if we may so speak, in the eagle-flight of her soul, ever on and on, and upward and upward, it was when she saw Jesus hanging His love on Joseph, and arraying with new and incomparable graces that soul which already in its grandeur surpassed all the saints. Eighteen years with God, knowing Him to be God, eighteen years of hearing, seeing, touching, being touched by, and governing the Creator of the universe! Is it possible for language to unveil the mysteries of such an epoch? Which is the most imitable of God's attributes by us His creatures? Strange to say, it is His holiness. So our Lord Himself declares. We are to be perfect as God is perfect. The product then of all these eighteen years in Mary's soul was sanctity, and if sanctity, therefore love. But by what means, in what ways, by the infusion of what gifts, at what rate of speed, by what accelerated flights, what mortal can so much as dream, but they themselves, Mary and Joseph, on whose souls God lay thus as it were upon a resting-place? If love belonged only to angels and to men, we should have to give it some other name, when it reached the height it did in Mary. But God Himself is love. So we have an infinity to move about in, and can call Mary's sanctity by the name of love without fear of uncrowning it of any of its highest elevations. But if our Blessed Mother could ill part with Jesus at the gate of Jerusalem eighteen years ago, how will this new universe of ten thousand different kinds of love of Him, which she holds in her heart, allow her to part with Him now? This is the one sense in which each dolour outstrips its predecessor, that it has more love to torture, and therefore more power of inflicting pain. So much, power it has, that omnipotence must stand by to hold the life in that dear heart which is dearer to Him than all the world beside.

The Eighteen Years come to an end, and the Three Years' Ministry begins. It is not clear to what extent our Blessed Lady was with Jesus during His Public Ministry. Most probably she was never long separated from Him. But Scripture affords us no decisive testimony on the point, and contemplative saints have differed upon the subject. It seems most likely it was not an actual separation from Him. If she was allowed to follow Him through His Passion, we can hardly suppose she was ever far removed from Him during His ministry. He began His miracles at her intercession at Cana in Galilee, and when on one occasion in the Gospel, she comes to seek Him, as it were, with a Mother's rights, the tone of the narrative would lead us to suppose, that on the one hand she was not continually with Him, and on the other that, although it was no common thing her joining Him at times, she did do so on occasions. Under any circumstances, whether in spirit, or through the revelations of the angels, or by some human channel, we cannot but suppose that she was aware of all His sayings and doings during those three years. The word of her Son can hardly be the common and accessible property of all of us, and not have been her portion also, and a means of her further sanctification.

To Mary the Three Years' Ministry was like a new revelation of Jesus. She saw Him from many points of view from which she had never seen Him before. Every variety in Him, however apparently trivial, could not be really trivial, and was full of wonder, full of beauty, full of grace. It was fresh food for love. It rung changes on the love which it drew from the Mother's heart. In the Infancy she had seen Him, as it were, in still life, giving out heavenly mysteries, as the fountain throbs out water, with a seeming passiveness, though not unconsciously. In the Boyhood the wonders of His activity had developed themselves. Her heart was taken captive afresh by His gracefulness. But He was with those He knew, to whom He trusted Himself, whom He loved unspeakably. He was at once the subject and the superior in the Holy House. But His Ministry was almost a greater change upon His Hidden Life, than His Hidden Life had been upon His Childhood. He had now to act out in the world, to be God, yet not to seem singular, to adapt Himself to numberless new positions, to address Himself to various classes of hearers. At one while He was gently maturing the vocations of His apostles, at another He was swaying multitudes, at another soothing sorrow, at another rebuking sin. Now He was unfolding the Scriptures, and unrolling the hidden folds of His deep parables, to the chosen few; now He saw quietly, and with easy wisdom, eluding the snares of His enemies, who had endeavoured to entangle Him in His talk. Every day brought its changes, its attitudes, its positions, its varieties. Every side of His Human Nature was brought out. Endless graces were elicited. It was like three years of heavenly music, rising and falling, changing and interweaving, hushing and raising, winding and unwinding its beautiful sounds for evermore. It was an indescribable combination of sweetness and power, of wisdom and simplicity, of accommodation and sanctity, of human and divine. There was not, there could not be, a trait, a tone, a gesture, a look, in the behaviour of the Incarnate Creator, which was not in itself, at once a revelation to Mary, and in a lower degree, to the angels also, and at the same time an unfathomable depth which His own eye alone could sound. It was more beautiful than the Infancy; it was more wonderful than the Hidden Life. Its effects upon Mary must have been astonishing.

We shall never approach to a true view of her, if we do not give the Three Years' Ministry its due place in the stupendous process of her sanctification. The epochs of her sanctification were more wonderful than the days of creation, and they are as distinctly marked. The Immaculate Conception with its fifteen years of growing merits was the first day. The Incarnation with the twelve years of the Childhood occupied the second. The Three Days' Loss with the eighteen years of the Hidden Life filled the third. The Three Years' Ministry occupied the fourth. The Passion was the fifth. The forty days of the Risen Life, with the descent of the Holy Ghost, engrossed the sixth. Then came the seventh, our Lord's Sabbath, when He had ascended into heaven and sat down at His Father's Right Hand, leaving the great world of Mary's sanctity to go on for fifteen years, but, as in the case of the material world, not without His ceaseless interference and watchful providence and real presence, yet without His Hands working at it as they did before. Then comes its end, her glorious death, her sweet doom, her blissful resurrection, and His second Advent with His angels to assume her into heaven. We can never estimate the graces of our Blessed Mother, if we break up and disjoin these seven days of her spiritual Genesis.

We must therefore consider the Three Years' Ministry as a most peculiar time, during which, under the influence of the adorable changes of Jesus, her love was growing, perhaps as it had never grown before. It seems unreal to talk of new breadth and depth and height, to that which was beyond all, even angelic, measurements long ago. Years since, her love had gone up so near to God, that the strong splendour of His vicinity confused its outlines and proportions to our ineffectual eyes. Nevertheless we must speak so, hardly knowing what we mean. Mary reached Bethany on the Thursday in Holy Week loving Jesus with a love which far surpassed the love she had for Him when the eighteen years of the Hidden Life had come to a conclusion. St. Joseph was gone, and although her love of him, ardent as it was, was no diversion from her love of Jesus, but rather a variety of it, and an addition to it, yet in some way, as all changes were with her, his death increased her love of our Blessed Lord. The apostles had come into Joseph's place. She knew all the secret designs of grace which our Lord had upon each of them. She saw His way with them all through, in the variety of their vocations and their gifts and their characters. It was a model to her, who was one day to be the queen of those apostles. Her love of them also in some way multiplied her love of Jesus. As in her other periods, so in this, everything which Jesus did was a fresh fountain of love within her heart. His sermons, His parables, His secret teaching, His austerities, His prayers, His tears, His miracles, His journeys, His weariness, His hunger, His thirst, His contradictions,—each one of them was an inexhaustible depth of love. So it was up to the eve of the Passion. All this incalculable augmentation of love was, from our point of view, a correspondingly increased capability of suffering. So the end of the Ministry arrives, and the possibilities of her heart are more wonderful than ever.

We seem to have wandered away from the dolour before us; but it is not really so. The seven dolours are not seven separate mysteries, neither can we understand them, if we look at them in that way. They have a unity of their own, and if we detach them from that unity, we miss their significance. They carry the whole of the Three-and-Thirty Years along with them. Each of them depends for its truth, for its depth, for its intensity, for its peculiar character, on a certain portion of those years, inseparable from it. Jesus grows more beautiful. Grace rises proportionately in Mary's soul. The growth of grace is the growth of love. It reaches a certain point, known to God, fixed by Him, capable of bearing a certain weight, of undergoing a given amount of elevating and sanctifying sorrow; and at that point, as by the operation of a law, one of the dolours comes, takes up the grace and love of the preceding times, of years as in the Childhood, of days as in the swift Passion, compresses them into the most solid and sublime holiness, flies away with the Mother's soul as if it had the strength of all the angels, and places her upon some new height, far away from where she was before. Thus each dolour is a distinct sanctification to her, a renewal, a transfiguration, another degree of divine union. Then the process begins again. Grace and love accumulate once more, with an acceleration and a magnitude in proportion to her new height, until once more, in the counsels of God, they reach the point where another dolour comes to do its magnificent work. Thus also we have two principles of comparison, by which we can contrast the dolours one with another. First of all, they differ in themselves. Each has its peculiar excess, like our Lord's sufferings in the Passion; and so each has its own perfection and its own pre-eminence. They are all equally perfect, but it is with a different and an appropriate perfection. The kind of excess in one may be more afflictive than the kind of excess in another. Thus it is that we call the third dolour the greatest. In this sense they do not rise by degrees, each exceeding its predecessor, and so culminating in a point. But there is a second sense in which they do. Each dolour as it comes, falls upon greater love, and also upon love that has suffered more, and therefore upon a greater capability of suffering. In this way each is worse than its predecessor; and they go on rising and rising in the terrible power of causing anguish, till the very last, till the Burial of Jesus, till the possibilities of woe seem to be exhausted, till the abysses of sanctifying sorrow contained in the huge world of the Incarnation have been dried up by the absorption of the single immaculate heart of the Mother of the Incarnate Word. This is the unity of the dolours; and each dolour really means, not what it looks like by itself, but what it is in the setting and order of the Three-and-Thirty Years.

The Passion may be said to begin on the Thursday in Holy Week in the house of Lazarus at Bethany. Mary, as might have been expected, opened the long avenue of sorrows, great epochs in substance, though brief in time. Jesus had entered Jerusalem on Palm Sunday in the modesty of His well-known triumph. He had spent that day teaching in the temple, as well as the following Monday and Tuesday. He returned however to Bethany at night; for no one in Jerusalem had the courage to offer Him hospitality, as the rulers were incensed with Him because of the recent resurrection of Lazarus, and none of those who had cried Hosanna on Sunday had the courage to put themselves forward individually, and so draw the resentful notice of the chief priests upon them. The Wednesday He is supposed to have spent in prayer on the Mount of Olives, and to have seen the elect of all the ages of the world pass before Him in procession, while He prayed severally for each. Judas meanwhile was arranging his treachery with the rulers. It is supposed also that our Blessed Saviour spent the Wednesday night out of doors praying in the recesses of the hill. On the Thursday morning He went to Bethany to bid His Mother farewell, and to obtain her consent to His Passion, as He had before done to His Incarnation. Not that it was necessary in the first case as it was in the last, but it was fitting and convenient to the perfection of His filial obedience. Sister Mary of Agreda in her revelations describes the affecting scene, how Jesus knelt to His Mother, and begged her blessing, how she refused to bless her God, and fell upon her knees and worshipped Him as her Creator, how He persisted, how they both remained upon their knees, and how at last she blessed Him, and He blessed her. Who can doubt but that He also enriched with a special blessing His beloved Magdalen, the first and most favoured of all the daughters of Mary? He then went to Jerusalem, whither His Mother followed Him, together with Magdalen, in order that she might receive the Blessed Sacrament. The last Supper, the First Mass, took place that night, our Lord's first unbloody Sacrifice, to be followed on the morrow by that dreadful one of blood.

By a miraculous grace she assists in spirit at the Agony in the Garden, sees our Lord's Heart unveiled throughout, and feels in herself, and according to her measure, a corresponding agony. She sees the treachery of Judas consummated, in spite of her intense prayers for that unhappy soul. Then the curtain falls; the vision grows dim; she is left for a while to the anguish of uncertainty. With the brave gentle Magdalen, she goes forth into the streets. She tries to gain admittance both to the houses of Annas and Caiphas, but is repulsed, as she was at Bethlehem three-and-thirty years ago. She hears the voice of Jesus; she hears also the blow given to her Beloved. Jesus is put in prison for the night, and St. John comes forth, and leads our Blessed Mother home to the house, in which the last Supper had been eaten. At all the horrors of the morning she is present. She hears the sound of the scourging, and sees Him at the pillar, and the people around Him sprinkled with His Blood. She hears the gentle murmurs, the almost inaudible bleatings of her spotless Lamb; she hears them, and omnipotence commands her still to live. In spirit, if not in bodily presence, she has seen the guards of Herod mock the Everlasting. She has beheld the ruffians in the guard-room celebrate the cruel coronation of the Almighty King. She has seen the eyes of the All-seeing bandaged, and the offscouring of the people daring to bend the knee in derision before Him who is one day to pronounce their endless doom. She has looked up to the steps of Pilate's hall, and has beheld, beautiful in His disfigurement, Him who was a worm and no man, so had they trodden Him under foot, and mangled Him, and turned Him almost out of human shape by their atrocities. She heard Pilate say, Behold the Man! and verily there was need some one should testify that He was Man, who if He had been only Man could never have survived the crushing of the wine-press, which the threefold pressure, of His Father, of demons, and of men, had inflicted upon Him. Then rose over the crowded piazza that wild yell of blasphemous rejection by His own people, which still rings in our ears, still echoes in history, still dwells even in that calm heaven above, in the Mother's ear who heard it in all the savage frightfulness of its reality. Now the Magdalen leads her home, whither John is to come with news of the sentence when it is passed.

Quietly, almost coldly, we seem to say these things. Alas! many words are not needed. Besides,—what words could they be? To Mary's heart, to Mary's holiness, to Mary's dolour, each minute of those hours was longer than sheaves of centuries bound together in some one secular revolution of the system of the world. Each separate mystery, each blow of the scourging, each fragment of action or suffering which we can detach from the mass, was far, far away of more value, import, size, reality, than if at each moment a new universe with all its immeasurable starriness had been called out of nothing, and peopled with beings more beautiful than angels. It is as if the course of all nature were quickened, and time accelerated, and all things bidden to take the speed of thought, and flash onward to the end which God appointed. Like the fearfulness of some gigantic machinery to a child, so to our eyes is the vision of our Lady's holiness, cleaving its way, like some colossal orb, in terrific velocity, through the darkness and the blasphemy and the blood. Can her soul be the same which left Bethany only yesterday afternoon? The saint in his beaming glory and the whitefaced querulous sick man on his dying bed are not further apart than the Mother of yesterday and the Mother of to-day, apart, yet cognisably the same. She has reached the point of the fourth dolour. She is ready now to meet Jesus with the Cross.

St. John at length returns to the house with the news of the sentence and other information. Our dearest Mother, broken-hearted yet beaming as with divine light in her tranquillity, prepares to leave the house with Magdalen and the apostle. The latter, by his knowledge of the city, will lead her to the end of a street, where she can meet Jesus on His road to Calvary. But has she strength for such a meeting? Not of her own; but she has as much strength to meet Him as He has to travel by that road. For she has Himself within her, the unconsumed species of the Blessed Sacrament. It is only with Jesus that we can any of us meet Jesus. It was so with her. We take Him in Viaticum, and then go to meet Him as our Judge. She took Him, in a strange sense, in Viaticum, and went to meet Him as condemned, and on His way to death. It was that unconsumed Blessed Sacrament, which had carried her through the superhuman brokenheartedness of the last twelve or fifteen hours. If that marvellous conjecture be true, as we think it is not, that it was at the moment when the species of the Blessed Sacrament were consumed in Himself, that our Lord cried out, My God, My God, why hast Thou forsaken Me? we can estimate the strength that sweet Sacrament was to her now.

Everywhere the streets are thronged with multitudes setting in one tide to Calvary. Heralds at the corners of the streets blow their harsh trumpets, and proclaim the sentence to the people. Mary draws her veil around her. John and the Magdalen lean their broken hearts on hers, for they are faint and sick. What a journey for a Mother! She hardly takes note of the streets, but with their shadows they fling into her soul dim memories of the Pasch twenty-one years ago, and the three bitter days that followed it. She has taken her place, silent and still. She does not even tremble. Some tears flow as if spontaneously from her eyes. But her cheeks are red? Yes—her tears were blood. The procession comes in sight; the tall horse of the centurion shows first, and leads the way. The trumpet sounds with a wailing clangour. The women look from the lattices above. She sees the thieves, the crosses, everything,—and yet only one thing, Himself. As He draws nigh, the peace of her heart grows deeper. It could not help it; God was approaching, and peace went before Him. Never had maternal love sat on such a throne as that one in Mary's heart. The anguish was unutterable. God, who knows the number of the sands of the sea, knows it. Now Jesus has come up to her. He halts for a moment. He lifts the one hand that is free, and clears the blood from His eyes. Is it to see her? Rather, that she may see Him, His look of sadness, His look of love. She approaches to embrace Him. The soldiers thrust her rudely back. O misery! and she is His Mother too! For a moment she reeled with the push, and then again was still, her eyes fixed on His, His eyes fixed on hers, such a link, such an embrace, such an outpouring of love, such an overflow of sorrow. Has He less strength than she? See! He staggers, is overweighed by the burden of the ponderous Cross, and falls with a dull dead sound upon the street, like the clank of falling wood. She sees it. The God of heaven and earth is down. Men surround Him, like butchers round a fallen beast; they kick Him, beat Him, swear horrible oaths at Him, drag Him up again with cruel ferocity. It is His first fall. She sees it. He is her Babe of Bethlehem. She is helpless. She cannot get near. Omnipotence held her heart fast. In a peace far beyond man's understanding, she followed slowly on to Calvary, Magdalen and John beside themselves with grief, but feeling as if grace went out from her blue mantle enabling them also to live with broken hearts. The fourth dolour is accomplished; but alas! we only see the outside of things.

Although this dolour seems to be but one step in the Passion, it has nevertheless strongly marked peculiarities of its own. The fact of its having been selected by the Church as one of the seven sorrows of Mary implies that it has a significancy belonging to itself. To our Blessed Lady it was the actual advent of a long-dreaded evil. It was the fulfilment of a vision which had been before her, sleeping and waking for years. It is the first of her dolours which stands clear of the mysteries of the Infancy, and belongs to the second constellation of her griefs, those of the Passion. There is a peculiar suffering of its own in the coming of a misfortune which we have long been expecting. There is such a thing as the unpreparedness of extreme preparation. We have imagined everything beforehand. We have tried to feel the very place where we were sure the blow would fall, and to harden it beforehand. We have placed the circumstances all round about the sorrow just in the order and position which is our liking. We have thought over and over again what we would think, what we would say, what we would do. We have practised the attitude in which we intend to receive the blow. We have left nothing unthought of, nothing unprovided for. We have made up our minds to it. It is before us like a picture, and though there has been no little suffering in the anticipation, familiarity has almost taken the sting out of our sorrow before it comes. And then it comes. O the cruel waywardness of the evil! It has not observed a single one of our many rubrics. It has come by the wrong road, at the wrong hour, with the wrong weapon, struck us in the wrong place, and bore no similarity, not even a distant family resemblance, to the romance of woe, for which we had prepared ourselves. It has taken us unawares. It has disconcerted us utterly. We feel almost more wronged by this, than by the evil in itself.

Moreover the tension of mind and body, to which we have strung ourselves up for the endurance, renders us peculiarly susceptible of pain, and disables us from bearing it one half so heroically as we had resolved. There are many men, who can meet punishment and death bravely, if it comes at the appointed hour: but if it is deferred, the powers of the soul, which had knit themselves up for the occasion, fall away, and disperse, and often become soft with almost an effeminate softness. And yet to us ordinary mortals, as the poet has justly said, "all things are less dreadful than they seem;" whereas in the case of our Blessed Lady's sorrows, the realities far outstripped the most ample expectations. They fulfilled to the uttermost the cruel pains which were foreseen, and brought many with them likewise, as if tokens of their presence, for which no allowance could have been made even in the clearest prevision granted to her. The sorrow that had been queening it over all other sorrows for three-and-thirty years, had now met her at last, in the streets of Jerusalem. It came to do its work for God, and it did it, as God's instruments always do, superabundantly.

Even with our Blessed Lady there is a great difference between sight and foresight, between reality and imagination.

There is a vividness, which could never be foreseen. There is the unexpectedness of the way in which the circumstances are grouped. There is a withdrawal of that medium of time and unfulfilment, which before existed between the soul and its sorrow, and which made it less harsh and galling in its pressure. Besides which, there is a life, an announcement, an individuality in the actual contact of the misfortune, which belongs to each misfortune by itself, is inseparable from it, and is unshared by any other sorrow whatsoever. It may be called the personality of the sorrow. Alas! we all know it well enough, in our degree. Many a time it has driven us to extremities. It is always the unbearable part of what we have to bear. It needs not to have lived a long life to be able to say from our own experience that there is no sameness in sorrow; likenesses there are, but not identities. We have never had two griefs alike. Each had its own character, and it was with its character that it hurt us most. So it was with our dearest mother. Her sorrows, when they lay unborn in her mind, were hard to bear; but when they sprang to life, and leaped from her mind, and with Simeon's sword clove her heart asunder, they were different things, as different as waking is from sleeping, or life from death.

There was another aggravation of her grief in this dolour in the knowledge that the sight of her increased our Lord's sufferings. In the preceding dolour He had been, as it were, her executioner; now she was His. Which was the hardest to bear? Is there any loving mother who would not rather receive pain from her son, than cause it to him? What must this feeling have been in Mary, who transcended all maternal excellence in the fondness and devotedness of her deep love? What must it have been to her whose Son was God? Each outrage which had been offered to Him, each stripe which had fallen upon His Sacred Flesh, had been torture to her beyond compare. She had been penetrated with horror as she thought of the cruelty and the sacrilege of which all, priests, judges, soldiers, executioners, people, had been guilty who had taken part in these atrocities. And behold! she herself was one of the number. She was adding to His load. She was more than doubling the weight of that heavy cross He was carrying. The sight of her face at the corner of that street had been worse a thousand times than the terrible scourging at the pillar. It was her face which had thrown Him down upon the ground in that third fall. What name can we give to a sorrow such as this? The records of human woe furnish us with no parallel to it, which would not dishonour the subject. Some have spoken of the meeting between Sir Thomas More and his daughter in the streets of London. But what is the result of the allusion? Only to take the beauty and the pathos out of that touching English scene, without reaching the level of the sorrow we are speaking of, or reaching it only to degrade it. It was part of the necessity which was laid on Mary. She was to be her Son's executioner, and, in the pain she inflicted, the cruellest of them all. This fourth dolour was the first exercise of her dreadful office. It was new to her; for she had never given Him pain before. But it was the Will of God, that Will which is always sweet in its extremest bitterness, always amiable when flesh and blood and mind are shrinking aghast from the embrace it is throwing round them. It was that Will which headed the procession to Calvary, that Will which was waiting on Calvary like a luminous cloud, that Will which was a crown of thorns round the brow of Jesus, and a Cross upon His shoulders, and a sword in His Mother's heart, and His Mother's heart a sword in His. Had ever saint such a Divine Will to conform to as Mary had? Had ever saint such conformity to any Divine Will he ever encountered? She is going up to Calvary, in brave tranquillity, to help to slay the Babe of Bethlehem.

There was another grief also in this dolour, which was new to her, and caused in her heart in an incomparable degree the acute pain which the sight of sacrilege causes to the saints. She saw Him in the hands of others who could touch Him and come near Him, while she was kept far off. How she longed to wipe the blood from His face with her veil, to part His tangled hair, to remove with lightest touch that cruel crown, to lift the Cross off His shoulders and see whether her broken heart would not give her superhuman strength to carry it for Him! O there were countless ministries in which a mother's hand was needed by that dear Victim of our sins! And think of the plenitude of the rights she had over Him, more than any mother over any son since the world began! He had acknowledged them Himself. He had made her assert them openly in the temple. But these men knew no more of the Mother of God, than poor heretics do. Moreover they, who had trampled her Son under foot, would have made but little scruple of her rights. In the times of Bethlehem and Egypt it had been her joy to touch Him, in the performance of her maternal office. Her love had risen so high, that it could find no vent except in breathless reverence, and it was the touch of His Sacred Body which hushed her soul with that thrill of reverence. Saints at the altar have exulted with the Blessed Sacrament in their hands, till they rose up from the predella in the light air, and swayed to and fro, like a bough in summer, with the palpitations of their ecstasy. How many times must we multiply that joy to reach Mary's? She had only not grudged Joseph the embraces of her Child, because she loved him with the holiest transports of conjugal affection, and best satisfied her love by giving him his turn with Jesus. The novelty had never worn off. The joy had never become thinner from use. The reverence only grew more reverent from custom. The thought of it came back to her now, and the waves of grief beat up against her heart as if they would have washed it away. She had seen the filthy hands of the public executioner grasping His neck and shoulder. She had seen the miry foot of some sinful soldier spurning His bruised flesh. She had seen them brutally knock the wooden cross against His blessed head, and drive the spikes of the thorns still further in. St. Catherine of Genoa had to be supported by God, lest she should die, when He showed her in vision the real malice of a venial sin. What if, with her eyes thus spiritually couched, she had beheld the malice which can trample the Blessed Sacrament under foot in the sewers of the street! The love of a whole Christian land will rise with one emotion to make reparation for a sacrilege against the Blessed Sacrament. They, who have been but too indifferent to their own sins, will then afflict themselves with fasting, and impair their own comforts by abundant alms. It is the instinct of faith's loyalty, and of the love which lies in reality, however appearances may be against it, at the bottom of every believing heart. In truth the feeling of sacrilege is like bodily pain. It is as if we were being cruelly handled ourselves. Holy people, both religious and seculars, have offered their lives to God in reparation of a sacrilege, and have rejoiced when He deigned to accept the offering. To die for the Blessed Sacrament,—that would be a sweet end, glorious also, but more sweet than glorious, because it would so satisfy our love! But the sacrilege that day in the streets of Jerusalem! Mary's woe is simply unimaginable. She would have died a thousand deaths to have made reparation. Ah! but, dearest Mother! thou must live, which to thee is worse far than death, and thy life must be thy reparation! All the evils which others find in death, thou findest in life, and many more beside. To thee it would be as great a joy, as all thy seven dolours all together were a sorrow, if thou mightest not outlive three o'clock that Friday afternoon. But there is a bar between thee and death,—a whole omnipotence. So thou must be contented, as thou ever art, and envy the accepted thief, and for our sakes consent to live!

There was also in this dolour a return of one of the worst sufferings of the Flight into Egypt, only now it was in a higher degree than then. It was terror. We always look at Mary as something very near to God, even though infinitely far off, as the nearest creature needs must be. It is a good habit, because it is the truth. But we must not forget that her heart was always eminently feminine. Fancy the sea of wild faces into which she looked in those crowded streets. Wild beasts in the desert would have been less dreadful. Every passion was glaring out of those ferocious eyes, rendered more horrible by their human intelligence, mingled with the inhuman fiery stare of diabolical possession. A multitude, with the women, possibly the children, all athirst for blood, raving after it, yelling for it as only a maddened populace can yell. It was a very vent of hell that voice of theirs, a concourse of the most appalling sounds, of rage, and hate, and murder, and blasphemy, and imprecation, and of that torturing fire in their own hearts, which those passions had fiercely lighted up. The sights and sounds thrilled through her with agonies of fear. She was alone, unsheltered, uncompanioned. For she was the companion to John and Magdalen; they were not companions to her. O for the loneliness of the desert, and its invisible panic, so much better to bear than this surging multitude of possessed men. They touch her, they speak to her, they jostle her. Visible by her blue mantle, she floats about on the billows of that tossing crowd, like a piece of wreck on the dark weltering waters of a storm. And she is apart from Jesus. He is perishing in the waves of that turbulent people. He is engulphed. She can stretch out no hand to save Him. The mother of the Machabees looked bravely on the fearful pomps and cruel pageants of the legal injustice which was to make her childless, and her name justly lives, embalmed in sacred history, and still more, in Christian hearts. But those faces and those cries—earth never saw, never heard anything so terrible; the demon-maddened creatures howling over their conquered God ! And to Mary it had such reality, such significance, as it could have to no one else. Surely the suffering of fear was never more intensely felt by any creature than it was by her on that Friday; and the many bitter chalices she had drunk during the preceding night and all that morning rendered her, in the ordinary course of things, less able to bear up against this violent assault of terror. Her fear was not so much for herself; it was for Him. Her fear, as well as her love, was in His Heart rather than in her own. The knowledge that He was God only deepened her terror. It was just that very thing which made the horror of the scene unsurpassed by any other the world had ever known, or ever could know again. The day of doom will be less terrible than Good Friday was. Nay, it is the fearfulness of Good Friday which will make the pomp of the last judgment so endurable, so calm, so full of reverent sweetness. O Mother! that day will pay thee back the terror of to-day; for thou wilt see thy Son in all the placid grandeur of His human glory, with those beaming Wounds illuminating the whole circle of the astonished earth, and thou wilt return from the valley of Josaphat with a family of other sons, that can be counted only by millions of millions, to be thine eternal possession in heaven, won for thee by the dread mysteries of this great Friday.

As we have said before, it belonged to the perfection of Mary's heart, that one ingredient of her sorrow did not absorb or neutralise another. She felt each of them as completely as if it were simply the whole sorrow. It possessed her, with an undistracted possession. Each feature was as if it were the entire countenance, the full face of each dolour, and it looked into her heart as if it, and it alone, expressed the fulness of the mystery. Thus her terror did not kill any other of the afflicting circumstances of this fourth dolour. As it did not perturb her peace, so neither did it confuse her feelings, or blunt her susceptibilities. This is always one of the peculiarities of Mary's griefs, which puts them beyond the reach of parallels. Thus it was an additional sorrow to her on the present occasion that, except St. John, the apostles were not following their Master to His end. The graces of each one of them came upon her mind. She revolved the peculiarities of the vocation of each, and all the minute tenderness and generous forbearance on the part of Jesus to which it testified. She saw the words of eternal wisdom pouring for those three years into their souls, in the communication of the sublimest truths, in the pathetic kindness of affectionate admonitions. She saw how omnipotence had placed itself in their hands in the gift of miracles. They, like her, only for fewer years, had fed upon the beautiful grace of Jesus. They knew the marvellous expressions of His venerable face. The tones of His voice were familiar to them. The touch of His hands, the look of His eye, the very significance of His loving silence, all was known to them. They had been drawn within the ring of its attractions. It had been to them a new birth, a new life, an anticipated heaven. To use our Lord's phrase, they had gone into their mother's womb again, and had been born anew of Mary, brothers of Jesus, resemblances of Jesus. She knew that next to the dignity of being the Mother of God, the world could have no vocation so high as that of being apostles of the Word, unless it were that of being His Foster-Father, or His Precursor. Eternal Wisdom had come to earth, and of all its millions He was to choose but twelve, who should know His secrets, who should reflect Him, perpetuate Him, hold His powers in vessels of flesh, and accomplish the work He had begun. They were more than angels; for no angels ever bore such messages to mankind, except the secret annunciation of Gabriel to the divine Mother.. They were kings as none ever were before; for they were not only to conquer the entire earth, but their thrones of judgment are set up round His in heaven. No blood of martyrs was more precious in their Master's sight than theirs. No doctors have ever attained to their science. No virgins have equalled their purity, whether it were the purity of innocence or the purity of penance. No confessors have ever confessed as much, or confessed it more bravely. No Bishops have used the keys more liberally, more discreetly, more blamelessly than they. No sovereign pontiff will let himself be called by Peter's name, because none else has worn the world's tiara so gloriously or so meekly as he. And these other Christs, gleaming with gifts, enriched with graces, the wide world's special souls, the new paradise which God had planted,—where were they now? Peter was in his lurking-place on Mount Sion, weeping bitterly over his fall. He went to Calvary only in his Master's Heart, and in Mary's. His love was not like hers. He could not bear to see the sufferings of Him, whom he loved far more than the others loved Him. The very penitent shame of his fall made him less able to bear so great a sorrow. The rest were hidden. They had fled from Gethsemane, and were dispersed, the prey of grief, uncertainty, and pity, the strength of love dubiously contending with the timidities of despair. They have left Jesus to tread the winepress alone. When He is risen, He will meet them with the old love, with more than the old love, and they will hear no word of reproach from His sweet voice, and they will see no look of reproach in the deserted Mother's eye. Only John is there, drawn by his Saviour's love of him, rather than urged by his own love of Jesus.*

The absence of the apostles was a keen aggravation of Mary's sorrow. It was a triple wound to her. It wounded her in her love of Jesus. She knew how deep the wound was which it made in His Sacred Heart. She saw how, far beyond the cruel scourging and the barbarous coronation, her Beloved was tormented by this cruel abandonment of

* On the question whether S. Peter or S. John loved our Lord most, Palafox (Excelleneias di San Pedro, lib. iii. cap. 39) says, Que San Pedro fuesse mas amante que San Juan, es tan llano que toca poco menos que en la Fe. Alexander Hales says our Lord loved S. Peter more than S. John, because as God He necessarily (in a sense) loved most those who loved Him most. S. Thomas says S. Peter loved our Lord most in His members, whereas S. John loved Him most in Himself. See Barradas in Evangelia, tom. v. lib. ii. cap. 12; Maldonatus in Joann. xxi.; also Newman, Discourses to Mixed Congregations, p. 78. Cardinal Bérulle however (Elévations sur Ste Marie Madeleine, cap. vi. 3) speaks of the two apostles as le mieux aimant et le mieux aimé. Some have said our Lord loved St. John most with His *human* will, but this is untenable. Others have said that He showed more outward signs of love to St. John. The words, Simon, son of John, lovest thou Me more than these? seem decisive of the question, while the expression, The disciple whom Jesus loved, implies no comparison whatever. But see Sylveira in Evangelia, lib. ix. cap. 8, which is in fact a beautiful treatise on the wonderful excellences and prerogatives of the great Evangelist.

Him by those whom He had loved beyond the rest of men. She could go near to fathoming the anguish which this was causing Him. Moreover, her own love of Him underwent a cruel martyrdom in seeing Him thus deserted, and by those whose very office should have taken them to Calvary, who should have been witnesses of His Crucifixion as well as of His Resurrection. There was something unexpected in it, although it was foreknown. So it always is with ingratitude. It is a knife with so sharp an edge, that we cannot help but start when it cuts us, however long and bitterly it has been anticipated. We excuse much to men who think, even though it be mistakenly, that they have been the victims of ingratitude; and thus we acknowledge the agony of the smart. But it wounded her also in herself. Her own love of the apostles made her value their love of her. It was true love, it was intense love. She knew it. Then why was John only with her in that encounter with her cross-laden Son, in that melancholy pilgrimage to Calvary? A broken heart like hers could spare no love, which rightly belonged to it; and when the love of Jesus towards her was working bitterness in her soul rather than consolation, she could the less afford to do without such love as would simply be a joy, a rest, a consolation. But she must not expect it. It is her place to console, not to be consoled. Her Son came to minister, not to be ministered to. She must participate in the same sublime office. She must empty her own heart of consolation, and pour it all out upon the rest, keeping for herself, what is not only specially her own, but what none else are able to receive, the untold weight of her exceeding sorrow. It would have been somewhat easier to have gone up to Calvary with the apostles round her. And yet for their sakes she was content to have John alone, content the others should be spared what it would so overwhelm them to behold. But their absence inflicted yet a third wound upon her heart, in the love which she herself bore to the apostles. Their weakness was a cruel sorrow to her love, and yet it strove with the sorrow that they should be suffering so much as that very weakness implied. She grieved also, because one day it would so grieve them that they had not been with Jesus to the last. She mourned likewise, because they lost so much in after thought by not having witnessed those appalling mysteries. There was not a varying sorrow in the heart of any one of them which she did not take into her own. For they had come to her in the place of Joseph, and she poured out on them the love she had poured out on him. He had been with her in her three first dolours; why were they absent from her fourth? And a gush of marvellous unavailing love to her departed spouse broke from the fountains of her heart, as she asked herself the question. O how wonderful are the ingenuities of suffering which love causes in the heart!

But Judas was almost a dolour by himself. We learn from the revelations of the saints, how she had striven in prayer for that wretched soul. She had lavished all manner of kindness on him, as if he had been more to her than either Peter or John. She had watched with unspeakable horror the gradual steps by which He had been led on to the consummation of his treachery. She had seen how sensitively the Heart of Jesus shrank from this cruel sin, and how many scourgings would have gone to make up the sum of pain which the traitor's single kiss had burned in upon His blessed lips. For a while it appeared as if Judas had been even more to her than Jesus, so had she occupied herself at that awful season to rescue the falling apostle, and to hinder that tremendous sin. Moreover, none could know so truly as herself the immensity of that sin, and the whole region of God's fair glory which it desolated. She saw it in the Heart of Jesus. It was as if she had been an eye-witness of the fall of Lucifer, from the heights of heaven to the inconceivable lowness of that abyss which is now his miserable and accursed home. Terrible as was the thought that an apostle could betray her Son, it seemed even yet more injurious to His honour that, although Judas should have stained himself with so black a crime, he should yet despair of mercy and doubt the infinity of his Master's love. She had lost a soul. She had lost one of her little company. Jesus was not the first son she was to lose. That grand apostolic soul, decked with gifts like a whole angelic kingdom, crowned with the splendours of earth's most beautiful vocation, canonised by the especial choice and outpoured love of Jesus, was gone, gone down in the most frightful hopeless wreck. Even Mary had some things to learn. This was her first lesson in the loss of souls. If we were more like saints, we should know something of what it meant. The Passion began by losing an apostle's soul, and ended by saving the soul of a poor outcast thief. Such are the ways in which God takes His compensations.

But we have to add physical horrors now to the agonies of mind and heart. They begin in this dolour, and are among its most marked peculiarities. There are few persons who have ever read a book on the Passion, from which they would not wish something to be left out. This is not from the weakness of their faith, but from the fastidiousness of a natural taste, which has not yet been fully refined by the supernatural love, whose one object St. Paul so significantly divides into two, Jesus Christ *and* Him Crucified. Truly penitent love would not shrink from the contemplation of those dread realities which the Son of God condescended to undergo for us, and into the horrors of which our own sins drove Him. When adoration cannot swallow up sentimentality, or invest it with a new character, it is a sign that we are wanting in a true sense of sin as well as a true love of our Blessed Lord. It is not well with a soul when it averts its inward eye from the Crucifixion, and fixes it on the secret mental agony of Gethsemane, because the three hours of the one are free from the frightful atrocities of the three hours of the other. Reverence will not allow us to deal thus either with our Saviour's Passion or with our Lady's dolours. Her broken heart was surfeited with physical horrors. It was part of her sanctification. She pressed her way through them all that day, steeling her shrinking nature. She would not have missed one of them for all the world.

It was a dreadful thing for a mother to walk the streets over her own son's blood. It was fearful to have her own feet reddened by the precious Blood, and the loss of Judas fresh in her afflicted soul. She saw the crimson track which Jesus had left behind. The multitude was mixing it up with the mud, which it tinged with a dull hue. It was on their shoes, and upon their garments. It went up the steps of their doorways. It splashed up the legs of the centurion's horse. No one cared for it. No heart was touched. None suspected the heavenly mystery at which angels were gazing in silent stupor. Mary too must tread upon it. It was sorrow almost literally trampling its own heart under foot. She must tread on that which she was worshipping. That which coloured the street mud, which blotched the paving stones, which clung half wet and half dry to the garments of the multitude, was hypostatically united to the Godhead. It merited the plenitude of divine worship. Mary was adoring it at every step. There was not a spot tinged with that dull red, not a garment laid by that night in a clothes-press with those spots upon it, over which crowds of angels were not stooping, and would remain to guard it till the moment of the Resurrection. Surely this is unutterable woe, over which the heart should spread itself in silence only.

In this dolour also we must notice particularly what has been observed before, the union in Mary of horror of sin with intense anguish because of the misfortune of sinners. She saw some, who were handling our Lord or shouting after Him, in completest ignorance, without so much as a suspicion of the dreadful work in which they were engaged. They were obdurate sinners hardened by ungodliness, who sinned almost as they would breathe the air or move their limbs. All ignorance of God was pain to her, now especially that souls were beginning to belong to her. But the ignorance of a seared conscience was a grief too deep for tears, a phenomenon she would have longed should not exist upon the face of God's weary earth. How dark it was, how hopeless! Even now Eternal Truth was looking it in the face, and alas! only blinding it! Then there were others whose malice was more intelligent, who were consciously satisfying some evil passion, hatred of purity perhaps, or the spite of untruthfulness against truth, or the envy which meekness always excites when it is very heavenly and heroic, or political vengeance, or the long-treasured anger against one who had reproved them, or the mere love of cruelty, and the excitement of human fury which the smell of blood causes in men as in beasts. All this she saw. She trembled at the horror of the vision. She was heart-stricken by the thought of Him, the gentle blameless One, against whom all this was concentrated. She was pierced also by the sharpest anguish from the love of the very sinners themselves. She would not have called fire down from heaven, as James and John were fain to do upon the Samaritan village. She craved not for judgments. She would have deprecated with all the might of her holiest impetrations the advent of a destroying angel. She must have those souls. She has lost Judas. She claims consolation. Into those dark minds the light of faith shall be poured. Over those blood-stained souls more Blood, more of the same Blood shall flow, but it shall be in gentlest fertilising absolutions. On those blaspheming tongues the Blessed Sacrament shall lie. She will travail in pain with them till they are born again in Christ. So she too goes up to Calvary with a work to do. Look well at her heart! She will accomplish it. There are few things the sanctity of human sorrow cannot do. God seems to treat it as a power almost coequal with Himself. But here in our Blessed Mother, what sanctity! what sorrow!

Then, as if the very contrast had called it forth, there rose up before her the most vivid vision of the beautiful Infancy. It was true that from the very first her life had been dismantled by an enduring sorrow. Nevertheless how peaceful and how sweet seemed the old days at Nazareth, and even the cool evening airs on the brink of the distant Nile, compared with the violence and noise, and bloodshed of this tearful Passion. Then, when her arms were round

P

Him, she had pressed at once her sorrow and her love to her bosom. She had held quiet colloquies with Him. He belonged only to her, for Joseph was most truly a second self. Now she had given Him away, not in thought only, not in the tranquillity of an heroic intention, but in reality. He was not only in the hands of others, but He was taken from hers. Any one could come near Him, except herself. She alone had lost her rights. Every action of the Holy Childhood came before her and found its bitter contrast in the scene that was then enacting in the streets of Jerusalem. She thought how she had washed Him, clothed Him, given Him food, nursed Him to sleep, and knelt down and worshipped Him when He was asleep, though she knew well He could see her even then. Every one of those things found their opposites with dreadful accuracy in the Way of the Cross. Earth, and blood, and shameful spittings defiled His face, and hands, and feet. His hair, from which handfuls had been pulled, was clotted, entangled, and deranged. His tunic clung painfully to the half-congealed blood of His wounds. Alas! for those baths of His childhood, and the reverent ministries of His loving Mother! We shall come to them again in the sixth dolour, and then how changed the circumstances! They have once torn His garments from the wounds, and made them bleed afresh. They will do so again at the top of Calvary. It was not thus she had undressed Him in the quiet sanctuary of Nazareth. He had had no food but the sins of men, and a very feast of ignominy, since the evening before. He was worn with want of sleep, but will never sleep again now. She thought of tears which ran silently down His cheeks in the days of His Childhood. Why should they not have redeemed the world, and washed all sin away, seeing their worth was infinite? O how busy memory was in that hour with its comparisons and its contrasts, and there was not one which did not heighten the misery of the present. Could she be a mere mortal to go up to Calvary with a will nestling so tranquilly alongside of the will of God, with a heart broken to pieces, yet out of whose rents not one breath of her peacefulness had been allowed to escape? Yes! she was mortal, but she was also the Mother of the Eternal, and loving hearts alone know how those two things contradict each other, and yet are true together.

Such was the fourth dolour. Let us now examine the dispositions in which she endured it. First of all, there was the unretracted generosity of the oblation she had made. Amid the multitude of thoughts, which in all her sorrows passed through her mind, her will lay still. So completely was she clothed in holiness from head to foot, that it never so much as occurred to her to think that the load might be lightened, or the pangs mitigated, or the circumstances be more tolerably disposed. When we have committed ourselves to God, we have committed ourselves to more than we know. John had not reckoned on the long years of weary waiting in the exile of life, when he said he could drink his Master's cup. So is it with all of us. We find that what God really exacts from us is more than we seemed to be promising. The more He loves us, the more exacting does He become. He treats us as if we were more royal-hearted than we are, and by His grace He makes us so. Our Lady knew more of the length and breadth, and depth of her oblation than any one else had ever done. It was this which made her lifelong sorrow so much more real and intense than the mere foresight of a prophet or a saint. Nevertheless even she probably, though she knew all, did not realise all. Probably she could not compress into a vision, no matter how piercingly clear, that slow pressure which the lapse of time lays upon a sorrowing heart. Thus in its totality, in the disposition of its circumstances, in the combination of its peculiarities, in their united pressure, and in the long years of their endurance, as well as the actual impressions of the senses, her sorrow was not more than she meant to promise, because she meant to promise all, she meant herself to be a holocaust, a *whole* burnt offering to the Lord, but it might be more than she realised at the moment that she promised. She was a creature. We need to be reminded of that, because the magnificence of her sanctity so often makes us almost forget it. St. Denys said he should hardly have known her to be a mere creature, if he had not been told.

Now this consideration renders still more wonderful the unretracted generosity of her offering. If she was not taken by surprise in any of her sufferings, she felt new things coming upon her. She was sinking into depths deeper than had been revealed to her. The actual horror of the present shut out some of the light, which had lighted her down the abysses, when she had explored them in mental anguish only. Yet she went on in tranquillity. God was welcome to it all, welcome to more if His omnipotence should see fit to anneal her heart to bear a stronger heat. She had cried out once. It was an awful moment. It was in the great temple of the nation, before the doctors of her people. But her Creator Himself had wrung it from her, partly because He yearned to load her with another world of graces, and partly because He loved to hear it, seeing that it worshipped Him so wonderfully. Job sanctified himself by the patience of his complaining. Low as we are, how imitable the virtue of Job seems by the side of Mary's generous endurance! Even great saints have begun to sink, when called, like Peter, to walk upon the waters. As to ourselves, even in our little sorrows, how hard it is to keep to God, and not to turn aside, and lie down, and rest our heads on the lap of creatures, and bid them whisper consolations in our ear, as a respite to us for a while from the oppression of God's vicinity! What does our perseverance look like at best but a running fight between grace and time, the one to win which chances, for it seems a chance, to have struck the last blow when the death-bell sounds? But are not those saints the most indulgent to others, who have been the most austere to themselves? Is it not ever the unmortified, who are the critical? Do not they always stoop lowest, who have to stoop from the greatest heights? So will Mary be all the better mother for us in the dust in which we creep, frightened, shrinking, and despairing, because of the sublimities of that generosity of hers which is always above the clouds, always with the eternal sunshine on its brow.

We must observe also the firm hand which our Blessed Lady kept upon her grief. Amid the jostling of the crowd, she seemed as if she were impassible. There was not a gesture or a movement which betrayed the slightest interior emotion. When they repulsed her from Jesus, and barbarously interposed between the embrace of the Mother and the Son, there was no impatience in her manner, no resentment on her countenance, no expostulation on her lips. She possessed her soul perfectly. The movements of the Blessed in the visible presence of God in heaven could not be more regulated than were hers. St. Ambrose has dwelt at length upon this excellence of hers. Yet we must not conceive of our Blessed Mother, as of a coldly graceful statue, never descending from her pedestal because she was heavenly marble, and not flesh and blood. Statues have not broken hearts. This calm imperturbability of her demeanour arose from the sublimity of her holiness, which itself arose in no slight degree from the intensity of her sorrow. The excesses of her suffering were commuted into excesses of tranquillity, which looked superhuman only because what is completely and perfectly and exclusively human is seen nowhere but in her. This is the picture we must always draw of our Blessed Lady. She is woman, true woman, but not mere woman. We shall sadly degrade her in our own minds, if for the sake of facility or effect we venture to exaggerate the feminine element beyond what we find it in the Gospels. It is easy to distort the image of Jesus. When men speak of His compassion to sinners, they often throw a sentimentality over the narrative, which is far removed from the calm gentleness of Scripture. They think they bring Him nearer to us by making Him as like ourselves as doctrine will allow them, and all the while they are excavating an impassable gulf between Him and us, and casting Him leagues and leagues away from us. Unfortunately this lowering process is yet more easy with Mary, for she has no divinity to save her in the long run. A merely feminine Mary is not the Mary of the Bible. Neither again is she a simple shadow of our Lord, or her mysteries a repetition of His. If we endeavour to establish any parity, even a proportionate one, between her and our Lord, we only meddle with Him without really elevating her. She had not two Natures; her Person was not divine; she was not the Redeemer of the world; she was not clothed in our sins; the anger of the Father never directly rested upon her; her innocence was not His sinlessness; Her Compassion was not His Passion; her Assumption was not His Ascension. She stands by herself. She has her own meaning, her appropriate significancy. She is a distinct vastness in God's creation. She is without a parallel. Jesus is not a parallel to her, nor she to Him. She fills up the room of a huge world in the universe of God, but the room she fills is not the room of the Sacred Humanity of Jesus, nor even like to it. She is Mary. She is the Mother of God. She is herself. Near to God yet every whit a creature, sinless yet wholly human, human in person, and not divine,—in nature human only, and not divine also. They who represent her as a pale shadowy counterpart of our Blessed Lord, changing the sex and lowering the realities, miss the real grandeur of Mary as much as they miss the peculiar magnificence of the Incarnation. Thus it comes to pass that, if in order to paint her sorrows in more striking colours, we exaggerate what is feminine about her, we obtain the same result with those who insist in finding in her all manner of unequal equalities with her Son, namely, an unworthy view of her as well as an untrue one. She is more like the invisible God than like the Incarnate God. She is more accurately to be paralleled with what is purely divine, than with what is human and divine together. She is a creature clothed with the eternal sun, as St. John saw her in the Apocalypse, the most perfect created transcript of the Creator. As the Hypostatic Union links

Creator and creature literally together, so Mary, the divinely perfect, pure creature, is the neck which joins on the whole body of creatures to their Divine Incarnate Head. She has her own place in the system of creation, and her own meaning. She is like no one. No one is like her. What she is most like is the Incomprehensible Creator. Thus of the three elements, into which the idea of Mary resolves itself in our minds, the feminine element, the element of the Hypostatic Union, and the divine element, it is this last which seems to control the rest, while all three are so inextricably commingled that we can detach none of them without injury to truth.

We must also not omit to mention here the union of Mary's sorrows with our Lord's. We have spoken of it before, but a new and very significant feature in this disposition of hers comes to view in the fourth dolour. There is such a gracious unity vouchsafed to us between our Blessed Lord and ourselves, between the Redeemer and the Redeemed, that we may, not in mere imagination or as an intellectual process of faith, unite our sufferings to His, and so make them meritorious of eternal life. It is chiefly the more excellent attainment of this union which distinguishes the saints from ourselves. Theologians have said that the great difference between the service of the Blessed in heaven and the service of the elect on earth is, that on earth the soul unites itself to God by the exercise of a variety of virtues, whereas in heaven Jesus Christ is the one virtue of the Blessed, the link which joins them to the Father. Some saints have been allowed in a certain measure, and by a very peculiar gift, to anticipate on earth this heavenly particularity, and to be clothed in an unusual way with the very spirit of Jesus. Cardinal de Berulle was even said to have the gift of communicating this spirit in a subordinate degree to the souls which he directed. Of course no saint, nor all the saints put together, ever possessed the spirit of Jesus so nearly to identity, as His Blessed Mother. Hence in all her dolours she suffered in the most unspeakable union with

Him. But in this one the invisible realities of the spiritual life seem to come up to the surface, and pass into outward facts, into the actualities of external sensible life. Her sorrows and His became almost indistinguishably one, in fact as well as feeling, in reality as well as faith, in endurance as well as love. It was His suffering which made her suffer. The way in which He suffered she suffered. His dispositions were her dispositions. Nay, it was rather in Him than in herself that she suffered. His very sufferings were her very sufferings. It was only as His that they were hers. And her sufferings made Him suffer; they were His worst sufferings. He suffered in her, as she in Him. They were exchanging hearts, or living in each other's hearts, all the while in that journey to Calvary. She seemed to have put off her personality, and to have become to Jesus a second multiplied capacity of suffering. Never was union more complete; never were the inner mystical life of the soul and the outward present life of tangible facts so identical before. We have no terms to express the union, which would not at the same time confound the Mother in the Son, and so be undoctrinal, unfaithful, and untrue.

In speaking of the peculiarities of this dolour, we have already seen how horror at the sight and sound of sin was united in our Lady's soul with the most inexpressible tenderness for sinners. But in our meditations we must remember to assign it its proper place among her dispositions. It has only been for the convenience of meditation that we have throughout treated separately two things which in reality are never disunited, the peculiarities of each dolour, and our Lady's dispositions under it. They both grow on the same stalk, and are often the same blossoms with different names.

There was yet another disposition of our Blessed Mother in this dolour, which was an effect of her eminent sanctity. In the breadth of the sorrow which lay heavily upon her, filled in, as we might have supposed it would have been, with a multitude of figures, she saw nothing, in the point of her soul, but God only. In that light all secondary causes vanished. They were submerged in her single view of the First Cause. There was no Pilate, no Herod, no Annas, no Caiphas; but only God, with His irresistibly sweet will streaming out of Him, and filling up every nook and corner where else perhaps some hungry agency might have been visible. If the secondary causes were there at all, they were far in the background, with the soft golden haze of God's merciful intentions upon them, or else behind the mist which His light and heat always raise when they beat full upon the earth. It is this grand singleness of vision, after which the saints are perpetually striving, and to which they hardly attain, even amid the many wonders of their holiness, at the end of a long life of ascetic straining and supernatural trial. It was a grace which Mary started with, and had always exercised; and in this fourth dolour it underwent a special trial, because the sorrow had so much more of an external life, and was produced by such a far greater crowd of outward agents and circumstances, than any of her others had been. If all exercises of all virtues were heroic in her, there were many times in which they went beyond heroic, and were godlike. So now, in this single vision of God only, there was a shadow of His blessed and eternal occupation with Himself, which belongs to Him who can have no end but His own adorable Self. What wonder so much sweetness, so much gentleness, so much patience, so much conformity, so much tender love of sinners, so much inexplicable outpouring of love upon Jesus, came from a grace which had its root so deep down and so high up in the mountain of God Himself!

This fourth dolour gives us also many lessons for ourselves. All the dolours have led us through strange realities; for it is the way of sorrow, above all other things in human life, even more than love, to make the things which lie around it peculiarly solid. But in this dolour our realities grow more real. They gain a new reality, from being integral parts of that last tremendous drama in which the salvation of the world was accomplished at an incalculable cost of pain, and shame, and agony. The three fountains of the Sacred Humanity were drawn dry by the exactions of most merciful justice for the sins of men. In His Body the abyss of pain was emptied, in His Mind all the possibilities of shame, in His Soul the depths of intellectual and moral agony. We have seen Mary's sufferings almost pass into His, and His revert to her. Have we no participation in this reality? Yes! one out of which the hot springs of devotion ought to be flowing always. We ourselves were part of our Mother's dolours, because we were an actual part of our Saviour's Passion. Thus they cease to be mere matters of history to us. They are not simple devotions, which attract us because they are so touching. They are not only a beautiful scriptural pathos, enhancing at every turn the lovely mysteries of the Incarnation, and clothing with fresh interest that which already kindles our faith and fascinates our love. We ourselves are part of them. We made ourselves felt in them. We were agents then, not simply spectators now. There is guilt attaching to us; and the sorrow which comes of guilt and shame is another thing from that which comes of gratuitous pity or affectionate compassion. It tells differently on our intercourse with our Blessed Mother. It changes our position. It makes our devotion part of our penance, instead of a free sentiment of our own religious choice or pious fancy. There are some devotions into which taste may lead us while we worship; but this is one in which justice is concerned, and into which duties flow. Forgiven love knows what it has to do. The dear Magdalen stands up for ever in the Church to tell us that we must love much, to whom much has been forgiven. We were cruel to our Mother, and when we had wounded her, and the weapon was yet in our hands, she pressed us to her bosom. Unmelted, we wreaked wrong after wrong upon her and she paid us back love, fresh love, always love, for every unkindly wrong. Seven times we went into her heart to hurt her. Seven times we took part in her chief mysteries of grief. Seven times we turned against her when she was loving us as never mother loved before. But seventy-times-seven would not nearly express the sum of graces which she has obtained for our barren and thankless souls. Ah! if we have been realities to her in those days of her dolours, is it not the least we can do, to let her dolours now be realities to us?

Every morning of life we begin anew. We go forth from our doors to encounter a new day on its passage to eternity. It has much to say to us, and we to it; and it carries its tale to God at sunset, and its word is believed, and its message remembered till the doom. Would it not be an unproductive day, in which we did not meet our Lord? For is not that the very meaning of our lives? If the day is meant for the sun to shine, it is but half a day, or rather it is night, if only the material sun shall shine, and the Sun of Justice also rise not on us with health upon His wings. We go out to meet Jesus in every action of the day; but we require this fourth dolour to admonish us that we must rarely expect to meet Him, except with the Cross, and that a new one. When we are in sorrow, He Himself "draws near and goes with" us, as He did with the disciples on the road to Emmaus. That is the privilege of sorrow. It is an attraction to our dearest Lord which He can seldom resist. Provided we seek not other comfort, He is sure to draw near and comfort us Himself. Oh! if unwary souls did but know the graces which they miss by telling their griefs and letting their fellow-creatures console them, how saints would multiply in the Church of God! We read the lives of holy persons, and wonder how ever they can have attained to such a pitch of union with God, little suspecting all the while that we have had sorrow enough to carry us further still than that, only we would not wait for Jesus; and if we will not let Him have the first word, He may perchance send His angels to fulfil our consolation, but He will not come Himself. But when we take the initiative, when we ourselves go out to meet Him, and we do so by our promises in prayer, by our open profession of piety, by our ecclesiastical vocation, by our religious profession, by the works of mercy to which we have now by usage committed ourselves, then it is always with the Cross that we encounter Him. Why then are we so amazed when crosses come? When it has happened thus so often, do we not see that it is a law, a law of the kingdom of grace, and that not to perceive it is to lose half its blessing by missing the promptitude of obedience? We lay ourselves in the arms of our Heavenly Father, knowing not what is to come, only that much is to come, more than without Him we could by possibility bear; let us lie still now that we are there, and not be surprised into retracting the offering we once have made. What cross we shall meet to-day, we know not: sometimes we cannot guess. But we know that, if we meet Jesus, we shall meet a cross, and evening will find us with the burden on our backs. Only let us remember this invariable peculiarity of these divine encounters, and then, if we are reverently wary in making promises, we shall also be reverently firm in keeping our resolutions.

Some men meet Him, and turn away. Some see Him far off, and turn down another road. Some come close up, and leap down the precipice at the side, as if He were a destroying angel blocking up the way. Some pass by, pretending they do not know Him. He has been walking cross-laden in thousands of earth's roads to-day; but He has had few honest greetings. Faith and love have made some men too timid, to pass Him or avoid Him, but they have expostulated with Him about the Cross, and have wept out loud when He persisted. Some follow in the sullenness of servile obedience, and drag their cross, and it jolts upon the stones, and hurts them all the more, and they fall, but their falls are not in union with those of His upon the old Way of the Cross. Few kneel down with the alacrity of a glad surprise, and kiss His feet, and take the Cross off His back, and shoulder it almost playfully, and walk by His side, singing psalms with Him, and smiling when they totter beneath the load. But oh! the beauty of that day's sunset to such as these! They "constrain Him, saying, Stay with us, because it is towards evening, and the day is now far spent. And He goes in with them." This is what we should do. Can we do it? No! but we can try, and then He will do it in us. But He *meets* us with the Cross. This implies much. It implies that we must turn back from our own road, and that all the way we went till we met Him was but waste of strength and fruitless travelling. We can only carry our crosses one way, and that is, heavenward. They keep our faces in that direction. They push us up hill; down hill they would prostrate us, and fall heavily upon us, and kill us. All the faces of cross-carriers are turned one way. The end, which is meant to go into the earth, points to the earth: the cross of the cross looks over our shoulders into heaven, and rights itself there, however unsteady we may be, like the needle always trembling in reverent fidelity towards the pole. So let us not miss our opportunity, but take up our cross at once, and turn round, and follow Him: for so only shall we fall into the Procession of the Predestinate.

But this dolour tells us more still. It teaches us that long rest is the ground in front of great crosses. Unusual crosses follow unusual quiet. The greater the peace now, the greater the cross presently. This is one of those lessons which every one knows, and no one remembers. Out of three-and-thirty years twenty-one ran out between the last dolour and the Passion. How often does the same thing happen to ourselves! Partly it is that God gives us a breathing-time that we may make the most of our past graces, and so gain new strength, and collect ourselves for higher achievements. Partly it is that the past graces, in which lie prophecies and preparations of graces yet to come, require time to develop themselves, and become established in the soul. Partly also the cross comes at the end of these quiet times in order to consolidate their graces, to acquire a permanent possession of them for the soul, and to crown them with the cross, which is the only reward on this side the grave. A grace uncompressed, unfixed, unmatured by sorrow, seems hardly yet our own, but a transitory thing which may or may not be realised. At best it is but income, and not capital. The refinement of sorrow is the last process of grace. After that, it becomes glory by the mere keeping. He, who forgets that the cross is coming, wastes his quiet. He misses the ends for which the calm was sent him, and renders himself less able to bear the cross when it comes, than he would have been if he had prepared for it. It is in these long seasons of quiet that most of those serious mistakes in the spiritual life are made, which have consequences almost irreparable. Sometimes we think we have attained the level of our intended grace, and therefore we persist in keeping upon it in spite of inspirations to higher things, resisting these as if they were temptations to evil, not attractions to good. We may thus mar the whole scheme of our sanctification. Sometimes we imagine our tranquillity to arise from dulness, weariness, and want of fervour. We overlook the operations of grace which are going on in our souls beneath the surface of the apparent calm, and extricate ourselves by a fatal effort from the groove in which we were intended to run, and adopt a spiritual life after a type and fashion of our own. It is less unsafe to be without spiritual direction in times of growth and trouble and change, than in these long seasons of comparatively untempted peace. There could be no lukewarmness, or self-trust, no falling back, no idle loitering, if only we remembered that the seeming quiet was merely the hush before the coming of a greater cross. It would then be to us at once a period of rest in God, and yet of ardent, tremulous, active preparation for a new and different manifestation of Him, which we know will break upon us like a storm, and be a serious trial of our worth.

This dolour also prepares us for another trial, which is by no means infrequent in the experience of the cross. We never seem to need our Blessed Lord's consoling presence and kind words more than when He has just loaded us with another cross. Nature groans under the burden, and becomes faint. If at the same moment our supernatural life becomes a cross to us also, how shall we bear it? Yet there are few of us who have not experienced this collision of an outward with an inward cross. We meet Jesus. He gives us our new cross without a word; even, so it seems, without a blessing. Often the expression of His Face says nothing. We are like servants with a master. We have simply to do His will, without any further directions than a sign. No confidence is imparted to us. No cheerful words of encouragement are uttered. There is no token that He is pleased or displeased with us, no token that we are doing Him a service in accepting this new cross, no token that He is other than indifferent whether we carry it or not. We have simply the material obedience to perform. He could not treat us otherwise, if we were mere machines. Then, when this cold dry ceremony of imposing the new cross upon us is performed, sometimes He walks by our sides without looking at us or speaking a single word, as if we were slaves carrying His burden for Him, and beneath His notice. Either He is occupied with His own thoughts, or He considers that anything like communicativeness will inflate us, and make us forget ourselves. But sometimes the trial is worse than this. He makes over His load to us, and then, like an unburdened man, walks on lightly with a quicker step than we can follow, laden as we are. We cannot keep up with Him. We do not know if He meant us to try to do so. Perhaps He intended us to fall behind, into our proper place as inferiors. Perhaps He would consider it a liberty if we endeavoured to overtake Him. On the other hand He may think us wanting both in diligence and respect, if we lag too far behind. Then He goes out of sight, and has not told us which road to take; and we come to a cross-road, and are in perplexity. Moreover, like a practised superior, He does all this so naturally, and with so much apparent unconcern, that we cannot divine whether it is meant to try us, or whether it is indifference, displeasure, or disdain. It comes at the very moment too when He has given us more work to do, and heavier weights to carry. Thus Mary met

Him; the meeting was in silence; He passed on out of sight; they met again on Calvary. There is not a step in this journey, which we have not sometimes to take. It is a peculiar trial, for which there is no possible preparation but love. The more we love Jesus, the more confidence shall we feel in His love of us; and while our humility will not be surprised by any show of indifference, when something far worse than that is merited by our vileness, our love will enable us to go on with a quiet suffering cheerfulness, convinced that the love of His Heart and the look of His Face are telling different tales.

We must also be prepared to find that one cross leads to another, and little crosses to great ones. For the most part crosses do not come single. They meet each other in our souls, as if it were at a given moment and on some previous understanding. Sometimes, especially after seasons of long tranquillity and the apparent inaction of grace, we suddenly pass into a region of crosses, just as the earth traverses a region of shooting stars at certain periods of the year. Then crosses follow each other in rapid succession, now one at a time, now two together, now two or three at once, so that we can hardly stand upright. Sometimes there is a storm of crosses driving right in our faces like vehement slanting hail, pelting so pitilessly that we can hardly make any way at all, or at least we have all the miserable feeling of making none. Sometimes they come upon us from behind, and if we are walking carelessly, we stumble and fall; and alas! who does not know that a fall with a cross on our shoulders, though it seems so much more pardonable, always hurts us far more grievously than a fall without one? It is the cruellest law of the spiritual life.

Some men have one lifelong cross to carry, and other crosses do not appear to be added to it. But even then it is much the same as if there were new crosses; for the burden is not equable. Sometimes the road is rougher; sometimes the day is hotter; sometimes we are ourselves unwell, and timorous, and weak; sometimes also the cross, by a sort of miracle, causelessly, so far as we can judge, grows far heavier, and galls us as it never did before, and, the reason being hidden, the remedy is hidden also. This lifelong cross, even when most equable, and unaccompanied by other crosses, is the hardest of all trials to bear. There is so much mutability in our nature, that even a change of punishment from sharp to sharper is in effect a relaxation. The satisfaction of the change is a greater good to our humanity than the increased severity of the pain is an evil. The dreadful thing to nature is to be tied down to a persevering uniformity. It is in this that the secret heroism of vows resides. Who has not felt relief in illness, when the pain has changed from one limb to another? So is it, and still more, with the sufferings of the soul. He, who carries one cross, for years, and carries it to his grave, must either be one of God's hidden saints, or must lie in low attainments as near to lukewarmness as is compatible with the salvation of his soul.

But sometimes the one lifelong cross remains always upon our shoulders, only as the abiding foundation of a very edifice of crosses, which God is for ever building up, and pulling down, and building up again, upon the old enduring cross, without ever shifting that. There are some souls God seems always to be experimenting upon, and only experimenting, and experimenting to the last; but it is real work. This unites the two sufferings of monotony and change together. All the epochs of life are variously represented by the transitory heaps of crosses, while the abiding cross is the deep undertone of the whole of life. Such men walk the world not merely as memorials to be wondered at, but as living fountains of devotion to all who see them. They are men of power; for it is to the secret intercessions of such souls that all spiritual renewals on the earth are owing. Not unfrequently they carry for a while the whole Church upon the top of their cross. They are monuments of God's love; for in them we see in fullest revelation the grand truth, which is true also in its measure of the very lowest of ourselves, that the cross is never only a chastisement, but always a reward as well, and the plentifulness of God's love to each created soul is measured by the abundance of its crosses.

There is one more lesson yet to be learned from this dolour. Jesus and Mary were both going one way; could it be any other way than the road to heaven? Yet the road they were travelling led over Calvary. Hence we infer that no one's face is towards heaven, when it is not towards Calvary. In life, whether we know it or not, we are always travelling to a sorrow. At the next turn of the road stands an unforeseen death of some one whom we love, or the breaking up of a circle in which it seems as if our very existence were bound up, or some disgrace which we never reckoned on. We look on to something next summer, and it is a joy to us to think of the good and happy work we then shall do, and there is a bed of sickness lurking in the way, and the summer's sun will only shine upon our useless and querulous convalescence. The long nights of winter are to find us at an occupation, which we only regret we have delayed so long, because it is so good, so full of God's glory, so full of our own sanctification. But before the shortest day has come, all life has shifted. Circumstances are changed. The good would be good no longer, or the means of doing it have slipped from our hands. The loss of the opportunity is an unhappiness to us; the delay by which we lost it is greater still. A good, which can be done now, can never be done afterwards. If it will be good to-morrow, then be sure it is not good to-day. God changes things when He changes times. This is the reason why unpunctual, procrastinating men are never holy, seldom affectionate, always selfish. So life slips by, and we manufacture our own sorrows by the want of promptitude. Devotion only means one thing in theology, and that one thing is promptitude.

Sometimes, however, we do see the sorrow towards which we are travelling. Perhaps this is the most common case of the two. We know that an illness is almost sure to return at a particular season of the year. Or we have an inevitable work to do, and the experience of the past assures us that the suffering, which will come of it, is as inevitable as the work itself. Or we are bending over a sister or a child, in whom insidious consumption is wearily eating its fatal way. A loss we cannot bear to think of is thus continually impending. It may be next spring, or it may be next spring year. Or it may be when the leaf falls this year, or when it falls two years hence. Or a sharp frost may nip the flower this winter, or the blood-vessel may break in sleep to-night. A son perhaps has wound his own manliness around an aged widowed mother; or a daughter so clings to a failing father, that she has never in her whole life been able to undomesticate herself from the hearth of her childhood, and to the last has remained more daughter than wife, more daughter than mother. In both cases the son and the daughter have before them an inevitable sorrow, inevitable if they live themselves, inevitable in the course of nature. It is only a work of time, and of no long time. In the majority of instances these foreseen sorrows are more sanctifying than the unforeseen. Life grows softer under the shadow, heavenlier during the eclipse of earth. It suits better with the common laws of grace, and is a less perilous process than the terrible surprises which make saints as money is minted, by one desperate blow, one sharp pressure when hot from the fire. O happy are they, did they but know it, who have a visible sorrow always waiting them a little further on the road! So has the path been garnished of by far the greatest number of the predestinate.

Thus the fourth dolour contains within itself the whole science and mystery of cross-bearing. This is the wisdom we learn from the picture while we gaze on Mary in the streets of the cruel Jerusalem. The eye of her soul sees the fair-haired Boy in the temple, whom she sought more than twenty years ago, while her bodily eye is fixed on the pale and bleeding and earth-stained Man, going with sound of trumpet and the chorus of earth's curses to His doom. And shall we, who gave Him that heavy Cross to bear, and kept weighting it after we had given it, as if our cruelty were not satisfied, refuse to bear the sweet grace-giving crosses which He binds on us, so little too as when we have borne them for a while we are forced to confess they are? O no! let us do now, as Mary did then,—look at Him who is on the road before us, and see how the beauty of the Sacred Heart sits with meek majesty and attractive love on the woe-worn disfigured Countenance.

CHAPTER VI.

THE FIFTH DOLOUR.

THE CRUCIFIXION.

THE world is a mystery. Life, time, death, doubt, good and evil, and the uncertainty which hangs about our eternal lot, are all mysteries. They lie burning on the heart at times. But the Crucifix is the meaning of them, the solution of them all. - It puts the question, and answers it as well. It is the reading of all riddles, the certainty of all doubts, and the centre of all faiths, the fountain of all hopes, the symbol of all loves. It reveals man to himself, and God to man. It holds a light to time that it may look into eternity, and be reassured. It is a sweet sight to look upon in our times of joy ; for it makes the joy tender without reproving it, and elevates without straining it. In sorrow there is no sight like it. It draws forth our tears, and makes them fall faster, and so softly that they become sweeter than very smiles. It gives light in the darkness, and the silence of its preaching is always eloquent, and death is life in the face of that grave earnest of eternal life. The Crucifix is always the same, yet ever varying its expression so as to be to us in all our moods, just what we most want and it is best for us to have. No wonder saints have hung over their Crucifixes in such trances of contented love. But Mary is a part of the reality of this symbol. The Mother and the Apostle stand, as it were, through all ages at the foot of the Crucifix, symbols themselves of the great mystery, of the sole true religion, of what God has done for the world which He created. As we cannot think of the Child at Bethlehem without His Mother, so neither will the Gospel let us picture to ourselves the Man on Calvary without His Mother also. Jesus and Mary were always one; but there was a peculiar union between them on Calvary. It is to this union we now come, Mary's fifth dolour, the Crucifixion.

The Way of the Cross was ended, and the summit of the mount has been attained a little before the hour of noon. If tradition speaks truly, it was a memorial place even then, fit to be a world's sanctuary; for it was said to be the site of Adam's grave, the spot where he rested when the mercy of God accepted and closed his nine hundred years of heroic penance. Close by was the City of David, which was rather the city of God, the centre of so much wonderful history, the object of so much pathetic divine love. The scene which was now to be enacted there would uncrown the queenly city; but only to crown with a far more glorious crown of light and hope, and truth and beauty, every city of the world where Christ Crucified should be preached and the Blessed Sacrament should dwell. It was but a little while, an hour perhaps, since the last dolour; so that only four hours have elapsed between the fourth dolour and the consummation of the fifth. Yet in sorrow and in sanctification it is a longer epoch than the eighteen years of Nazareth. In nothing is it more true, than in our sanctification, that with God a thousand years are but one day. These hours were filled with mysteries so divine, with realities so thrilling, that the lapse of time is hardly an element in the agony of Mary's soul. She comes to the Crucifixion a greater marvel of grace, a greater miracle of suffering, than when an hour ago she had met the cross-laden Jesus at the corner of the street.

They have stripped Him of His vestments, from the shame of which stripping His Human Nature shrank inexpressibly. To His Mother the indignity was a torture in itself, and the unveiled sight of her Son's Heart the while was a horror and a woe words cannot tell. They have laid Him on the Cross, a harder bed than the Crib of Bethlehem in which He first was laid. He gives Himself into their hands with as much docility as a weary child whom his mother is gently preparing for his rest. It seems, and it really was so, as if it was His own will, rather than theirs, which was being fulfilled. Beautiful in His disfigurement, venerable in His shame, the Everlasting God lay upon the Cross, with His eyes gently fixed on heaven. Never, Mary thought, had He looked more worshipful, more manifestly God, than now when He lay outstretched there, a powerless but willing victim: and she worshipped Him with profoundest adoration. The executioners now lay His right arm and hand out upon the Cross. They apply the rough nail to the palm of His Hand, the Hand out of which the world's graces flow, and the first dull knock of the hammer is heard in the silence. The trembling of excessive pain passes over His sacred limbs, but does not dislodge the sweet expression from His eyes. Now blow follows blow, and is echoed faintly from somewhere. Magdalen and John hold their ears; for the sound is unendurable; it is worse than if the iron hammer were falling on their living hearts. Mary hears it all. The hammer is falling upon her living heart; for her love had long since been dead to self, and only lived in Him. She looked upward to heaven. She could not speak. Words would have said nothing. The Father alone understood the offering of that heart, now broken so many times. To her the Nailing was not one action. Each knock was a separate martyrdom. The hammer played upon her heart as the hand of the musician changefully presses the keys of his instrument.

The Right Hand is nailed to the Cross. The Left will not reach. Either they have miscalculated in the hole they have drilled to facilitate the passage of the nail, or else the Body has contracted through agony. Fearful was the scene which now ensued, as the saints describe it to us in their revelations. The executioners pulled the left arm with all their force; still it would not reach. They knelt against

His ribs, which were distinctly heard to crack, though not to break, beneath the violent pressure, and dislocating His arm they succeeded in stretching the Hand to the place. Not more than a gentle sigh could be wrung from Jesus, and the sweet expression in His eyes dwelt there still. But to Mary,—what imagination can reach the horror of that sight, of that sound, to her ? There was more grief in them than has gone to the making of all the saints that have ever yet been canonised ! Again the dull blows of the hammer commence, changing their sounds according as it was flesh and muscle, or the hard wood, through which the nail was driving its cruel way. His legs are stretched out also by violence; one Foot is crossed upon another, those Feet which have so often been sore and weary with journeying after souls; and through the solid mass of shrinking muscles the nail is driven, slowly and with unutterable agony, because of the unsteadiness of the Feet in that position. It is useless to speak of the Mother; it is idle to compassionate her. Our compassion can reach no way, in comparison of the terrible excess of her agony. But God held His creature up, and she lived on.

Now the Cross is lifted off from the ground, with Jesus lying on it, the same sweet expression in His eyes, and is carried near to the hole, which they have dug to receive the foot. They then fasten ropes to it, and, edging it to the brink of the hole, they begin to rear it perpendicularly by means of the ropes. When it is raised almost straight up, they work the foot of it gradually over the edge of the cavity, until it jumps into its socket with a vehement bound which dislocates every bone, and nearly tears the Body from the nails. Indeed, some contemplatives mention a rope fastened round His waist, with such cruel tightness that it was actually hidden in the flesh, to hinder His Body from detaching itself from the Cross. So one horror outstrips another, searching out with fiery thrills, like the vibrations of an earthquake, all the supernatural capabilities of suffering which lay like abysses in the Mother's ruined heart. Let us not compare her woe to any other. It stands by itself. We may look at it, and weep over it in love, in love which is suffering as well. But we dare not make any commentary on it. Sorrowful Mother! Blessed be the Most Holy Trinity for the miracles of grace wrought in thee at that tremendous hour!

Earth trembled to its very centre. Inanimate things shuddered as if they had intelligence. The rocks were split around, precipices cloven all along the most distant shores of the Mediterranean, and the mystical veil of the temple rent in twain by the agitation of the earth, as if a hand had done it. At that moment, so one revelation tells us, there rose up from the temple courts a long wailing blast of trumpets, to mark the offering of the noonday sacrifice, and they, that blew the trumpets, knew not how that day they rang in heaven as the noonday trumpets never rang before. Darkness began to creep over the earth; for the satellite of earth might well eclipse the material sun, when the earth itself was thus eclipsing the Sun of Justice, the Eternal Light of the Father. The animals sought coverts where they might hide. The songs of the birds were hushed in the gardens beneath. Horror came over the souls of men, and the beginnings of grace, like the first uncertain advances of the stealthy dawn, came into many hearts out of that sympathetic darkness. A moment was an age, when men were environed by such mysteries as these.

The first hour of the three begins, the three hours that were such parallels to the three days, when she was seeking her lost Boy. In the darkness she has come close up to the Cross; for others fell away, as the panic simultaneously infected them. There is a faith in the Jews, upon which this fear can readily graft itself. But the executioners are hardened, and the Roman soldiers were not wont to tremble in the darkness. Near to the Cross by the glimmering light they are diceing for His garments. Their coarse words and rude jests pierced the Mother's heart; for, as we have said before, it belonged to her perfection, that her grief absorbed nothing. Everything told upon her. Everything made its own wound, and occupied her, as if itself were the sole suffering, the exclusively aggravating circumstance. She saw those garments, those relics which were beyond all price the world could give, in the hands of miserable sinners, who would sacrilegiously clothe themselves therewith. For thirty years they had grown with our Lord's growth, and had not been worn by use, renewing that miracle which Moses mentions in Deuteronomy, that through all the forty years of the desert the garments of the Jews were not "worn out, neither the shoes of their feet consumed with age." Now sinners were to wear them, and to carry them into unknown haunts of drunkenness and sin. Yet what was it but a type? The whole of an unclean world was to clothe itself in the beautiful justice of her Son. Sinners were to wear His virtues, to merit by His merits, to satisfy in His satisfactions, and to draw at will from the wells of His Precious Blood. As Jacob had been blessed in Esau's clothing, so should all mankind be blessed in the garments of their elder Brother.

Then there was the seamless tunic she herself had wrought for Him. The unity of His Church was figured there. She saw them cast lots for it. She marked to whom it had fallen. One of her first loving duties to the Church will be to recover it for the faithful as a relic. Then it was that the history of the Church rose before her. Every schism, which ever should afflict the mystical Body of her Son, was like a new rent in her suffering heart. Every heresy, every quarrel, every unseemly sin against unity, came to her with keenest anguish, there on Calvary, with the living sacrifice being actually offered, and the unity of His Church being bought with so terrible a price. All this bitterness filled her soul, without distracting her from Jesus for a single moment. As holy pontiffs, with hearts broken by the wrongs and distresses of the Church, have been all engrossed by them, yet never for an instant lost their interior union with Jesus, so much more was it with His Mother now. It was on Calvary she felt all this with an especial feeling, as it is in Lent, and Passiontide, and in devotion to the Passion, that we learn to love the Church with such sensitive loyalty.

Fresh fountains of grief were opened to her in the fixing of the title to the Cross. It had come from Pilate, and a ladder was set up against the Cross, and the title nailed above our Saviour's Head. Every blow of the hammer was unutterable torture to Him, torture which had a fearful echo also in the Mother's heart. Nor was the title itself without power to extend and rouse her suffering. The sight of the Holy Name blazoned there in shame to all the world, the Name which to her was sweeter than any music, more fragrant than any perfume, this was in itself a sorrow. The name of Nazareth also, how it brought back the past, surrounding the Cross in that dim air, with beautiful associations and marvellous contrasts. Everywhere in the Passion Bethlehem and Nazareth were making themselves felt and seen and heard, and always eliciting new sorrow from the inexhaustible depths of the Mother's heart. If He was a king, it was a strange throne on which His people had placed Him. Why did they not acknowledge Him to be their king? Why did they wait for a Roman stranger to tell it them as if in scorn? Why did they not let Him rule in their hearts? Ah! poor people! how much happier would it be for themselves, how many sins would be hindered, how many souls saved, how much glory gained for God! King of the Jews! would that it were so! Yet it was really so. But a king rejected, disowned, deposed, put to death! What a load lay upon her heart at that moment! It was the load of self-invoked curses which was to press to the ground that poor regicide people. She would have borne all her seven dolours over again to abolish that curse, and reinstate them as of old in the predilection of the God of Abraham, Isaac, and Jacob. It was too late. They had had their day. They had filled up the measure of their iniquity. It rose to the brim that very morning, and the breaking of Mary's heart was a portion of their iniquity.

But at least over her heart Jesus was acknowledged king and reigned supreme. So was it with the dear Magdalen and the ardent John, and as she thought of this, she looked upon them with a very glory of exceeding love. Is it that Jesus breaks the hearts over which He reigns, or that He comes of special choice to reign in broken hearts? But as the sense passed over her of what it was to have Jesus for a king, of the undisputed reign which by His own grace He exercised over her sinless heart, of the vastness of that heart far exceeding by His own bounty the grand empire of the angels or the multitudinous perfections of the saints, and of the endless reign which He would have in that, beautiful "ivory palace" of hers which made Him so glad, her love burst out afresh upon Him, as if the dykes of ocean had given way, and the continents were being flooded with its waters; and every gush of love was at the same time an exquisite gush of pain.

She had enough of occupation in herself. But sorrow widens great hearts, just as it contracts little ones. She had taken to herself the thieves for sons. She was greedy of children. She felt the value of them then, in the same way in which we know the value of a friend when we are losing him. His dead face looks it into us, and means more than his living expression did. She has wrestled in prayer for those two malefactors, and God has given her to see the work of grace beginning in the heart of one of them. Does this content her? Yes! with that peculiar contentment which comes of answered prayer, that is to say, she became more covetous, because of what she had got. She counted that only for a beginning. She pleaded, she insisted. One would have thought such prayer at such a time resistless. It is not heaven that resists. Graces descend from above like flights of angels to the heart of the impenitent thief. They fluttered there. They sang for entrance. They waited. They pecked at the heart of flesh. They made it bleed with pain, with terror, with remorse. But it was its own master. It would not open. So near Jesus and to be lost! It might well be incredible to Mary. Yet so it was. The thief matched his hardness against her sweetness, and prevailed. Mary may not be queen of any heart, where Jesus is not already king. But oh the unutterable anguish to her of this impenitence! His face so near the face of Jesus, the sighs of the spotless victim dwelling in his ear as silence dwells in the mountains, the very Breath of the Incarnate God reaching to him, the Precious Blood strewn all around him, like an overflow of waste water, as if there was more than men knew what to do with, and in the midst of all this to be damned, to commute the hot strangling throes of that crucifixion for everlasting fire, to be detached by his own will from the very side of the Crucifix, and the next moment to become a part of hopeless hell! Mary saw his eternity before her as in a vista. She took in at a glance the peculiar horror of his case. There came a sigh out of her heart at the loss of this poor wretched son, which had sorrow enough in it to repair the outraged majesty of God, but not enough to soften the sinner's heart.

Such were the outward, or rather let us call them the official, occupations of Mary during the first hour upon the Cross. Her inmost occupation, and yet outward also, was that which was above her, overshadowing her in the darkness, and felt more vividly even than if it had been clearly seen,—Jesus hanging upon the Cross! As our guardian angels are ever by our sides, engrossed with a thousand invisible ministries of love, and yet all the while see God, and in that one beatifying sight are utterly immersed, so was it with Mary upon Calvary. While she seemed an attentive witness and listener of the men dividing our Lord's garments amongst them, and of the nailing of the title to the Cross, or appeared to be occupied with the conversion of the thieves, she did all those things as the saints do things in ecstasy, with perfect attention and faultless accuracy, and yet far withdrawn into the presence of God and hidden in His light. A whole hour went by. Jesus was silent. His Blood was on fire with pain. His Body began to depend from the Cross, as if the nails barely held it. The Blood was trickling down the wood all the while. He was growing whiter and whiter. Every moment of that agony was an act of worship fully worthy of God Himself. He was holding ineffable communion with the Father. Mysteries, exceeding all mysteries that had ever been on earth, were going on in His Heart, which was alternately contracted and dilated with agony too awful for humanity to bear without miraculous support. It had divine support: but divine consolation was carefully kept apart. The interior of that Heart was clearly disclosed to the Mother's inward eye, and her heart participated in its sufferings. She too needed a miracle to prolong her life, and the miracle was worked. But with the same peculiarity. From her also all consolation was kept away. And so one hour passed, and grace had created many worlds of sanctity, as the laden minutes went slowly by, one by one, then slower and slower, like the pulses of a clock at midnight, when we are ill, beating sensibly slower to reproach us for our impatient listening.

The second hour began. The darkness deepened, and there were fewer persons round the Cross. No diceing now, no disturbance of nailing the title to the Cross. All was as silent as a sanctuary. Then Jesus spoke. It seemed as if He had been holding secret converse with the Father, and He had come to a point when He could keep silence no longer. It sounded as if He had been pleading for sinners and the Father had said that the sin of His Crucifixion was too great to be forgiven. To our human ears the word has that significance. It certainly came out of some depth, out of something which had been going on before, either His own thoughts, or the intensity of His pain, or a colloquy with the Father. Father! forgive them; for they know not what they do! Beautiful unending prayer, true of all sins and of all sinners in every time! They know not what they do. No one knows what he does when he sins. It is his very knowledge that the malice of sin is past his comprehension, which is a great part of the malice of his sin.

Beautiful prayer also, because it discloses the characteristic devotion of our dearest Lord! When He breaks the silence, it is not about His Mother, or the apostles, or a word of comfort to that affectionate forlorn Magdalen whom He loved so fondly. It is for sinners, for the worst of them, for His personal enemies, for those who crucified Him, for those who had been yelling after Him in the streets and loading Him with the uttermost indignities. It is as if at Nazareth He might seem to love His Mother more than all the world beside, but that now on Calvary, when His agony had brought out the deepest realities and the last disclosures of His Sacred Heart, it was found that His chief devotion was to sinners. Was Mary hurt by this appearance? Was it a fresh dolour that He had not thought first of her? O no! Mary had no self on Calvary. It could not have lived there. Had her heart cried out at the same moment with our Lord's, it would have uttered the same prayer, and in like words would have unburdened itself of that of which it was most full. But the word did draw forth new floods of sorrow. The very sound of His voice above her in the obscure eclipse melted her heart within her. The marvel of His uncomplaining silence was more pathetic now that He had spoken. Grief seemed to have reached its limits; but it had not. That word threw down the walls, laid a whole world of possible sorrow open to it, and poured the waters over it in an irresistible flood. The well-remembered tones pierced her like a spear. The very beauty of the words was anguish to her. Is it not often so, that deathbed words are harrowing because they are so beautiful, so incomprehensibly full of love? Mary's broken heart enlarged itself, and took in the whole world, and bathed it in tears of love. To her that word was like a creative word. It made the Mother of God Mother of mercy also. Swifter than the passage of light, as that word was uttered, the mercy of Mary had thrown round the globe a mantle of light, beautifying its rough places, and giving lustre in the dark, while incredible sorrow made itself co-extensive with her incalculable love.

The words of Jesus on the Cross might almost have been a dolour by themselves. They were all of them more touching in themselves than any words which ever have been spoken on the earth. The incomparable beauty of our Lord's Soul freights each one of them with itself, and yet how differently. The sweetness of His Divinity is hidden in them, and for ages on ages it has ravished the contemplative souls who loved Him best. If even to ourselves these words are continually giving out new beauties in our meditations, what must they be to the saints, and then, far beyond that, what were they to His Blessed Mother? To her, each of them was a theology, a theology enrapturing the heart while it illumined the understanding. She knew they would be His last. Through life they had been but few, and now in less than two hours He will utter seven, which the world will listen to and wonder at till the end of time. To her they were not isolated. They recalled other unforgotten words. There were no forgotten ones. She interpreted them by others, and others again by them, and so they gave out manifold new meanings. Besides which, she saw the interior from which they came, and therefore they were deeper to her. But the growing beauty of Jesus had been consistently a more and more copious fountain of sorrow all through the Three-and-Thirty Years. It was not likely that law would be abrogated upon Calvary. And was there not something perfectly awful, even to Mary's eye, in the way in which His divine beauty was mastering everything, and beginning to shine out in that eclipse? It seemed as if the Godhead were going to lay Itself bare among the very ruins of the Sacred Humanity, as His bones were showing themselves through His flesh. It was unspeakable. Mary lifted up her whole soul to its uttermost height to reach the point of adoration due to Him, and tranquilly acknowledged that it was beyond her power. Her adoration sank down into profusest love, and her love condensed under the chill shadow into an intensity of sorrow, which felt its pain intolerably everywhere as the low pulsations of His clear gentle voice rang and undulated through her inmost soul.

The thought which was nearest to our Blessed Saviour's Heart, if we may reverently venture to speak thus of Him, was the glory of His Father. We can hardly doubt that after that, chief among the affections of the created nature, which He had condescended to assume, stood the love of His Immaculate Mother. Among His seven words there will be one, a word following His absolution of the thief at Mary's prayer, a double word, both to her and of her. That also shall be like a creative word, creative for Mary, still more creative for His Church. He spoke out of an unfathomable love, and yet in such mysterious guise as was fitted still more to deepen His Mother's grief. He styles her "Woman," as if He had already put off the filial character, He substitutes John for Himself; and finally appears to transfer to John His own right to call Mary Mother. How many things were there here to overwhelm our Blessed Lady with fresh affliction! She well knew the meaning of the mystery. She understood that by this seeming transfer she had been solemnly installed in her office of second Eve, the mother of all mankind. She was aware that now Jesus had drawn her still more closely to Himself, had likened her to Himself more than ever, and had made their union more complete. The two relations of Mother and Son were two no longer; they had melted into one. She knew that never had He loved her more than now, and never shown her a more palpable proof of His love, of which however no proof was wanting. But each fresh instance of His love was a new sorrow to her; for it called up more love in her, and with more love as usual more sorrow.

But what a strange annunciation it was, this proclamation to her of the Maternity of men, compared with the Annunciation of her Divine Maternity! The midnight hour, the silent room, the ecstatic prayer, the lowly promptitude of the consent, the swift marvel of the adorable mystery,—all these were now exchanged for the top of Calvary in the dun light of the eclipse, with her Son hanging bleeding on the Cross. O what surpassing joy went with the first Motherhood, what intolerable anguish with the second! Yet while God sent His Angel to make the first Annunciation, He Himself, with His sweet Human Voice, condescended to make the second. But in Mary's soul there was the same tranquillity, in her will the same alacrity, of devout consent. When we are in deep sorrow, every action, which we are constrained to do, seems to excite and multiply our grief. Even the very movements of the body disturb the stillness of the soul. An interruption, an external noise, the scene that meets the uplifted eye, these are sufficient to burst the bounds, and throw the mass of bitter waters once more over the soul. So when Mary's whole nature rose to meet this word of Jesus, and threw itself into the consent she gave, and turned her forcibly as it were from Jesus to John, it was as if the whole anguish of the Crucifixion gained a new life, a fresh activity, a more potent bitterness, a more desolating power. The thought of Him, while it was the most terrible of all her thoughts, was also the most endurable. She felt most, when other thoughts usurped the place of that. Who has not felt this in times of mourning? He whom we have lost is our most terrible thought. Yet there is a softness, a repose, in thinking of him. The thought sustains our grief. But to think of other people, of other things, brings with it a rawness, a disquietude, an irritable dissatisfaction, an inopportune diversion, which makes our grief intolerable. So now Jesus Himself brought sinners uppermost in Mary's mind. He turned her thoughts from Himself to the Church, to His enemies, His persecutors, His murderers. He unsphered her, so to speak, from the sweet circle of her Motherhood, and placed her in the new centre of her office and official relation to mankind. For even when He spoke to her and of her, it was still rather sinners than herself, which seemed to be uppermost in His affections. The suffering of all this was immense, worse than any other woe which that prolific morning had brought her yet. So the second hour upon the Cross elapsed, an age of wonders which ages of angelical science and seraphic contemplation cannot adequately fathom. Jesus still lived; the

Blood was still flowing; the Body still growing whiter in the eclipse; the silence tingling all around, except when His beautiful words trembled lightly on the air, deepening, as it seemed, both the darkness and the silentness.

The third hour began, the third epoch in which this long dolour was working at the grand world of Mary's heart. His first word in this last hour was worse than Simeon's sword to our dearest Mother. He said, I thirst. Well might He thirst. Since the blessed chalice of His own Blood the night before, nothing had crossed His lips, but the taste of wine and gall, the pressure of the sponge with vinegar against His mouth, and His own Blood which had trickled in between His lips. Meanwhile the nails were burning like fires in His Hands and Feet; His limbs from head to foot had been scorched with the thongs and prickles of the brutal flagellation; endless thorns were sticking like spikes of flame through His skull, until His brain throbbed with the intolerable inflammation. Drop by drop His Blood had been drawn from Him, with all the moisture of His Body, and the fountains in the Heart were on the very point of failing. Surely we may well believe that there was never thirst like His. No shipwrecked sufferers have ever burned with a more agonising thirst, or have ever pined and died with tongue and lips and throat more dry and parched than His. Yet we know that single torture has been enough with strong men to sweep reason from its throne, and that there are few deaths men can die more horrible than death from thirst. We cannot doubt that our Blessed Lord suffered it beyond the point when without miracle death must have supervened. How fearful must have been the pressure of that physical suffering, which caused the silence-loving Sufferer to exclaim! If ever it was marvellous that in all her woe Mary had displayed no signs of feminine weakness, no fainting, no sobbing, no outcry, no wild gesture of uncontrollable misery, it was doubly marvellous now. Not only was this exclamation of Jesus a most heart-rending grief to her, but there came upon it that burden, which human grief can never bear, and the grief of a mother least of all, the feeling of impotence to allay the agony of those we love. She looked into His dying Face with a face on which death was almost as deeply imprinted as on His. She saw His parched, swollen, quivering lips, white with that whiteness of the last mortal struggle, which is like no other whiteness. But she could not reach, not even to wipe with her veil the Blood that was curdled there. It was vain, and she knew it, to appeal to the cruel men that were scattered about the mount. For a cup of cold water to those lips, through what new scenes of sorrow would she not be eager to pass! But it might not be. She remembered how He had once looked down into the cold sparkling water of Jacob's well, and longed in His fatigue and thirst for one draught of that element which He Himself had created, and then how He had forgotten both thirst and weariness in His loving labour of converting that poor Samaritan woman. But now, and it was an overwhelming thought, water was as far from the lips of the dying Saviour as it was from those of Dives in the endless fires, out of which he had appealed if it were but for a single drop. No! her dearest Son must bear it. He has at last complained of His physical tortures. But of what use was it except to break His Mother's heart again, and to call forth the love and adoration of countless souls through ages and ages of His Church! To Him it brought no relief. It was for our sakes that He complained, that, even at the expense of more agony to Mary, we might have one additional motive to love our Crucified Brother.

But this was not the only thirst that word was intended to convey. His Soul thirsted as feverishly for souls as His Body did for the water of the well. He brooded over all coming ages, and yearned to multiply the multitudes of the redeemed. Alas! we have approximations by which we can measure His torment of physical thirst: but we have no shadow even, by which we can guess of the realities of that torment in His Soul. If the love, which the Creator has for creatures whom He has called out of nothing, is unlike any other love either of angels or of men, if its kind is without parallel, and its degree an excess out of the reach of our conception, so also is the spiritual love of souls in the Soul of the Saviour of the world. Saving love is without similitude, as well as creative love. As all the loves of earth are but sparks of creative love, so all apostolic instincts, all missionary zeal, all promptitude of martyrdom, all intercessory penance, and all contemplative intercession, are but little sparks of that saving love of which Calvary is at once the symbol and the reality. The torment of this thirst was incomparably beyond that of the other thirst. Mary saw it, and no sooner had she seen it, than the very sight translated her, as it were, into a fresh unexplored world of sorrow. She saw that this thirst would be almost as little satisfied as the other. She saw how Jesus at that moment was beholding in His Soul the endless procession of men, unbroken daily from dawn to dawn, bearing with them into hell the character of baptism and the seal of His Precious Blood. See! even now, while the Saviour is dying of thirst, the impenitent thief will not give Him even his one polluted soul to drink! So was it going to be evermore. Mary saw it all. Why had He ever left Nazareth? Why had He gone through all this world of unnecessary suffering, only to succeed so inadequately at last? Was God's glory after all the end of Calvary, rather than the salvation of men? Yes! and yet also No! Mary, like Jesus Himself, grudged not one pang, one lash, one least drop of Blood that beaded His crowned brow. She too thirsted for souls, as He did, and her heart sank when she saw that He was not to have His fill. O poor miserable children that we are! how much of our own souls have we not kept back, which would have somewhat cheered both the Mother and the Son that day!

But Jesus had to go down into an abyss of His Passion deeper than any which He had sounded hitherto. Into that deep, Mary must go down also. Not merely for us was the word He was now to utter.* It is beyond us. It comes like a mysterious far-off cry out of the depths of spiritual anguish, to which even mystical theology can give no name. It is God abandoned of God, the creature rejected of the Creator, although united to Him by an Hypostatic Union, the Sacred Humanity abandoned by the Divine Nature to which it is inseparably assumed, a Human Nature left Personless because the Divine Person, who never can withdraw Himself, has withdrawn, the Second Person of the Holy Trinity deserted by the Other Two! What wild words are these! We know they cannot be, simply cannot. Yet when we put the dereliction of Jesus into words, these are the impossible expressions in which we become entangled. My God! My God! why hast Thou forsaken Me? Was there ever a more truly created cry? Yet He who uttered it was Himself the Creator. Not merely for us then could such a word be spoken. It was wrung from Him by the very spirit of adoration in the extremity of His torture. Some have conjectured that it was at that moment that the hitherto unconsumed species of the Blessed Sacrament was consumed, and so that mysterious union of Himself with Himself withdrawn. But this does not recommend itself to us. Why should He derive comfort and strength from His own sacramental Flesh and Blood, when He was exposing both Flesh and Blood to unheard-of torments? Why derive comfort at all, when He was studiously making all things round Him, even His Mother's heart, fresh instruments of torture? Why should His Divine Nature in the Blessed Sacrament be a sweetness and restorative to Him, the loss of which extracted such a cry, when even in the Hypostatic Union, which was an incomparably closer union than that of the Blessed Sacrament, He was cutting off the supplies

---

* The reader will observe that the order in which the seven words are here arranged is not meant to be historical. They are placed for a special purpose in the order which seems best for the present object, to throw light upon our Lady's Dolours. Hence the Deus meus is put here as if it came after the Sitio, whereas the former was the fourth word, and the latter the fifth.

of His Divine Nature from His Human, excepting the single communication of His omnipotence to enable Him to live, in order that He might suffer more? The sense of the faithful, that instinct which so seldom errs, points without hesitation to the Eternal Father, as the cause of that suffering, and as addressed in that word.

But is there cruelty in God? No! Infinite justice is as far removed from cruelty as infinite love can be. Yet it was the Father, He who represents all kindness, all indulgence, all forbearance, all gentleness, all patience, all fatherliness in heaven and earth, who chose that moment of intensest torture, when the storm of created agonies was beginning to pelt less pitilessly because it was now well-nigh exhausted, to crucify afresh, with a most appalling interior crucifixion, the Son of His own endless complacency. With effort, unutterably beyond all grace ever given, except the grace of Jesus, Mary lifted up her heart to the Father, joined her will to His in this dire extremity, and in a certain sense, as well as He, abandoned her Beloved. She gave up the Son to the Father. She sacrificed the love of the Mother to the duty of the Daughter. She acknowledged the Creator only as the last end of the creature. She had done this at the outset in her first dolour, the Presentation of Jesus, and it was consummated now. O Mother! how far had that exacting glory of God led thy royal heart? She saw Jesus abandoned. She heard the outcry of His freshly crucified Soul, pierced to the quick by this new invention of His Father's justice. And she did not wish it otherwise. She would have Him abandoned, if it was the Father's will. And it was His will. Therefore with all her soul, with the most unretracted, spontaneous consent, she would have Him abandoned. She would go down from the top of Calvary this moment, if the Father bade her. But her love rose up, as if it were desperate, to meet this uttermost exigency. No one would have dreamed that a human soul could have held so much love as she poured out upon Jesus at that moment. Was her heart infinite, inexhaustible? It really seemed so. For at that hour it combined, multiplied, outstripped all the love of the Three-and-Thirty Years, and rushed into His soul as if it would fill up with its own self the immense void which the dereliction of the Father had opened there. Everything went out of her, but the horrible bitterness of her martyrdom. Sorrow, pure, sheer, sharp, fiery sorrow was flesh and blood and bone and soul and all to her. All else was gone into the Heart of Jesus, which thereupon sent forth upon her an outpouring of love which deluged her with a fresh ocean of overwhelming woe. And by one miracle, they both lived still.

Now, Blessed Mother! that thou standest on such incredible heights of detachment, the end may come! It was finished. All was finished. Chiefly creation. It had found a home at the grave of the First Adam, under the Cross of the Second. The Father had left Him. He must go to the Father. It is impossible They should be disunited. Creatures had done what they could. They had filled to the brim the Saviour's cup of suffering, and He with pitiable love had drained it to the dregs. But there was one created punishment still left, created rather by the creature than the Creator, created chiefly by a woman. It was the punishment of death, the eldest-born child of the first Eve. But could death hold sway over the living Life of eternity? Could Eve punish God? Was He to inherit the bitter legacy of the sweet Paradise? How could it be? How could He die? What could death be like to Him? Mary's heart must be lifted to the height of this dread hour. High as it is, it must be raised higher still, to the level of this divinest mystery. The Three-and-Thirty Years are ending. A new epoch in the world's history is to open. The most magnificent of all its epochs is closing. What will death be like to Him? Ah! we may ask also, what will life be like to her when He is dead? What will Mary herself be like without Jesus? She was not looking up, but she knew His eye was now resting on her. What strange power is there in the eyes of the dying, that they often turn round the averted faces that are there, and attract them to themselves, that love may see the last of its love ? His eye was resting on the same object on which it rested the moment He was born, when He lay suddenly on a fold of her robe upon the ground while she knelt in prayer, and when He smiled, and lifted up His little hands to be taken up into her arms, and folded to her bosom. His arms were otherwise lifted up now, inviting us to climb up into them, like fond children, to see what the embrace of a Saviour's love is like. She felt His eye, and she looked up into His face. Never did two such faces look into each other, and speak such unutterable love as this. The Father held Mary up in His arms lest she should perish under the load of love, and the loud cry went out from the hill-top, hushing Mary's soul into an agony of silence, and the Head drooped towards her, and the eye closed, and the Soul passed her, like a flash, and sank into the earth,—and a wind arose, and stirred the mantle of darkness, and the sun cleared itself of the moon's shadow, and the roofs of the city glimmered white, and the birds began to sing, but only as if they were half reassured, and Mary stood beneath the Cross a childless Mother. The third hour was gone.

Such was the fifth dolour, with its creative periods of sanctity and sorrow. She had stood through it all, notwithstanding the agonising yesterday, the sleepless night, the long morning crowded with its terrible phenomena. In the strength of her unfailing weariness she had stood through it all, and Scripture is careful to mark the posture, as if this miracle of endurance was of itself a revelation of the greatness of the Mother's heart. It is, as it were, a reward for her dolour, that we cannot preach Christ Crucified, unless Mary be in sight. It is something else we preach, not that, —unless she be standing there. And now she stands on Calvary alone. It is three hours past noon of the most awful day the world shall ever see.

Something still remains to be said of the peculiarities of this dolour, notwithstanding that so much has been unavoidably anticipated in the narrative. Above all things, the Crucifixion has this peculiarity, that it was the original fountain of all the other dolours, except the third. That stands apart. It is Mary's own Crucifixion, her Gethsemane and her Calvary. But the two dolours which came out of the Infancy, and the four which represent the Passion, have the Crucifixion for their centre. The Three Days' Loss does not belong to the Infancy, and the shadow of the Passion is no more thrown over it than it was over the whole life of Mary. It was the act of Jesus Himself, which seemingly had an especial relation to His Mother. The third dolour, which prefaces the Eighteen Years at Nazareth, was to her sorrows what the Eighteen Years were to her life generally, something between Jesus and herself, a mystery of a different sphere from those in which both He and she were concerned in the fulfilment of the world's redemption. But the sword in Simeon's prophecy was the Crucifixion. The Flight into Egypt was to hinder the cruelty of Herod from anticipating the moment of our Saviour's death. The Meeting with the Cross was the road to Calvary. The Taking down from the Cross and the Burial, were sorrows which flowed naturally out of the Crucifixion, and were in unbroken unity with it. The Crucifixion was therefore the realisation of her lifelong woe. The fountain was reached. She had tracked it up to Calvary. What remained was the waste water, or rather the water and blood which flowed down from the mount, and sank in at the threshold of the Garden Tomb. Compared with the Crucifixion, the other dolours, the third always excepted, were almost reliefs and distractions stirring on the fixed depths of her unfathomable woe. The Crucifixion was a sorrow by itself, without name or likeness. It was the centre of the system of her dolours, while the independence of her third dolour betokens the existence of that vast world which Mary is in her own self, a creation apart, brighter than this world of ours, and more dear to Jesus. It is a mysterious orb allowed to come in sight of this other system, where we are,—a disclosure of all that world of phenomena which is hidden from our eyes in the Eighteen Years, during which Jesus devoted Himself to her. It ranks with the Immaculate Conception, the Incarnation, and the Assumption, all which belong to Mary's world, and would have been even if sin had not been, though they would have been different from what they were. But that third dolour shows how the fallen world of sin and the necessity of a passible Incarnation, told on her world, as it did on His, and passed upon the lineaments of the Maternity as well as upon those of the Incarnation. There are certainly few mysteries in the Gospel, which we understand less than the Three Days' Loss.

Another peculiarity of the Crucifixion is the length of time, during which the tide of suffering remained at its highest point without any sign of ebbing. The mysteries which filled the three hours, seem too diversified for us to regard them, at least till we come to the Dereliction, as rising from less to greater in any graduated scale. They are rather separate elevations, of unequal height, standing linked together like a mountain chain. But the lowest of them was so immensely high that it produced immeasurable agony in her soul. The anguish of death is momentary. The length of some of the most terrific operations which can rack the human frame seldom exceeds a quarter of an hour. Pain pushed beyond a certain limit, as in mediæval torture, is instantaneous death. In human punishments, which are not meant to kill, the hand of science keeps watch on the pulse of the sufferer. But to Mary the Crucifixion was three hours, three long hours, of mortal agony, comprising hundreds of types and shapes of torture, each one of them intolerable in itself, each pushed beyond the limits of human endurance unless supported by miracle, and each of them kept at that superhuman pitch for all that length of time. When pain comes we wish to lie down, unless madness and delirium come with it, or we are fain to run about, to writhe, gesticulate, and groan. Mary stood upright on her feet the whole weary while, leaning on no one, and not so much as an audible sigh accompanied her silent tears. It is difficult to take this thought in. We can only take it in by prayer, not by hearing or reading.

It was also a peculiarity of the Crucifixion that it was an heroic trial of her incomparable faith. Pretty nearly the faith of the whole world was in her when she stood, with John and Magdalen, at the foot of the Cross. There was hardly a particle of her belief which was not tried to the uttermost in that amazing scene. Naturally speaking, our Lord's Divinity was never so obscured. Supernaturally speaking, it never was so manifest. Could it be possible that the Incarnate Word should be subject to the excesses of such unparalleled indignities? Was the light within Him never to gleam out once? Was the Wisdom of the Father to be with blasphemous ridicule muffled in a white sack, and pulled about in absurd, undignified helplessness by the buffooning guards of an incestuous king? Was there not a point, or rather were there not many points, in the Passion, when the limit of what was venerable and fitting was overstepped? Even in the reserved narrative of the Gospels, how many things there are, which the mind cannot dwell on, without being shocked and repulsed, as well as astonished! Even at this distance of time do they not try our faith by their very horror, make our blood run cold by their murderous atrocity, and tempt our devotion to withdraw, sick and fastidious, from the affectionate contemplation of the very prodigies of disgraceful cruelty, by which our own secret sins and shames were with such public shame most lovingly expiated? Is not devotion to the Passion to this day the touchstone of feeble faith, of lukewarm love, and of self-indulgent penance? And Mary, more delicate and more fastidious far than we, drank all these things with her eyes, and understood the horror of them in her soul, as we can never understand it. Think what faith was hers.

The Divine Perfections also suffered a strange eclipse in the Passion. Sin was triumphant. Justice was condemned. Holiness was abandoned even by the All-holy. Providence seemed to have withdrawn, as if under constraint. God was trodden out, and creatures had creation to themselves; nay, more than that, they had the Creator in their power. There was no divine interference, just when it appeared most needed and most natural. If men could have their own way then, surely they could have it always. One while God looked passive, another while cruel. Oh it required angelic theology to reconcile the providence of that day with the attributes of the Most High! Then the angels themselves might be a trial of her faith. Were there such things, such beings as angels? She had seen them so often, she could not doubt it. She had seen St. Michael but the night before, bending in adoration by the side of Jesus in His agony, a glorious being, fit for that strange exceptional mission of consoling the Son of God in His inconsolable distress. But where was their zeal for the Incarnate Word, that grand grace by which they had all been established in their final perseverance? Where were the double-edged cherubic swords that guarded the entrance into Eden from all but Henoch and Elias? Ah! there were legions of them pressing forward, yet ever beaten back, like a storm-cloud striving to plough its way up against the wind, eager and burning, yet with difficult obedience bending backwards before the meek admonishing eye of Jesus. Then, again, who could have believed, when they saw the beauty of Jesus and fathomed the depth of His prayer, as Mary only could see the one or fathom the other, that divine grace really had power to convert human hearts? He was the very beauty of holiness. During His Passion men themselves tore away every veil which humility and reserve could hang about His sanctity. His humility, His sweetness, His patience, His modesty, all stood disclosed with the fullest light upon them, exercised openly and heroically in the midst of the grossest outrage. And yet men were not won to Him! There were the guards who had fallen backwards in the garden the night before. There were those who had stood nearest to Him during the scourging, those who had talked with Him as Pilate had, those who had taken Him to Herod and brought Him back again. There was the impenitent thief close by His side. Grace was going out from Him every moment. His effectual prayer was incessant. Mary's intercession itself was busily engaged. Yet when the sun set on Friday how little visible harvest had all that grace gathered into its garners! Never did any one so walk by faith, simple, naked faith, as Mary did that day. There was faith enough to save a whole world in her single heart.

Another peculiarity of this fifth dolour is to be found in the seven words which our Lord uttered from the Cross. They were as seven sharp thrills in Mary's heart, reaching depths of the human soul to which our griefs never attain. It was not only the well-known accents of her dying Son, with their association inconceivably heightened by the circumstances in which they broke upon the stillness. It was not only the exceeding beauty of the words themselves, disclosing, as death sometimes does with men, an unexpected interior beauty in the soul. It was not only that, like the unuttered music of poetry in a kindred soul, they waked up in her the remembrances of other words of His, and gave light to many mysteries in her mind, and played skilfully upon the many keys, and with the various stops, of her wonderful affections, saying, as they did to her, what they do not say to us, and what we cannot so much as guess. But they were the words of God, such words as are spoken of in the Epistle to the Hebrews,* "living and effectual, and more piercing than any two-edged sword, reaching unto the division of the soul and the spirit, of the joints also and the marrow, and discerning the thoughts and intents of the heart." Such was their operation in the heart of Mary, penetrating her as the blast of a trumpet seems to penetrate the recesses of our hearing, and in their subtlety and agile swiftness carrying grief into the crevices of her nature, whither it could not else have reached. She was the broken cedar, the divided flame of fire, the shaken desert of Cades,

* iv. 12.

in the twenty-eighth psalm. "The Voice of the Lord is upon the waters; the God of majesty hath thundered, the Lord upon many waters: the Voice of the Lord in its omnipotence, the Voice of the Lord in its magnificence. The Voice of the Lord breaketh the cedars, yea, the Lord shall break the cedars of Libanus. The Voice of the Lord divideth the flame of fire. The Voice of the Lord shaketh the desert, and the Lord shall shake the desert of Cades."

We have already spoken of the parallel between the Crucifixion and the Annunciation, which is another peculiarity of the fifth dolour. She became our Mother, just when she lost Jesus. It was as it were a ceremonial conclusion to the Thirty-Three Years she had spent with Him in the most intimate communion, and at the same time a solemn opening of that life of Mary in the Church, to which every baptized soul is a debtor for more blessings than it suspects. In the third dolour He had spoken to her with apparent roughness, as if her office of Mother was now eclipsed by the Mission which His Eternal Father had trusted to Him. In this fifth dolour, He as it were merges her Divine Maternity in a new motherhood of men. Perhaps no two words that He ever spoke to her were more full of mystery than that in the temple, and now this one upon the Cross, or ever caused deeper grief in her soul. They are parallel to each other. With such a love of souls as Mary had, immensely heightened by the events of that very day, the motherhood of sinners brought with it an enormous accession of grief. The multitudes that were then wandering shepherdless over the wide earth, the ever-increasing multitudes of the prolific ages, all these she received into her heart, with the most supernatural enlightment as to the malice of sin, the most keen perception of the pitiable case and helpless misery of sinners, the clearest foresight of the successful resistance which their free-will would make to grace, and the most profound appreciation of the horrors of their eternal exile amidst the darkness and the flames of punishment. Our Lord's word effected what it said. It made her the Mother of men therefore, not merely by an outward official proclamation, but in the reality of her heart. He opened up there new fountains of inexhaustible love. He caused her to love men as He loved them, as nearly as her heart could come to His. He as it were multiplied Himself in the souls of sinners millions of millions of times, and gave her love enough for all. And such love! so constant, so burning, so eloquent, so far above all earthly maternal love both in hopefulness, tenderness, and perseverance! And what was this new love but a new power of sorrow? We cannot rightly understand Mary's sorrow at the Crucifixion under any circumstances, simply because it is above us. But we shall altogether miss of those just conceptions, which we may attain to, unless we bear in mind that she became our Mother at the foot of the Cross, not merely by a declaration of her appointment, but by a veritable creation through the effectual word of God, which at the moment enlarged her broken heart, and fitted it with new and ample affections, causing thereby an immeasurable increase of her pains. It was truly in labour that she travailed with us, when we came to the birth. The bitterness of Eve's curse environed her spotless soul unutterably in that hour of our spiritual nativity.

We must not omit to reckon also among the peculiarities of this dolour that which it shares with the fourth dolour, and in which it stands in such striking contrast to the sixth, her inability to reach Jesus in order to exercise her maternal offices towards Him. So changeful can sorrow be in the human heart that the very thing, which will minister sorrow to her by the fulness of its presence in the Taking down from the Cross, is a sorrow to her here by its absence. But they have mourned little, too little for their own good, who have not long since learned to understand this contradiction. It is hard for a mother to keep herself quiet by the deathbed of her son. Grief must be doing something. The wants of the sufferer are the luxuries of the mourner. The pillows must be smoothed again, the hair taken out of the eyes, those beads of death wiped from the clammy brow, those bloodless lips perpetually moistened, that white hand gently chafed, that curtain put back to give more air, the weak eyes shielded from the light, the bed-clothes pressed out of the way of his difficult breathing. Even when it is plain that the softest touch, the very gentlest of these dear ministries, is fresh pain to the sufferer, the mother's hand can scarcely restrain itself; for her heart is in every finger. To be quiet is desolation to her soul. She thinks it is not the skill or the experience of the nurse, which dictates her directions, but her hard-heartedness, because she is not that fair boy's mother; and therefore she rebels in her heart against her authority, even if the chances of being cruel do in fact restrain her hands. Surely that foam must be gathered from the mouth, surely that long lock of hair must tease him hanging across his eye and dividing his sight, surely that icy hand should have the blood gently, most gently, brought back again. She forgets that the eye is glazed and sees no more, that the blood has gone to the heart, and even the mother's hand cannot conjure it back again. And so she sits murmuring, her sorrow all condensed in her compulsory stillness. Think then what Mary suffered those three long hours beneath the Cross! Was ever deathbed so uneasy so comfortless, as that rough-hewn wood? Was ever posture more torturing than to hang by nails in the hands, dragging, dragging down as the dead weight of the Body exerted itself more and more? Where was the pillow for His Head? If it strove to rest itself against the Title or the Cross, the crown of thorns drove it back again: if it sank down upon His Breast, it could not quite reach it, and its weight drew the Body from the nails. Slow streams of Blood crept about His wounded Body, making Him tremble under their touch with the most painful excitement and uneasiness. His Eyes were teased with Blood, liquid or half-congealed. His Mouth, quivering with thirst, was also caked with Blood, which His breath seemed less and less to moisten. There was not a limb which was not calling out for the Mother's tender hand,

and it might not reach so far. There were multitudes of pains, which her touch would have soothed. O mothers! have you a name by which we may call that intolerable longing which Mary had, to smooth that hair, to cleanse those eyes, to moisten those dear lips, which has just been speaking such beautiful words, to pillow that blessed Head upon her arm, to ease those throbbing hands, and hold up for a while the soles of those crushed and lacerated feet? It was not granted to her; and yet she stood there in tranquillity, motionless as a statue, not a statue of indifference, nor yet of stupor and amazement, but in that attitude of reverent adoring misery, which was becoming to a broken-hearted creature who felt the very arms of the Eternal Father round her, holding her up to live, to love, to suffer, and to be still.

We must also remember that the abandonment of Jesus by His Father was something to her which it cannot be to us. In religious mysteries we are continually obliged to take words for things. We speak of the Eternal Generation of the Son and of the Eternal Procession of the Holy Spirit, but we cannot embrace the wisdom, the brightness, the love, the tenderness, the pathos, if we may venture on the word, which those acts of the Divine Life imply. Consequently the words do not call out in us an intelligent variety of feelings and sentiments and emotions: we meet them by a simple act of adoring love. Yet they mean more to theologians than to uneducated Christians, more to saints than to theologians, more to the blessed in heaven than to the saints on earth. But according to our knowledge so should be our love, and in heaven it is so. Thus, while the dereliction of Jesus on the Cross fills our minds with a sacred horror, we only see into it confusedly. We rather see that it *is* a mystery, than in what the mystery consists. It is often the very indistinctness of divine things which enables us to endure them. Who could live, if he realised what hell is, and that every moment immortal souls are entering there upon their eternity of most shocking and repulsive punishment? We smell a sweet flower, and just then a soul has been condemned. We watch with trembling love the elevation of the Host and Chalice, and meanwhile the gates of that fiery dungeon have closed on many souls. We lie down upon the grass, and look up at the white clouds, dipping through the blue sky as if ether had waves, and catching the sun on their snowy shapes, and all the while hell is underneath that grass, within the measurable diameter of the earth, living, populous, unutterable, its roaring flames and countless sounds of agony muffled by the soil that covers the uneasily riveted crust of the earth. What agony would this be, if our minds were equal to it, or co-extensive with its reality! Nay, if we realised it, as sometimes for a moment we do realise it, we could not survive many hours, even if we did not die upon the spot. For if the guilt of one venial sin shown to His saint by God would have produced the immediate separation of body and soul, unless He by miraculous interference had supported her, what must the vision be of the countless enormities of hell, with the additional hideousness of final impenitence, and the unspeakable horror of its punishments? So was it with this dereliction of our Blessed Lord; none understood it as Mary did. The whole of the marvellous theology that was in it was perhaps clear to her. At least she saw in it what no one else, not even an angel, could see. Hence while it called out in her a variety of the most vivid emotions and most sensitive affections, it also plunged her into fresh sorrow, by transferring all at once the Passion of Jesus into another and more terrific sphere.

The universality of her suffering is also another peculiarity of the fifth dolour, and in this it was a sort of shadow of the Passion. Who can number the variety of the pains which those three hours contained? What portion of her sinless nature was not covered with its appropriate suffering? There was no spot whereon a sorrow could be grafted, where the hand of God had not inserted one. She was as completely submerged in grief, as a fish is submerged in the great deep sea. The very omnipresence of God round about her was to her an omnipresence of suffering. As the fires that punish sin are so dreadfully efficacious, because God intended their nature to be penal, so the supernatural sorrows of our Blessed Mother on Calvary were fearfully efficacious, because they were intended to carry suffering to the utmost limit which the creature could bear, that so her holiness, her merits, and her exaltation might exceed those of all other creatures put together except the created nature of her Son. There was not an inlet of any one of the senses down which pain was not flowing masterfully, like clashing tides in a narrow gulf. There was not a faculty of her mind which was not illuminated, or rather scorched, by a light which hurt nature and gave it pain. Her affections had been cruelly immolated at the foot of that altar on Calvary, one after another, and the zealous Priest had not spared His victims. Her will was strained up to the height of the most unheard-of consents, which the devouring justice of God had demanded of her. Her soul was crucified. Her body was the shrinking prey of her mental agony. Her feet were weary with standing, her hands wet with His Blood, her eyes filled with her own. "How hath the Lord covered with obscurity the daughter of Sion! Weeping she hath wept in the night, and her tears are on her cheeks. There is none to comfort her among all them that were dear to her. From above He hath sent fire into my bones, and hath chastised me: He hath spread a net for my feet; He hath turned me back; He hath made me desolate, wasted with sorrow all the day long. The Lord hath taken all my mighty men out of the midst of me. He hath proclaimed against me a time, to destroy my chosen men. The Lord hath trodden the wine-press for the virgin daughter of Juda. Therefore do I weep, and my eyes run down with water, because the Comforter, the relief of my soul, is far from me. My children are desolate because the enemy hath prevailed. My heart is turned within me, for I am full of bitterness. Abroad the sword destroyeth, and at home there is death alike. O all ye that pass by the way ! attend, and see if there be any sorrow like to my sorrow; for He hath made a vintage of me, as the Lord spoke in the day of His fierce anger!"*

Last of all, there was her inability to die with Him. Many a time to die with the dead would be the only true consolation of the bereaved. One heart has been the light of life, the unsetting light of long years of various fortune, bright in the blue sky of prosperity, brighter still in the black clouds of adversity. Now that light is put out by death. Why should we survive? Henceforth what significance can there be to us in life? That cold heart was the end of all our avenues. Every prospect terminated there. We valued no past where that heart was not. We saw no future in which it did not play its part. All our plans ended there. The weight of our expectations was concentrated on that one point, and now it has given way, and we are falling through, we know not whither. Ah! this loss is truly the end of life, more truly far than the mere physical dissolution of soul and body. The apostles, especially the quick affectionate Thomas, wished to go and die with Lazarus, simply because Jesus loved him so. Surely we can all remember days, which were the world's end to us, days which it seemed impossible should have a morrow! There was a bed, laden with a sad weight, with a beautiful terror, which was to us the end of time, the edge of the world, the threshold of eternity. It has been long looked for, and yet words would not tell how cruelly unexpected it came at last. All our hopes and fears and loves were gathered up, as if the Judge were coming then to settle them. Common things could not go on after that. Daily duties must not recur. Habits were run out. It was an end, an end of so much,—so much so cruelly ended. It was as fearful to have no prospect, as it is to have no hope; and therefore we longed to lie down and die, on the same bed, and be buried in the same grave, though it seemed strange that any one should remain behind to bury us, so completely did it seem a universal end.

* Lamentations I.

This is a wild extremity of human grief. Our Lady's dolour was something else than this. The end of the Thirty-Three Years was not like any other end. Her Son was God. It all lies in that. Think, after that, of the unutterable misery of the Mother's life protracted, when His was done. It will not bear explaining. It cannot be explained. But we can feel it, below the world from which words come; we can see it, a light beyond the region where thought can grasp things,—that actual sundering of Jesus and Mary, the dissolution of that union which had been the world's divine mystery for all those wonderful and wonder-peopled years! Which of us can tell what grief is like, when it has gone beyond the point at which it would kill us, and we only live by a miracle external to ourselves? Such grief was our Mother's when our Lord breathed out His Soul into His Father's hands.

But let us turn from the peculiarities of the fifth dolour to the dispositions in which our Blessed Lady endured it. Yet the task of describing these is impossible. We read the lives of the saints, and see in each one of them a peculiar inward sanctity, sometimes different from that of all others that we know, sometimes congenial to the spirit of another saint, sometimes, though not often, allowing itself to be grouped in numerous classes. Many of the graces, which we read of, have no names in the nomenclature of the virtues of their kindred dispositions. We wonder as we read. We are dazzled by the lights which keep appearing in the beauties of holiness, in splendoribus sanctorum. Yet we know that what we see is as nothing to that which we do not see. As the queen of the south said of Solomon, not the half is told. All that comes to the surface is a mere indication of the depths which are below, hardly enough to let us guess at the interior beauty which the eye of God beholds in the saintly soul. But if this is the case with the saints, how much more so is it with our Blessed Lady! It is expressly said of her that the beauty of the king's daughter is all within, and when our Lord in the Canticle describes her loveliness, He adds twice over, "besides that which lieth hid within." It is therefore impossible to speak worthily of the interior beauty of Mary. As we have considered each dolour it has become more difficult to speak of her dispositions. We are obliged to use common words for things which are singular, and only akin to what is common. The realities keep rising taller and taller above the words, until these last almost mislead us, instead of elucidating the subject; and we have to repeat the same words for dispositions which have become different in the transition from one sorrow to another, as well by the novelty of their exercise as by the increased magnificence of their heroism. Thus the depth and grandeur of our Blessed Mother's inward life are sufficient of themselves to hinder our doing it justice. Mary is one of those divine visions which expands before expanding holiness, and even like the Blissful Vision itself, excites hunger in the beholder even while it is satisfying his soul unutterably.

But there is another reason also of this difficulty, which bears especially upon her dolours. It is the comprehended reality of the present. We must explain our meaning. It hardly ever happens to us either in sorrow or in joy fully to take in the present at once. We realise our sorrows and our joys piecemeal. We are constantly finding new features in them, and coming across peculiarities which did not strike us at the first. In everything which happens to us there is always far more implied than is expressed. This is what we mean when we speak of a growing sorrow. It is not the sorrow that grows, it is our own appreciation of it. It belongs to the imperfection of our minds that this process should be gradual. All that years unfold, apply, bring home to us, was in the transient act, whether death, misfortune, or disgrace, when it was present; only we were unable to embrace it. Hence it is that we often seem more heroic in sorrow than we really are. We bear no more of our burden than what we see, and we see but a portion of it. Our Heavenly Father lets it down gradually upon us, dividing the weight between His own hand and our shoulders, till use enables us to bear the full pressure without being crushed. We commit ourselves to Him, engaging ourselves to what is implied, while our eyes are fixed upon what is expressed. Our venture succeeds, not so much by our own courage, as by His grace. It even sometimes happens that we lose a friend, whose death affects us very moderately. Somehow the light of life is not thrown on the chasm that he has made in leaving. Years pass on, and circumstances change. All at once, or by degrees, we miss him. We cannot do without him. He is a want which just at this particular moment must be supplied, and cannot be supplied. The loss is irreparable, and is now fast becoming intolerable. It seems as if something which had to be gone through, cannot be gone through, simply because he was the part of our life needful to the going through with it, and now he is not here. A false, a cruel, a suspecting friend we lose before he dies. But we never miss him. It never comes out that he is wanted. He is found to have been always in reality outside of our lives; and he is dismissed from our minds with a sad sort of relief that we have done with him, and the pious consolation that after all no love is ever wasted, which at any time or for any object has been mixed up with God. But it is not so with a true friend. The loss of him is never over; it is continually reappearing, and making our hearts as strangely tender as if his spirit were touching them at the moment. All this comes of the present being too much swollen with realities, so that we cannot get into our souls at once. Thus we are always behindhand with life, understanding ourselves and others, and, most of all, God, when it is too late. We cannot keep up with the present by intelligence or sentiment. We can only keep up with it by a spiritual quickness which prompts us to act, to suffer, and, above all, to compromise ourselves, at the bidding of the instincts of grace. Thus it is that sorrows are mostly less hard to bear, than they seem; for we are almost unconsciously bearing them by degrees.

Now it was not so with our Lady. She took in the present in its fulness; she embraced it in the tranquillity of her vast comprehension. A sorrow revealed itself to her in its completeness, and thus pressed with all its weight upon her soul at once. Thus her sorrows are greater than they seem. They grow upon us, but they did not grow upon her. This is very much to be remembered, when we speak of her dispositions in her sufferings. Her endurance was of another kind from ours, because of her complete realisation of the present, and hence her dispositions, while the poverty of language compels us to call them by the same names, must be magnified and multiplied into something quite different from what they were before.

Having premised this, we must look first of all, as we have had to do in the other dolours, at our Blessed Mother's tranquillity. If we pass in review the manifold horrors of the Crucifixion, and see the various assaults of grief of which her soul was the centre, it will seem as if tranquillity was just that grace, the exercise of which would be impossible. If we did not know that God was everlasting peace, there would appear something almost incongruous, and out of keeping with the scene, in a holiness which was stayed in the deepest calm at such a time. With us depth of feeling is for the most part accompanied by agitation, which makes it difficult for us to conceive the union of the liveliest sorrow and the most delicate sensitiveness with a tranquillity which looks as if it were impassible. Among men calmness in grief is but a token of insensibility. Our Lady's peace is like that of God, undisturbed amid the sounds of ten million worlds, unruffled by the portentous revolt of sin, and self-possessed in the very profusest outpouring of intense and burning love. Nothing discloses to us more astonishingly her union with God, than this unbroken calm. Where God is, there can be no trouble; and there was not a recess in our Lady's nature where God was not, and which He did not possess with the most undivided sovereignty. Hence, while horror followed horror, there was no amazement in her soul, no stupefaction, no bewilderment. As the mystery unfolded strangest depths of suffering, even the counsels of God did not seem to take His chosen creature by surprise. In what an abiding presence of God must her soul have dwelt! How trained must each faculty of the mind have been, to fall in with the ways of God as it met them, and with such unquestioning promptitude, with such unstartled dignity! In what subordination must every affection have been to the instantaneous dominion of grace, a subordination which would so increase their freedom as to augment their powers of loving and of sorrowing a thousandfold! There was no effort, no struggle, no pause, no token that her inward life felt the pressure of outward circumstance. The creature kept step with the Creator, and the angels marvelled at the divine repose of her beautiful dependence.

Out of this calmness came her silent courage. We must remember that, although her surviving so great a sorrow was miraculous, her endurance of the sorrow was not a miracle, but a grace. Her life was kept in her by the hand of God; but she received no such support in her endurance as for one moment interfered with the perfection of its merit. It was fortitude such as the most glorious spirit in the choir of Thrones could not attain to. It was a courage the very silence of which showed at once the severity of its trial and the earnestness of its generosity. The silence itself was another proof of Mary's amazing union with God. For they, who are much with Him, lose their habits of speaking, and acquire in their stead habits of supernatural listening. She spoke not, because she reposed in God. She did not even gather herself up to bear, or prepare her courage for the combat. She let the burden take her as it found her. She neither quickened her pace nor slackened it. How could a resolution so quiet be at the same time so strong? This is the question which our limited notion of sanctity is tempted to ask. The answer is easy; its strength was in its very quietness. But, if we understand the words, do we comprehend the thing? Do we fathom the disposition of Mary's soul in which this grandeur of strength was wedded to this childlike simplicity of unwondering quietness?

Out of her quietness we pass into her silent courage, out of her silent courage into her generosity. They are like ample halls within her soul, where we dare hardly speak above a whisper lest we wake the echoes, and where we gaze, without questioning, on the wonderful trophies which hang upon the walls. A creature has but one will to give away to God, and when he has given it irrevocably, what further oblation is left? All generosity then is but a perseverance in the first grand generosity, and if perseverance is a grander thing than the act or disposition in which we persevere, it is so only in its completeness, and not in each of its separate stages. Yet it seemed as if Mary had endless wills to give to God, and as if they came as fast as He could call for them. The Divine Will tried her everywhere, and everywhere it found the most entire conformity. There was no failure, no lagging behind, nothing unequable. There was a strain certainly. How shall the creature not strain who has to keep up with God, especially when His awful justice was urging its chariot wheels through the Red Sea of the Passion? But it was a strain of the most heavenly peace, of the most graceful adoration. When God went quicker, she went quicker. Her will actually entered more promptly into His will, in proportion as it exacted more from her. Her soul seemed to become more inexhaustible the more it was exhausted, like the souls of the Blessed, endlessly loving, endlessly adoring, as they sink deeper still and deeper in the Vision of the Holy Trinity.

But the very thought of these impossibilities of Mary's generosity turns us from her dispositions to the lessons, which this fifth dolour teaches to ourselves. The last dolour taught us how to carry our crosses, this one how to stand by them. We must not leave the Cross. We must not come down from Calvary until we are crucified, and then the Cross and ourselves will have become inseparable. But Calvary is a great place for impatience. Many have the courage to march up the hill, shouldering their cross with decent manfulness. But when they get there, they lay their cross on the ground, and go down again into the city to keep the remainder of the feast with the people. Some are stripped, and then leave, refusing to be nailed. Some are nailed, but unfasten themselves before the Elevation. Some stand the shock of the Elevation, and then come down from the cross, before the three hours are out, some in the first hour, some in the second, some, alas! when even the third hour is drawing to its close. In truth the world is full of deserters from Calvary, so full that politic or disdainful grace seems to take no trouble to arrest them. For grace crucifies no one against his will. It leaves that work to the world, and treacherously and tyrannically does the world do it. Men appear to believe that to breathe the fresh air on the top of Calvary for half a minute is to act upon them like a charm. Crucifixion, like a plunge in the cold sea, the briefer it is, will have the healthier glow and the more sensible reaction. But unfortunately it is not so. Sorrow is a slow workman, and crucifixion a long business. A tree takes root in a new ground quicker than the cross in a new heart. But all this is by no means agreeable to rapid, impulsive nature. It will allow sanctification to be like an operation, sharp but soon over. It cannot wait if it comes in the shape of a gradual cure. Yet who is there that has ever tried to kill self in any one of its least departments, and has not almost despairingly wondered at its amazing and provoking vitality? How many great minds are there, who have travelled far along the road of sanctity, before they are out of sight of personal feeling and wounded sensibility? O then for the grace to remain our three full hours on the top of Calvary! Can there be a sadder sight on earth than that which tells how often and how easily great heights in heaven are missed, those half-crucified souls we meet in all companies, so strangely out of place, such mournful monuments of the impatience of nature and the jealousy of grace!

God is very exacting. They, who love Him, can say so without loving Him less. Nay, to them the very thought is an additional degree of love. He is not content with our remaining on Calvary our three full hours. When we are not nailed to our cross, we must stand. There must be no sitting, no lying down, no leaning on our cross, as if forsooth that was meant for our support which is waiting there only to crucify. Indeed, and this is significant enough, kneeling is not so good as standing. We go there to suffer, not to worship. Our suffering will turn into worship. We are not to adore our cross, or say fine words about it, or put ourselves into sentimental attitudes before it. We are to do the commonplace thing of standing by it, which is the posture of men. Standing is what the ceremonial of Calvary prescribes. Here again what sad sights we see! It is well if we do not play a part in them ourselves. There are souls whose Way of the Cross is full of promise, and yet who spoil everything on the top of Calvary. Perhaps if they had been crucified at once, they might have done well. But that was not God's Will. Waiting has unmanned them. Their courage has oozed out among the grim skulls that strew the faded herbage of the mount. They have sat down, because the delay was long. Or they have knelt to pray that the cross might pass from them. Foolish souls! that belongs to Gethsemane, not to Calvary. We must not put our beginnings, where our end should be. Or the preparations frighten them, the digging of the fosse, the measuring of the breadth from hand to hand, done so carelessly as it seems to be, and yet a matter in which the least carelessness may be infinite torture, the repointing of those blunt nails, and then those cruel unnecessary flourishes of the hammer. Some shrink from stripping in the cold air, and have to be stripped almost by force. Some are terrified by the eclipse, which hides friends' faces and the consolations of creatures. Some cry out and jump up when the cold iron touches the palm of the first hand. Most fail then. Is it not better to go down from Calvary, in the honest confession of our cowardice, than to behave so weakly on the summit of that sacred hill? O no! it is better far to stay. Better a reluctant crucifixion, than none at all. Let us stand, if we can; if we cannot, let us be rolled about like logs, as if we had died of fright, and be nailed by force or in unconsciousness. Only let us be crucified;—gracefully, if it may be, but ungracefully rather than not at all.

Why do so many fail? Because they are not silent. Endurance depends much on silence. Power escapes with words. It is only by the help of the grace of silence that the saints carry such heavy crosses. A cross, for which we have received sympathy, is far heavier than it was before, or it may be that the sympathy has unnerved ourselves, so that the weight seems greater, and the wound in our shoulder sorer. Silence is the proper atmosphere of the cross, and secrecy its native climate. The best crosses are secret ones, and we may be silent under those that are not secret. Indeed silence creates a sort of secrecy even in public. For at least we can hide how much we suffer, if we cannot hide altogether the fact that we are suffering. We can conceal how often we are almost at the point of sinking beneath our burden. We can keep to ourselves those individual peculiarities of suffering, which are far its sharpest points, and which feed the sympathy of others more than greater things can do. In some way or other human sympathy desecrates the operations of grace. It mingles a debasing element with that which is divine. The Holy Spirit withdraws from its company, because it is "of the earth, earthy." The Comforter gives His best consolations only to the inconsolable of earth. They, who seek creatures first, must be content with creatures; for they will not find God afterwards, let them seek ever so much. They, to whom God is not enough by Himself, but must have comforting creatures mixed with Him, will never find out their sad mistake; for to them God will never open those treasures which will show them how different He is from creatures. But all this is hard to nature. Nature never yet breathed freely on the top of Calvary.

Men do not take their ease on mountain-heights. They hardly rest there, except to admire the magnificence of the view, because the breathing is so difficult. It is very hard to put away all consolation from ourselves. Sympathy seems often to be just that which makes our pain endurable. Well then! let us go down a step lower. Let us not put it away; but do not let us ask it. Let it find us out without our seeking. As the world goes, we shall not greatly peril what is divine in our sorrows, by being simply passive about sympathy. But even this passiveness is hard. How should it be anything else but hard, when it is part of our crucifixion? It is Calvary's hardest lesson. Let us take it to ourselves, although we fear it; neither let us be cast down because we fear. Who ever did anything well which he had not first feared to do? What is there upon earth that is worth doing, which is not worth fearing also?

But there is a true consolation, deeply hidden indeed, yet near at hand, in this putting away of human consolation. It is in the darkness of nature that we realise the vicinity of Jesus. It is in the absence of creatures that we are held up in the sensible embrace of the Creator. Creatures bring obscurity with them, wherever they intrude. They are for ever in our way, intercepting graces, hiding God, defrauding us of spiritual consolations, making us languid and irritable. They so fill our outward senses, that the inner senses of our souls are unable to act. We often wish our lives were more divine. But they are in fact much more divine than we believe. It is sorrow which reveals this to us. It comes like a shroud around us. By degrees our horizon narrows in, and our great world becomes a little world. Onward still it creeps, first one object disappears, and then another. We are growing less and less distracted. Our inward life is more awake. Our soul gets strong. Now the line of darkness has touched Jerusalem itself. Even the consolations of the spiritual city have disappeared. The helmets of the Roman soldiers catch the light for a moment above the level of the cloud, as if they were floating away on a dark current. The greenness of the mount grows black. For a moment it blinds us; then by degrees the white Figure of Jesus comes out in the dim obscurity. We feel the warm blood on our hands as we grasp the Cross. It is no apparition: it is life. We are with God, with our Creator, with our Saviour. He is all our own. The withdrawal of creatures has made Him so. But He has not come. He was always there, always thus within our souls, only He was overpowered with the false brightness of creatures. He comes out in the dark like the stars. The white moon of noonday does not allure us by its beauty; it enchants us only in the night; so it is the darkness of a spiritual Calvary which covers our souls with the soft shining of our beautiful Saviour.

But the couching of our spiritual sight is not the only operation which the senses of our soul undergo on Calvary. All souls are hard of hearing with respect to the sounds of the invisible world. The inner ear is opened upon Calvary. The sounds of Jerusalem travel up to us through the darkness, and perhaps the sounds of labour in the gardens near. But they rise up as admonitions rather than as distractions. They come to us softly and indistinctly, and do not jar with the silence of our endurance, or the low whisperings of prayer. Least of all do they muffle the clearness of our Saviour's words when He vouchsafes to speak. Down below, how the world deafened us by its tumultuous noises, and jaded our spirit with its multiplicity of sounds! We knew that Jesus was at our sides, and yet we could not converse with Him. It was like trying to listen, when the loud wheels are rattling harshly along the streets, when listening is no better than an unsuccessful strain, or a perplexed misunderstanding. The mere noise the world makes in its going so amazes us that it hinders our feet upon the road to heaven. It is only on Calvary that earth is subdued enough to make music with heaven; for it is there only that God is heard distinctly, while the low-lying world murmurs like a wind, a sound which is discordant nowhere, because it is rather the accompaniment of a sound than a sound itself.

We see but two things on Calvary, Jesus and Mary; and from each we learn a lesson, one about our own deaths, and one about the deaths of others. Jesus vouchsafes to teach us how to die. If He in His great hour would have His Mother by Him, how shall we dare to die without her? In all things must we imitate Jesus, although it be in a sphere so infinitely below Him. But most of all, it is of importance to us to imitate Him in His death. If it had been well, He would have loved to spare her that terrific scene, though she perhaps would have accounted her absence a cruel mercy. It was there, at that deathbed, that she became our Mother. There is surely not one of us into whose mouth faith does not many times a day put that universal prayer, the prayer of the pope and the peasant, of the doctor and the scholar, of the rich and the poor, of the religious and the secular, that the Mother of God may assist us in the hour of death. But we must imbed this petition into all our prayers. Let us leave to God, without dictation or even wish, the time, and place, and manner, of our death, so only that it be not an unprovided death, and above all things not unprovided with Mary. The hour of death is a thirsty time, and exhausts great graces. Unsuspected chasms open suddenly in the soul, and swallow up past years, old habits, and a thousand other things we can ill spare then. The devil reserves his worst weapons for the last. It is very terrible not to be able to die twice, lest the novelty get the better of us the first time,—and it is a tremendous stake. There are great sacraments for that hour, but not greater than are needed. Watch a dying man! See how absolutions sink swiftly into his dry soul, like summer rain into the gaping ground. And yet the battle is still coming and going in his eyes. Let us have Mary. Whether she be there visibly or invisibly, whether she speak and work, or work without speaking, let it be an agreement of long standing, a pledge not to be broken, that she shall be present to conduct for us a ceremonial so difficult and yet of such unutterable import. It is worth while to spend a whole life in asking this, if only we gain the object of our petition at the last. What is a good life worth if it be not crowned by a good death? Yet a good life is the nearest approach in our power to a good death. There have perhaps been comparatively few good deaths, which have not come at the end of good lives. And those few, so all the believing world says, have been contrived by Mary. But a good life is the likeliest of all things to bring her to our bedsides in that hour. A cross-bearing life is for ever meeting Mary. At crucifixions she is present as it were officially. If Jesus would not die without her, she will love us all the more if we refuse to do so either. However long the agony has been, however troubled in spirit the poor passing soul, blessed above all the dead are those, whose eyes Mary herself has closed!

Such is the lesson which Jesus teaches us about our own deaths. We learn one from Mary about the deaths of others. It is, that devotion for those in their last agony is a Mary-like devotion, and most acceptable to her Immaculate Heart. There is not a moment of day or night in which that dread pomp of dying is not going on. There are persons, like ourselves, or better than ourselves, and whose friends have with reason loved them more than ever ours have loved us, who are now straitened in their agony, and whose eternal sight of God is trembling anxiously in the balance. Can any appeal to our charity be more piteously eloquent than this? When we think of all that Mary had done for each of those souls, those who ceaselessly, momentarily fixing their eternity in death, when we call to mind the long train of graces which she has brought to every one of them, and consequently the yearning of her maternal heart for their final perseverance and everlasting salvation, we may form some idea of the gratefulness of this devotion to her. The deathbed is one of her peculiar spheres. She seems to exercise quite a particular jurisdiction over it. It is there that she so visibly co-operates with Jesus in the redemption of mankind. But she seeks for us to co-operate with her also. She would fain draw our hearts with hers, our prayers to hers. Is she not the one Mother of us all? Are not the dying our brothers and our sisters in the sweet motherhood of Mary? The family is concerned. We must not coldly absent ourselves. We must assist in spirit at every death that is died the whole world over, deaths of heretics and heathens, as well as Christians. For they too are our brothers and sisters; they have souls; they have eternities at stake; Mary has an interest in them. And their eternity is in more than double danger. How much more must they need prayers, who have no sacraments? How much darker must their closing scene be, where the full light of faith shines not? How much more earnest must be the prayers, when, not ordinary grace, but a miracle of grace, must be impetrated for them? Alas! they will have none of our other gifts; at least, and affectionately in their own despite, they shall have our prayers. We must remember also that we too have to die. We shall one day lie in the same strait, and need unspeakably the same charitable prayers. The measure which we mete to others shall be measured to us again. This is the divine rule of retribution. Nothing will prepare a smoother deathbed for ourselves, than a lifelong daily devotion to those who are daily dying. Mary assisted her Son to die in many mysterious ways. By His will, and in the satisfaction of her own maternal love, she has now assisted at the deathbeds of many millions. She has great experience by this time, if we might so speak, and is wonderfully skilled in the science of the last hour. By prayerful thoughts, by pious practices, by frequent ejaculations, by the usages the Church has indulgenced, let us win a bright and gentle end for ourselves, by following Mary everywhere to the deathbeds she attends.

Such are the lessons we learn from the fifth dolour. The Crucifixion can never be rightly understood without Mary, because without her it is not truthfully represented. What a picture it is, the High Mass of the world's redemption, offered by Jesus to the Eternal Father, while the countless angels are the audience and the spectators! When the

Host is elevated, the whole frame of inanimate nature trembles with terror and adoration, and earth darkens itself, which is to be a rubric it is to observe in the presence of Jesus for all ages. But what is Mary's part? Her Immaculate Heart is the living Altar-stone on which the Sacrifice is offered; it is the Server, the beatings of whose broken heart are the responses of the liturgy; it is the Thurible, in which the world's faith, the world's hope, the world's love, the world's worship, are being burnt like incense before the slain Lamb that taketh away the sins of the world; and finally the same Immaculate Heart is the Choir, the more than angelic Choir of that tremendous Mass; for did not the silence of her beautiful sufferings sing unutterable, voiceless songs into the ravished ear of the Bleeding Host?

CHAPTER VII.

THE SIXTH DOLOUR.

THE TAKING DOWN FROM THE CROSS.

THE darkness of the eclipse had passed away, and the true shades of evening were beginning to fall. The Cross stood bare on Calvary against the light which the setting sun had left behind it in the west. The spectacle of the day was over, and the multitudes of the city were all gone, and the current of their thoughts diverted elsewhere. A few persons moved about on the top of the mount, who had been concerned with the taking down of Jesus from the Cross, or were bringing spices from the city to embalm Him. Mary sat at the foot of the Cross, with the dead Body of her Son lying across her lap. Is Bethlehem come back to thee, my Mother, and the days of the beautiful Childhood?

There are many varieties of human sorrow. It is difficult to compare them one with another; because each has its peculiarity, and each peculiarity has an eminence of suffering belonging to it, in which no other sorrow shares. Thus it may easily happen that a sorrow, which in itself looks less than another, may in reality be greater, because of the time at which it comes, or the circumstances under which it occurs, or the position which it occupies in a series of other griefs. This is the case with the sixth dolour, the Taking down from the Cross. It is the grief of an accomplished sorrow, and in this respect differs at once from the strain of a distressing anticipation, or the active struggle of a present misery actually accomplishing itself. This difference cannot be unknown to us in our own experience. When we are in the act of suffering we are not fully conscious of the efforts we are making. Our whole nature rises to meet what we have to endure. Capabilities of pain, of which we had hitherto no suspicion, disclose themselves. Perhaps also we have a greater amount of supernatural assistance than afterwards. But when the pressure is lightened, when the strife is over, then we become conscious of the drain which grief has made upon our strength. The weariness of sorrow, like bodily fatigue, comes when all is over. We stiffen, as it were, and our heart begins to ache more sensibly, in the seeming tranquillity which follows the misfortune. The reaction makes itself felt in a peculiar depression, which is almost more hard to bear than actual suffering, not so much because it is intrinsically greater than actual suffering, but because it comes after it, and, being itself the exhaustion of our powers of endurance, it has nothing under it to support it.

It happens also for the most part that, by a merciful cruelty of Providence, our ordinary duties, or even sometimes new duties to which our sorrow has given birth, present themselves before us, and require our energy and attention. But, while this often hinders the reaction of sorrow from going too far, it is also in itself hard to bear. We are seldom in greater want of grace than in this moment of resuming the duties of our station after an interruption of more than common sorrow. It is like beginning life again at a disadvantage. We have perhaps more to do, when we are less able to do it. We have used up our power of bearing grief; and just when the rawness of our misery is passing off, new duties come which, either by contrast or by association, open the old wounds afresh, and how are we to endure it? Moreover, excessive grief, even when it lasts but for a short time, seems to have a peculiar power to destroy habits. Things, even hard things, are easy to us, because we are accustomed to them. But after violent sorrow, everything appears new and strange. We have lost our old facility.

Things have changed places in our minds. Easy things are now hard, because of this very novelty. Yet life is inexorable. It must go on, and under the old laws, like a ruthless machine which cannot feel, and therefore cannot make allowances. Now perhaps is a greater trial of our worth than when we were enduring the blows which misfortune was dealing upon us. This is the account of the sixth dolour; this is the place it occupies in the sorrows of our dearest Mother. Think of the Crucifixion, and all that it involved, and is not the reaction after that likely to be something which it is quite beyond our power adequately to conceive! Immense as is the holiness of her Immaculate Heart, sorrow can still find work to do, and can build the edifice higher, as well as embellish what is built already.

The Soul of Jesus passed into the earth at the foot of the Cross, and descended to the limbus of the fathers. Mary was still at the foot of the Cross. She comprehended in its completeness the vast mystery of the separation of that Body and Soul, the death of the Son of God. The soul has left her, but she has the Body still. In the next dolour that will go also, and then the Mother will be indeed alone. For the most part it is not God's way to withdraw Himself all at once. He spares the weakness of the soul, and passes from it almost insensibly, after special favours and more intimate union, as the perfume gradually exhales out of a jar where it has been kept. The two thieves are still in their agony close to the dead Body of Jesus. To one of them it is like the soothing presence of the Blessed Sacrament, which we all of us in trouble know so well, because it is unlike any other feeling. To the other there is no consolation now. There is time for him still. Mary still prays, for she never ceases while the fondest hope has any foothold left to which it can cling. The living Jesus is not so far off, but He can hear him if he cries. But he has made his choice, and keeps to it. The life that remains in him is every moment desecrating Calvary.

Crucifixion is a slow death, and includes many sorts of

pain. Among these is to be reckoned the breaking of the legs of the sufferers, either to add to the torture already inflicted, now that its duration has become wearisome and without interest to the ministers of vindictive justice, or by a sort of fierce mercy to hasten its termination. The executioners therefore approach the top of Calvary thus to consummate the punishment of the three whom they had crucified, armed with a strong hammer or heavy bar of iron, of such weight as speedily to fracture the limbs when they are struck. It was a fearful sound for Mary to hear, the dull crashing of the flesh and bone, and the agonising cries of the miserable sufferers, one of them too the son of her second motherhood, the firstborn of her prayers. But words will not tell the anguish with which she saw them approach the Body of Jesus. Earth held nothing one half so sacred. Dead as it was, it was joined to the Divinity, and therefore was entitled to the fullest honours of divine worship. One rude touch of it were an appalling sacrilege; but to crush the limbs, to break the bones, was a profaneness too horrible even for the mind to dwell upon. The thought was an intense grief to her religion. But her love, was not it also concerned? It is true, life was gone; but was the lifeless Form less an object of her love than when beautiful life had filled it? Let the hearts of those who have mourned their dead reply. Never does love pour itself out in more soft sadness over eyes bright with life than over those that are closed in death. To the eye of love the pale face has become doubly beautiful. The graces of old years have passed upon it. The intensity of its unmeaning quiet has a charm of its own. The compressed lips speak with a dumb eloquence which belongs to them. The cold body has to satisfy two claims of love, its own claim, and the soul's, and it satisfies them well. We call it "*him*," not "*it*," because to fond love it is so really the person, the self, whom we are loving. So mothers have wept over sons, from whose caresses the dignity of great manhood has separated them for years, but now the old times have come back, and the familiarities of childhood, with more than its passive helplessness, have come back, and perhaps the old childish look as well, and grief feeds itself sweetly out of the marble beauty of its dead. Who does not know this? But if we common mourners, whose grief is so soon distracted, can feel all this with such intensity, what must have been the unspeakable love of Mary for the Body of her Son, her Son who was God as well? She spoke not. Her voice broke not the silence, mingled not with the moans of the dying thieves; but the silence of her prayer was loud in heaven. The rude men saw that Jesus was dead, and desisted from their purpose. "These things were done, that the Scripture might be fulfilled, You shall not break a bone of Him."

But there was another Scripture also to be fulfilled, "They shall look on Him whom they pierced." Mary's prayers shall cause the first Scripture to be fulfilled, but not that any sorrow may spare the Mother's Heart. It shall accomplish the word of God, but it shall not spare the sacrilege. Truly this second Scripture shall be one of Simeon's swords. Whether it were from doubt of our Lord's being really dead, or whether it were in the mere wantonness of authority little used to give account of itself in such times and places, one of the soldiers drew near, and drove his spear into our Lord's right side, across His Body, and through His Sacred Heart, and immediately there issued forth from the sacrilegious wound both Blood and Water, some of which it is said sprang upon the limbs of the penitent thief as if it were an outward baptism or a visible absolution, where inward grace had already accomplished its heavenly work. It were long to tell of how much pathetic love this wound in our Saviour's Heart was the figure and the symbol. It has been the sweet contemplation of countless saints. The spear has opened a home, a refuge, a hermitage, in that wounded Heart in which souls in all ages, in these latter days especially, have nestled in all their sorrows and trials, having renewed themselves in the weariness of their exile, and have hidden themselves from the strife of tongues and from an evil world.

It is the very glory of devotion to the Precious Blood that this wound of the Sacred Heart proves that our dearest Lord shed every drop of His Blood for us. To us therefore, for these and many other reasons, the piercing of His Heart is one of our greatest spiritual consolations. But we have to regard it here as one of Mary's chiefest sorrows.

There is something in the thought of our Blessed Lord's dead Body which overshadows the mind, and bends the soul down in profoundest reverence. It hung there upon the Cross in the light of the March afternoon, white, with seams of dark blood all over it, and disfigured with almost countless wounds. There was no object on earth so sacred as itself. It was worshipful with the divinest worship. Throngs of invisible angels were adoring all round. Yet, while it was adorable, it was helpless also. It was as if the Blessed Sacrament had been left upon a mountain top, over which there was a thoroughfare for men. This object of divine worship was the property of the rulers, who had just consummated the unutterable sin of the Crucifixion. Practically speaking, it was in the power of base executioners to do what they would with it, certain that no ignominy which they could work upon it would be reproved. There was something very dreadful in a thing which was so sacred being left in such insecurity, in such vicinity of evil, to such probability of appalling outrage. The Mother was there, her heart full of worship, but helpless as the Body itself. Were she to plead, her pleading would but suggest sacrilege. It would but stimulate the ruffian nature of those with whom she had to deal. But there it hung upon the Cross, anybody's right, anybody's property, rather than hers, out of whose sweet blood the Holy Ghost had made it. Two wretched criminals were writhing in their last agonies on either side. The city was keeping feast below, and preparing to commence its Sabbath-rest. That Victim-Body had begun its Sabbath already. Its pain had ceased, and it was resting. The executioners are returning. The Roman soldiers ride up and down the mount. The relics of the execution must be cleared away before the Sabbath begins. That Body does not belong to the Cross. It belongs to an unimaginable supernal throne, at the Right Hand of the Eternal Father. No one is here who knows it, but the silent Mother; and she is silent because she has no right to speak, and because her speaking would do harm. O how often in the world does God frighten us by this seeming abandonment of Himself and of all He holds most dear! And it appears as if it were the very strength of our love, which makes our faith so weak. We fear most timorously for that which we love most tenderly.

The love of God brings many new instincts into the heart. Heavenly and noble as they are, they bear no resemblance to what men would call the finer and more heroic developments of character. A spiritual discernment is necessary to their right appreciation. They are so unlike the growths of earth that they must expect to meet on earth with only suspicion, misunderstanding, and dislike. It is not easy to defend them from a controversial point of view; for our controversy is obliged to begin by begging the question, or else it would be unable so much as to state its case. The axioms of the world pass current in the world, the axioms of the Gospel do not. Hence the world has its own way. It talks us down. It tries us before tribunals where our condemnation is secured beforehand. It appeals to principles which are fundamental with most men, but are heresies with us. Hence its audience takes part with it against us. We are foreigners, and must pay the penalty of being so. If we are misunderstood, we had no right to reckon on anything else, being as we are out of our own country. We are made to be laughed at. We shall be understood in heaven. Woe to those easy-going Christians, whom the world can understand, and will tolerate, because it sees they have a mind to compromise!

The love of souls is one of these instincts, which the love of Jesus brings into our hearts. To the world it is proselytism, the mere wish to add to a faction, one of the selfish developments of party spirit. One while the stain of lax morality is affixed to it, another while the reproach of pharisaic strictness! For what the world seems to suspect least of all in religion is consistency. But the love of souls, however apostolic, is always subordinate to love of Jesus. We love souls because of Jesus, not Jesus because of souls. Thus there are times and places when we pass from this instinct of divine love to another, from the love of souls to the hatred of heresy. This last is peculiarly offensive to the world. So especially opposed is it to the spirit of the world, that even in good believing hearts every remnant of worldliness rises in arms against this hatred of heresy, embittering the very gentlest of characters, and spoiling many a glorious work of grace. Many a convert, in whose soul God would have done grand things, goes to his grave a spiritual failure, because he would not hate heresy. The heart, which feels the slightest suspicion against the hatred of heresy, is not yet converted. God is far from reigning over it yet with an undivided sovereignty. The paths of higher sanctity are absolutely barred against it. In the judgment of the world, and of worldly Christians, this hatred of heresy is exaggerated, bitter, contrary to moderation, indiscreet, unreasonable, aiming at too much, bigoted, intolerant, narrow, stupid, and immoral. What can we say to defend it? Nothing which they can understand. We had therefore better hold our peace. If we understand God and He understands us, it is not so very hard to go through life suspected, misunderstood, and unpopular. The mild self-opinionatedness of the gentle undiscerning good, will also take the world's view and condemn us: for there is a meek-looking positiveness about timid goodness which is far from God, and the instincts of whose charity is more towards those who are less for God, while its timidity is daring enough for a harsh judgment. There are conversions where three-quarters of the heart stop outside the Church, and only a quarter enters, and heresy can only be hated by an undivided heart. But if it is hard, it has to be borne. A man can hardly have the full use of his senses, who is bent on proving to the world, God's enemy, that a thoroughgoing catholic hatred of heresy is a right frame of mind. We might as well force a blind man to judge on a question of colour. Divine love inspheres us in a different circle of life, motive, and principle, which is not only not that of the world, but in direct enmity with it. From a worldly point of view the craters in the moon are more explicable things than we Christians with our supernatural instincts. From the hatred of heresy we get to another of these instincts, the horror of sacrilege. The distress caused by profane words seems to the world but an exaggerated sentimentality. The penitential spirit of reparation, which pervades the whole Church, is in its view either a superstition or an unreality. The perfect misery, which an unhallowed touch of the Blessed Sacrament causes to the servants of God, provokes either the world's anger or its derision. Men consider it either altogether absurd in itself, or at any rate out of all proportion, and if otherwise they have proofs of our common sense, they are inclined to put down our unhappiness to sheer hypocrisy. The very fact that they do not believe as we believe removes us still further beyond the reach even of their charitable comprehension. If they do not believe in the very existence of our sacred things, how shall they judge the excesses of a soul to which those sacred things are far dearer than itself?

Now it is important to bear all this in mind, while we are considering the sixth dolour. Mary's heart was furnished, as never heart of saint was yet, with these three instincts regarding souls, heresy, and sacrilege. They were in her heart three grand abysses of grace, out of which arose perpetually new capabilities of suffering. Ordinarily speaking, the Passion tires us. It is a fatiguing devotion. It is necessarily so, because of the strain of soul which it causes, as well by its horrors, as by the profound adoration which it is every moment eliciting. So, when our Lord dies, a feeling of repose comes over us.* For a moment we are tempted to think that our Lady's dolours ought to have ended there, and that the sixth dolour and the seventh are almost of our own creation, and that we tax our imagination in order to fill up the picture with the requisite dark shading of sorrow. But this is only one of the ways, in which devotion to the dolours heightens and deepens our devotion to the Passion. It is not our imagination that we tax, but our spiritual discernment. In these two last dolours we are led into greater refinements of woe, into the more abstruse delicacies of grief, because we have got to deal with a soul rendered even more wonderful than it was before, by the elevations of the sorrows which have gone before. Thus the piercing of our Lord with the spear was to our Blessed Lady by far the most awful sacrilege which it was then in man's power to perpetrate upon the earth. To break violently into the Holy of Holies in the temple, and pollute its dread sanctity with all manner of heathen defilement, would have been as nothing compared to the outrage on the adorable Body of God. It is in vain that we try to lift ourselves to a true appreciation of this horror in Mary's heart. Our love of God is wanting in keenness, our perceptions of divine things in fineness. We cannot do more than make approaches, and they are terrible enough.

We have spoken already of mothers watching the deathbeds of their sons. It is the form of human woe, which comes most naturally to us, when we are with Mary upon Calvary. When the long struggle is at last over, and the breaking heart has acknowledged at least a kind of relief in the fact that the object of her love has no more to suffer, when that same heart has taken quiet possession of the beautiful dead form before it, as if it were a sanctuary, almost a refuge from grief itself, would not the least rough-

---

* This impatience of Holy Week and eagerness for Easter was strikingly exemplified in the Venerable Mother Frances of the Blessed Sacrament, the Carmelite nun to whom so many remarkable revelations about the souls in Purgatory were made.

ness, the least inconsiderateness, the most trivial dishonour to the dead body, be a new and fearful sorrow to the mother? Is there a mother on earth who could bear to see with her own eyes even the kindly hand of science, which she has herself invoked, endeavouring to discover in what recess it was that the mysterious ailment lodged itself, which has now made her childless? Would it not be as if she saw a hallowed object desecrated before her eyes? In the dire necessities of the pestilence, with its swift burial and rough ministers and horrible dead-cart and quicklime pit, how much more terrible would the outrage be! She still fills the lifeless figure with the life of her own love, and before she has drunk her fill of love by gazing on it, before the red blood has had time to curdle or the limbs to grow cold, it is torn from her, as if it was not hers, by some stern officers, not the tenderest of their kind, for their office is the rudest, rude even in the wise mercy it fulfils, and is flung upon the dead-cart, with a heap of other pest-stricken victims, and so borne onward to a dishonourable grave, a promiscuous charnel-house. And fresh grief is so tender, so raw, can so little bear handling! Is it not fearful to think of? Yet it is as nothing to our Lady's agony, when the Body of Jesus was outraged by the spear. It is an immeasurably less sorrow in itself, and falls upon a heart, which however sweet and meek and loving, is immeasurably less capable of suffering than Mary's was. But it is an approach to Mary's sorrow, and a shadow of it.

Let us rise higher still. A saint is at the altar, overwhelmed with the dread action which he is performing. His heart is fit to break for love of God, of that incarnate God who lies before him on the corporal. Wild and sinful men break in upon him, whether in popular tumult or from other cause. He is driven off in his sacred vestments with violence, while he is clinging to the altar as an animal clings to its young when they are being torn from it. He sees the Blessed Sacrament flung upon the ground, the Precious Blood streaming over the altar-steps and both the

Body and the Blood trodden with scorn and blasphemy beneath the feet of the ruffian invaders. Because he is a saint, the sight would kill him, did not God miraculously support him. But the accumulated sorrows of a long life are nothing to this. The vision of that hour has been burned in upon his soul as by a fiery brand. Nothing of it will ever be forgotten. No excesses of penance will be sufficient to satisfy his yearning appetite for reparation. Years after, he will shudder in his prayer, and the tears course swiftly down his cheeks, as he calls to mind the boundless horror of that appalling sin. It is a sort of grief beyond common griefs, a grief in a shrine, of which holy and chosen souls only may participate. Yet what is it to Mary's sorrow, when she saw the spear touch the dead side, and the lifelike movement the Body made as the Heart was pierced, and the pulselike throbbing with which the Blood and Water followed the lance as it withdrew? As far as the saint is below Mary in sanctity, so far is his grief inferior to hers. An angel told St. Bridget that so tremendous was the shock to her, that she would have died instantly, but for a miracle. A sword in her own heart would have been a thousand times less dreadful.

It is strange how close to great sins great graces will often lie. Longinus had sinned in ignorance of that which peculiarly aggravated the horror of his act. Nevertheless it was a cruel action, the more cruel, if he knew that the mother was standing by. Wantonness too was the less excusable in him, upon whom, if tradition speaks truly, the hand of God was laid not lightly. He is said to have been suffering from some disease of the eyes, which threatened total blindness; and it may have been that his imperfect sight did not allow him to be certain of the death of Jesus, and that on that account he went beyond his commission, and pierced the Body with his lance. Some drops of the Blood fell upon his face, and tradition tells that, not only was the disease in his eyes instantaneously cured and the full use of his sight restored to him, but also, a still more wonderful miracle, the vision of his soul was made bright and clear, and he at once confessed the Divinity of Him whose Body he had thus dared to insult, at the risk of becoming in his own person the murderer of our Blessed Lord. For if he doubted of His death, he ran no less a risk than that of slaying Him himself. No one will wonder when Mary of Agreda tells them that, as with the penitent thief, so with Longinus, the grace of conversion was the answer to Mary's prayer. The very fact of his having been an instrument to increase her sorrows would give him a special claim upon her prayers.

Another small body of men is now approaching the summit of Calvary, and from their fixed looks it is plain that Jesus is the object of their coming. Is it some fresh outrage, some new sorrow for Mary? It is a new sorrow for Mary, but no fresh outrage. It is Joseph of Arimathea and Nicodemus, together with their servants. Both of them were disciples of our Blessed Lord, but secretly; for they were timid men. Joseph was "a counsellor, a good and just man," who had not "consented to the counsel and doings" of the others, because he "himself looked for the Kingdom of God." Nicodemus was a man learned in the Scriptures, the same who had come to Jesus by night for fear of the Jews, and had learned from Him the doctrine of regeneration. Joseph had gone in to Pilate, to whom he probably had access in his capacity as counsellor, and had begged the Body of Jesus, which had been granted to him. He had then, as St. Matthew tells us, got "a clean linen cloth" to wrap it in, and had called on Nicodemus to accompany him to Calvary. Nicodemus, as St. John tells us, brought with him "a mixture of myrrh and aloes, about an hundred pound weight." They also brought their servants with them to assist. They approached our Blessed Lady with the profoundest reverence and sympathy, told her what they had done, and asked her permission to take the Body down from the Cross. With hearts full of the tenderest devotion to the dolours of the Immaculate Mother, they drew nigh to the Cross, and made their preparations. They fixed the ladder against the Cross. Joseph mounted first, and Nicodemus after him. Mary, with John and Magdalen, remained immediately beneath them. It seemed as if some supernatural grace issued forth from the Adorable Body, and encircled them round, softening and subduing all their thoughts, making their hearts burn with divine love, and hushing them in the deepest and most thrilling adoration. Old times came back upon the Mother's heart, and the remembrance of the other Joseph, who had been so often privileged to handle the limbs, and touch the Sacred Flesh of the Incarnate Word. It would have been his office to have taken Jesus down from the Cross. But he was gone to his rest, and one that bore his name supplied his place, and it was both sweet and grievous to Mary that it should be so. One Joseph had given Him his arms to lie in, the other should give Him his own new monument to rest in; and both should pass Him from their own arms to those of Mary. It is strange too how often the timid are unexpectedly bold. These two disciples, who had been afraid to confess their Master openly when He lived, are now braving publicity when even apostles remain within the shelter of their hiding-place. Happy two! with what sweet familiarities and precious nearness to Himself, is not Jesus recompensing their pious service at this hour in heaven!

With gentle hand, tremblingly bold, as if his natural timidity had developed into supernatural reverence, Joseph touches the crown of thorns, and delicately loosens it from the head on which it was fixed, disentangles it from the matted hair, and without daring to kiss it, passes it to Nicodemus, who reaches it to John, from whom Mary, sinking on her knees, receives it with such devotion as no heart but hers could hold. Every blood-stained spike seemed instinct with life, and went into her heart, tipped as it were with the Blood of her Son, inoculating her more and more deeply with the Spirit of His Passion. Who can describe with what reverential touch, while the cold Body was a furnace of heavenly love burning against his heart, Joseph loosened the nails, so as not to crush or mutilate the blessed Hands and Feet which they had pierced. It was so hard a task that we are fain to believe angels helped him in it. Each nail was silently passed down to Mary. They were strange graces, these which were now flowing to her through the hands of her new son; yet after all not so unlike the gifts which Jesus had Himself been giving her these three-and-thirty years. Never yet had earth seen such a worship of sorrow as that with which the Mother bent over those mute relics, as they came down to her from the Cross, crusted too as they were, perhaps wet, with that Precious Blood, which she adored in its unbroken union with the Person of the Eternal Word. But with what agony was all this worship accompanied, what fresh wounds did not all these instruments of the Passion make in her heart, what old ones did they not re-open!

But a greater grief was yet to come. The Body was detached from the Cross. More and more thickly the angels gathered round, while thrills of love pierced with ecstatic bliss their grand intelligences. Mary is kneeling on the ground. Her fingers are stained with Blood. She stretches the clean linen cloth over her arms and holds them out to receive her Son, her Prodigal come back to her again, and come back thus! And was He not a Prodigal? Had He not wilfully gone out from her quiet home into the wildest and rudest of worlds, leagues and leagues distant from the purity and love of her spotless heart? Had He not spent all His substance on companions, worthless and despicable? Was it not a riotous spending, a riot of some eighteen hours' duration? Had He not been prodigal of His Precious Blood, of His beauty, His innocence, His life, His grace, His very Divinity? And now He was coming back to her thus! Can such a sorrow, such an accumulation of concentering sorrows, have any name? Can she bear the weight? Which weight? The sorrow or the Body? It matters not. She can bear them both. From above, the Body is slowly descending. She remembers the midnight hour when the Holy Ghost overshadowed her at Nazareth. Now it is the eternal Son who is so strangely overshadowing His kneeling Mother. Joseph trembled under the weight, even while Nicodemus helped him. Perhaps also it was not the weight only which made him tremble. Wonderfully must grace have held him up to do what he did. Now it is low enough for John to touch the sacred Head, and receive it in his arms, that it might not droop in that helpless rigid way, and Magdalen is holding up the Feet. It is her old post. It is her post in heaven now, highest of penitents, most beautiful of pardoned spirits! For one moment Mary prostrates herself in an agony of speechless adoration, and the next instant she has received the Body on her extended arms. The Babe of Bethlehem is back again in His Mother's lap. What a meeting! What a restoration! For a while she remains kneeling, while John and Magdalen, Joseph and Nicodemus, and the devout women adore. Then she passes from the attitude of the priest to the attitude of the mother. She rises from her knees, still bearing the burden as lightly as when she fled with Him into Egypt, and sits down upon the grass, with Jesus extended on her lap.

With minutest fondness she smooths His hair. She does not wash the Blood from off His Body. It is too precious; and soon He will want it all, as well as that which is on men's shoes, and the pavement of Jerusalem, and the olive-roots of Gethsemane. But she closes every wound, every mark of the lash, every puncture of the thorns, with a mixture of myrrh and aloes, which Nicodemus has brought. There was not a feature of His blessed Countenance, not a mark upon His Sacred Flesh, which was not at once a sorrow to her, and a very volume of profoundest meditations. Her soul went through the Passion upon His Body, as men trace their travels on a map. The very quietness of her occupation, the very concentration of her undistracted thoughts, seemed to enable her to go deeper and deeper down into His sufferings, and to compassionate them with a more interior bitterness than before. In none of the earlier stages of her sorrow had there been more demand upon her to control the common gestures and outbursts of grief, than when she sate in the light of that spring evening with her Son's dead Body on her lap, smoothing, anointing, and composing the countless prints of shame and suffering which had been worn so deeply into it. In vain for her were the birds trilling their even-song, the weight of the eclipse being taken off their blithe little hearts. In vain for her were the perfumes of the tender fig-leaves rising up in the cool air, and the buds bursting greenly, and the tender shoots full of vernal beauty. Her grief was past nature's soothing. For her Flower had been cruelly gathered, and lay withered there upon her knee.

She performed her task as an act of religion, with grave assiduity, not delaying over it to satisfy the grief of which her heart was full. The dead Body seemed as obedient to her as ever the Babe had been in Bethlehem, obedient in all things but one. She told St. Bridget that the extended arms could not be closed, and laid by His side or crossed upon His breast. We ought rather to say they *would* not, than they *could* not, be closed. He will not relinquish those outstretched arms which seem to invite the whole world into the utmost width of their embrace. There was room for all within them, a harbour large enough for all creation. If the lifting up of His Hands upon the Cross was an "evening sacrifice" to the Eternal Father, the outstretching of them was as it were a sacramental sign to men, that none were excluded from His invitation and His welcome. He would carry with Him to the tomb the form and figure of one crucified; and Mary understood why the arms were rigid, and forebore the gentle violence she was about to use. He must be swathed in the winding-sheet in that shape as well as may be, preaching large, wide, welcoming love even to the end. Mary must now take her last look of that dead Face. Mothers live lives in their last looks. Who shall tell what Mary's was like? Who would have been surprised if the eyes of the dead had opened, and His lips parted, under the kindling and the quickening of that look! With heroic effort she has bound the napkin around His Head, and has folded the winding-sheet over the sweet Face. And now there is darkness indeed around her. The very dead Body had been a light and a support. She has put out the light herself. Her own hands have quenched the lamp, and she stands facing the thick night. O brave woman! Hours of ecstatic contemplation over that silent-speaking Countenance would have passed like moments. But it was a time for religion, not for the indulgence of her tenderness; and she pierced her own heart through and through with the same hand with which she hid His Face. But, O Mary! thou seest that Face now, and art drinking thy fill of its beauty, and thou wilt do so for evermore, and never be satisfied, even when always satisfied, happy blessed Mother!

When we pass from the narrative of the sixth dolour to treat of its peculiarities, we are struck at the outset by a characteristic which runs all through it. It surrounds us perpetually with images of the Sacred Infancy and of the Blessed Sacrament. The Passion seems to sink out of view, as if it were a foundation only; the superstructure is carved all over with symbols of Bethlehem and the Altar. There is scarcely an action or attitude of Mary in all the dolour, which does not bring to mind at once either the old days of the Mother and the Child, or the coming days of the Priest and the Host. When she kneels to receive the Body, and remains kneeling with it in her arms for the others to adore, when she ministers to it and with tender reverence manipulates it, when care and responsibility for the Lord's Body is the anxiety of her heart, and her grief comes from the fear of sacrilege, we cannot avoid having the Blessed Sacrament continually before us. Her outward demeanour appears as if it were the model from which the Church had drawn its rubrics for mass, benediction, or procession. Her inward temper seems the ideal of those interior dispositions which should belong to all good priests in virtue of their being custodians of the Blessed Sacrament. In its measure the same prophetical forth-shadowing of the worship of the Blessed Sacrament is visible in the actions and gestures of Joseph and Nicodemus, of John and Magdalen. Thus an entirely new set of ideas comes in with this dolour. While it looks as if it were but the complement of the Crucifixion, and divisible from it only by an imaginary line, we find its inward spirit, its examples, allusions, doctrine, and figures, to belong to an entirely different region from that of the Passion. This reveals to us the real distinction there is between this dolour and the two which have preceded it. The mystical connection of the Blessed Sacrament with the Sacred Infancy has been dwelt upon at length elsewhere.* The Blessed Sacrament is, as it were, the real perpetuation of His Infancy in memory of His Passion. Thus in the sixth dolour it appears as if our Lord had no sooner consummated the work of His Passion, than He at once began to shadow forth that state in which it was His sweet will to abide with His Church for ever in the Sacrament of the Altar. From that instant the old images of Bethlehem rose up again, as if they had been kept down by force for awhile; and they return more determinately and plainly in the shape of forebodings of the Blessed Sacrament. This is not so much a separate peculiarity of this dolour, as its very soul and significance, running through every feature of it, tincturing Mary's dispositions under it, and giving a special character to the lessons which it conveys to ourselves.

There is a peculiarity of this dolour, which it is impossible for us fully to understand, but which must be borne in mind throughout, because it indicates the greatest depth of sorrow which this mystery reached in the soul of our Blessed Mother. It was the withdrawal of the life of Jesus. She herself perhaps did not know till now how much it had supported her, nor how many offices it had fulfilled towards her. For three-and-thirty years she had lived upon His life. It had been her atmosphere. There had been a kind of unity of life between them. Her heart had beaten in His

* Blessed Sacrament. Book Second.

Heart. She had seen with His eyes, and had heard with His ears, and had almost spoken with His lips, and thought with His thoughts, as she had done when she composed and sang the Magnificat. Mother and son had never before been so fused into each other. Two lives had never seemed so inseparably one life, as these two had done. And how shall one of them, and that the weaker and inferior, now stand alone? The sundering of body and soul looks a less effectual separation than the dividing of the life of Mary from the life of Jesus. Perhaps it was on this account, to supply this mysterious want of the Human Life of Jesus, that the species of the Blessed Sacrament remained incorrupt within her during the remainder of her life from one communion to another. We have sometimes seen mothers and sons approximate to this unity of life, especially when the son has been an only child, and the mother a widow. It has been also in these cases, as with our Lady, that it is the mother's life which is drawn into the son's, not the son's into the mother's. The sight of such a mother and son is one of the most pathetic which earth can show; pathetic, because its roots have always been, not in the palpable sunshine of overflowing happiness, but in the unwitnessed depth of domestic sorrow. The grandeur of its beauty has been in proportion to the fiery heat of that furnace of agony in which the two lives have been melted into one. But when we looked, we have trembled to think how the inevitable separation of death would ever be endured. Yet how faint a shadow of Jesus and Mary are these filial and maternal unities on earth!

In order then to understand the intolerable suffering which the withdrawal of the life of Jesus caused in the heart of Mary, we must know what His life had been to hers throughout. But this is not within the reach of our comprehension. We can but guess at it, and calculate it, and then be sure that the reality has far outrun our boldest calculations. Yet here also the annals of human sorrow help us by comparison. Who has not known instances of that perfection of conjugal love, when husband and wife have so lived into each other, that the life of one is apparently imbedded in the life of the other ? Each has borne the other's cares. Heart has leaned on heart, and they have throbbed together in one pulse. They have used even each other's senses with such an affectionately borrowed use, that we have sometimes been fain to smile at such simplicity and dependency of love. Voice, expression, gesture, gait, manner, and a thousand little nameless ways, have been only the outward disclosure of the intense unity of love within. Long years have formed habits which it would seem downright death to break. The chequered experiences of life, with their dark and bright, their tears and smiles, their losses and their compensations, have still more effectually moulded those two hearts into one. The two personalities are confused; God alone sees them clear and distinct, each in its own sphere of praise and blame, of merit and demerit, in His account. Death comes. There is not a power in nature but inexorable death, which would dare to rend asunder so exquisitely delicate a union. And what has been the consequence? It has become plain that there was almost a physical reality in this oneness of two loving lives. For now that one is left alone, the stream can hardly flow. It shrinks and runs dry, like a fountain in summer. It is not self-sufficing. It cannot feed itself. The one spring cannot do the work of the two. The survivor is unable to face life. His mind succumbs distracted under the least burden. It is not merely that one half of his strength is gone. It is something more than that. He is truly as feeble and faint, as a man bleeding to death; but he is incomplete also. He has no front to present to the common tide of daily life, and breast it as it comes. No matter how calmly life may flow, it is too much for him. He droops, and pines, and dies, in as many months as physical decay may require; and his death is not so much a death in itself as a part and completion of that other death. The lives were one, the deaths are one also. Who has not seen this? But we do not mourn over it. It is best and completest as it is. Here also we have but a partial shadow of the union of Jesus and Mary; yet it helps us to see what an overwhelming sorrow to her sensitive heart must have been the cessation of the life of Jesus. It was the deepest depth to which the sixth dolour reached.

Another peculiarity of this dolour is the reappearance of responsibility, which formed so weighty a part of the third, but had not come to view at all during the fourth or fifth. It is Mary's feeling of responsibility about His Sacred Body, now that it had reverted to more than the original helplessness of childhood. No one understands the adorableness of that Body as she does. Who is to care for it but herself? And she also is helpless. It is the same feeling which pervades the whole Church with regard to the Blessed Sacrament. In the Church, if it is a feeling of anxiety, it is also a feeling of amazing joy. But with Mary it was a manifold sorrow. In the midst of sorrow responsibility is itself a new sorrow. Yet it is one of the providential laws of grief, that it almost always brings new responsibilities to view, and just when we seem least capable of rightly discharging them. Grief is one of those things which concentrate, yet do not simplify, as most concentrations do. It is a perplexity rather than a light. It gives us more to do, rather than less to do. A man in great grief has less leisure than any other man on earth. Nothing thickens life so much as sorrow. Nothing precipitates the great work of experience as it does. Nothing endows our nature with more magnificent accessions of power. A life of joy is, too often, thin and shallow. Few heroisms can be manufactured out of gladness, though it also has its sunny depths which are full of God. But sorrow is the making of saints, the very process of the transmutation of drossy earth into purest heaven. This is why God seems to bear so hard upon us in sorrow. His wisdom makes His love cruel. These unendurable new responsibilities, whose apparently inopportune advent in seasons of grief is so depressing, are almost his choicest gifts. There is a crisis of life perhaps in every one of them.

But our Lady's responsibility for our Lord's Body was also a grief to her, because of the circumstances of the time and place. Violence and cruelty reigned supreme. Savage executioners and ruffian soldiers were the kings of Calvary. The chances of outrage and defilement were hardly chances. To human calculation, they were inevitable necessities. The breaking of the legs, the spear of Longinus, the hurry to get everything cleared away for the beginning of the Sabbath, the malice of the Jews, the way in which Pilate had truckled to them, the ordinary lot of the bodies of those whom justice had put to death, the very convenience of the Golgotha where the crosses were erected, the fact that there were three bodies to dispose of, and not one only—all these things were so many terrific risks which the inviolate safety of that adorable Deposit, which was in Mary's care, had now to run. Furthermore, her responsibility was in a third way of grief, because of the sense of utter helplessness which came along with it. What could she do? How was it in her power to stave off, or even to divert into another channel, any one of these numerous ill-boding consequences, which were pressing upon her? And yet the consequences of a failure were too appalling to contemplate. Even to our thoughts in quiet meditation there is something almost more shocking in the idea of the Dead Body of Jesus in the polluted hands of those fierce men, than the dear and living Lord Himself. We shudder at the possibility. What then must have been the agony of Mary's adoring heart, to which these horrors were visible and imminent, with the feeling that the care was hers, and the knowledge that she was helpless as the merest mother of an odious criminal could be, nay, all things considered, even more helpless, for her claims would have provoked insult where those of the common mother would have elicited compassion?

Out of this responsibility came again the misery of terror. It was a new kind of terror, the dread of sacrilege. No observant person, and love makes all of us observant, can avoid being struck with the part which terror plays in the dolours of our Blessed Mother. It comes out strongly as almost a universal characteristic of them. In treating of the second dolour we have seen what a huge aggravation of sorrow fear always is. Let us try now to conjecture why it is that fear fulfils so prominent an office in Mary's griefs. In the first place, it may have been as an especial trial to that which was her especial grace, tranquillity. This tranquillity, as we have already seen, is an essential element in the true idea of Mary. It is not perhaps so much a distinct grace, as the firmament, most rightly named a firmament, in which her purity, humility, and generosity were set to shine. In each of her sorrows, and the same remark is applicable to her joys as well, there was always something peculiarly trying to her tranquillity, from the Annunciation to the Descent of the Holy Ghost, something, which by its suddenness, or its vehemence, or its horror, or its exultation, or its strain upon human nature, was especially likely to disturb her inward peace, and to ruffle and arrest for a moment the calm onward majesty of her queenlike repose. But fear is, of all things, the most opposed to tranquillity; and hence, those varieties of terror, which we have discovered in her dolours, sometimes looming in the distance, sometimes frowning close at hand, now visible upon the surface, now working underneath in the recesses of her heart, may have been sent to try, and by trying to perfect and enhance, her heavenly tranquillity. In the second place, it was necessary that such immense sanctity as that of our Blessed Lady should be tested by trials in proportion to its grandeur. Now several distinct worlds of the most grievous temptations were impossible in her case, because of her gift of original justice, while the consummate sensibilities of her beautiful and delicate nature would make terror a most agonising trial to her, just as Jesus "began to fear and be heavy," when the Crucifixion of His Soul was reaching its highest point in the garden of Gethsemane. Thus, in her case, terror may have had to condense within itself the energies, properties, and pains of innumerable temptations, and to accomplish in her the ends which it was not permitted those other things to try, because of her utter sinlessness. Such, we may reverently conjecture, might be the reason of the amount of terror in our Lady's sorrows; but whatever becomes of the explanation, the fact is one of which we must never lose sight, if we would form a true idea of what she suffered.

But responsibility does not bring out fear only; it brings out loneliness also. We may be alone in the world, without knowing how much we are alone. Our kindred may have failed us, and the bond, which unites us to those immediately around us, may be formed of far frailer materials than the blood of relationship. But we are well and strong. Life as yet is sparing us its worst. We feel tolerably sufficient for ourselves. In a beautiful place, on a fine day, in perfect health, the feeling of solitude is little more than poetry. But sorrow comes,—not to strip us of our domestic world—that has lain long unpeopled, a wistful weary blank; but it comes to show us that we *are* stripped, and makes us feel the dreariness of being alone. Alone too perhaps, without Cain's consolation, of being able to wander. Then, when new responsibilities supervene on recent sorrow, the sentiment of our desolation is complete. We want some one every moment. We wait, but they do not come. It is a folly to wait; they cannot come who ought to come. We know it; nevertheless we wait. There are voices which ought to speak to us now, in counsel as of old, but they are mute. There were arms we used to lean upon; and we feel for them in the darkness, and they are not there. Every moment a fresh want knocks at the grave of something which has long been buried, and the heart sinks at the hollow echoes which the knocking wakes. And all this is the worse to bear, because it is so deep down in the unpeopled hollows of the soul. We are alone. The fact is old and familiar; but the feeling is new and terrible. Thus loneliness was part of this sixth dolour. It was not utter loneliness yet. That point had to be reached in the seventh sorrow. But it began in this. When the soul of Jesus left her, the world seemed a most awful solitude. Her feeling of responsibility about His Body deepened this sense of loneliness till it ached. Deeper down, and with more anguish, it penetrated together with her sense of helplessness, and deeper still was it carried, as by swift piercing shafts, by her terror lest some sacrilege should be committed. She was fearfully alone, and yet had to diffuse herself into those around her to be their comfort and support. As the life of Jesus had been her life, so was hers now the life of Magdalen and John. But she was not utterly alone. She had the Body still. Dead as it was, it was marvellous companionship. Dead as it was, it was like no other Body, for it was still united to a living and eternal Person. It was not a relic, such as love clings to and weeps over. It was a sanctity for worship and adoration. The loneliness therefore could not yet be desolation. But such as it was, it was a weight of grief, which no soul but Mary's could have borne.

It was also a peculiarity of the suffering of this dolour, that it consisted in prostration rather than in agony. It followed immediately upon the exhausting scenes of the Passion. It came upon a nature, which of itself was on the point of dying from the excruciating severity of its martyrdom, and whose miraculous support never allowed itself to be felt in the shape of refreshment or sensible consolation. The Hand that held her up was a hidden support, like that which the Divine Nature ministered to the Human in our Blessed Lord during the Passion. Thus, naturally, Mary felt every moment as if she had reached the ultimate term of endurance. It had worn her soul through, and the next pressure would be death. She felt in her soul the unrestful aching which overfatigue produces in the body. Her spirit was fatigued to death, not in a figure of speech, but in literal truth. Life was become a sensible burden, as if it were external to herself. She supported it; it did not support her. This exhaustion was more harassing than pain, more distressing than sharp suffering would have been. It was a collapse after the rack, bringing no relief, because the cessation of pain is not sensible when one is utterly crushed. We have got what is like a new being, capable of suffering quite in a different way. Yet this trial also her tranquillity bore unshaken. It did not become stupid, passive, inert, as the victims of cruelty sometimes are under torture. It did not perform the duties which came to it with the feverish energy and impatient precipitation common to fatigue. It was a broken-hearted peace, but also gentle, collected, considerate, unselfish, full of majesty, and working with the noiseless promptitude and slow assiduity which always betokens the presence of God within the soul. As at the Crucifixion she stood three hours beneath the Cross, so now she knelt and held the heavy Burden on her outstretched arms, with the same becoming and unforward bravery. Never was any soul so prostrate as Mary's in this sixth dolour, never was any so upright in its prostration. But do we not stand cold and trembling on the shores of such an icy sea of sorrow?

In such a state kindness was unkind, not in its intention, but in its effect. Thus when Joseph and Nicodemus, John and Magdalen, gathered quietly round her, as she was composing and embalming the Body, their very kindness somehow brought out the loss of the compassion of Jesus. When she stood under the Cross, she had not thought about herself. She was compassionating Him. She considered only the sorrow her sorrow was to Him, not the compassion towards herself which it was causing in His soul. But she discovered now how great a support that compassion had been to her all the while. Like all divine operations, she saw it more plainly now that it was past; and it rose up in gushing memories which were full as much kindlings of sorrow as of joy. He was gone who alone could understand her heart. He Himself had overwhelmed her with grief by the implied comparison between Himself and John, when He had given her the apostle for her son in His stead. And now the gentle sweetness, the graceful tenderness of loving sorrow and filial compassion, which John was showing, while it filled her heart with love of his virgin soul, awoke memories against its will, and instituted comparisons in spite of itself, which filled her with sadness, and with that sorrowful feeling which is regret in us, but which could not be so in her, because there is something in the holiest regret which does not altogether square with the will of God. Besides which the past reflected itself in all those kind faces round. John was in the place of Jesus, and he was like Him too, as true friends always are to their friends. Jesus was mirrored in the eyes of the sorrowful enthusiast Magdalen, and Mary saw Him there. None could be so high in grace as that seraphic penitent, and not resemble, even in their lineaments, the Bridegroom of their souls. Joseph had come to live again in him of Arimathea, and was standing where Joseph had so often stood, close by the lap on which Jesus lay, looking, as Joseph looked, at Him and not at her. Nicodemus too, with his myrrh and aloes, had renewed the offering of the Three Kings, no longer in prophecy, but when the spices were needed for His burial. And while Mary herself anointed Him, she did not forget how Magdalen had anointed His Feet already "against the day of His burial." And in the midst of them was Jesus Dead. A very cloud of sorrowful remembrances rose up from the group, and enveloped the soul of Mary in pathetic shadows.

Indeed there was altogether a quiet intensity about this dolour, which was suitable to a state of prostration, and which contrasted visibly with the more active and changeful endurance of many of the sorrows past. It was the first dolour, which had been running in a subterranean channel under all the others, which was now coming to the surface again, with its lifelong volume of sorrow, undistracted, unimpetuous, in self-collected simplicity of suffering. This prostration is as if it were simply that old lifelong sorrow risen to its natural high tide, and pausing for an instant

THE TAKING DOWN FROM THE CROSS.

before it ebbed. It had all the Three-and-Thirty Years in it. It joined the Infancy with the Passion, and confused in beautiful orderly confusion Bethlehem and Calvary together, and the life Jesus lived on earth in His visible Flesh with the life He leads there now in the invisible Flesh and Blood of His adorable Sacrament. Nay, the Infancy and the Passion are both actually present in that scene, visible to the eye, palpable to the touch, bound together in the one divine mystery of that Body lying over the Mother's lap. There was the Passion written, engraven, or rather deeply sculptured on those limbs. Every sin had fiercely inscribed its own reparation there. From the Head to the Feet, from the Feet to the Head, the Way of the Cross was winding up and down. Each Station had left its mark, its dread memorial, its noticeable wound. Every mystery was represented there. Mary's ardent contemplations fitted every mark with life, put a piteous voice into every wound, and kindled over again in her scathed and bleeding heart those fires of human cruelty which had burnt themselves out from very violence, even before death had withdrawn their Victim beyond their reach. But the Infancy was there as well. The Child was on His Mother's knee. That other Joseph was standing by. Those maternal ministries were all such as beseemed a child in its uncomplaining helplessness. There was the old gracefulness of the Mother's ways, as she parted His hair, and smoothed His limbs, and swathed Him again in His last swaddling clothes. Her sorrow now was the counterpart of the old joys; nay, rather it was the continuation and completion of the old sorrows. In Bethlehem, in Egypt, at Nazareth, she had long foreseen this hour. And now it was come. She was down in unfathomable depths of woe, where the eye can hardly reach her, but it is visibly the same Mother, indubitably the same Child. This is her payment for the old nursing. Strange payment! but it is God's way, and she, if any one, understands it well. Alas! to us the beauty of the sorrow almost distracts us from its bitterness!

Such were the peculiarities of the sixth dolour. Foremost amongst the dispositions of Mary's soul in her endurance of it, we must reckon the calm clearness with which she saw and followed the will of God through the darkness of her sorrow. Grief indulged troubles the vision of faith. It is because we give way to the tenderness of nature that we are so backward in discerning the will of God, and so stupid in interpreting its meaning. When a mourner calls God's ways inscrutable in his affliction, it is the result of a pardonable dimming of his faith's lustre. Pardonable, because we are so weak, and none knows our weakness so well as God. God's ways are for the most part inscrutable in joy, inscrutable above all to us, who know what we are, and what we deserve. But they are seldom inscrutable in sorrow. Sorrow is God's plainest time. Never are the clouds, which curtain His throne, put so far back as they are then. A grief, quietly considered, is generally a revelation. But to the most moderate self-knowledge how can it be a mystery? We are always startled afresh with the wonders of the Passion, though we have known them from our childhood. But Mary found nothing strange even in the tremendous realities, present to her, and almost crushing the life out of her. Her eye was single. It looked out only for God's will; and that will always came at the right time and in the right place. It is faith's peculiar habit to see what we may call the naturalness of God's will. To faith it always seems so fitting, we cannot conceive what else could suitably have happened, except the very thing which has happened. It almost appears strange that we did not prophesy it beforehand. We see all this wonderfully illustrated in the lives of many of the saints, but never so wonderfully as in our Blessed Lady. The most exacting, the most uncommon, the most apparently unseasonable will of God always finds her prepared, just as if it was an orbit traced by a law which she knew beforehand, so that she had nothing to do but to glide in it like a star in its proper heaven. This was the reason why no time was lost, no grace uncorresponded to, no grace to which the correspondence was not generous and prompt. The will of God was her sole mystical theology. It was her compendious way to that perfection for which the abstrusest mystical theology can find no name.

Another disposition, which was admirably exhibited in this dolour, was her union of reverence with familiarity. There is no truer index of union with God than this. It can only come out of great holiness. No rules can be laid down for it, just as no precise rules can be laid down for good manners. It is an instinct, or what we call breeding, or an inborn delicacy, which enables a man to comport himself faultlessly. So is it heavenly breeding, an instinct of the Holy Ghost, a refinement of high and unusual grace, which enables a man to unite familiarity and reverence in his dealings with the Most High. It cannot be learnt. The utmost which can be taught is to avoid a familiarity, to which in our low estate we have no right. We must be long conversant with God's love and long conversant with our own nothingness, before the first indications of this choice and beautiful grace will be discerned upon the surface of our conduct. But what a model of it is our Blessed Mother, embalming the Body of her Son! We can tell how dear to her is that Body, even though she gives way to no outward gesture of endearment. We can tell how sacred it is, though there is no visible display of worship. We could almost divine it was the Body of God, from the very undemonstrative self-collection of her demeanour, so completely does it blend that familiarity and reverence which belong only to an object of adoration. See her face, watch her fingers, sound her heart, it is all one grace playing everywhere! Yet there are few lessons in the world of the Incarnation deeper than these—that Mary knew that Jesus was God, and yet dared to use the rights of maternal tenderness towards Him, and that she lived with Him as her Son for Three-and-Thirty Years in the most amazing intercourse of familiar love, and yet never for one moment either forgot that He was God or forgot what was due to Him as God. Out of these two truths alone must we perforce build a pedestal for our Lady, whose top shall be far above out of our sight; and where then shall she be, who is to be raised thereon?

We must note also her spirit of studious, minute, and special reparation. Not the love of all possible worlds would be enough to pay Jesus back for the least pain He suffered for us, or for one single drop of the copious streams of Blood which He vouchsafed to shed. As God, the least of His humiliations is utterly beyond the reach of our compensations. The saints in all ages have marvellously loved and adored His Passion, and by supernatural penances and in mystical conformities have imitated its dread mysteries. Yet all their love together came not so nigh a just reparation to Him, as the worship of Mary while she prepared Him for the grave. The near sight of what He had really endured was something quite different from her presence at the Passion, while its various mysteries were being enacted at some distance from her. It took her down into the depths of the Passion, close to our Lord Himself, and whither no contemplative has ever penetrated. Her science and her Mother's heart combined to read and interpret those fearful documents, which were written within and without His Body, like Ezekiel's book, "lamentations, and canticles, and woes," as neither angel nor saint could read or interpret them. Ever as her fingers moved with the embalming, acts of worship and reparatory love out of the interior magnificences of her soul went along with them. She saw the number and the weight and the kind and the aggravation of all those sins which found there their proper and distinct expiations; and for each and all she made the most wonderful reparations. This spirit of reparation is one of the instincts of divine love. While the angels by our sides perform their ministries of vigilant affection, they never cease beholding God. So in like manner the servants of God go forth into the world in search of God's outraged glory, to make reparation for it, while in the meantime they never stir out of that abiding sense of their own sinfulness, which is the atmosphere of true humility. But Mary had no sense of sin, and her humility was more deeply rooted than that of St. Michael himself, the most zealous of the angels, because he was also the most humble. The reparations of Mary therefore were in a sphere by themselves. The saints are in a measure expiating their own sins, even while they are expiating the sins of others. But Mary's reparations were the worship of a sinless creature. As Christ satisfied for us, because we could not satisfy for ourselves, so Mary worshipped His Passion for us as well as for herself, because we are unable to do it worthily ourselves, and she is our mother; and by our Lord's own gift, what is hers is in some most real sense ours also. It was not time for reparation until now. Its natural place is in the sixth dolour, when the work of cruelty has ceased, and the huge world-sin has been consummated. Where complaint, or virtuous indignation, or loud appeals to divine justice, would have come in others, there came in Mary a busy, silent, tender reparation. O it is a joy to think that, if our sins were in the lashes of the scourge and the spikes of the thorny crown, our hands also were in our Mother's hands, composing and embalming the Body of our Saviour, and filling in as if with posthumous healing those deep red hieroglyphics which sin had left thereon!

We have already spoken of the perseverance of our Lady's tranquillity through the varying phases of her martyrdom. But we must not omit to enumerate it here among the heroic dispositions in which she endured her sixth dolour. It is by far the most wonderful thing about the interior life of her soul, so far at least as we are allowed to see into it. There seems to be no height of holiness which may not be predicated of such a marvellous tranquillity. It is a token, not so much of a process of sanctification still going on, as of the deification of a human soul completed. It comes nearest of all graces to the denial of created imperfections. Inequality, surprise, mutability, inconsistency, hesitation, doubt, vacillation, failure, astonishment,—these are all what might be called in geological language the *faults* in created sanctity. They are the imprints which human infirmity has left upon the work, before it was set and hardened. They are the marks of catastrophe, which is itself a mark of feebleness. From all these, so far as we can see, our Lady's incomparable tranquillity preserved her. To her there seems to have been communicated some portion of that peace of God, which Scripture says "surpasseth all understanding," and whose special office towards ourselves is "to keep our hearts and minds in Christ Jesus." No one thing explains so much of our Blessed Lady's grandeur as this heavenly calm. Apparent exaggerations find their place, their meaning, and their connection, when they are viewed in the light of this tranquillity. Graces, which sound impossible when stated by themselves, settle down in this tranquillity, disclosed distinctly by its light, and at the same time softened and made natural by its beauty. The Heart of Jesus alone can read the riddle of Mary aright; but this dovelike peace, this almost divinely pacific spirit, is the nearest reading of the riddle of her immense holiness to which we can attain. It is as if God had clothed her with His attribute of mercy for our sakes, and with His attribute of peace for her own.

We learn two lessons for ourselves in this sixth dolour. Our Lady is at once a model to us of devotion to the Blessed Sacrament, and a model also of behaviour in time of grief. We have already seen how allusions to the Blessed Sacrament flit before us continually in this dolour. From Mary's demeanour we may now gather what our own devotion to that dread mystery ought to be. For the sixth dolour is as it were perpetuated in the Church until the end of time. As our Blessed Lord is daily offered in the Mass, and the selfsame sacrifice of Calvary continued and renewed without intermission day and night around the world, so are Mary's ministries to His mute yet adorable Body going on unceasingly upon thousands of Christian altars and by the hands of thousands of Christian priests. Yet, as is ever the case with those things which we have from Jesus and Mary, what was intense bitterness to her, to us is exultation, privilege, and love. When she had gently laid aside the crown and nails, as precious relics, with what profound reverence did she kneel to receive the Body of her Son! It was not the attitude of a Mother towards a Son, but rather of the creature towards the Creator. She adored it with divine worship. She held it in her arms until the rest had adored it also. Her rights as a Mother were merged in her service as a creature. Yet the Blessed Sacrament is the living Jesus, Soul as well as Body, Godhead as well as Humanity. Worshipful as was His dead Body, because of its unbroken union with the Person of the Eternal Word, the Blessed Sacrament, if it were possible, demands of us a worship more full of dread, more self-abasing, more profound. We have no mother's rights. We are not, like Joseph of Arimathea, doing Jesus a service by ministering to His Body. The obligation is all on our side. He has come down again from heaven to us. We are not gone up to the Cross to take Him down. With what immense reverence then ought we not to worship this divine Sacrament! Our preparation for Communion should be full of the grand spirit of adoration. Our act of receiving should be a silent act of holy eager fear and breathless worship. In our thanksgiving we ought to be lost in the grandeurs of His condescension, and not too soon begin to ask for graces, until we have prostrated ourselves before that living Incarnate God, who at that moment has so wonderfully enshrined Himself within us. We should behave at Mass, as, with all our present faith and knowledge, we should have behaved on Calvary. At Benediction, and when praying before the Tabernacle, the Blessed Sacrament should breed in us continually a spirit of unresting adoration, unresting as that incessant cry which the astonished Seraphim and Cherubim are continually uttering at the sight of the unimaginable holiness of God.

To this reverence we must add tranquillity, or rather, out of this reverence will come tranquillity. The spirit of worship is a spirit of quietness. We must not disquiet ourselves in order to deepen our reverence. We must not disturb ourselves by making efforts. We must gently submit ourselves to be over-ruled, constrained, and gradually calmed by the present majesty of God. Neither must we look into our own souls to see if we are worshipping, nor make any other reflex acts upon the processes which are going on within us. Under the pretence of keeping up our attention, all this is but so much occupation with self, and so much distraction from the presence of Jesus. Hence it is that so many Communions bring forth so little fruit. It is from the want of quietness. An unprepared Communion can hardly ever be a quiet one. The very object of the preparation is to clear our hearts of the worldly images which possess them, and which, if not expelled beforehand, will become importunate distractions at the very moment when adoration should rule within us tranquil and alone. Hence also it is that the best preparation for the Blessed Sacrament consists by no means in endeavouring to stimulate our affections by devout considerations, in order to warm our cold hearts and raise our fervour to a proper pitch. In truth it is not in our power to do so. For the ardour, or the seeming ardour, which we produce, is unnatural because it is violent, and so it is not only short-lived, but it is followed by a reaction proportioned to the efforts we have made. A feeble fire is extinguished by the bellows, and even where it is blown up into a noisy crackling flame, it burns black and dull for long afterwards, when the artificial blast has ceased to play. The best preparation is that which is rather of a negative character, and which consists in emptying ourselves of self, so far as may be,—in banishing distractions, in realising our own needs and poverty and nothingness and malice, and so coming to Jesus in the same temper that the humble sufferers came to Him in the Gospel to be healed of their diseases. Whatsoever is empty and unoccupied in our hearts He will fill, when He enters there. Hence the more room there is for Him, the more grace will there be for us. A quiet Communion with but little sensible fervour is a far deeper thing than a Communion which thrills through us with a pleasant agitation of great thoughts. Tranquillity is thrilling also, but it is so in a higher and more supernatural way. The preparation of peace is the best adornment of the heart in which we are to hide the Blessed Sacrament: for the presence of Jesus is itself peace, and works greater things where it finds peace already, and has not to lose time by making room for itself and expelling intrusive images.

It is out of peace that love will come, such burning yet such humble love as becomes the worship of the Blessed Sacrament. Our reverence cannot have been right at the first, if love does not follow. When fear and shrinking and avoidance come to souls with regard to the Blessed Sacrament, it is not so much the want of love to which we must look, as the want of reverence. Reverence infallibly provides for love. But the love of the Blessed Sacrament must be a growth of inward peace and spiritual tranquillity. Very often we love less than we should love if we made less effort to love. Our faith tells us such overwhelming things of this divine mystery, that it seems a shame, almost a sin, that we are not burning with sensible love all the day long. Jesus Himself so near, so accessible, so intimately uniting Himself to us, Bethlehem, Nazareth, Calvary actually here, and we so cold, so moderate, so commonplace! Surely we ought to be burnt up as with the fires of the Seraphim. It is true. Yet for all that we cannot force ourselves. It is better to turn our vexation into self-hatred and self-contempt, than to try to create an interior vehemence which after all is a different thing from divine love. The love of the Blessed Sacrament is daily and lifelong. Surely it is not likely that such a love should be always, or even most often, sensible. Do we go to Mass on week-days at our own inconvenience? Are we punctual and reverential in our daily visit to the Blessed Sacrament? Do we hear Mass with devout attention? Are our preparations for Communion, and our thanksgivings after it, among those actions which we practically confess to rank as the most important of our lives? Do we give up exercise, pleasure, visiting, study, and the like, or at least interrupt them, to go to Benediction when it is in our power? These are better proofs of an acceptable love of the Blessed Sacrament than the warmest transports or the most glowing heat in our hearts. Perseverance is the real divine heat in our hearts.

But out of love must come familiarity. Yet as the love itself comes out of reverence, the familiarity must be of a peculiar and noticeable kind. It must have nothing in it of forwardness, of presumption, of carelessness, of indifference, or even of freedom. It implies a spirit accustomed to the divine visitations, and therefore not taken unawares by them, nor flurried, nor excited, nor discomposed, nor forgetful of properties. Some ecclesiastics are well versed in the sweet science of the rubrics and ceremonial of the Church, so that if they are suddenly called upon to take part in some great function, they are not confused or oblivious. They know what to do. They fall into their place naturally. They are parts of a whole, and do not cause disturbance on either side of them by ignorance or precipitation. They are slow and yet ready, calm and yet interested, dignified and yet bashful. Their greatest praise is that they go through the ceremonial in such a natural and unaffected way, that men for the most part do not notice how well they have fulfilled their office, and how completely they are at home in the rubrics of the function. This is an illustration of spiritual familiarity. It is at home with God, not in the sense of ease and freedom, but in the sense of understanding its part, of receiving Him with the proper honours, of calmly and mindfully fulfilling all the ceremonial which His presence requires, and so practically of forgetting self, because there is no need to remember it, and of being occupied reverently and lovingly and tranquilly with Him only. This is the true idea of holy familiarity; and when we consider how frequent and how common Mass, Communion, Benediction, and Visit are, we shall see at once how essential an element it is in our devotion to the Blessed Sacrament. Mary was never but once at the deposition from the Cross, and yet with what beautiful familiarity did all her ministries to the Sacred Body take their place, as if they were daily occurrences among the maternal offices of Bethlehem and Nazareth!

Then, last of all, a continual spirit of reparation must preside over all our devotion, a reparation which is the immediate growth of familiarity, or rather which is the loving familiarity itself with its eye resting on the reverence out of which all our devotion springs. To the devout mind Jesus habitually presents Himself as one who has not got His rights. He is injured and wronged with every heightening circumstance of pathetic injustice. There is no time when love pours itself out from the deepest and purest fountains of the heart with more self-abandonment, than when the object of our love has been wronged. The very thought is so pitiable that it creates new love, such love as we never felt before, and the spirit of self-sacrifice beats in it like a heart. It is no longer a mere private joy of our own, a luxury of sentiment, a romance of feeling, which, while it enveloped the object of our love, reflected also no little radiance back upon ourselves. Self is more at home in love than in any other of the affections. It is an humbling and unpoetical truth, but nevertheless a truth. Now the position of being wronged invests the object of our love with a kind of sanctity. Affection assumes something of the nature of worship, and then self can live there no longer, because worship is the only real incompatibility with self. Hence it is that the love of reparation is a pure and unselfish and disinterested love. But this is not all. Jesus not only habitually presents Himself to us as one who is suffering, because He is defrauded of His rights, but also of one who is in some mysterious way dependent on our compassion to console Him, and upon our reparation to make good His losses. This adds tenfold more tenderness to our love, and self returns again, but only in the shape of sacrifice, of generosity, of work, of sorrow, of abandonment. The spirit of reparation is a beautiful spirit, a spirit of human beauty fit to wait on the Humanity of our dearest Lord. It is the true Mary's lap within our souls, in which the Blessed Sacrament should ever lie, the pure white corporal of our most disinterested love !

Such should be our devotion to the Blessed Sacrament, as taught us by our Mother ministering to the Body of Jesus on the top of Calvary. It should consist of reverence, tranquillity, love, familiarity, and reparation, rising out of each other in this order, and connected with each other in the supernatural logic of a devotional spirit.

But Mary is also our model of behaviour in grief. Grief may either be the solid foundation on which a vast supernatural edifice of sanctity is to be raised, or it may be the very thinnest and most diluted of all human affections, a mere clumsy ingenuity of selfishness, the most self-seeking of all the kinds of love; for there can be little doubt that sorrow is a kind of love. Thus the very highest and at the same time the very lowest things may be predicated of grief. The reason of the difference is to be found in the way in which we bear it. Grief is a difficult thing to manage. There is no time when our correspondence to grace requires to be more active, more vigilant, or more self-denying than in seasons of affliction. If we once begin to indulge our grief, a great work of God is frustrated. Everything which happens in the world, happens with reference to our own soul. But sorrow is the tool with which God finishes the statue, and animates it with its beautiful expression. It is sad for us when we take it into our own hands. If God condescends to resume His work, and succeeds us when we have done, He must disfigure us with suffering again, before we shall be once more in a condition for Him to commence His gracious work anew. Now we have all of us a great temptation, and the more tender-hearted we are the greater our temptation, to induge in grief as if it were a luxury. To endure, to hold fast by God, to do our duty, to supernaturalise our adversity, to carry our cross, to aspire heavenwards, all these things are fatiguing. They give us the sensation of toiling up a steep. We have all the weariness of an ascent without the satisfaction of any visible elevation; for we seem to make no way at all. Whereas to indulge our grief, to give way unreservedly to the ready inundation of comfortable tears, to complain, especially if we bring in a vein of religion, like a vein of poetry, into our complaining,—these things bring with them the relieving sensation of going down hill. Of a truth it is the most earthward process through which a heart can well go. Thus a tender-hearted man ought to be as much on his guard against sorrow as an intemperate man should be against wine. There is a fascination in it which may easily become his ruin. What makes the temptation more dangerous is that the world applauds the indulgence as if it were a moral loveliness, and looks shy at the restraint as if it were hardness and insensibility; and to be suspected of coldness and indifference is almost more than a tender-hearted man can bear. There is no need to do physical violence to ourselves to hinder tears. The effort will make us ill, without bringing any profit either to body or soul. God does not dislike to see His creatures weeping. We creatures even like to see those we love weeping sometimes. All which our Lady's example counsels, is moderation. Let us relieve our hearts. It will make us less selfish. But let us not foster, embrace, rekindle, and indulge our grief. For then our sorrow is a selfish and luxurious fiction, a ground in which the Holy Spirit will not dig; for He knows there is no gold underneath.

Neither is the indulgence of grief content to stop in the mere luxury of sentiment. It goes on to do positive evil. It prompts us to dispense ourselves from the duties which our hand finds to do. It seems hard to work when we are grieving; but it is just this hardness which renders the work so heavenly. We think that sorrow makes us privileged persons, forgetting that our privileges are only an increase of our responsibilities. They think deepest and most truly of their responsibilities, who most habitually regard them as privileges. The world's work is not to stop for our sorrow. We are but units in a multitude. We must roll round from west to east with our fellows; we must meet life as life meets us; we must take joy and sorrow as they come; they mostly come both together; both are at work at once, both unresting, both unimportant; but both lie upon our road to the only thing which is of importance, and that is God. Self-importance is the canker-worm of Christian sorrow. We must not make too much of ourselves; yet this is what the world's stupid consolations try to do with those who are in grief. Dispensations are always lowering, but there is nothing which they lower so much as suffering and sorrow. Our grief is part of the world's rolling, because it is part of our own way to God. It is a going on, not a standing still, a quickening of life's time, not a letting the clock run down and stop. For the great clock goes, while ours stands so that we gain nothing, but lose much. We pull down the blinds, and strew the streets, and muffle the bells, and go slowly, and tread lightly, when sickness is in the house: but let us take care not to do so to sorrow in our own souls. For sorrow is by no means a sickness of the soul; it is its health, and strength, and vigour. Sins of omission may be more venial in times of sorrow, but they none the less unjewel our crown, and intercept the generosity of God.

Sorrow is a sanctuary, so long as self is kept outside. Self is the desecrating principle. If a time of sorrow is not the harvest-time of grace, it is sure to be the harvest-time of self. Hence, when we find people indulging in the sentimentality of their sorrow, we are almost certain to find them inconsiderate towards others. They are the centres round which everything is to move. Everything is to be subordinate to their mourning. Thus they pay no attention to hours. They disturb the arrangements of the household. They make the servants carry part of the burden of their wretchedness. They diffuse an atmosphere of gloom around them. They accept the service of others ungracefully, sometimes as if it was their right, because they are in grief, sometimes as if the kindness were almost an intrusion, which politeness only constrains them to endure. If this goes on, so rapid is the process of corruption when self has tainted sorrow, childhood works up again to the surface in middle life or age, and we have ill-temper, peevishness, petulance, quick words, childish repartee, self-deploring foolishness, grandiloquent exaggerations, attitudes and gestures of despair; in short, the long-banished ghosts of the nursery come back again, in proportion as sorrow with literal truth is allowed to unman us. A Christian mourner notes the least acts of thoughtfulness, and is full of gratitude for them. He feels more than ever that he deserves nothing, and is surprised at the kindness which he receives. He is for ever thinking of the others in the house, and legislating for them, and contriving that the weight of his cross shall be concentered upon himself. He smiles through his tears, takes the sorrow carefully out of the tone of his voice, and makes others almost gay while his own heart is broken. A saint's sorrow is never in the way. To others it is a softness, a sweetness, a gentleness, a beauty; it is a cross only to himself.

We must be careful also not to demand sympathy from others, and if possible, not even to crave for it ourselves. What is it worth when it comes, when we have demanded it? Surely the preciousness of sympathy is in its being spontaneous. There is no balm in it, when it is paid as a tax. Not that it is wrong to hunger for sympathy, when we are in sorrow. We are not speaking so much of right and wrong, as of fittest and best, of what God loves most, of what makes our sorrow heavenliest. The more consolation from creatures the less from God. This is the invariable rule. God is shy. He loves to come to lonely hearts, which other loves do not fill. This is why bereaved hearts, outraged hearts, hearts misunderstood, hearts that have broken with kith and kin and native place and the grave of father and mother, are the hearts of His predilection. Human sympathy is a dear bargain, let it cost us ever so little. God waits outside till our company is gone. Perhaps He cannot wait so long, for visits to mourners are apt to be very long, and He goes away, not angrily, but sadly, and then— how much we have missed!

Where self comes, unreality will also intrude. This unreality is often shown in shrinking from painful sights and sounds, which it is necessary or unavoidable for us to see and hear. Much inconvenience is often occasioned to others by this, and the generous discharge of their duties in the house of sorrow rendered far more onerous and disagreeable than it need have been. It is just those who are cherishing most the sight or the sound in their morbid imaginations, who shrink with this unreal fastidiousness from the substance of that on which they are perversely brooding. There is none of this unworthy effeminacy of sorrow about those who are all for God. Such men neither seek nor avoid such shadows of their grief as come across them. They are supernaturally natural; and this is the perfection of mourning. Neither must we fail to exhibit the utmost docility to the arrangements of others. If this righteous unselfishness is hard to bear, it is a legitimate part of the sacrifice which grief brings along with it. Sorrow tends to eccentricity. The strain of endurance makes men curiously fanciful. All this we must restrain, make it part of our immolation, and offer it to God. If our sorrow intrinsically weighs an ounce, a pound of self-sacrifice must go along with it. We must bear harder upon ourselves than God bears upon us. This is royal-heartedness. The whole theology of sorrow may be compressed into a kind of syllogism. Everything is given for sanctification, and sorrow above all other things; but selfish sorrow is sorrow unsanctified, therefore unselfishness is grace's product out of sorrow.

To all these counsels we must add yet another. There must be in our grief a total absence of realising the unkindness or neglect of human agents. Nobody is in fault but God, and God cannot be in fault; therefore there is no fault at all; there is only the divine will. Faith must see nothing else. It must ignore secondary causes. It takes its crosses only from Jesus, and straight from Him. It sees, hears, feels, recognises no one but God. The soul and its Father have the world to themselves. O what a herculean power of endurance there is in this sublime simplicity of faith! But all these are hard lessons; and sorrow, if it is not peculiarly teachable, is the most unteachable of all things. Yet we could hardly expect Mary's lessons to be easy ones, least of all when she gives them from the top of Calvary.

Let us gaze at her once more, as she swathes the Body in the winding-sheet. How like a priest she seems! How like a Mother! And are not all mothers priests? For, rightly considered, all maternities are priesthoods. Ah Mary! thy maternity was such a priesthood, as the world had never seen before!

CHAPTER VIII.

THE SEVENTH DOLOUR.

THE BURIAL OF JESUS.

THE shades of evening fall fast and silently round that Mother, sitting at the foot of the Cross with the covered Head of her dead Son upon her lap. The very earth is weary with the weight of that eventful day. The animals were fatigued after the panic of the eclipse, whose darkness they had mistaken for the night, so that the beasts slunk to their lairs, the birds to their roosts, and the lizards went to rest in the crevices of the rocks. Men themselves were outworn with sin and the impetuous activity of their own evil passions, while the scattered few, who composed the Church, were weary with shame, and fear, and sorrow, and the agitation of accumulated thoughts. The well-known sounds of night begin to succeed to the sharper and more frequent noises of the day. There is a divine light in the heart of Mary, more golden than that last lingering rim of departed sunset, that sun which seemed so glad to set after the burden of such a day, and she is resting on it for a moment, before she girds up her whole nature to meet her seventh sorrow and her last.

It was a strange station for a mother to choose for her repose, just at the foot of the cruel tree on which her Son had died, and which was yet bedewed with His Precious Blood. Yet it is also just the very spot, where, with Mary-like instinct, the mourners of eighteen centuries have come to rest, and have found peace there, when there was no peace, at least for them, in any other corner of the earth. It is a place of spells, since Jesus hung there and since Mary sat there. Here tears have been dried, which it had seemed would never cease to flow. Here hearts have consented to live, which a while ago were fain to die. Here the widow has found another and a heavenly Husband. The mother has had her lost children restored to her. The orphans have gone there in the dark, and when they were done sobbing, they found the arms of their new Mother Mary round them. Here thousands of hearts have discovered how good a thing it was to have been broken; for through the rent of their own hearts they saw God. When Mary sat on that hill-top, and enthroned the dead Christ upon her knee, she left an inexhaustible legacy of blessings behind her to all generations, with the condition of residence on the top of Calvary attached to their enjoyment.

It was not therefore for herself, but for us, that she sat there, and rested for a moment. But the time has now come, and she signifies with calm self-collection to the disciples round to form the procession to the tomb. There was Joseph of Arimathea and Nicodemus, John and Magdalen, the devout women who had come up to the Cross, some of the trusted servants of Joseph and Nicodemus, and to these was now added the converted centurion who at the moment of our Lord's death, had confessed that He was the Son of God. Perhaps also some of the apostles and other disciples may by this time, as some of the saints have conjectured, have been gathered to the Cross. It seemed sad to break up so fair a scene of beautiful sorrow; but it was time to fulfil the Scripture. With calm heroism, yet not without the direst martyrdom, Mary gave up the treasure which lay across her lap. Who had any right to touch Him but herself? Ah Mother! thou knowest we have all of us got those rights now. He has become the property of the world, the inheritance of sinners, and thou thyself too art the universal Mother. What the poor old heathen called the earth, that art thou to us, and much more also. But she had borne Him into Egypt. Should she not bear Him also to the tomb? No, Mother! God hath given thee strength by miracle, that thou mightest suffer; but He will not give thee strength to do that which will be a consolation to thy woe! There is that other Joseph, haunting thee with his sweet look of reverence and love through these last two mysteries of thy sorrow. He and Nicodemus will bear the burden, while John and Magdalen will go along with thee.

The rude world intruded not upon the silence of that wonderful procession. The multitude had long since flowed back, like an ebb tide, from that sacred hill. The earthquake had sobered many hearts, which diabolical possession had maddened in the morning. The crowded city had enough to think of for itself. Easter even will not put a term to the panic of this day. There are to be strange portents still. The joys of the Church are to be, now as afterwards, fresh troubles to the world. For there will be processions in the streets of Jerusalem, strange processions, such as will make men seek their homes, and close their doors, and speak low, and think of God. A shadow will lie over all hearts. The dead will walk. The earthquake had burst the tombs open, and like those impatient prognostics which so often usher in a divine work, had laid bare the bodies of the saints, who should rise with Christ. The old saints of the land, the dead of other generations, will go about the city, and be seen of many, with their beautiful threatening faces speaking unutterable silent things. Even already the memory of the day hung like a cold stone around the souls of many. In others it was burning like a hot restless fire, the harbinger of converting grace. Many wept, many more were sad, and all were weary, dulled by a shadow, oppressed by a divine terror. Hell had lighted a volcano in the people during the morning. Now it was burnt out, and human nature could hardly find its place again in many of the hearts from which it had been so awfully displaced. There was therefore no interruption from the city. The city was brooding over itself, like a disconsolate bird over its robbed nest. The very trumpets of Titus were almost in its ears, and might have been heard by prophetic listening. Poor Jerusalem! God has loved thee long, and loved thee with a mysterious fondness; but to-day's disloyalty has filled up thy measure, and thy doom has received its orders, and is now upon its way. From the top of that hill, brown in the dusky twilight, they are carrying to His tomb the Body of thy rejected King!

What awful shapes and shadows, of history, of prophecy, of dim divine decrees, gather like waving banners in the darkness, round that sacred procession! Has creation come to this, that a few faithful creatures are bearing the Dead Creator to a tomb in the rock, and that a mortal Mother, who numbers less than fifty years, is chief mourner there as the veritable Mother of the Eternal? The songless angels are marshalled round in serried phalanxes.

Their science almost makes them afraid, so overwhelming is the mystery. Now they have passed over the grave of Adam, the First Man, in which the Cross had been set up. The Soul of Jesus had already gone to Adam to give him the Beatific Vision. Now his descendants were treading on his grave. His daughter Mary the second Eve had been sitting there awhile ago with the second Adam on her lap. The bones and skulls of malefactors, luckless tokens of the fall, strewed their path, half bedded in the tufts of faded grass, or lying loose upon the smooth herbage which the goats had cropped. They are descending now into a garden, another Eden, to plant a tree there in the rock, better incomparably than all the trees of that old Paradise, better even than the tree of life, and which should bloom in three days with an inconceivable blooming. It was a garden where the vines grew, and the olive-trees dropped fatness. But this tree should give forth wine more gladdening to the heart of man than any which ever bled in the wine-press from the vine, were it from the rarest clusters of Engaddi. It should yield oil, as no olive ever yielded it, an oil to heal all wounds, and to be the inexhaustible balsam of the world. There were no flowers on earth like that withered one upon the bier, none to compare with it for beauty or for fragrance, none that should have so vernal a spring as He should have when but another sun was set. So they went onward to the garden, a whole cloud of divinest mysteries, accomplished types, fulfilled prophecies, historical consummations, resting on them as they went: and over all was poured the soft light of the paschal moon, hanging low in the western heavens, as if it were the light escaped from Mary's heart which was making all the scenes so deeply sad, so sadly beautiful.

Slowly they went, and in silence as soft as the foot of midnight itself. If they had sung psalms, the restless city might have heard. But in truth what psalms were there which they could sing? Not even the inspired harp of David could have shed sweet sounds fit for a dirge for such a funeral. No one spoke in all that company. What should they say? What words could have expressed their thoughts? "Out of the abundance of the heart the mouth speaketh." But there are times when the heart is over-full, and then it cannot speak. So it was with that procession. A deeper shadow of sorrow had never fallen upon men, than the gloom which fell on those who now were wending from the top of Calvary to the garden-tomb. There was grief enough to have darkened a whole world in Mary's single heart. Human suffering is not infinite; but it is near upon it, and she had come by this time to its very uttermost extremity. There was only one sacrifice she could make now, and she was in the very act of making it. She was going to put away from herself and out of her own power, to hide in a rocky tomb and let Roman soldiers come and keep watch over it, that Body which though it was dead was more than life to her. Then indeed she would stand upon the highest pinnacle of evangelical poverty, to which God had promised such mighty things. She would only keep for herself that which she could not part with, and would not have parted with if she could, a broken heart utterly submerged in such waters of bitterness as had never flowed round any living creature heretofore. There never would have been joy on this planet again, if her accumulated woe had been divided into little parcels, and distributed to each child of Adam as he comes into the world. Men look with eyes of admiring wonder at adventurous travellers and the successful explorers of unknown lands. Look now at Mary, as she closes the funeral procession. That woman is a creature of the Most High more exalted than any angel in heaven. The throne that awaits her is one of the marvels of the heavenly court. She is as sinless as the sunbeam, and her empire is over all creation. The Three Persons of the undivided Trinity will themselves perform her coronation. But she has explored now all the vast realms of pain. She has sounded the depths of every heart-ache man can know. She has traversed vast regions of suffering which none ever traversed before her, and whither none can follow her. She has been with the Incarnate Word in abysses of His Passion, which theology has never named, because not even saints have ever imagined their existence. She has exhausted all the possibilities of mortal anguish. Her dolours have outreached the tall science of the angels. They are known to none but Jesus and herself. At this present moment she is drawing near to the term of that which is so nearly infinite. The mystical border is close at hand. The outside of possible suffering, like the end of space, is inconceivable. A few more footsteps, and she will have reached that indescribable point of human life. Who would have dreamed of such a possible suffering as the Dead Body of the Living God? There is only one suffering beyond it: it is the parting with that Body, and going back into the world alone, in such a solitude as never creature knew before.

But now the garden-tomb is reached, the new Eden of the second Adam. It was hewn in the solid rock, and was new. Joseph had meant it for himself. But no man had ever lain there yet. All things were fitting, and full of all manner of meanings and proprieties. The tomb of this new Joseph was to be to Him what the arms of the other Joseph had often been before, His resting-place awhile, when Mary had to part with Him. But in those days there had never been such partings as this was to be. Mary enters the tomb with Joseph. It was his help she chose. Her hands arranged everything. How gently they lowered His Head into the tomb! As to His arms, perhaps they now allowed her to close them to the Body,—or perhaps, if there was room, He rested even in the grave with that wide crucified embrace, ready to receive a whole world of sinners. We are not told. She adjusts and composes the winding-sheet, and puts the feet together, which had been so painfully together those three hours upon the Cross. The instruments of the Passion too she takes, and kisses them, and deposits them in the tomb. There is no unnecessary delay over each action, such as marks the weakness of common grief. All was done in order, assiduity, and silence. Then came perhaps the last look. Perhaps she lifted up the cloth to see that the moving of the Body had not discomposed the venerable features. How pale it must have looked by the wan torchlight inside that rocky tomb! The eyes were closed, whose single look had converted Peter. The lips were shut that but awhile ago uttered those seven marvellous words upon the Cross, the sound of which had not yet died out of her listening ears. Slowly the cloth was replaced; and on her knees she made her last act of adoration of that lifeless Body. Never surely had any anguish so awful, any woe so utterly superhuman, desolated the soul of living creature. There have been many last looks in the world. Many graves have closed on earth, shutting in worlds of hope and love, and imprisoning often more of the survivor's life than death has robbed from the departed. Yet none has ever come nigh this. It stands alone, a grief without a parallel; because she who mourned and He whom she mourned were alike incomparable. Perhaps in none of her dolours was there any single isolated moment, that for accumulated and intense woe could be reckoned along with this. She was widowed and orphaned as none else were before. She sank down in depths of widowhood and orphanhood which had never opened to any one else. But what are father and mother and husband and child compared with an Incarnate God ? To be fatherless, motherless, husbandless, and childless, how little a measure of grief do these dismal words represent compared with that for which there is no real word ! For a soul to be Christless, is simply heathenism and hell. For Mary, His own Mother, to be Christless, and on the night of such a day—O the sorrow lies out dark before us, like the sea at night, and we know no more !

All who were present at the burial genuflected before the Body, and adored profoundly, and then turned away, as though they were tearing themselves from a strong attraction, and departed in silence. Joseph, as St. Matthew tells us, rolled a great stone to the door of the monument, and then went his way also. Mary, with John and Magdalen, return slowly over the summit of Calvary. She will need repose after the terrific agony of that moment in the tomb. But repose is far away from that broken-hearted Mother yet. Her soul, shattered by that last assault of suffering, has yet to pass through a fearful ordeal before she reaches the house of John in Jerusalem. After that, there is to be no respite to the anguish of her desolation for three days, three scriptural days, from this Friday evening till the dawn of Sunday's sun, the aurora of the Resurrection.

The Cross lies in their path across Calvary. The fatal tree is still discernible in the darkness, for the light of the low moon creeps up over the earth, and lights objects from below. But its dimensions look larger and more swollen than before. Mary rests a while, and falls down upon her knees to adore the bloodstained Cross. She kisses the wood, partly as if it were in sign of reconciliation with it after its cruel yet blessed office of the day, and partly as if it were the most precious object she could touch now that the Body, which had hung on it, was laid in the tomb, and partly also in sign of love and worship of the Precious Blood. When she rose up, her lips were stained with it. Dreadful seal of love which the Son has printed on His

Mother's mouth and cheek, from those lips of His which were "as lilies dropping choice myrrh!" O Mother! "thy cheeks are as the bark of a pomegranate, beside what is hidden within thee!" O Bloodstained mouth! giving voice to that heavenly soul, how much has passed since thou didst sing that wonderful Magnificat! Thy silence now is as eloquent before God as thy song was then!

She turns from the Cross. Below her lies the guilty city, magnified and indistinct in the murky air, with a few restless lights glancing here and there, and the irregular broken sounds of night rising up into the air. There were no words of reproach upon her lips, no look of reproach in her eyes. She took it all in, from the stately temple to the outer gateways of the city. She saw the host of Titus beleaguering its walls, and the mothers that slew their little ones for food. She saw the old predilection of God withdrawing from His ancient Sion, as a golden cloud follows the sunset under the horizon. But she yearned over Jerusalem. Not a week had passed since He, whom she had just buried, had shed tears of vexed love and lingering fondness over that chosen city of the God of Abraham and Isaac and Jacob. Since then, how had it done penance? Alas! it had crucified Him who wept, Him whom its little ones out of their pure hearts had greeted with Hosannas. Poor Jerusalem! She knew that it was doomed. But there was room in her broken heart for the guilty city as well as for the slaughtered Son. A cloud of beautiful history rests over its dreary sanctuaries to this day, even in its dishonour; and Mary's entrance into it that night, next to the tears of Jesus, is one of the most pathetic of its memorials. Half buried in its ruins, no city upon earth is so dear to the believer's heart, a city he will assuredly one day see, when he goes to meet his Saviour, whom it slew, come to judge the tribes of men in the valley of Josaphat hard by. Through the same gate, by which she had left the city in the morning, she re-entered it that night. As men count time, some ten hours or so had passed: but in the purposes of God, in the annals of grace, in the chronicles of that broken heart, it was a long secular epoch, longer than the years that had fled since Abraham's day. It was that Friday which we name The Good, partly to veil the bad deed it held, and partly because out of that injustice comes to us an infinity of mercy.

In order to understand the agony which our Blessed Mother had now to suffer, we must take several circumstances into consideration. There was too much of the satiety of bitterness in her soul to allow her to feel sensibly the pain of hunger. She had not done so during the Three Days' Loss. But her long fast told grievously upon her strength. No food had crossed her lips since the evening before. No sleep had visited her eyelids on the Thursday night, and there was little hope of her sleeping now, while Jesus lay in the tomb. Moreover the twenty-four hours had been filled with the most astonishing events, gigantic mysteries following each other in almost indistinguishably rapid succession. Her soul had been on the rack of extremest torture the whole while. Her mind, serene and capacious as it was, had been stretched and fatigued incessantly by the very comprehension of what was going on around her. Her nature had been shaken to its centre by terror. She was worn out by the bodily fatigue of standing so many hours. The very intensity of her sustained adoration had preyed upon the supplies of her life. That indescribable moment in the tomb had been eclipse and earthquake in her soul, both at once. Now, fasting, thirsty, footsore, her eyes tingled with sleeplessness, her limbs aching with fatigue, her mind burning with terrible memories and still more terrible understandings, her heart crushed and desolate within her, a very wreck which the tempests of supernatural woe have been unable to submerge, she enters, at the gate of Jerusalem, on another course of the most dire and heartrending affliction.

She is retracing the morning's pilgrimage, and making the stations of the Cross from last to first, instead of from first to last. Slowly she traversed the intolerable scenes of the morning. Not a gesture had escaped from her retentive memory that evening, just as none had escaped the vigilant anxiety of her eye before. She heard His low soft sighs upon the nightwind. His beautiful disfigured face looked at her through the darkness. Here He fell, and her feet burned and trembled as she stood upon the spot. She knew that she was treading on the pavement stained with His Blood, though the night veiled the ruddy traces from her eyes. There the Cyrenian had taken His Cross. There He had spoken His gentle words, yet words of saddest doom, to the daughters of Jerusalem, whose women's hearts had melted in them at the cruelty of which He was the victim. There He had impressed His adorable lineaments on the cloth which Veronica had brought Him. There was the corner of the street where Mary herself had met Him. It seems ages ago. Those eyes were on her still. That look was in her soul, burning with a fire of love whose heat was torture to the weakness of mortality. There was the guard-room where He was crowned, and there the pillar of the scourging. She knew what lay around the foot of it; from her mind's eye at least the darkness could not veil it. There were the steps of Pilate's judgment-hall, where He had been shown with derisive pity to the raging people. The silent air seemed still to ring with their cries of Barabbas. Verily His Blood was on them and on their children now. It was an awful pilgrimage, and her heart bled within her as she made it. It is always a great trial to love, to revisit scenes of deep sorrow. Even when time has closed the wound, it is a bitter pain to bear, bitter although our love may drive us to seek it of ourselves. Eyes weep then that have not wept for years. Strong men sob as if they were weak women, and are rightly not ashamed of it. Hearts are broken afresh, which patient dutiful endurance had pierced together as well as might be. Fountains of bitterness from underneath, long closed and almost unsuspected, now break up and flow, and inundate the soul with gall. All this too takes place when use has blunted the edge of grief, so that it cannot cut as deeply or as fiercely as it did before. But what is this compared with Mary's backward Way of the Cross, the second she had made that day? The peculiar horror of the mysteries, the incomparable sharpness of the anguish, the crushed and broken heart of the sufferer, her intense bodily fatigue and fainting lassitude, and the rawness of the Recent Passion, bear her sorrow far beyond the limits of all comparison.

In such unutterable woeful plight it was that the streets of Jerusalem beheld their unknown queen that night, wending her weary way to the house of John.* This was the home she had received in exchange for the House of Nazareth. John is her son now instead of Jesus. He is the man and she the woman. But he must lean on her, not she on him. He, who last night pillowed his tired head on the Sacred Heart of Jesus, must now, in spirit at least, find his repose upon the Immaculate Heart of the sorrowing Mother. The door closed upon her. She was now at home. Home! surely the word was mockery. It was less of a home to her than the chance cave is to the wounded wild beast. How could she have a home except where Jesus was? Bethlehem had been a home, and distant foreign Heliopolis, and sequestered Nazareth, and the open hill-top of Calvary, and the inside of the garden-tomb. They were homes, because Jesus made a home for her wherever He was. It was when she left the tomb that her true homelessness began. The first step from that sad second Eden was the beginning of her exile. And John's house too, had it no dreadful associations which would weight heavily and haunt darkly a broken heart? Who does not know how, in the extremity of sorrow, the eye and the mind busy themselves, not in despite of us, but to our complete unconsciousness, with all the minutest details of the place in which we are? The furniture, the position in which it stands, the pictures on the

---

* The private revelations of the saints, however, *for the most part*, speak of her returning to the Cenacolo.

wall, the pattern of the carpet, the exact folds of the curtains, the lines across the ceiling, the mouldings of the cornice, little things that are crooked and awry, or out of place, are all indelibly transferred to our souls, never to be forgotten; and each detail, each outline, can hereafter become a well of dark associations replenishing for ever the fountains of our tears. So was it with Mary. In that room, with her spirit at Gethsemane, she had spent the three hours of the agony; and the look of the room brought it all back to her, living and real and unbearable. From that room she had gone forth with John and Magdalen to try to gain admittance to the house of the high-priest. To that room she had returned, when Jesus was thrown into the dungeon for the night. In that room she had spent such a vigil as no other mother could have spent without forfeiting either her reason or her life. And now she had come back to it again, the most bereaved, the most desolate, among all the countless creatures of our Heavenly Father, and all this because she was nearest to Him, and His best beloved.

There, with the silent companionship of John and Magdalen deepening the utter solitude, she abode for more than four-and-twenty hours. Her grief meanwhile remained preternaturally at its height, because it was beyond the reach of use and time and calm. None could assuage it but God; and His time was not come yet. In fact it rather grew than otherwise. Like all divine works, its dimensions were in such exquisite proportion that it looked less than it really was. Its vastness, which was hidden from the eye, manifested itself to experience. The storm also grew and thickened in her soul, without flash or sound; yet a true and fearful storm it was, lightening invisibly in the very centre of her fixed tranquillity, an imprisoned storm, but painful and desolate exceedingly. It kept up the swiftness, energy, and vitality of her sorrow, that it might penetrate the more piercingly into every part of her nature. It settled down into the depths of her soul, filling up every void, commuting to itself, absorbing, and transforming, all other things which it found there. So that her faith became an agony, her love an agony, and even her hope an agony. Every faculty of her mind was on the rack. Her reason was deep suffering. Her imagination brought with its exercise acutest pain. Her memory thronged into the avenues of every one of her senses, filling them up with fire and bitterness and terror. Her will, weighted with all these mysterious dolours, hung suspended as on a sort of rack, in the most agonising tension, yet calm and brave, uttering no cry, letting no sign of torture pass on its features, but peaceably and passively abiding all for God. It is not impossible also that the outward divine abandonment, in which she was, might have its fearful inward counterpart, as was the case during the Three Days' Loss, of which this seventh dolour is in many ways itself the counterpart. It was a complete possession of sorrow, a miraculous transfiguration of a human life, grander and broader than other human lives, into a living impersonation of unutterable grief.

Such was the mystery of the seventh dolour, or rather of those few outskirts of it which escape from the secrecy of Mary's heart, and come within the range of our limited vision. If it has been hard to tell the story, it will be harder still to specify the peculiarities. The greatest peculiarity of this dolour consisted in its being the last. Very much is implied in this. No one can have failed to perceive that our Lady's dolours are a divine system, a world governed by laws of which we have but a very partial intelligence. We have already classified them on different principles, and have seemed to gain light by doing so. Nevertheless our view of them is by no means complete. Perhaps it never can be. We feel, as if by instinct or divination, that there is a unity in them which we have been unable to grasp, and that they are one in the same way that the Passion is one, though the method is beyond our view. There are lights now and then, strong lights, in dark places. But they only prove to us that we do not see the whole. Like a landscape by moonlight, all is mottled, and visionary, shadows and objects confused together, heights and distances falsified, a view which is seen through an inadequate medium. All is real and recognisable, but it is with a visionary reality. Her sorrows were beyond all doubt a very special divine work. The Church does not leave us in any uncertainty as to that question. Now the end of a divine work must be worthy of its beginnings, and in keeping with them, and as it were a crown of grandeur to them. Thus the seventh dolour, whatever may be the peculiar kind of sorrow, which it brought along with it, must have been an adequate and congruous consummation of the rest. We have seen what they were; what then must this have been?

From this it follows further, that the sorrow of the seventh dolour was a sorrow without a name, a grief which cannot be classed as belonging to the family of any other known grief. It is a class of its own. If we give it a name, it would be an arbitrary one, because we have no similitudes or analogies to guide us in imposing the name. The numerous resemblances, which we can trace between the seventh and the third dolour, are enough to satisfy us that this last sorrow must have been one of colossal stature. We cannot tell what suffering is like when the heart has got beyond life's possibility of suffering, and the victim is kept alive by power external to himself, not power which mitigates the pain or alleviates the capability of endurance by alleviating and consoling, but sheer power of miracle. We have seen this even in her earlier sorrows. Now here, in like manner, we cannot tell what grief is when it has outrun all the actual experience of the griefs of men, and attained the solitary term beyond which grief cannot go. All possibilities are finite; the possibilities of grief therefore among the rest. He only is truly infinite, who is not a possibility but an Eternal Simple Act. But what can we know of the uttermost territories of possible sorrow? Only as a mysterious place where the Mother of God has been, and where she was when she knelt to make her last adoration of the Body in the tomb. We call it the seventh dolour, and we can call it nothing else. So far as our intelligence goes, her third dolour was her greatest. But her seventh dolour is beyond our intelligence, both in kind and in degree, and therefore was her greatest in another sense. The circumstances, which formed the material of the sorrow, were without parallel on earth. They have happened only once, and the unassisted science of the wisest angel would never have dreamed that such things could have happened at all in the bosom of God's creation, rife as it is with unexpected wonders. Mary's heart also was an instrument unparalleled on earth, now that the Sacred Heart was cold and motionless in the tomb. Even when it lived and beat, its union with the Divine Person took it out of the parallel. Mary's state at the close of this vast system of dolours, through which she had revolved, was also quite without parallel, both in respect of holiness, of powers of suffering, and of the miraculous holding together of her shattered life. Thus everything about this dolour is without parallel. We can but shadow forth in our spirits some nameless immensity of grief, and say it was the seventh which our Mother bore.

Another peculiarity of this dolour, and immediately connected with what has been said, consisted in its being beyond the reach of consolation. It was this which kept its bitter and tempestuous waves unnaturally poised in the air during those four-and-twenty hours in the house of John. It could not be assuaged. It had no power of itself to ebb. It was beyond the laws of grief's common tides. It had nothing to do with creatures, and therefore creatures could not minister consolation to it. The cruelty of men and the rage of devils reached to the death upon the Cross. In the fifth dolour therefore they found their term. Human agency could not reach the seventh dolour. It struggled feebly and faintly, or at least comparatively so, in the sixth; it reflected itself, depicted itself there; it failed and died out before the seventh, and fell short of that moment at the tomb. Like the third dolour, its affliction was altogether divine. We may guess the proportions of a sorrow coming express from

God, and from Him to a creature such as Mary, when compared with the sorrows men or devils can inflict. But here again we do not know what it is to be beyond the reach of human consolations. Men tell us, with the usual flattery of comfort or the monitory commonplaces of edification, that our griefs are beyond human consolation. But it is not really so. Time consoles us inevitably, even though it may do its work tardily. Kindness consoles us, even while it irritates us. Life consoles us by the very importunity of its distractions. But Mary was further removed even than this. She was beyond the consolations, not only of common grace, but of that prodigious grace which she herself brought down from the top of Calvary. What is a creature like, who is beyond the consolations both of nature and of an unparalleled grace, and whom God Himself can alone console by immediate union with Himself?

We think of those who lie on the bleak confines of creation, in eternal exile from their Father! O woe is their unutterable and yet ineradicable life! Yet there the mighty cloud of an unanswerable justice casts something softening and tolerable over their endless solitude of pain, by the very fact that it renders it even to their blackened spirits so confessedly reasonable. But Mary was beyond consolation, even when she was meriting more divine sweetnesses than all the angels and the saints together. So that she is not to be paralleled for woe of that kind, even with the lost. Moreover, if we may so dare to speak, love is in some sense a more energetic agent than justice. Thus there is a sense in which an inconsolable desolation prepared by eternal love to inflict suffering must be a more penetrative and overwhelming thing, than an inconsolable desolation prepared by eternal justice for the punishment of sin. Nay, the Blood of Jesus somewhat quells the fierceness of the flames of hell; whereas it was that very Blood which was kindling the flames in Mary's soul, and heating the furnace of her heart sevenfold hotter than it was before. So that even the desolation of the lost may not compare itself in its excess with that mystical inconsolable affliction, which was God's last trial of His Mother's heart. Even He, so seemed it, had no more trials whereby unutterable sanctity might be tested and established.

But there are some lesser peculiarities, lying on the outside of this seventh dolour, which we must not omit to notice. We saw that the loneliness of the sixth dolour had not yet reached the point of desolation, because Mary still had the companionship of the Body. It became desolation, when the great stone was rolled to the door of the monument, and she went forth from the garden of His sepulture. This has been a well-known moment in the grief of all of us. All was not over when death was over. We spoke of the lifeless frame in the masculine or feminine, as if the body was the real self of the one we loved. The house was not forlorn, at least not utterly forlorn, though it was darkened and silent. The dead furnished it, peopled it with one exclusive growing life, and filled it with a mysterious attraction. It made home more home. It was now a consecrated home. It had but been a common home before. Oh there was such manifold companionship in the dead! Its white face was so eloquent. It did not tell of pain just passed, and the gnawing of hungry disease, and the blight of pestilence. But it spoke of old times, of simple childish years. It was a very resurrection of bygone looks, of almost forgotten expressions, of innocent youthful pleasantness of countenance, blooming above death like the snowdrops above the hoarfrost. The compressed lips smiled at us. The closed eyes looked at us, without opening. The blue-veined hands were full of meaning. It was a dark hour when the coffin closed, but the spell was not gone yet. The moment of desolation did not come when the blue spires of incense up-curled themselves out of the damp grave, and the clods rattled on the coffin lid, and the hollow sound was like a frightening echo of eternity. But it came when the mourner set his first step again on the threshold of his door, having left the partner of his life, or the child of his hopes, or the mother of his boyhood, behind him in the grave. Then the house was empty indeed, and his heart was empty too, and desolate. If we substitute Mary for ourselves, and Jesus for the love we lost, and make allowance for those wide disparities, like grief was Mary's when she turned away from the garden-tomb. This it is within our compass to understand, and there are dark days in our own past to testify to its reality.

It is another peculiarity of this dolour, which it shares with the sixth, and which we have already alluded to repeatedly, that Mary was surrounded in it by images of the Sacred Infancy. These were a twofold fountain of sorrow, both in their contrasts and their similitudes. His imprisonment in the tomb was an image to her of the nine months He had spent in her blessed womb. But she had borne Him then herself over the hill-country of Judæa, with swiftest exultation, while each thought was a Magnificat within her soul. Joseph of Arimathea reminded her of him who was chosen of all men by the Eternal Father to be the foster-father of Jesus. But he had gone to sleep peaceably with his head on the bosom of Jesus, while Joseph of Arimathea was just reversing the pleasant sadness of that older mystery. When she laid Jesus in the tomb, and arranged the winding-sheet, she remembered the crib of the manger, wherein she had laid Him at Bethlehem. But between the crib and the tomb there was all the vast interval which lies between the poles of Christian devotion, Christmas and Passiontide. The two mysteries were so alike, and yet so different! He was more helpless now than ever He was then. What was loveliest obedience then is rigid passiveness now. His silence was voluntary then; so is it now, but with a different kind of will. He had noticed her then; He takes no notice now. When He slept as a Babe, and His eyes were closed, she knew that He was thinking, loving, worshipping, all the while; and His sleep was in itself a beauty, and a charm. But now the heart was cold and motionless, worshipful because of its union with the Godhead, but not beating with conscious love of her. They had had one strange union since

His death. It was when she had knelt with Him extended on her arms, and they two together had made the figure of one Crucifix, and it was neither altogether Jesus who was crucified, nor altogether Mary, but God's one victim out of two lives. That was a figure with a strong divine light upon it, never to be forgotten, though we should soon sink out of our depth in its theology of love.

Yet the Passion was there as well as the Infancy. They met upon that ground. That marble Body, many-streaked with inter-twisted red and livid blue, was no monument of Bethlehem. The whole Passion was elaborately written out upon His limbs; nay, it is gorgeously illuminated on His Hands and Feet and Side this hour in heaven. Those instruments of the Passion too, those precious relics, which are deposited in the tomb, tell not of Bethlehem and Nazareth, but of Jerusalem and Calvary, of the Prætorium and of Golgotha. Others touching, handling, carrying Him rather than herself,—this painful characteristic of the Passion, which had cut so deep into her soul in the fourth dolour, was renewed in the sixth and seventh. It was a sort of token of the presence of the Passion. But tokens were hardly needed, and if present were scarcely preceptible, in a mystery which breathed the aromatic bitter of the Passion in all its bearings and in each minutest incident. In the Sacred Infancy she had none to lean their weight on her weariness and weakness; for she and Joseph both leaned on Jesus, and rest and peace and joy are all one abiding thing to those who lean on Him. But she had to carry the Church in her heart at the Passion. When Jesus died, Peter, the Rock, leaned his repentant faith and love on hers. She upheld by her gentle bravery both John and Magdalen. Joseph and Nicodemus would scarcely have had nerve to detach the Body from the Cross, if she had not been there to inspire them with her own tender fortitude. Yet this leaning of others made her heart ache. It was a fresh sorrow of itself. It multiplied the number of dear hearts in which she had to suffer, while it was also a strain upon her own.

The Passion reached its height in Mary, not when the Soul of Jesus sank through the greensward at the foot of the Cross, but during that final moment at the tomb.

Here also the Three Days' Loss, that mystery which shines apart, finds something like its fellow. The essence of the sorrow is the same in both cases. It is the loss of Jesus. The time which the loss endures is mysteriously the same. There is the same absence of human agency and secondary causes. The occupations of the absent Jesus are not unlike in both cases. In the first He was illuminating the doctors of His nation. In the second He was giving beatific light in the limbus of the Fathers, the older doctors of His people. There was a Joseph to sorrow with Mary at the tomb, as there had been a Joseph to sorrow with her in the temple; and both Josephs were the choice of God Himself. The nature of the suffering was the same in both cases, because it came from a divine abandonment. Desolation was equally the form of sorrow then and now. She had lost Him both times in the same place, just outside the gates of Jerusalem. There can be little doubt that the Three Days' Loss was a prophetical foreshadowing of the present separation. But there was one notable exception to all these similitudes. The darkness in the seventh dolour arose from the impossibility of consolation. The darkness in the third was a mysterious ordeal of supernatural ignorance. Here she knew everything. She had watched the Passion to its close with heroic fidelity. She had embalmed Him herself. She had helped to lay Him in the tomb. She knew where He was, and how He had been lost, and she knew of the Resurrection that was to come on Easter morning. But as one deep calleth to another in the ways of God, so doubtless the third dolour calls to the seventh, and the echoes answer to the call. The voices of both agree in telling us that they both have abysses, which we cannot sound, and that beyond the deep places, in which we have nearly lost ourselves, there are deeper places still, which we suspect not.

But the seventh dolour had a prerogative of its own. The

THE BURIAL OF JESUS.

Hypostatic Union had long been an object of blissful contemplation to Mary, just as it was the work of God into which the delighted science of the angels most desired to look. The Union of our Lord's Body with His Soul, and the Union of both Body and Soul with His Divine Person, as the Eternal Word, the Second Person of the Most Holy Trinity, had been to her the type of all unions, the monument of immutability in the mutable works of the Creator. Like the mystery of the Holy Trinity itself, it had seemed to her as that threefold cord, of which Scripture says with significant moderation, that it is not "easily broken." There was something like a break in it now, and the very thought of such a thing is too terrible for words. What the Word once assumed, that He never put away. The Hypostatic Union could not by possibility be broken. The Body, the Soul, the Blood on the Cross, on the pavement, on men's sandals, and on Mary's garments, all, awaiting the Resurrection, were united to the Person of the Eternal Word, all equally so, though all apart. But the Flesh and Blood were sundered, both worshipful, but both separate. The Blood, precious and divine, was outlying in all directions, in the most unthought-of places, in the most degraded mixtures, in the most complicated inextricable confusion, as if it was not in its generous, prodigal, world-saving nature to be cooped up in one place as the Body was, and be inactive in a tomb. Its colours should be its voice, and its mute red should preach stirringly wheresoever it might be scattered. But this separation of Flesh and Blood was a fearful invasion of the sanctuary of that heavenly Union. Yet, more awful far was the sundering of Body and of Soul, that old dread mystery which God had first invented as a punishment for sin. Here, too, which is more terrible still, it had been done as a punishment, and as a punishment for sin. In the first moments of the Incarnation there had been no succession. The Soul was not an instant before the Body, nor the Body before the Soul, nor either of them an instant without the Divinity. But the Union, which was effected in the womb, was broken in the grave, and Mary ministered to both the mysteries. The grief, which this appalling separation caused in Mary's heart, must have resembled in its pain the disruption which caused it, and it is one of those things which have to stand alone, because God willed that they should be mysteries without mates in His vast creation.

Thus it appears that this seventh dolour was a sort of centre, or a harbour, in which all the various lines of mysteries of the Thirty-Three Years converged. Bethlehem and Calvary, Nazareth and Jerusalem, the Infancy and the Passion, the Boyhood and the Ministry, were all represented here. The possibilities of sorrow were exhausted. Simeon's last sword is sheathed in the Mother's heart. If none can tell the sorrow that she bore, so none can tell the holiness she reached. The frenzy of man's sin and the pressure of divine justice had separated the Body and Soul of Jesus. Both of them combined could do no more, and so the Passion ended. Mary's woes had been mounting, various in their cruelty, inventive in their ruthless tortures, and with her too separation is the last. She is separated from Jesus, from His Soul first of all in the fifth dolour, and from His body now. Her last separation is from that which she herself gave Him,—His Sacred Flesh. Man's sin and the ever-blessed cruelty of divine love have forced the Mother and the Son asunder, though for three-and-thirty years their union had been second to none in creation, save that of the Hypostatic Union. Jesus was without Mary, and Mary was without Jesus, that darkest of all desolations which the evil one and heresy can imagine in order to rob a poor perishing world of the Precious Blood. Ah! venerable Simeon! thy last sword is indeed sheathed in the Mother's heart. Thou hast departed in peace, according to thy prayer. Thou art gladdening thyself now in the light of Jesus. Yet thy peace beyond the grave is not more glorious than that peace of hers, which for these so many years thy prophecy has turned into inexpressible bitterness!

From these peculiarities of the seventh dolour we may

turn now to the dispositions in which our Blessed Mother suffered it. It was the characteristic of our Lady's holiness that it consisted in a perfect correspondence to grace. All holiness is of course simply a correspondence to grace; but with ordinary men, and even with the saints, there is a great deal of failure, of fluctuation, of falling and then rising again, and consequently of imperfect correspondence to grace. Self-will diverts grace from its legitimate channel, and impresses its own character even upon its divine action. Sin also leaves its prints and vestiges even upon our holiness. Temper and disposition too are clearly cognisable in the structure when it is completed. Thus there is something human, something special, something strongly savouring of their natural bent and individual character in the holiness of the saints. By it we distinguish one saint from another. It is an attraction to our devotion, a stimulus to excite us, a model to copy. This arises from their sanctity not being merely a correspondence to grace, but a result of struggle, of temptations, revolutions, catastrophes, and even ruinous accidents. It is a divine work, but inextricably mixed up with what is human. It is almost a beauty in our eyes that it should be so. Our Lady's holiness was of quite a different character. It was a simple, unmixed, unthwarted, perfectly accomplished transmutation of grace into holiness, without delay, as the fresh grace came. Hence it is altogether a divine work, sustained by a human will. Sin has left no trace there. There is no vestige of catastrophe, but only the beautiful uniformity of calm and equable law, acting with resistless power upon the most glorious theatre in unspeakable pacific majesty. There is no alloy with the pure gold, and as far as our dim eyes can see, but little individual character. Not that she was without character of her own, and doubtless a very marked one. But it is too near God for us to see it. It is hidden in the vicinity of the intolerable light, as a planet would be if it lay close to the shores of the sun. It is this divine purity of her holiness, which, when we reflect maturely upon it, is far more wonderful than its colossal proportions, and distinguishes her with a more nearly infinite distinction from the saints.

A single grace from God is a marvellous thing. Theologians have said that one communion is enough to make a saint. Even in the very commonest graces experience sometimes enables us to discover the most manifold capabilities, the most incredible power of duration, the most extraordinary empire over the soul. It seems occasionally as if a single grace was sometimes a fountain of spiritual miracles within us, or had power enough of itself to turn the helm of our whole lives, and to contain all heaven and the width of eternity within its own compass. A saint perhaps corresponds to a thousandth part of His grace, we to much less. So far is our meanness, even when it strives, from matching the free magnificence of God. But a grace corresponded to instantly brings another grace, and that another, and so on through an endless series rising in number, in multitude, in beauty, and in efficacy. Thus the irresistible swiftness of the process of sanctification dawns upon us almost as a thing to fear. The possibilities of sanctity cannot be thought of without trembling. The holiness of creatures dazzles us, while the holiness of the Creator seems ever removing and removing further off from us, at the very time it is drawing us onward towards itself in breathless adoration. But our imperfect correspondence frustrates the work. We tie up the liberality of God. We squander, corrupt, dilute His grace, even when we use it, and we delay as if we wished to let it stand and evaporate and lose its peculiar celestial freshness before we take heart to use it. Thus, if we may reverently say it, God with His grace in men's souls is like a man whose thoughts are eloquent and beautiful, but who has not the gift of speech, and cannot utter them, or only in a stammering way which both hides and spoils them. He has not free scope with us. He can but produce a very inferior work at best, because His materials are wilfully incapable of a better. Grace was never so gloriously unbound as it was in Mary's soul, except in the Human soul of Jesus, which is out of all comparison. In her heart it expatiated as if it were in heaven, and developed itself in all its unhindered magnificence. She corresponded to every grace to the very uttermost. Her graces were gigantic, immeasurable, even when compared with the graces of the apostles, and yet she corresponded perfectly to their vastness. Thus every moment of life was bringing down fresh inundations of grace, which were foliage, flower, and fruit, almost the moment they had touched the virgin soil of her immaculate heart. Days went on adding themselves to days, and years to years; and like some fabulous machinery, with overwhelming force and with invisible speed, the process of correspondence and sanctification went on, multiplying itself in one short hour beyond the figures of all human sums. Her life moved too amid tall mysteries, each of which was a universe of sanctification in itself. The march of her soul was amongst immaculate Conceptions, adorable Incarnations, Hidden Lives of God, Passions of the impassible, Defeats of the Omnipotent, Birth and Growth and Death of the Immutable and Eternal, the Government of a God, mysterious prodigies of Dolour, Descents of the Holy Ghost, Queenships of Apostles, and the like. What oceans of grace might not such a life of supernatural heroism absorb, and convert into a holiness, which, soberly speaking, is unimaginable by angel or by saint? No wonder we always speak so unworthily of Mary. It is one of those sad human infirmities from which we never can escape; for all language is so inexpressibly unworthy of her, that the most glowing praise and the coldest commonplace sink down into one level from such a distance as the inaccessible mountains of her holiness. Love alone can feel its way far on towards her; and happy is he whose love for her is ever growing. He is enjoying in time one of the choicest blisses of eternity.

This view of Mary's holiness, that it is a purely divine work, because it is simply God's own grace realised, and realised to the utmost, by correspondence, not only gives us the true height of her sanctity, and shows that its world-wide dimensions are not magnified by any mists of affectionate exaggeration, and that all that ever has been said of her by Bernard, Bernardine, and the rest, is far below the level of her tremendous grandeur, but it also explains to us the difficulty we have in getting any clear conceptions of her interior dispositions. In the first place, we are obliged to use the same words to express correspondence to different graces. We speak of her conformity to the will of God, or her generosity, or her fortitude, or her union, when the change of circumstances and the varying refinements of grace have caused the words really to mean different things at different times. We have not keenness or subtlety of spiritual discernment to distinguish between these niceties of grace, these shadings of heavenly beauty. Yet we know them to be so real, that one shade of one of Mary's graces would produce a different kind of saint from another shade of the same grace; and we know them also to be so great and powerful, that each single shade of any one of her graces could fill with colour and splendour the souls of a multitude of saints, or the spirits of a hierarchy of angels. But there is such a thing as an eloquent stammering, when we are discoursing on the things of God; and we must speak, even though what we say is far below what we mean, and what we mean is but a wavering likeness of the reality which we see blindedly in the burning fires of the majesty of God.

In the second place, if Mary's holiness consists in tranquil, adequate, congenial correspondence to grace, it is that correspondence which must give the name and character to her dispositions. But, if the graces are far out of our sight, if their abysses are not registered in our theology, (and who can lay down soundings for the unfathomable?) then must her correspondence also be far out of our sight, and with it those conceivable dispositions which form her interior loveliness and grandeur. We can do no more than hazard guesses, and imagine shadows, which shall stand for those invisible realities. We can but make calculations, and then allow for errors from our knowledge of the superlative excellence of the

Mother of God, and then let the sum stand, not as an accuracy, but as a mere help to getting an idea. Each succeeding dolour the difficulty of speaking of her dispositions has been greater; and yet we could not be silent, because her dispositions were the graces of her sorrows in blossom, passing on to the fruit of solid holiness. For Mary was no mere monument of marvels, upon which God had hung external dignities, and endless banners, and figurative emblems, and the external spoils of a redeemed world. The bewildering glory outside, and truly it was bewildering, was as nothing compared to that which was within. Mary was a creature, a woman, a mother, a sufferer; and by stupendous correspondence to them, she had made God's gifts her own. They are at this moment not mere ornaments, or privileges, or decorations, or offices conferred, or prerogatives communicated, or even inalienable jewels; neither are they simple attributes, or perfections referred to her, or glories separable from her, or wonders predicated of her, or merits imputed to her; in heaven they are Mary's own self, her own human, maternal, characteristic, loving, quiet self: a self which is in glory what God made it twice over, in nature and in grace. O it is sweet to think that our Heavenly Father has such a daughter, to be ever at His feet worshipping Him with the little greatness of her love!

Of all the interior dispositions of the saints, the one which strikes us as the most magnificent, more magnificent than the spirit of martyrdom, is that of perseverance in a complete sacrifice. Perseverance is in itself the most uncreaturelike of graces. It is as if the immutability of the Creator had dropped like a mantle upon the creature, and became him well. There is something at once more graceful in its movements and more heroic in its demeanour, than characterised the beautiful fervour in which the soul irrevocably committed itself to the first generous sacrifice. There is more of heaven in its stateliness while there is also more of a man's own in the courage of the sustained effort. But the glory of perseverance is greatly increased when it is in a complete sacrifice. There is a completeness and unity about the whole work, which seems to render it an offering worthy of the divine compassion. Strange to say, while many souls fail under the effort while the sacrifice is yet incomplete, there are not a few who dishonour it in its completeness. Nature gives way and seeks repose, when it has attained the summit that was before it; and it seldom happens on earth that there is not something ignoble and unworthy about repose. Others look back on what they have done almost with cowardly regret; for it is rarely the case that any sacrifice is strictly speaking complete in itself. A man has committed himself by it to something further, something higher. All efforts in the spiritual life, properly speaking, have to be sustained till the end. The difficulty, and therefore the costliness, of perseverance, consists in its tension never being relaxed. It is on this account that perseverance is an uncreaturelike grace, a supernatural similitude of God. Others again do not regret the efforts expended or the sacrifices made; but they look at once for their reward. They lower the nobility of what they have done by a want of disinterestedness. We are not offended when little services look for their reward. But great services remind us of God, and do not look so palpably unworthy of Him, and therefore they offend us by the mention of their recompense. So it is that in one way or other there are few souls, who do not somewhat disfigure and impair their sacrifice, and take the unearthly freshness from it. Thus when we see any one persisting in his complete sacrifice, with the same ardour, and fortitude, and magnanimity, and patience, almost gracefully unconscious that he has done or is doing any great thing, not that he does not understand what he has done, but because when all his thoughts are fixed on God, there are none left for attention to himself, then do we call it the most magnificent of all interior dispositions, a shadow of the rest of the unfatigued Creator, when His sabbath succeeded to the making of the world. Such was Mary's disposition in this seventh dolour. It was the sabbath of her world of sorrows. But when we think of the sacrifice which she had made, of the completeness with which she had made it, and then of her quiet bravery in that desolate solitude of creatures which was all around her uncompanioned soul, we may conceive how far it is beyond our power to realise the intrinsic majesty of such a disposition, and how much we should lower it, if we strove to compare it with the corresponding disposition in the saints, to which in the paucity of words we are fain to give the selfsame name. God rested on Himself in the hollow of uncircumscribed eternity, when His dread sabbath came. Can a creature share in such a sabbath ? Yet to what else shall we liken Mary in the repose of her dolours finished ?

Another disposition of her soul in this dolour was her detachment from all spiritual consolations and the sweetness of divine things. This is a height of love, which he, who practices it not on earth, loses the opportunity of practising for ever; for there can be no such love in heaven. We talk so often of the love of suffering, urging it on others and on ourselves, that we almost forgot how high and rare a grace it is, and how rash the pursuit of it is to common souls. There are few indeed to whom such a grace is a reality, and fewer still with whom it is at home, or amidst whose other graces it finds a place that fits it. Even saints, who have loved such suffering as creatures could inflict upon them, have shrunk from those processes of suffering which God Himself immediately imposes on the soul. Many, who have willingly parted with the light of the earth, have drawn back trembling from the darkness of heaven, when it threatened to descend upon them, and have averted it by the energy of their prayers. There have been saints who for the love of God would forego His spiritual sweetnesses and consolations, who yet could not bear to have His blessed Self laid upon them as a dread instrument of mysterious pain. The cloudy solitudes of divine abandonment have been trodden by very few, and they for the most part, when they had entered into the obscurity, let us know how far they had advanced by the cries of anguish which escaped from them as from wounded eagles, in their torture. Jesus Himself had cried aloud as He sank down into that appalling death. Mary in this dolour was allowed to try this perilous descent, and to share still further than she had done beneath the Cross the dereliction of our Blessed Lord. As this came upon Him at the end of his Passion, as the crowning sorrow, just when it was least possible for nature to endure it, so hers came on her at the end of her Compassion, as the crowning dolour, when suffering had left nature but as a wreck amid the abounding waters of divinest grace. The two sorrows, His and hers, ended in the same mysterious divine affliction, whither we cannot reach, but where we know that out of speechless woe there rose unutterable beautiful light from out their souls, which worshipped God with the perfection of created worship, carrying as on some mighty resistless wave the offering of human love far beyond the highest point which the tide of angelical intelligence was ever known to reach.

There are also two growths of heroic sorrow which we must not forget to notice, and which we may assuredly reckon among her dispositions in this dolour, the spirit of intercession and the spirit of thanksgiving. The products of grace are not unfrequently the contradictories of nature, even while they are grafted upon them. It would seem as if the natural result of sorrow were to make us selfish, by forcibly occupying us with ourselves, and concentrating our attention upon our sufferings. Yet we know that the proper grace of sorrow is unselfishness. It is as if the very multitude of things we had to bear made large room in our hearts, and caused a leisurely tranquillity there, which enabled us to think of others, and to legislate with the most minute and foreseeing consideration for their comfort. The spirit of intercession is part of the unselfishness which comes from the sanctification of sorrow. Our kindliness towards others takes especially a religious and supernatural form, because we are bearing our sorrow in the presence of God, and our whole being is softened by it, and drawn into deeper and more heavenly relations with Him. The spirit of intercession belongs to hearts which are victims, victims voluntary or involuntary of God's loving justice. Every Christian, who is in sorrow, is so far forth a living copy of Christ Crucified, and the spirit of expiation is an inevitable element in his grace. Moreover human agents are generally more or less concerned with our griefs, and for the most part not innocently or unintentionally so; and our thoughts, in being occupied with ourselves, are necessarily occupied with them. Thus Jesus prayed for His murderers upon the Cross. Thus the martyrs prayed for their tormentors. Thus also to wrong a saint has generally been the royal road to his choicest prayers. Who can doubt therefore, and especially in those critical circumstances of the world and out of the very abysses of the mysteries of redeeming grace, that Mary's soul, the more it was overwhelmed with the waters of bitterness, with all the more quiet intensity poured itself out on others; and inasmuch as her prayers were her treasures, treasures that could enrich the world far beyond its own suspicion or belief, it would necessarily be in intercession that the largeness and exuberance of her love found vent, especially when this spirit of intercession was at the same time the most efficacious reparation to Jesus for the wrongs He had sustained.

But while sanctified sorrow melts the heart in kindliness towards others, much more does it absolutely liquefy it, to use the favourite word of mystical writers, in kindliness towards God; and this, in the same spirit of contradiction to nature, takes the form of thanksgiving. On natural principles the times of sorrow are the times when we have least to thank God for; but to an enlightened and discerning faith they are the times into which blessings are miraculously compressed, miraculously both for number and for greatness. Yet even here there is something also which is deeply natural. When a friend has wounded us in any way, his change of conduct somehow brings out his love for us in our hearts, and the past is brightly magnified from behind the present cloud. Thus in our relations with God, sorrow makes us feel our own unworthiness more deeply, so that the contemplation of past mercies fills us with a humble astonishment, whose only voice is wondering praise and the thanksgiving of happy tears. This is that glorifying of God in the fires, which is one of the magnificences of tried souls. As we crush the aromatic leaves of the cypress and the bay to extract their fragrance from them, so God presses our hearts, till they bleed, that they may worship Him with the perfume of their gratitude, and draw Him closer to themselves with the new delight and love with which they inspire His compassion and His tenderness. Who can doubt that as Mary sank deeper down and deeper in those amazing gulfs of her dolours, her Magnificat became evermore louder and deeper and quicker and more full of adoring significance in the enraptured ear of God?

Last of all, the magnitude of her faith, in the dark hour of that seventh dolour, did of itself worship the Holy Trinity most incomparably. This is another of the many resemblances which there are between the seventh dolour and the third, the immensity and the repose of faith in unutterable darkness, faith without the light of faith, the sense of faith, the enjoyment of faith, without the ever-present self-reward as well as self-conviction which faith ordinarily brings with it. Here also is the same spirit of contradiction to unregenerate nature. We believe God the more readily, the more firmly, the more lovingly, just the more incredible He vouchsafes to make Himself to us. He never seems more good, than when we ourselves have least cause to think Him good, never more just than when He looks as if He were positively unjust. Faith is a gift which grows under demand, and becomes the more inexhaustible when its waters are let loose. It is in itself a worship of the truth of God, and in this perhaps resides the secret of its apparently unaccountable acceptableness with Him. Hence the more clearly we see this eternal truth in the midst of blinding darkness, so much the more firmly do we adhere to it in spite of seeming evidence to the contrary, and so much the less are we moved by difficulties; or rather, the less we apprehend them *as* difficulties, so much the more worship does our faith contain. Though He slay me, yet will I trust in Him, were the grand words of Job. Hence too it follows that calmness enhances faith. It is a testimony to its reality, and an evidence of its empire. Tranquil faith is sweetest worship because it seems to say that all is at peace because God is concerned. There is no need of agitation, or of trouble, or of any manner of unquietness: God is His own guarantee: all must be right and best and most beautiful because it is from Him. His word is dearer to us than knowledge, easier to read than proof, and nestles deeper in our hearts than a conviction. Yet, never was faith exercised under such circumstances as by Mary in this dolour, never was faith greater, nor ever faith more tranquil. The faith of the whole of the little scattered Church was in her, and there is not more faith to-day in the whole of the huge world-wide Church Militant, than was in her single heart that night.

All this gives us but a very faint idea of the inward beauty of our Blessed Lady in the endurance of this seventh dolour. Unknown graces were accompanied by unknown dispositions. The heights which she had reached are inaccessible to our mystical theology. God only can tell how beautiful she was within, and into what new unions with Himself she had by this last sorrow been permitted to enter. It is enough for us to know that, next to the Body of Jesus, her immaculate heart was the most wonderful thing on earth that night.

The seventh dolour contains also many lessons for ourselves, which are quite within the scope of those who are endeavouring to serve God in an ordinary way, while, at the same time, like all the other sorrows of our Blessed Mother, it calls us to serve Him with a higher, more detached, and more disinterested love, than we have ever done before. We learn from the promptitude with which she left the tomb to do her work, and to fulfil in her cheerless desolation the will of God, how we ourselves should put duty before all other considerations, and, in comparison with it, estimate as nothing the highest spiritual consolations. Now, as if Providence arranged it so on purpose, duty seems often to lead from the sensible enjoyment of Jesus. Even in common domestic life the unselfishness of daily charity will lead us to sacrifice what looks like a religious advantage, to forfeit what it is hard not to persuade ourselves is a spiritual improvement, for an agreeableness which others do not particularly value, and which appears to be only a growth of acquired politeness or of natural kindliness, and not at all an obedience to a supernatural bidding of grace. It is hard at all times to persuade ourselves that there is no spiritual advantage to be compared to the giving up of our own will, and that petty mortifications, which concern our own private ways, and the use of our time, and habits even of devotion, are, so long as they are painful to us, amongst the highest methods of sanctification. It is necessary to add, *so long as they are painful to us*, for, unlike other mortifications, when they cease to be painful, they cease to be mortifications, and become symptoms of the world having got the better of us, and then unfortunately there is no discretion left us but the apparently selfish rudeness of those who have real cause to be afraid about their souls. If the ordinary civilities of society may often claim our time and attention, at the seeming sacrifice of spiritual sweetness and communion with our Lord, much more imperative is the jurisdiction which charity may lawfully exercise over us in this respect. Unfortunately spirituality tends to be selfish. Our nature is so bad that good things acquire evil propensities, from their union with us, and it is the best things which have the worst propensities. Thus even the love of our Blessed Lord, when discretion does not guide it, may interfere with our love of others, and so come at last to be an untrue love of Him. Untrue, because merely sentimental; for there is no divine love which is not at the same time self-denying. To have to give up our own ways to those of others, to have our times of prayer at hours which we dislike, to accommodate our habits of piety to the habits of others, is certainly a delicate and perilous process, one needing great discretion, safe discretion, and an abiding fear of worldliness. Nevertheless it is often a most needful means of sanctification, especially to those whose duties, health, or position do not allow them to lead mortified and penitential lives. The use of time, whether we consider the annoying weariness of punctuality and the supernatural captivity of regular hours, or whether we look at the unwelcome interruptions and somewhat excessive demands upon it made by the inconsiderateness and importunity of others, is a most copious source of vigorous and bracing mortification for those who are trying to love God purely amid the inevitable follies and multifarious distractions of the world. It is the especial mortification of priests. But if manners and charity may lawfully draw us from the sensible enjoyment of Jesus, it would be simply unlawful to deny the claims of duty to compel such an act of self-denial. Yet it is a point in which pious people, especially beginners, almost invariably fail. There are few households or neighbourhoods in which the spiritual life has got an unjustly bad name, where the mischief has not been caused by the indiscretion of an ill-regulated piety in this respect, and while it is to be hoped that we look upon such households or neighbourhoods with an entirely unsympathetic coldness, it is not the less sad that the evil should be there, because it is not the less true that our Blessed Lord is the sufferer. Beginners cannot easily persuade themselves that Jesus can be more really anywhere than in the sensible enjoyments of intercourse with Him. The more advanced souls know well that Jesus unfelt is a greater grace than Jesus felt, in a multitude of instances; yet even with them practice falls below knowledge, because nature rebels to the very last against whatever limits the prerogatives of sense.

If Mary sought for no consolation in the house of John, but abandoned herself there to her desolation till Easter morning, does it not seem as if there was some kind of justification for those who cherish their grief and brood over it? We must distinguish. Grief in divine things so far differs from grief arising from earthly losses and bereavements, that we have no right to put it away from ourselves, or to seek consolation, until the impulses of grace bid us do so. The suffering of divine sorrow is so different a thing from that of common sorrow, that there is no danger of sentimentality, or effeminacy, or selfishness, arising from it. The endurance of divine sorrow is not the indulgence of it, but the continuation of a crucifixion; whereas the endurance of common sorrow soon ceases to be sorrow, and becomes an indulgence, an elegant and interesting self-importance, and a dissipating softness of luxurious melancholy. Thus sorrow for sin, sadness because of the sins of others, grief because of the vicissitudes of the Church, grief because of our Lord's Passion, or sorrowing sympathy with our Lady's dolours, are not so much events of human sadness which befall us, as direct operations of grace, and therefore aiming at different ends and working by other laws. Such griefs should be cherished, their remembrances kindled, and their shadows be perhaps with some slight degree of violence retained, when they seem as if they were departing. All this is unlawful with ordinary sorrows. Yet even in the case of divine sorrows it is to be remembered that any grace, which is out of the jurisdiction of discretion, is a phenomenon utterly unknown to the highest theology of the saints.

Since there are so many resemblances between the seventh dolour and the third, it is not surprising that they should in some respect teach the same lessons. We learn from this last sorrow that there is no darkness like the darkness of a world without Jesus, such as Mary's world was on that fearful night. It is darker than the darkness of Calvary; for that is a darkness which cheers, refreshes, and inspires. Jesus is there. He is the very heart of that darkness. He is felt more plainly than if He were seen. He is heard more distinctly, because all is so dark about Him, and other sounds are hushed by the gloom. It is like being in the cloud with God, as tried souls often are. It is truly a darkness, and brings with it the pain of darkness; yet there is hardly a loving soul on earth to whom such darkness would not be more welcome far than light. But the darkness of the absence of Jesus is as it were a participation in the most grievous pain of hell. If it is by our own fault, then it is the greatest of sorrows. If it is a trial from God, then it is the greatest of sufferings. In either case we must not let the light of the world tempt us out of the darkness. In such a gloom it is indeed dreadful to abide; but the consequences of leaving it by our own self-will are more dreadful still. It is not safe there to think of creatures. We must think of God only. It is the sanctuary of "God Alone," the motto of the saints and of the saintly. We must deal only with the supernatural, and leave Him who brought us there, whether for chastisement or fervour, to take us out when it shall be His will. Meanwhile we should unite ourselves to the dispositions in which Mary endured her seventh dolour, and this will bring us into closer union with God.

One more lesson still she teaches. She did her work in the world, as it were with all her heart, and yet her heart was not there, but in the tomb with Jesus. This is the grand work which sorrow does for all of us. It entombs us in the will of God. It buries our love, together with our sorrow, in the Blessed Sacrament. Sorrow is, as it were, the missionary of the Divine will. It is the prince of the apostles. The Church is built upon it. The gates of hell shall not prevail against it. Our Lord is with it always to the end. It is sorrow that digs the grave of self, and blesses it, and burns incense in it, and buries self therein, and fills it up, and makes the flowers grow upon the tomb. The great secret of holiness is never to have our hearts in our own breasts, but living and beating in the Heart of Jesus; and this can rarely be accomplished, except through the operation of sanctified sorrow. Happy therefore is he who has a sorrow at all hours to sanctify!

We have now brought our Blessed Mother to the threshold of those mysterious fifteen years, which followed her dolours and the Ascension of our Lord. She began with fifteen years without Him, and so in like manner she ended with fifteen years without Him. Only as in the first fifteen years the image of the Messias was engraven upon her heart, and the shadow of His coming lay over all her growths in holiness, so in the last fifteen years He dwelt bodily within her in the unconsumed Blessed Sacrament from Communion to Communion, and was the living fountain of all those nameless and unimaginable growths in holiness which during that time went on within her soul. The destiny of the Mother of God was a destiny of unutterable sorrow, exhausting at once the possibilities of woe and the capabilities of the creature. This might be expected, since it was by sorrow, shame, and the Passion, that the Incarnate God came to save the world. The dolours of our Blessed Lady therefore are inseparable from her Divine Maternity. They are not accidents of her life, one way out of many ways in which God might have chosen to sanctify her. They were inevitable to her as Mother of God, of God who took flesh to suffer and to die. Thus, rightly considered, Mary's dolours are Mary's self. Her first fifteen years, commencing with the Immaculate Conception, were a preparation for her dolours. Her last fifteen years, commencing with the descent of the Holy Ghost, were the maturity of her dolours. During them her sea of sorrow settled till it became a clear, profound, translucent depth of unmingled love, whose last act of taking the tranquil plenitude of possession of its glorious victim was the dislodging of her soul from her body, by the most marvellous and beautiful death which creature could ever die. Such an edifice of sorrow, as the Divine Motherhood was to bring along with it, could not rest on foundations less broad and deep than the immeasurable graces of her first fifteen years. What then must have been the grandeur of the graces which came upon that edifice when it was completed, and were its domes, and towers, and pinnacles? We have often wondered what could be done to Mary, in the way of sanctification, at the Descent of the Holy Ghost. What was left to do? In what direction was she to grow? The mere fact of the delaying of the Assumption meant something; and what could it have meant but increase of holiness and multiplication of grace? If she was kept on earth to nurse the Infant Church, as she had nursed the infant Saviour, to be herself a living Bethlehem with the Blessed Sacrament for ever in her, and her queenship of the apostles an external ministry of Bethlehem to the childhood of the Church, still untold and incalculable augmentations of grace and merit are implied in the very office, as well as in the fact that it was God's Mother who fulfilled the office. It was her dolours, which opened out in her soul fresh abysses for eager grace to fill. It was the dolours which rendered her capable of that other new creation of grace in the Descent of the Holy Ghost. His graces are absolutely inexhaustible: her capacities of grace are practically inexhaustible, to our limited comprehension. The grace, which prepared her for the Divine Maternity, prepared her also for her singular and lifelong martyrdom. Her martyrdom prepared her for those ineffable augmentations of grace and merit, which were compressed into her last fifteen years. Thus her dolours are, as it were, the centre of her holiness. They reveal Mary to us as she was in herself, more than any other of her mysteries. Indeed they are hardly to be called mysteries; they are more than that; they are her life, her self, her maternity. They enable us to understand her holiness. They help us to see, that what theologians say of the momentary accumulation of her merits is not so incredible, as it often seems to those who have not loved and meditated their way into Mary's greatness. There is nothing about Mary which unites in itself so much of Mary's part in the Incarnation, of her own peculiar personal holiness, and of her similitude to God, as the system of her dolours. They are at once the plainest and the completest, as well as the most tender and pathetic revelation, of the Mother of God. As her first fifteen years were secret, so are her last fifteen; but over the marvellous processes of grace, which fill them both, lies the shadow of her dolours, the shadow of a coming time in the one case, the shadow of a lofty mountainous past in the other. He, who would learn Mary, must enter into her broken heart to do so. It is the "dolorous Mother" who illuminates the Immaculate Conception on the one side and the fair pomp of the Assumption on the other.

Look once more at the great Mother as she leaves the garden of the sepulture. Eve going forth from Eden was not more sorrow-laden, and bore with her into the unpeopled earth a heart less broken and less desolate. That woe-worn woman is the strength of the Church, the queen of the apostles, the true mother of all that outspread world, over which the blue mantle of darkness is falling fast and silently. Sleep on, tired world! sleep on beneath the paschal moon, and the stars that are brightening as it sets; thy mother's heart watches and wakes for thee!

CHAPTER IX.

THE COMPASSION OF MARY.

At first we stood on the shore of Mary's sorrows, and gazed upon them as one vast ocean. We then sounded, one after another, the seven abysses of that ocean, which the Church selected and presented to us. Now we look at her dolours again as one, but pouring their waters through the strait of Calvary into the mightier ocean of the Precious Blood. This peculiar point of view is called the Compassion of Mary, the right understanding of which involves several grave theological questions, and yet is most necessary to make our devotion to the dolours real and profound. There are in fact seven questions for us to consider; the divine purpose of her Compassion, its nature and characteristics, what it actually effected, the relation in which it stands to our own compassion with her, a comparison of the Passion with Mary's Compassion, the seeming excess of the Compassion over the Passion, and lastly, the measures and dimensions of her Compassion.

SECTION I.

THE DIVINE PURPOSE OF MARY'S COMPASSION.

First of all, then, we have to consider the divine purpose of her Compassion. It is very questionable whether we might ever say of anything in God's works that it was merely ornamental. There is something in the idea of mere ornament which seems at variance with the actuality of God, with the magnificence of His simplicity, with His adorable reality. To suppose our Lady's dolours to be so much ornamental pathos, added to the Incarnation even for the holy end of exciting some additional degrees of love, would involve still further questions regarding the character and perfections of God, His tenderness towards His creatures, and the merciful significance which there is in every pain and sorrow through all creation. It is not easy to see how he, who should hold such a view of our Blessed Lady's sorrows, could be excused from the highest irreverence, or even from implicit blasphemy. God certainly had a purpose in them. He has a purpose in everything which He ordains. But His purpose in so very marked a feature of the Incarnation, as the unutterably woful destiny of the Mother of God, must have been proportioned to the magnitude of the mystery itself, and of that larger mystery of which it is a part. It could not have been a simple pathos. God could not have martyred one of His creatures only to throw a poetical halo round the intense realities of Calvary. Neither could it have been merely a lesson to us. For much of her Compassion is not only inimitable by us, and so beyond our reach, but also incomprehensible to us, and so beyond our understanding. It is true we learn lessons from it, because there is teaching in all that God does. But this is a different thing from God's having no further intention in a mystery, than that it should be a lesson to us. Neither can it have been only for her sanctification, though no doubt this was one great purpose in it. She had become the Mother of God before her dolours commenced; and they were a consequence of her Divine Maternity, not a preparation for it. They did sanctify her. Indeed they were in an especial sense the sanctification of one who, being sinless, could not be sanctified as the saints have been, by struggle, evil propensity, or inward temptation. But it is hard to contemplate them at all studiously, and believe that their purpose ended here. We crave a deeper and diviner purpose, and one more closely knit to the whole scheme of the Incarnation; and we may be sure that such an one exists, even though it may be beyond our discovery.

If then we reject all the views mentioned above, as unreal and unworthy, and clearly at variance with the phenomena to be explained, are we on the other hand to suppose that our Lady's Compassion was part of the redemption of the world, that the salvation of souls was merited by it, and that sin was expiated by it? Many writers have used language which seems to imply as much as this. Saints and doctors have united in calling our Blessed Lady co-redemptress of the world. There is no question of the lawfulness of using such language, because there is such overwhelming authority for it. The question is as to its meaning. It is merely the hyperbole of panegyric, the affectionate exaggeration of devotion, the inevitable language of a true understanding of Mary, which finds common language inadequate to convey the whole truth? Or is it literally true, with an acknowledged and recognised theological accuracy attached to it? This is a question which has presented itself to most minds, in connection with devotion to our Blessed Mother, and there are few questions to which more vague and unsatisfactory answers have been made, than to this. On the one hand, it seems rash to assert of language used both by saints and doctors, that it is only exaggeration and hyperbole, flowery phraseology intended to startle, but without any real meaning hidden beneath it. On the other hand, who can doubt that our most Blessed Lord is the sole Redeemer of the world, His Precious Blood the sole ransom from sin, and that Mary herself, though in a different way, needed redemption as much as we do, and received it in a more copious manner and after a more magnificent kind in the mystery of the Immaculate Conception? Thus, so far as the literal meaning of the word is concerned, it would appear that the term co-redemptress is not theologically true, or at least does not express the truth it certainly contains with theological accuracy. We are distracted between the desire to magnify our Blessed Mother, the authority of the saints and doctors, and the supremely sovereign requirements of a sound theology. We certainly shrink from asserting that the language of the saints has no meaning, or is inadvisable; and at the same time we have no doubt that our Blessed Lady is not the co-redemptress of the world in the strict sense of being redemptress, in the unshared sense in which our Lord is Redeemer of the world, but she is *co*-redemptress in the accurate sense of that compound word. But these are not times in which it is desirable to use words, the real meaning of which we have not distinctly ascertained. Hence, while it would be sad indeed for any one to attempt to deprive Mary of a title which saints and doctors have conferred upon her, for we are living in days when the growth of devotion to our Blessed Mother is our surest augury of a better future, at the same time it is of importance, even in a devotional point of view, for us to know what we mean by a title, which certainly conveys a real truth, and a truth which could not very easily be otherwise expressed. The following conclusions may perhaps be taken as true, finding truth in the mean, and avoiding both the somewhat violent alternatives of censuring the saints, or of infringing on the prerogatives of our Blessed Lord.

1. Our Blessed Lord is the sole Redeemer of the world in the true and proper sense of the word, and in this sense no creature whatsoever shares the honour with Him, neither can it be said of Him without impiety that He is co-redeemer with Mary.

2. In a secondary dependent sense, and by participation, all the elect co-operate with our Lord in the redemption of the world.

3. In the same sense, but in a degree to which no others approach, our Blessed Lady co-operated with Him in the redemption of the world.

4. Besides this, and independent of her dolours, she co-operated in it in a sense, and after a manner, in which no other creatures did or could.

5. Furthermore, by her dolours she co-operated in the

redemption of the world in a separate and peculiar way, separate and peculiar not only as regards the co-operation of the elect, but also as regards her own other co-operation, independently of the dolours.

These five propositions seem to place the whole question in a tolerably clear light. It does not appear to be necessary to say anything about the first. It is of faith that our Blessed Lord alone redeemed the world. The elect co-operate with Him in this work as His members. They have become His members by redeeming grace, that is, by the application to their souls of His sole redemption. By His merits they have acquired the ability of meriting. Their works can satisfy for sin, the sins of others as well as their own, by their union with His. Thus, to use St. Paul's language, by their sanctified sufferings or by their voluntary penances, they "fill up in their bodies that which is lacking of the sufferings of Christ, for His Body's sake, which is the Church." Thus by the communion of the saints in their Head, Jesus Christ, the work of redemption is perpetually going on by the accomplishment and application of the redemption effected on the Cross by our blessed Lord. It is not a figurative and symbolical, but a real and substantial, co-operation of the elect with our Blessed Redeemer. There is a true secondary sense in which the elect merit the salvation of the souls of others and in which they expiate sin and avert its judgments. But it is by permission, by divine adoption, by participation, and in subordination to the one sole and complete redemption of Jesus Christ. But the holiness of all the saints together does not even approximate to the holiness of Mary. Her merits have a sort of infinity as compared with theirs. Their martyrdoms and dolours are little more than shadows, when placed by the side of hers. Thus in their own sense of co-operation, she exceeds them in degree immeasurably, so that her co-operation with our Lord almost throws theirs into the shade. On this account she might be called co-redemptress with a truth, which would be far less applicable to the saints.

But this is not all. She co-operated with our Lord in the redemption of the world in quite a different sense, a sense which can never be more than figuratively true of the saints. Her free consent was necessary to the Incarnation, as necessary as free-will is to merit according to the counsels of God. She gave Him the pure blood, out of which the Holy Ghost fashioned His flesh, and bone and blood. She bore Him in her womb for nine months, feeding Him with her own substance. Of her was He born, and to her He owed all those maternal offices which, according to common laws, were necessary for the preservation of His inestimable life. She exercised over Him the plenitude of parental jurisdiction. She consented to His Passion; and if she could not in reality have withheld her consent, because it was already involved in her original consent to the Incarnation, nevertheless she did not in fact withhold it, and so He went to Calvary as her free-will offering to the Father. Now this is co-operation in a different sense from the former, and if we compare it with the co-operation of the saints, their own co-operation in which Mary herself alone surpassed them all, we shall see that this other peculiar co-operation of hers was indispensable to the redemption of the world, as effected on the Cross. Souls could be saved without the co-operation of the saints. The soul of the penitent thief was saved, with no other co-operation than that of Mary, and, if our Blessed Lord had so willed it, could have been saved without even that. But the co-operation of the Divine Maternity was indispensable. Without it our Lord would not have been born when and as He was; He would not have had that Body to suffer in; the whole series of the divine purposes would have been turned aside, and either frustrated, or diverted into another channel. It was through the free will and blissful consent of Mary that they flowed as God would have them flow. Bethlehem, and Nazareth, and Calvary came out of her consent, a consent which God did in nowise constrain. But not only is the co-operation of the saints not indispensable of itself, but no one saint by himself is indispensable to that co-operation. Another apostle might have fallen, half the martyrs might have sacrificed to idols, the saints in each century might have been a third fewer in number than they were, and yet the co-operation of the saints would not have been destroyed, though its magnificence would have been impaired. Its existence depends on the body, not on the separate individuals. No one saint, who can be named, unless perhaps it were in some sense St. Peter, was necessary to the work, so necessary that without him the work could not have been accomplished. But in this co-operation of Mary she herself was indispensable. It depended upon her individually. Without her the work could not have been accomplished. Lastly, it was a co-operation of a totally different kind from that of the saints. Theirs was but the continuation and application of a sufficient redemption already accomplished, while hers was a condition requisite to the accomplishment of that redemption. One was a mere consequence of an event, which the other actually secured, and which only became an event by means of it. Hence it was more real, more present, more intimate, more personal, and with somewhat of the nature of a cause in it, which cannot in any way be predicated of the co-operation of the saints. And all this is true of the co-operation of Mary, without any reference to the dolours at all.

But her dolours were of themselves another co-operation still more peculiar. The Incarnation might have taken place without its sorrowful mysteries. Indeed, if there had been no sin, it would have taken place in glorious and impassible Flesh, and of the same Mother with a different destiny, a destiny of joy as marvellous and inexplicable as was in fact her destiny of sorrow. The joys of Mary are like flashes from some other set of divine decrees, which was not wholly overlaid by the present dispensation. This is their peculiarity. They are tokens of a mystery existing in the mind of God, but which to us is no more than a possible world, or rather a world which our sin would not allow to realise itself. Thus it is impossible to separate the dolours of Mary from her divine Maternity. They follow from it in the way of consequence as necessarily as in the free divine counsels the Incarnation of shame and suffering followed from the necessity of expiating sin. Her sorrows were caused by and inextricably commingled with His sorrows. They came from the same source; they led into the same depths; they were connected with the same circumstances. The two sorrows were but one sorrow afflicting two hearts. Besides this, as we shall see afterwards, there were many peculiar points, not only of striking resemblance, but of actual union between her dolours and His. Yet, though we cannot separate her dolours from her Maternity in fact, her Maternity is quite conceivable without her dolours, and its peculiar co-operation with our Lord in the redemption of the world depends on other things than the dolours, things to which the dolours are by no means indispensable. So in like manner, or rather as a consequence, the co-operation of her dolours was a distinct co-operation from that of her Maternity, and has a character of its own.

Thus Mary has three distinct rights to the title of Coredemptress. She has a right to it, first of all, because of her co-operation with our Lord in the same sense as the saints, but in a singular and superlative degree. She has a second right to it, which is peculiar to herself, because of the indispensable co-operation of her Maternity. She has a third right to it, because of her dolours, for reasons we shall see presently. These last two rights are unshared by any other creature, or by all creatures collectively. They belong to the incomparable magnificence of the Mother of God.

It has been our privilege, more than once during the course of our inquiry into our Lady's dolours, to ascend some fresh height from which a new view of her grandeur has presented itself to us. Like the great summits in the mountain ranges of Alps, Andes, or Himalay, each new aspect of Mary's glory looks grander than the others. In truth it is with her greatness as with the greatness of sublime mountain scenery; we cannot carry its magnitude away with us in our minds. We see it, and appreciate it, while we are actually gazing on it; but when we turn away, the image of it in our minds is less than the reality. So, when we see the mountain again, from whichever side we get the view, it looks larger than it did before, because it is larger than our remembrance of it. So is it with our Blessed Lady. The moment we cease to rest our eye upon her in deep meditation, our idea of her is less than it ought to be. We never do her justice except when we gaze upon her. Perhaps it is so with all God's greatest works, as we know it is with God Himself. Hence it is that we so often hear objections to statements about the glory of Mary, coming even from pious believers. Their eye is not on her, and therefore what is said is incredible to them. Nay, they are the more convinced that the statements are exaggerated, because they so far transcend the image of Mary which is impressed upon their minds. They believe more of her, and they believe it more readily, as her feasts come round, for then their eye is on her, and they conceive more justly of her vastness. In nothing is she more like God than in having to be thus learned in order to be understood, and in having to be kept before us in vision, because our memory is not wide enough to hold her vast proportions, when she is out of sight.

This co-operation of our Blessed Lady is, therefore, another summit from which we gain a fresh view of her magnificence. It is the grandest privilege of the creature to be a fellow-labourer with the Creator, just as it will be our home and blessedness to enjoy His everlasting sabbath. But what is to be said of co-operating with Him in such a work as the redemption of the world, and co-operating in it with such efficacy, intimacy, and reality, nay, with a co-operation simply indispensable to its accomplishment? What an idea does it convey to us of immeasurable holiness! What gifts and graces does it not pre-suppose! What marvellous union with God does it not imply! It is as if He vouchsafed to select the very things about Him which are most incommunicable, and in a most mysteriously real way communicate them to her. It is as if in those things in which He stands alone and solitary, He drew her so nearly to Himself, that to us it should seem as if He was not solitary, because she was with Him. See how He had already mixed her up with the eternal designs of creation, making her almost a partial cause, and partial model of it. Yet this, while it accounts also for her share in the redemption, does not make her co-operation less wonderful. Divine works grow more wonderful in our eyes, as we discern more of their consistency and unity. No wonder then the saints should have sought to invent a word, a bold and startling word, which should express such an indescribable grandeur in a creature, as is involved in this three-fold co-operation of Mary in the redemption of the world. Our Lord had taken a created nature, in order that by its means He might accomplish that great work; so it seemed as if the highest honour and the closest union of a sinless creature with Himself should be expressed in the title of Co-redemptress. In fact there is no other single word in which the truth could be expressed; and far off from His sole and sufficient redemption as Mary's co-operation lies, her co-operation stands alone and aloof from all the co-operation of the elect of God. This, like some other prerogatives of our Blessed Lady, cannot have justice done it by the mere mention of it. We must make it our own by meditation before we can understand all that it involves. But neither the Immaculate Conception nor the Assumption will give us a higher idea of Mary's exaltation than this title of Co-redemptress, when we have theologically ascertained its significance. Mary is vast on every side, and as our knowledge and appreciation of God grow, so also will grow our knowledge and appreciation of her His chosen creature. No one thinks unworthily of Mary, except because he thinks unworthily of God. Devotion to the Attributes of God is the best school in which to learn the theology of Mary; and the reward of our study of Mary lies in a thousand new vistas that are opened to us in the

Divine Perfections, into which except from her heights we never could have seen at all.

What then is the place which our Lady's Compassion holds in the purposes of God? This grandeur of co-operation in a great measure answers the question. Her dolours were not necessary for the redemption of the world, but in the counsels of God they were inseparable from it. They belong to the integrity of the divine plan; and they doubtless perform many functions in it which we are unable to apprehend, and which perhaps we do not so much as suspect. According to God's ordinance, without shedding of blood there is no remission for sin. One of our Lord's infantine tears had enough in it of worth, of humiliation, of merit, and of satisfaction to redeem the sins of all possible worlds. Yet as a matter of fact we were not redeemed by His tears, but only by His Blood. Hence Bethlehem was not necessary for our salvation, nor the worship of the three kings, nor the presentation in the temple, nor the flight into Egypt, nor the disputing with the doctors. Nazareth was not necessary for our salvation, with all the beautiful mysteries of those eighteen years of hidden life. The public ministry, with its three years of miracles, parables, sermons, conversions, and vocations of apostles, was not necessary to our salvation. Indeed our Lord might have suffered as a Child, or He might have come full-grown like Adam, and simply suffered death at once. His Blood was all that was absolutely necessary. But Bethlehem and Nazareth and Galilee belonged to the integrity of the divine plan. They were not only congruous and beautiful, and significant and full of teaching: but there are deeper mysteries in them, and a diviner reality, simply because God planned it so. All His works partake in their degree of His perfections: in what degree then must the mysteries of the Thirty-Three Years partake of His perfections? The creation of the world was as nothing compared to the spiritual cosmogony of those Thirty-Three Years, except that it was the root of them. No one would dream of thinking lightly of the mysteries of our Blessed Lord's Sacred Infancy, because we were not redeemed by them. They are part of a whole, a divine whole. We do not know what would have happened, or what we should have lost, and what eternal consequences might have come, if they had not been there. So it is with our Lady's dolours. Her Maternity was indispensable to the Passion. Her dolours do not appear to be so. But they were an inevitable consequence of her Maternity under the circumstances of the Fall. They take their place among the Gospel mysteries. They rank with the mysteries of Bethlehem and Nazareth, not perhaps in their intrinsic importance, but in the relation in which they stand to the redemption of the world. Indeed we may be allowed to say that even in their intrinsic importance they might be compared with some of our Lord's own mysteries. For is it quite clear that His mysteries and hers can be divided off in this way? Are not her mysteries His, and His mysteries hers? Is not the Immaculate Conception a glory of His redeeming grace? Is not her Purification as much His mystery as His own Presentation? And in the case of the dolours the union of the Mother and Son is greater than in any other mystery. He is Himself her one dolour seven times repeated, seven times changed, seven times magnified. In our belief the dolours of our Blessed Lady rank very high indeed among the divine mysteries, and have a more privileged precedence there than is commonly suspected. But at any rate, so far as their relation to the redemption of the world is concerned, they are not further off from it than the unbloody mysteries of Jesus, and perhaps nearer, because of the immediateness of their connection. The truth appears to be, that all the mysteries of Jesus and Mary were in God's design as one mystery. We cannot break it up and divide, and parcel it out, and classify the importance of its various glories. This is a task beyond our science. Who can doubt, that it is true to say that many, who now are saved, would have been lost except for Mary's dolours; while yet her dolours do not bear the same relation to us as the Passion of our Blessed

Lord, even in their subordinate degree? The whole of the Three-and-Thirty Years, and the Hearts of Jesus and Mary in all the mysteries of those Years, are tinctured with the Passion: yet outside the Passion itself, where are the colours deeper, and the traits more life-like, than in the Mother's dolours? Mary's Compassion was the Passion of Jesus, as it was felt and realised in His Mother's Heart.

Is this then the whole account of the matter, that the Passion was necessary, and the Compassion unnecessary? Who would venture to say so? Who would dare to say that the Hidden Life of Nazareth was unnecessary? There is surely a very grave sense in which all the component parts of a divine work are necessary; for God is not such an artificer as man. If we are to rest simply on the doctrine that it was precisely blood-shedding by which our redemption was accomplished, then in the Passion itself were there not many things which were by no means necessary? There were the mental agonies, the public shame, the varieties of corporal torture, the insults, the lassitude, the thirst, the fear, the dereliction on the Cross. In that sense none of these things were necessary for our redemption. Even in the matter of Blood-shedding one drop would have sufficed; why was it all shed? Why the Sweat, the Scourging, the Crowning, the violent Unvesting, the Piercing after death? The profusion of the infinite was surely unnecessary, in our sense of that word. Now these are precisely the mysteries among which we ought to rank the dolours of Mary. They belong to the class of what we call the Unnecessary Sufferings of the Passion.* Indeed they were literally our Lord's own Unnecessary Sufferings; for were not her sorrows by far the most cruel instruments of His Passion? Her co-operation with the Passion by means of her dolours is wanting certainly in that indispensable necessity which characterises the co-operation of her Maternity. But it far more than compensates for that by the heroic detailed endurance of such

* For an account of these sufferings see the Second Chapter of the Author's Treatise on the Passion.

griefs, the overflowing fountain of freewill and promptitude, the unmingled and disinterested suffering, and its immediate contact with the Cross of Christ, which distinguishes it. In her Maternity she had joy as well as sorrow, and an unexampled dignity. Her consent to it was given once for all: and the co-operation of her Motherhood with the Passion was rather material than formal. This second co-operation of her dolours had more of herself in it and more similitude to her Son; it cost her more, and the very absence of necessity for it made the sacrifice the more generous and wonderful. Her maternity had to do with the Incarnation as the Incarnation: her dolours with the Incarnation as it was Redemption also.

SECTION II.

THE NATURE OF HER COMPASSION.

Having thus considered the divine purpose of Mary's Compassion, as far as it is in our power to do so, we may now pass to our second question, the nature and characteristics of her Compassion. What do we mean by the word Compassion? All sorrow for our Lord's Passion is compassion with Him. The contemplations of the saints, their painful ecstasies, their stigmata and thorny crowns, the engraving of the emblems of the Passion on the flesh of their hearts, and the miraculous inward sympathies with the Passion in their souls, are all but so many forms of Compassion, in the theological sense of the word. In like manner the tears and prayers and devout meditations of common Christians, the penances of Holy Week both among seculars and religious, the frequency of making the Stations or joining in other devotions to the Passion, are also Compassion, in the same strict sense. Hence it would appear that all sorrow of which the Passion is the cause, all sorrow which is the echo of the Passion in our hearts, no matter whether this sorrow takes the form of prayer, of penance, or of merciful deeds to others, is what we mean by Compassion. It is a great part, and truly an indispensable part, of the deep inward life of every believer. The more holy the heart in which it exists, the closer is its union with the life-giving Passion of our Lord. The intimacy and mystical beauty of this union depend on the vigour of the operations of grace, on the intensity of the will in identifying itself with the will of our Saviour, on the absence of all sin and self-seeking to mar the completeness of the union or retard the processes of grace, and finally on the tenderness of heart and the self oblivion of ecstatic love which accompany it. Now in all these respects our Lady's Compassion is beyond all comparison with the Compassion of the saints, so far beyond it that we may use the word Compassion of her companionship in the Passion, and use other and commoner words for the union of the saints with the sufferings of our Lord.

But as in the matter of co-operation, our Lady not only co-operated with Jesus in the same sense as the saints, only in a superlative degree, but also co-operated more intimately with Him in ways the saints could not share, so is it with her Compassion. It was actually contemporaneous with the Passion, and took place in the presence of the Passion. Indeed it is remarkable that all our Lady's dolours are compressed within the Thirty-Three Years. None fell in the fifteen years before, none fell in the fifteen years after. They came from the presence of Jesus. They were the very contact of His Heart with hers. The actual presence of our Lady's Compassion at the time and place of the Passion gives it a union therewith, which no other sorrow for our Lord can share. It was part of the living mystery itself. It was not the gradual result of long meditation. It was not a sorrow felt in the calm seclusion of the undistracted cloister, or a pious emotion roused by the marvellous ceremonial of a believing Church. It did not come from literature, or ritual, or history, or private revelation, or mysticism, or art, or poetry: but from the sights and sounds of the very Passion, in which it was immersed, and of which it formed an integral portion. It was part of our Blessed Mother's life. It was a series of events which happened to herself, outward sorrows of her own making these inward wounds. She had distinct rights, by which she was entitled to share in the Passion. It needed not to be transferred to her by grace, or love, or participation, or the power of faith. It was hers already as a mother. She suffered it in all the rawness and dishonour of its existing reality. She was in the crowd; she was jostled in it, and derided by it; she was distracted by the tumult; her inward tranquillity was assailed by the agitation and horror of the senses. All this is true of her Compassion, and of hers only.

Moreover her Compassion was part of the Passion, in the sense of having actually increased the Passion. With Judas and Annas and Caiaphas, with Pilate and Herod, with the Roman soldiers and the Jewish rabble, we must reckon Mary among those who wrung our Saviour's Heart with sorrow. Except the dereliction of His Father, we may well suppose that there was no pain in all His Passion equal to that which the vision of His Mother's broken heart supplied. Thus her Compassion was an integral part of His sufferings. Beautiful as it was, and exceedingly holy, a very worship in itself, and a very growth of heaven, to Him it was simple anguish. Intensely as He loved each soul of man, and therefore loved all souls collectively with an amount of burning desire which bewilders our conjectures, the single soul of His Mother was with Him an object of amazing love far beyond what He felt for all other creatures together. To see her therefore tempest-tossed on a dark ocean of unutterable woe was of itself a fearful torture to Him; but that woe was caused by Himself; it was being poured out of His soul into hers each separate moment, at each separate shame, pain, outrage, and indignity. It was He who was stretching her on the rack, He who was turning the instruments of her torture perpetually beyond the limits of human endurance, He who was thickening the inconsolable darkness round about her. It was He only who was doing all this. Without Him she would have had no dolours. It was her embrace of Him that was her agony. He was a fiery sharp-edged cross to the heart He loved best of all. Then all the incalculable bitterness that He had poured out of Himself into her, He took back into Himself without taking it away from her. It re-entered His Sacred Heart as another separate Passion, another great creation of sorrow by itself, and overwhelmed Him with a very deluge of tempestuous grief. Thus her Compassion came out of the Passion, and went into it again, so that there was rather an identity between the two, than a union of them. Her Compassion was the Passion taking a particular form. Her words to St. Bridget express this;* " The sorrow of Christ was my sorrow, because His Heart was my heart. For, as Adam and Eve sold the world for one apple, my Son and I redeemed the world with one heart."

From the Compassion of Mary being contemporaneous with the Passion, and indeed an integral part of it, there flowed into it the character of sacrifice and expiation which belonged to the Passion, and this in a degree and after a kind which does not belong to the sorrows of the saints. As the Passion was the sacrifice which Christ made upon the Cross, so the Compassion was the sacrifice of Mary beneath the Cross. It was her offering to the Eternal Father. It was an offering made by a sinless creature for the sins of her fellow-creatures. Their gain was her loss. The lightening of their hearts was the burdening of hers. Her darkness was their light. Their peace was her agony. Her son was their victim. Their life was her tremendous martyrdom. Her offering rose to heaven together with the offering of Jesus. They were as two grains of incense on the burning coals of one thurible. With various fragrance they rose up to the throne in the same thin circles of blue smoke, perceptibly different, yet utterly inseparable. When the sound of the scourging went up to heaven, the smothered sighs of Mary's bursting heart went up with it. When the Barabbas

* Rev. lib. i. c. 35.

of the multitude rang fiercely in the hollow vaulted sky the agony of Mary went floating up, sweet music mid the fierce clamour, to the Father's ear. With the dull knockings of the hammer, the beatings of her heart went up and lay down at the foot of the throne, and did not pass unheeded. Her voiceless aspirations flew upward in equal flight with the seven words which Jesus uttered on the Cross. His loud cry at the end was heard twice in heaven, the second time as it echoed thither out of Mary's heart. Thus, during those hours of the Passion, each oblation was a double one; the offering of Jesus and the offering of Mary were tied in one. They kept pace together; they were made of the same materials; they were perfumed with kindred fragrance; they were lighted with the same fire; they were offered with kindred dispositions. Thus there is a sacrificial and expiatory character in Mary's Compassion which is peculiar to itself. The world was redeemed by the Passion of our Lord. But there never was, in the ordinance of God, such a thing as a Passion of Jesus disjoined from the Compassion of Mary. The two things were one simultaneous oblation, interwoven each moment through the thickly crowded mysteries of that dread time, unto the Eternal Father, out of two sinless Hearts, that were the Hearts of Son and Mother, for the sins of a guilty world which fell on them contrary to their merits, but according to their own free will. Never was any sanctified sorrow of creatures so confused and commingled with the world-redeeming sorrow of Jesus, as was the Compassion of His Mother.

Furthermore, the Compassion of Mary was an example to the whole Church. It is part of the teaching of the four Gospels. It performs a function for all ages of the world. It is a continual source of holiness in the midst of each generation of the faithful. It is a living, grace-diffusing power among the children of God. It actually leads multitudes of souls to Jesus. It breaks the bonds of sin and evil habits. It melts cold hearts, and stimulates the lukewarm affections of the torpid and the worldly. It pours light and tenderness, and a spirit of prayer, and a love of suffering, and a thirst for penance, into countless souls, between the sunrise and sunset of each day, and in the whole breadth of the world from pole to pole. It models saints; it animates religious orders; it is the type of a special spiritual life to individual souls. It rises up to heaven like an endless angelic song. Everywhere in the Church there is a sound of it. Out of seven deep places it echoes everlastingly. Time and space have nothing to do with it. Simeon still prophecies, and we hear it, and a life-long sadness runs thenceforth alongside of our perseverance in the ways of grace. Still Mary flies with Jesus into Egypt, and dwells there, and the Nile lapses by, and the shadows in our souls are the substances of grace. Still for three days does the childless Mother wander with darkened spirit, seeking for her Child, and finding Him at last in the temple. Still is she meeting Him again and again with the heavy Cross upon His shoulders, and we the while meeting Him in her. Still is she at the foot of the Cross, alluring all her children to her. Still is she at the Deposition from the Cross, and at the Burial, acting over again and again those pathetic mysteries in the new hearts which the children of each generation give her. Thus her compassion is not merely her own. It authoritatively and authentically represented the whole Church on Calvary. She was present at the Passion, as it were officially, and in a double capacity, as co-operating with the Redeemer, and as representing the redeemed.

The Compassion of our Lady may also be regarded in a two-fold point of view, according as we consider our Lord as God or as Man, as God His Divine Nature was fearfully outraged by the Passion. Not all the sins of the world put together so dreadfully and sacrilegiously violated the glory of God, as that particular sin out of which He worked the redemption of the world. Never did the disloyalty of a rebellious creation make so deep an impression upon the divine honour, or seem so inexpressibly to endanger the sovereignty of God. This is a view of the Passion which we must never lose sight of. It needed another Passion to expiate itself. It needed a second Passion to make reparation to God for the first. Mary's Compassion occupies this place. The sin produced a double Passion, one in Jesus and one in Mary; but it produced it without double sin. So that her Compassion needed no expiation; though, had it done so, there was expiation enough in the Passion to satisfy for itself and for her Compassion. But she stood at the foot of the Cross as the minister of God's glory. Her sorrows, even while they are fresh sorrows to Him, were also the nearest approach to a perfect reparation which creatures could make. We have seen in the preceding chapters that reparation is an essential element in all holiness. Now if the collective sanctity of all the apostles, martyrs, confessors, and virgins through all time had dedicated itself, on the earth until the day of judgment, to the sole work of making reparation for His Passion (and rightly considered, the whole action of His Church is in effect reparation for the Passion), it could not by the end of the world have produced a reparation anything like so complete as the Compassion of Mary. It exceeded in efficacious holiness all other reparation. It was offered to our Lord's Divine Nature instantaneously, indeed simultaneously with the outrage, and almost co-extensively with its excess. It came from His own Mother, which added to it an incomparable acceptableness. It fitted His Passion in kind, fashion, method, and degree, as nothing else could fit it. Lastly, it drew its efficacy, not merely or so much from its own intrinsic worth, as from its real and vital union with His Passion. Mary's Compassion was the reparation she made to her Son as God.

If Mary at the foot of the Cross was the minister of our Lord's glory as God, she was no less the minister of His Sacred Humanity. In a merely human point of view, we might be surprised at Mary's presence upon Calvary. It was not a fitting place for a mother, the scaffold of her Son, and her Son, we might have expected, would have spared her the agony. But she was the minister of the Incarnation. She was His sole human parent. She represented in herself the human obedience under which the Incarnate Word had lived, and which was, as the Apostle has remarked, to characterise His death as perfectly as it had modelled His life. He had waited for her consent, before He took flesh of her. When He had inflicted her worst sorrow on her by leaving her at the age of twelve, He also in the same mystery especially showed forth His obedience to her in returning to Nazareth for eighteen years. He began His miracles at her suggestion. He had her permission for His public ministry. He had vouchsafed to ask her leave and blessing for His Passion. Perhaps His Heart may have silently asked her heart leave to die. From the first, Jesus and Mary had never been separated. It seems to have been a sort of law of the Incarnation that they should be together. Her Assumption, Coronation, and Mediatorial Throne, would be but the final instances of the operation of this law. Now that God has let us see the Thirty-Three Years in their perfection as a whole, we perceive that the absence of Mary from Calvary would have offended our Christian instincts as much as her absence from Bethlehem or Nazareth. She was the minister of the Incarnation: it all lies in that. She had no more right to come down from Calvary, than a priest would have to leave the altar in the midst of the sacrifice of the Mass. There would have been an incongruity in it. On one twenty-fifth of March she had given Him His Precious Blood; on another twenty-fifth of March she must minister at the shedding of it. She must swathe the Man as she had swathed the Child. She must lay Him in the tomb, who had already laid Him in the manger. She must preside at the end as she had presided at the beginning. There must be an overshadowing of the Holy Ghost at the last, as there had been one at the first. As she had waited fifteen years for His coming, she must wait fifteen years after His departure. Her priesthood consisted in this continuity of ministry to Him.* Her maternity was not to Him a mere means, occasion, instrument, or access, but an enduring ministry under which His obedience was consummated. Mary's Maternity was her Compassion at Bethlehem; Mary's Compassion was her Maternity at Calvary.

SECTION III.

THE ACTUAL EFFECTS OF HER COMPASSION.

We are now in a condition to inquire, thirdly, into the actual effects of Mary's Compassion. These may be classed under three heads, inasmuch as her Compassion was itself part of the Passion, as it fitted her for her office in the Church, and as it regarded her co-operation in the work of redemption. Yet, although these three things may be conceived of as separate, they are in reality so intertwined that, in classifying them apart, we run the risk of falling into some repetition, a risk however which, for the sake of clearness, it is worth while to incur.

As it was a part of our Lord's Passion, Mary's Compassion has a share in the effects which the Passion produced, in the same sense, though of course in a far lower degree, in which His dereliction by the Father, assisted in producing the results of the Passion. This is but a material co-operation: yet as it is a fact, it serves to show the reality of the Compassion, and the existence of a purpose in it as part of the divine plan. Its effects upon our Blessed Lord were so terrible, that it seems probable the agony it caused Him would have put an end to His life, if His Divinity had not miraculously sustained Him in order that He might suffer more. Our Lady revealed to St. Bridget, that when Jesus saw the bitterness of her grief, He was so affected by it

---

* Mary of Agreda tells us that our Lady's grace to minister to Jesus was *a special* grace: and that she received it at the same moment she received the grace of being His coadjutrix. The two graces went together. *Mistica Ciudad*, p. ii. l. iii. c. 12.

Himself that He became comparatively insensible to the pain of all His wounds, because of the much greater pain which the sight of her sorrow caused Him.* St. Bernard calls His vision of her grief "an inexplicable woe, an ineffable reciprocation of holy love." Thus her Compassion was not only an intrinsic part of the Passion, but among its chief and most efficacious elements. Moreover her dolours alone approached, after the Father's abandonment, to satisfy that thirst of suffering, which the immense love of Jesus still felt, even while He was hanging on the Cross, and this was in itself one of their most remarkable functions. All this is very obvious. Nevertheless we hardly do our Lady's dolours justice, as divine mysteries, from our habit of regarding them too exclusively as her sorrows, and not as His sorrows also, and perhaps more His than hers. We have already expressed a doubt whether we can, without peril of inaccuracy and misapprehension, divide our Lady's mysteries from our Lord's. For the whole spirit of the Gospel narrative, as well as the action of what is apparently a great law of the Incarnation, seems to bring Jesus and Mary together, and make them inseparable. Now, if we detach her mysteries from His, or look at her for a moment as apart from Him and possessing anything independently of Him, we run one of two risks. Either we shrink from the language and views of the great saints and doctors of the Church, because we have already in our own minds made Mary into some kind of gigantic saint, instead of the Divine Mother, the "Woman clothed with the Sun," in the Apocalypse, and so, looking at her standing by herself, we dare not use of her the almost godlike words which are common with the saints; or the authority of the saints overrules us to use their language, and to force ourselves into their beliefs without understanding them, and so we may come to attribute to our Lady by herself what only belongs to our Lord, and thus we disturb the analogy of the faith, and bring devotion to our Blessed Mother into discredit by what is manifestly

* Rev. l. i. c. vi.

an exaggeration, as well as an infringing of the honour of our Lord.

In a certain sense the saints may stand alone, with their own individual characters. Mary cannot do so. She is too near God to do so. If there be a peculiar kind of saint with a marked character and a recognisable individuality of her own, whose name is Mary, hidden under the Divine Maternity, lurking as it were at the bottom of the mysteries of Bethlehem, Nazareth, and Calvary, it is at least indistinguishable to us, because of the excess of that light of the Eternal Sun in which she is all arrayed. It is not in our power to detach it from the Divine Maternity. It never works its way to the surface. If it exists, it is known to God only. If we are ever to know it, it must be by the light of the Beatific Vision, and not here or now. To us she must be simply the Mother of God, not more like John than she was like Peter, not bearing a greater resemblance to St. Francis than to St. Dominic, to St. Teresa than to St. Catherine of Siena, to St. Philip than to St. Ignatius. We cannot look at her both as a saint and as the Mother of God. If we attempt to do so, one or other of the two characters will suffer. The inevitable result will be a lowering of her from the heights upon which the great doctors of the Church were wont to contemplate her grandeur, a grandeur which is not only solitary, but incomparable and incommunicable. They never looked at her as apart from Jesus. To their eyes she was blended with Him; and what she possessed, she possessed in common with Him. She was filled with His light, clothed with His magnificence, and, as it were, imbedded in the mystery of the Incarnation. The very thing which startles us about her, and which made St. Denys say he doubted for a moment if she was not a God, is that similarity to God which she appears to receive from the Divine Nature of her Son, in return for that Human Nature which she ministered to Him. This has always been to me the most noticeable thing about her, her likeness to the Word as God, who is so like her as Man. It is this very privilege of the Divine Maternity, which seems at times to raise her above the sphere of the Incarnation, and place her in such an unspeakable vicinity to the invisible God. The saints appear to have looked at Mary as a created person and nature, on which all the communicable splendour of God Himself was laid which a mere creature could, within the limits of the divine economy, be enabled to bear. Hence they looked at her so completely as she was in God, in the lap of His divine magnificence, that they did not shrink from using language of her, which cannot fail to be misunderstood by those who contemplate her from a different point of view. It is very important to bear this in mind. For at first sight those who love our Lady feel a kind of sorrow at the apparent denial to her of an individual character, which should be distinctive and her own. It seems to put her at a distance from them, and so to be unloving. But a little more reflection will show them in what devotional, as well as theological difficulties, the other view cannot fail of ultimately entangling them.

With regard to the dolours, however, there can be no question of their being simply unintelligible, if we view Mary in them as apart from Jesus. Whatever may be said of other mysteries, these are undeniably His as much as they are hers. Neither shall we ever attain to a right view of them, unless we regard them as sorrows in His Heart, as well as sorrows in hers; and thereby as helping to effect the Passion, and having in the Passion a very prominent and peculiar place assigned to them. Mary's Compassion was the way in which her Maternity was concerned with the Passion.

Her Compassion had also the effect of fitting her for her offices of Mother of Men, Queen of Mercy, and Refuge of Sinners. As we have said in the first chapter, she acquired what look like rights by her dolours. They were voluntary heroic sacrifices over and above the absolutely indispensable sacrifices which the Divine Maternity entailed upon her. Jesus was as it were indebted to her for them. It was in them that the glorious empire over the Sacred Heart, which she exercises this day in heaven, was chartered and took deepest root. It was in them that her almost identity with Jesus attained its highest point and most indistinguishable union. Neither can we doubt that her endurance of such fearful and at the same time such varied sorrow enlarged her heart, and rendered her more capable than she would otherwise have been of sympathising with the sorrows of humanity. The saints learn much from sin. Apostolic zeal and charity have roots in the experience of sin as well as in the pure love of God. From all such learning our Blessed Mother was absolutely precluded. Sorrow therefore had to teach her what sin was not allowed to teach. No science of the malice of sin or of the necessity of grace could make her feel that loss of Jesus, which is sin's primest unhappiness, as the Three Days' Loss taught it to her. Her intercession also derives an immense power of impetration, as well as a more impressive reality, from her experience of sorrow, and the union of her sorrows with those of Jesus. Even if we look at her dolours simply as enormous accumulations of merit, they assume a considerable importance in reference to her offices towards us. There can hardly be a shade of human sorrow which is not familiar to her heart. The manifold inventions of grief are known to her. The secrets of its alliance with grace, as well as its tendencies to conspire with the unworthy weaknesses of our nature, are no secrets to her. She, who is to be the prophetess of a sorrowing race, is by her own experience the grand doctress in the science of sorrow. Her Compassion also gives to her yearning to increase the harvest of the Passion an intensity, like to the blessed excesses of the Sacred Heart for souls, which perhaps she could not have had without it. Indeed her sorrows upon Calvary were the very birththroes in which all men were born as Mary's children, and thus her Compassion was not merely a fitness to be our Mother, but her very delivery of us as her children. In like manner, as it was in her Compassion that we were born to her, so in her

Compassion do we reach that wide and deep foundation on which our filial confidence may be built. Were our dearest Mother only the bright glad marvel she would be with her Immaculate Conception, her Divine Maternity, and her glorious Assumption, we should not trust her as we trust the broken-hearted Mother beneath the Cross. She would seem further off from us. We should feel towards her with feelings akin to those with which we regard the angels, full of love and worship, of tenderness and reverence, of wonder and congratulations, of holy envy and desire of union with them. We should not feel, as we do now, that she belongs to us, is near to us, and is our real Mother. It is the Compassion which throws this filial character over our devotion to the mighty Mother of God. But this is not all. As it was in her Compassion that we were born to her, as it is in her Compassion that we find our motives for filial confidence in her during life, so it was in her Compassion that we gained our right to die in her maternal arms. For it was then that she herself received the right of the patronage of death-beds, because of her attendance at the death-bed of our Lord; and her ministry to us, as to Him, in the hour of death is part of her office upon which the Church dwells most strongly by naming it in the Ave Maria. Thus is her Compassion inseparably bound up in the manifold offices of mercy, which by the ordinance of God Mary discharges to us.

The third effect of Mary's Compassion is her co-operation with Jesus in the redemption of the world. We have already spoken of this, but somewhat more yet remains to be said. The co-operation of Mary has sundry characteristics of which we must not lose sight, in considering the question. It was the co-operation of a sinless creature with the Incarnate Creator in redeeming the world from sin. She had no sin of her own, and yet she suffered, and moreover suffered for sin. This at once distinguishes her co-operation from that of the saints who had sinned, and the angels who could not suffer. It is peculiar to herself. Besides this her Compassion was, as we have said, one simultaneous and indeed identical sacrifice with His; so that one of the older theologians has said, "The will of Christ and Mary was altogether one, and their holocaust one; both offered alike to God, He in the Blood of His Flesh, she in the blood of her heart."* Hence her satisfactions have a place with His in the treasury of the Church, which does not belong to the satisfactions of the saints. They are more Christlike, as well as more abundant and more precious. When we offer our Blessed Lord to the Father, we are offering what is not in any proper sense ours to offer. It is only ours by the artifices of grace and the ingenuities of the communion of saints. They make it really ours in a Christian sense, a supernatural sense. But Jesus belonged to Mary, and was obedient to her, in quite a different sense. She had a right to offer Him, in which we cannot share. While our spiritual offerings cost us nothing, hers cost her a broken heart. She impoverished herself to enrich us. Moreover by offering Jesus to the Father, she did more than all creation put together could do to make reparation to His ever blessed majesty which sin had outraged. All angels and all saints must fall no less short than infinitely short of what she did: because her offering was infinite. Consequently it made ample reparation, a reparation worthy of God and equal to God, because what she offered was the Incarnate God, who was likewise her obedient and loving Son. When Mary had made her offering, not a vestige of the outrage of sin remained upon the glory of the Creator. All wound was healed, all void filled up, all darkness illumined, if we may dare to use human words of such a mystery, inadequate as they must necessarily be. Nay, this was not all,—by Mary's offering, which was her own and which she had a right to make, a very world of glory encompassed the throne of God; which He would not have had perhaps, if sin had never been. Sin became as it were an immensity of new matter, out of which the sacrifice of Jesus and the offering of Mary evoked a fresh world of glory,

* Arnold Carnot ap. Novatum i. 380.

vaster than all material worlds, for the Majesty of the Most High. Even this is not enough. Mary went into the sacrifice yet deeper. She became a living crucified part of it. Her dolours, next to the dereliction of the Father, were the deepest, the bitterest, and the most extensive part of our Saviour's Passion, and therefore co-operated, with the Divine Abandonment and the sinful cruelty of men, in enabling Jesus to offer to the Father that magnificent and super-sufficient satisfaction, which there was in the sacrifice of the Cross. These were the marvellous effects of her Compassion. We almost tremble to write of them, because we know so well how, through spiritual blindness and want of a truer love of our dearest Mother, we are stating them far below the splendour of their reality.

SECTION IV.

OUR COMPASSION WITH HER COMPASSION.

We have now to speak of our compassion with Mary as an imitation of her compassion with Jesus, or, in other words, of our compassion with her as itself a worship of Jesus and a true compassion with Him. First of all, devotion to the dolours of our Blessed Lady is most acceptable to our Lord Himself. We quoted in the first chapter His revelation to the Blessed Veronica of Binasco, in which He told her that tears shed over His Mother's sorrows were more precious in His sight than tears shed in memory of His own. We may perhaps venture to explain this as teaching us, what appears to be certainly true in itself, that devotion to the seven dolours brings with it by a kind of necessity devotion to the Passion, whereas devotion to the Passion does not seem so necessarily to include devotion to the dolours. Devotion to the Passion in which the right place and participation are not assigned to Mary, is not a scriptural devotion; and in many ways, which it would be out of place to enter upon here, it betokens an imperfect and unworthy view of the Passion itself. Yet it is not uncommon to meet with this partial devotion, and it rather tends to keep devotion to the dolours at arms' length than to lead to it. It is based upon that untheological mistake which some deceive themselves into thinking a theological nicety and a controversial felicity, namely, a sort of jealous ignorant accuracy in keeping Jesus and Mary apart, and not letting one intrude on the sphere of the other, as if to speak as slightingly as they dare of the Mother of God would make truth more attractive in the eyes of a misbelieving world, to which the incredible abasement of Jesus in His Sacrament is already a far greater stumbling-block than the incredible exaltation of His Mother. On the other hand, we see that devotion to the dolours brings with it as its invariable practical result a deep, tender, accurate, minute, and reverential devotion to the Passion. Again, we may venture to read in our Lord's words a loving intent to have reparation made to Mary for her Compassion, just as her Compassion was the grand reparation of His Passion. By inspiring saints and religious orders with this devotion, and sending forth His mighty grace and efficacious blessing to accompany it, He repays her for the beautiful reparation of her Compassion. But whatever other meanings there may be in this revelation to the Blessed Veronica, and although its force as a revelation was, as in all private revelations, intended for herself, it proves at least as much as this, that the devotion to our Lady's dolours is one of peculiar acceptableness in the eyes of our Blessed Saviour.

This devotion has also a remarkable connection with great interior holiness. This is proved by experience. Neither is it to be wondered at. For it is a devotion which naturally makes us unworldly, because we live and breathe in an atmosphere of sorrow. It brings out the unreality of worldly joys. It sobers our thoughts. It keeps them close to Jesus Christ, and to Him crucified. It communicates to our souls the spirit of the Cross; and the enviable gift of love of suffering full often brings in a prayerful familiarity with the sorrows of our Blessed Mother. More than most devotions it tends to supernaturalise the mind, because it keeps us in a sphere of heavenly beauty, whose look and odour gradually pass upon ourselves. It is a sphere in which the most wonderful divine operations mingle with the common woes and sorrows of a suffering world, and so it expresses that union of self-abasement and self-oblivion in which all the greater graces of the spiritual life take root. Moreover the prevailing ideas to which it weds our minds are just those which are the most solid and essential in any persevering endeavours after holiness. For it unites us to an abiding sorrow for sin, sin which caused Mary's sorrow, sin which caused the sorrow over which Mary sorrowed, sin of our own which was actually present and influential in both those sorrows, wronging at once the Mother and the Son. It equally unites us to the perpetual sense of needing grace, of absolute dependence upon grace, and of that ready abundance of grace on which our filial confidence reposes. It is all stained with the Precious Blood; and thus it puts us into the very depths of our Saviour's Sacred Heart. There is no soul, which worldliness finds it harder to attack, than one which is entrenched within the dolours of our Blessed Lady. There is nothing which the world can graft itself upon in that devotion. There is nothing congenial to the spirit and way of the world in it, nothing even which the world can falsify for its own ends or fraudulently divert for its own purposes. Moreover it was in the dolours that the grandeurs of Mary's sanctity were fabricated, and fabricated out of materials which in their degree are common to every one of us her sons and daughters. It is hard to live in the bosom of great examples, and be uninfluenced by them. The lessons which the dolours teach us are wanted at almost every turn of life, and are most appropriate to the very seasons when grace is wont to be most active in us; and they are imparted with such loving tenderness, with such pathetic simplicity, and in the midst of such countless similitudes between our sinless Mother and our sinful selves, that it is difficult to conceive of a school in which so much heavenly wisdom is taught so winningly as in the Compassion of Mary.

Furthermore, this devotion to the dolours of Mary is reckoned by theologians among the signs of predestination. Certainly a special attraction of grace is a sweet prophecy of our final perseverance; and it is by a special attraction of grace that we addict ourselves to this devotion. Perhaps our Lord's revelation to St. John the Evangelist, cited in the first chapter, of the four graces which it was His blessed will to attach to this devotion, one of which concerned the gift of perfect contrition before death, and another our Lady's protection in the hour of death, may have led to its being included in the catalogue of signs of predestination. For sorrow for sin is well-nigh the queen of graces; enclosing as it does within itself the grace and more than the grace of sacraments. Contrition is nearest of kin to perseverance, and the promise of our Lady's assistance at the hour of death is not far removed from an assurance of our salvation. Cartagena says,* "A man may put before himself as the most assured sign of predestination, the fact that he has had compassion for this most afflicted Mother; for the ancients tell us that it was conceded to the Blessed Virgin by Christ the Lord, that whoever should revolve in his mind her maternal dolours, might be sure of impetrating any favour which concerned the salvation of his soul, and especially the grace of true penance for his sins before death."

Thus also devotion to the dolours is one of the best preparations for death, not only because of the precise graces promised to it in the hour of death, but also because it concerns our Lady's ministry to our Lord at the hour of His blessed death. Hence there is a congruity between this devotion and death. And after all, what should life be but a preparation for death? And what graces should more attract our humility than those which promise us their suc-

* Ap. Sinischalch. xvi.

cour in that tremendous hour? Alas! it is not for such as we are to look forward to death with triumph, or even with impatience. We are not saints. Triumph therefore would be unseemly in us, and impatience is surely premature. It is enough for us, in our low attainments, to be content to die, and to fear bravely that which we are contented to endure. Fine words are easy, and love is very profuse of them, when we are not tempted, and when God is flooding us with that inward sweetness which gives us such a facility in prayer. But when we are tempted we grow silent; and when to our temptation is added spiritual dryness, querulousness and peevishness are added to our silence. We are soon prostrated; and we learn thereby the good lesson of our own real inward misery and helplessness. But if dryness and temptation bring such changes, what will death bring? It will bring such an unutterable, speechless, terrified, agonising necessity of grace as it is appalling to think of, when we bend our thoughts seriously to it. What will a devotion be worth to us then, which has two special death-bed promises attached to it? Gold and pearls could not reckon its price. But the devotion must have been a lifetime devotion in order legally to inherit the death-bed promises.

It is unnecessary to speak of the authority of the Church, of the liberality of her indulgences, of the examples of the saints, or of the records of numberless conversions, all attesting the power and acceptableness of this devotion. They have already occupied our attention in the first chapter. But we must not forget that our Blessed Lady has a special claim upon our devotion to her dolours. It is part of the duty of sons to their mother to compassionate her in her trials and sorrows, of whatever nature they may be, or from whatever cause they may spring. But this is very far short of our duty towards the sorrows of Mary. We ourselves were part of them. We were the causes of her suffering. It was not only for our good that she suffered, but it was by our evil that she suffered. Hence there is no devotion to her to which we are so bound as to her dolours. There is no expression of our love more fitting and indeed more imperative upon us, than compassion with her Compassion. It is the most inclusive of all devotions to her. It comprehends the greatest number of her mysteries. It keeps closest to her when she is in the closest union with Jesus. It goes deepest down into her immaculate heart. It throws the strongest light on the summits of her Divine Maternity, and at the same time it is the special devotion of her Motherhood of us. It best satisfies our obligations to her, while it is most vividly kindling our love. It at once befits the necessities of our lowliness, and the splendours of her magnificence.

Let us add to its perfection as a devotion to Mary, its perfection also as a devotion to Jesus, and the picture is complete. The highest devotion to our Blessed Lord is to possess ourselves of His spirit, to appreciate it, to welcome it, to feel in it, to act in it, to suffer in it. The more we can do and suffer all things in union with Him, the more excellently are we His disciples. We have to become Christ's. It is the business of grace to multiply all over the world copies and likenesses of the Incarnate Word. Union with Jesus is the shortest definition of holiness, and one which is equally applicable to all its numberless varieties. Now Mary is our model of this. The special grace of all devotions to Mary is union with Jesus. This is what they all teach. They not only teach it as a lesson, but they are the vehicle by which it is conveyed into our souls as a real predominant spirit, a substantial transforming grace. She is inseparable from Jesus. Her spirit is the greatest possible communication of His. He is her meaning, her significance, her motive, her aim, her life. The action of Jesus and Mary is as nearly one action, as a twofold action can be one. Jesus is our model; but we must copy Him as Mary copied Him. It is her office to teach us this, to be our model of imitation. We must do all things in union with Mary, and then shall we best do them all in union with Jesus. But devotion to her dolours leads us most directly, most speedily, and most universally to do all things in union with her. For her sorrows were lifelong; they were the most constant of all her dispositions; they were the dispositions in which she was the most closely united with Jesus, and followed Him with the most minute and changeful fidelity through the mysteries of the Three-and-Thirty Years. Thus it comes to pass that devotion to her dolours leads us most directly, most speedily, and most universally to do all things in union with Jesus; and therefore it is the highest devotion to Him, the perfection of devotion to Jesus, as well as the perfection of devotion to Mary. Thus our compassion with Mary partakes of the beauty, power, and blessing of her Compassion with Jesus, and is part of hers, as by hers it is won to Jesus, and by hers closed in His loving embrace, with the tenderest union of which we are capable, with our unspeakably tender and loving Lord.

SECTION V.

THE PASSION AND COMPASSION COMPARED.

Our fifth point was to compare the Compassion and the Passion together. But a great deal of this has already been done by implication in the course of the preceding enquiries. The first point of similitude is in its interior character. The mental sufferings of the Passion went far beyond its bodily tortures, not merely because anguish of heart is worse to bear than pain of body, but also because they were of a far more awful description, and because they were of longer duration. The inward agony, by which the shame and guilt of sin was expiated, was far more terrific than the blows and wounds and diversified atrocities which the cruelty of sinners could inflict upon the Body of Jesus. His inward pains were more numerous, more various, more vehement, burned deeper, and lasted longer. The abandonment of the Father and the weight of His angry justice were of course the most intolerable sufferings of the Passion, and both those were interior. Next to them we must rank the sorrows of Mary, and they chiefly affected Him inwardly. Sin, the third of His executioners, tortured His soul more than His Body. Thus, though our intention is naturally most drawn to His outward Passion, we shall never rightly conceive even of that, unless we remember that by far the greater portion of His Passion was interior. The visible Passion was but the tossing surface of an invisible deep. Mary's Compassion also was interior, in her heart, as well as His. It was drawn too from the same afflictive sources. It had passed through His Heart before it entered into hers. At the same time there is certainly a contrast in this respect as well as a similitude. For she had no outward Passion to correspond with His. Her interior agony was not of course without aching exhaustion of the frame, bitterest smarting and crushing of the fleshly heart, and intolerable burning of the brain. Her body suffered as well as her soul. It had to hold fire, and the fire burned it through and through. Nevertheless there was nothing at all to answer to the outward Passion of our Blessed Lord. Her outward Passion was the fifteen years of wearisome suffering delay, which was her lot when He had ascended into heaven.

The Passion and the Compassion may also be compared together, in that each was the cause of the other. Both were causes, and both were effects. It was our Lord's Passion which filled our Lady's heart to the brim with bitterness; and it was our Lady's Compassion which was one of the main ingredients in our Saviour's Passion. Only our Lady's Compassion was not co-extensive with the Passion, as its cause, while it was co-extensive with it as an effect, because it took it all in, embraced it, assimilated it to itself, and made it utterly its own. The contents of our Lady's heart could not fill our Lord's, but hers could hold the contents of His. The Mother crucified the Son, and the Son, crucified as He was, went and placed Himself with all the implements of His Passion in His Mother's heart, making it large enough by breaking it. It was not only that each pain of the Passion was represented in her Compassion. It is most likely that she really felt it all, just as it was, not in all its intolerable reality, but in such dread reality at least as was according to the measure of her immense capabilities of suffering. The saints have felt it so, in their lesser measure, great in our eyes as that lesser measure was. They have been invisibly stigmatised, and they have been led in horrible inward unimaginable tortures through all the mysteries of the Passion, miraculous power often being needed to prevent the separation of body and soul. Can we imagine that this inward real compassion was granted to them, and that she was without it? It is also another similitude between the Compassion and the Passion, that just as saints have been allowed in mystical ways to feel the sufferings of our Blessed Lord, so have they also been allowed mystically to participate in the sorrows of Mary. Both the Compassion and the Passion have been recognised fountains out of which have flowed some of the most singular and at the same time the best accredited phenomena of mystical theology.

SECTION VI.

THE SEEMING EXCESS OF THE COMPASSION.

But there is another point in the resemblance between the Passion of Jesus and the Compassion of Mary, which must not be omitted. It is the seeming excess of her sorrows over His. We call it *seeming*, because no one in his senses would dream of saying that Mary's sufferings equalled those of our Blessed Saviour. But her Compassion, as we have seen, is a divine work, a divine mystery, and inasmuch as this semblance is an undeniable feature of it, it must have been intentional. Everything in a divine work is notable, and we learn from it by the mere noting of it even where it is beyond our powers of explanation. It was in the joint mystery of the Compassion and Passion that the Mother and the Son saddened each other. Now, in proportion as His beauty exceeded hers, His power to increase her sorrow exceeded her power to augment His. It was a more terrible thing for the Mother to see the Son expiring on the Cross, than for the Son to see His Mother broken-hearted at the foot of the Cross. But when we remember that He was God, and that her whole love of Him was what it was because He was God, still more disproportioned will her suffering appear to His, and she too the weaker vessel, the less capable of enduring such highly wrought agony as that on Calvary. We must bear in mind also that inward pain is greater than outward pain, and that as she had no visible Passion to compare with His, the sorrow, which each outward pain and outrage of His caused in her, must have been inward also. His bodily Passion produced a mental counterpart in her. She was inwardly scourged, inwardly crowned with thorns, inwardly stripped, inwardly nailed to the Cross, and she died inwardly. All that was outward in Him was obliged to be inward in her. So also, when the Passion ended, the Compassion had at least three hours, perhaps six, of agony crowded with dreadful mysteries, yet to run. The fear of His limbs being broken, the wound of the lance, the taking down from the Cross, the embalming, the burial, and the desolation, all these sorrows were crucifying Mary's woe-weary heart while He was flashing light and beauty and glory through the caverns of Limbus, and being worshipped by the congratulations of all the patriarchs, kings, and prophets of the olden time. Moreover she was left behind to mourn for fifteen years, and what was that delay but a prolongation of all that was hardest to bear in each of her seven dolours through more than twice seven years? The words are easily written, but what hidden worlds of heroic endurance and desperate heart-worn life do they not imply! And there was one thought through all that scene on Calvary which she alone could have, and which must have reigned supremely over her mind, inspiring her with an incredible hatred of sin, and throwing a peculiar light upon the Passion, which it is not easy for us to conceive. It was the knowledge that Jesus was at that moment paying the price of her Immaculate Conception, that His Passion was for her redemption, and so principally for hers,—that it was more for hers than for that of the rest of the world together. Who then shall say what the Passion looked like to Mary's eye?

SECTION VII.

THE MEASURES OF MARY'S COMPASSION.

Lastly, we must say a few words of the measures and dimensions of her Compassion. We have drawn such a picture of it as we are able. It not only falls far below the truth, but it sensibly falls far below the real image of it in our own minds. A thousand unexpressed thoughts are teasing us at this moment, but the difficulty is how to express them fitly. Words do not seem to be measures for them. They are thoughts of love; and love does not speak; it burns. Moreover there must be limits to all things except loving. There are no limits there. Love is an eternal work. Love alone can measure the Compassion of Mary. Think of the sufferings of Jesus. They open at our feet like a huge abyss. Can we fathom their dreadful depths? Or do we not rather shrink in conscious nothingness from a task so hopeless and so rash? Yet Mary's Compassion contains that world-wide abyss, measures it, and holds it miraculously within its own dimensions. If we speak of the beauty of Jesus, straightway the vision of a shoreless sea, which no horizon bounds, over which the sun is rising and setting at the same moment, the half disc sunken in the west already rising in the east, and the waters rolling on and on for evermore. Yet as are the waters of that beauty, so were the waters of Mary's bitterness. By an opposite miracle to that of Moses, the

2 D

wood of the Cross thrown into those waters of beauty has converted them into bitterness. If we think of men's cruelty in the Passion, it is a mystery nearer to our understanding, yet is not that nearness almost an infinite distance? Are we not obliged to call to our aid the theory of diabolical possession? Even then the horrors of the Passion are almost incredible, because they are so nearly inconceivable. Yet these horrors were but a part of Mary's Compassion; and truly, compared with the wrath of the Father, and the beauty of Jesus, they were the very least part of it. If we think of her deep love of Jesus, it is only to delight in its interminable magnificence. It is beyond our definitions, out of the sphere of our comprehension. We make wild comparisons of all angels and of all saints, indulge in fanciful arithmetic, repeat our superlatives, but we only do so to convince ourselves more satisfactorily that it is all beyond us, just as a man uses violence with himself to be sure he is awake. Yet the dimensions of that love do not reach to the dimensions of her Compassion, because there is another love yet, to which it marvellously outstretches. It is the deep love of Jesus for her. Who can tell it? Who can speak of it even figuratively; for where is our figure to come from? Yet the breadth, and the depth, and the height of that love of Jesus for His Mother are the only true dimensions of her Compassion. Here are five abysses, five measures, five standards, His sufferings, His beauty, men's cruelty, her deep love of Him, His deep love of her. We must do our poor best with them all, and we shall reach a view of our Blessed Mother's Compassion which will be good for us and acceptable to her, but it will be below the truth. A work which Jesus and Mary made together, out of God's wrath, and man's sin, and the Hypostatic Union, and the sinlessness of a pure creature, must be a marvel about which at best we can but stammer, and lovingly go wrong; and such a work is Mary's Compassion. Our task is ended, and love will give our poor thoughts a truth of its own which will make them good for souls.

It is a beautiful and a dread sight, to see all the sorrows of fallen earth resumed in the broken heart of our own Mother. Has it moved us? Then why not for the rest of life, in sober panic at the world and worldliness, go and sit at our Mother's feet and meditate her griefs? Is there a fitter work for prodigals come back to their Heavenly Father? Compassion with her is already compassion with Jesus; and we may say that compassion with the Invisible Creator Himself is the devotional feeling out of which we shall serve Him most generously, and realise Him most tenderly as our Eternal Father,—eternal because he has been, blessed be His Majesty! from all eternity, and eternal because we shall be, blessed be His compassion! with Him, His happy sons, His pardoned sons, to all eternity. Truly Mary lays us evermore in the lap of God. Truly by some celestial logic of their own, all Christian things, be they doctrines or devotions, come out at last in that one compendious, melodious, alone-sufficing word, Eternal Father!

INDEX.

ABRAHAM, sacrifice of, 170
Academy, the, of the temple, 165
Adam, 159; site of the grave of, 246, 264, 341
Aelred, St., on the words of our Lord to His Mother, 172
Agony, the, of the martyrs, 9; of our Lady during the Passion, 37; in the Garden, 93; on the Cross, 254; prayer for those in their, 290
Agreda, Mary of, 51, 65; on the third dolour, 169, 188; on the Passion, 206; on the conversion of Longinus, 305; on the grace of our Lady, 400, *note*
Ambrose, St., on our Lady's tranquillity, 229
Ammonius, on the sojourn in Egypt, 112
Andrew Avellino, St., 122, *note*
Angels, the, abandon our Lady in the third dolour, 169; ministries of guardian, 253; quiescent during the Passion, 269
Anna, in the temple, 72, 76
Annas, 208, 233
Annunciation, the, 94, 257, 271
Anselm, St., on the dolours of our Lady, 8, 66
Anticipation, 293
Apostles, the, sufferings of, 4; love of our Lord, of, 187; our Lady's love of, 204, 221; sorrow of our Lady at the desertion of, 218; dignity of, 219; our Lady's dolours made greater by, 221
Archelaus, 112, 160

Arms, the, of our Lord on the Cross, 309
Art, evil of untheological, 51
Ascension, the, 55
Assumption, the, 21; delay of, 377
Attractions of the Sacred Humanity, 29
Attributes, communication of, 37

Barabbas, 348, 395
Baronius, on the sojourn in Egypt, 112
Barradius, on the sojourn in Egypt, 112
Beads, 122
Beatitude, the life of God, 52
Beginners, apt to disesteem forms, 121; mistake of, 373
Benedictus, the, 74
Benvenuta, the blessed, 57, 167
Bernard, St., 50, 51, 364, 401
Bernardine, St., of Siena, 364; on the dolours, 8
Berulle, de, Cardinal, on interior suffering, 144; an effect of the spiritual direction of, 231
Bethania, 204
Bethlehem, mothers of, 105, 128, 129; the shepherds of, 200; the life in, reproduced in the sixth dolour, 310
Blood, the precious, 39; in the streets of Jerusalem, 224, 359; shedding of, 258, 273; on the wood of the cross, 345; effects of, in hell, 354; the sole ransom for sin, 381

INDEX.

Body, the, of Jesus dead, 296; adoration of, by our Lady, 326
Bollandists, the, 39; *note*, 57
Boyhood, the, of our Lord, 155, 164, 200, 204
Bridget, St., on the dolours, 8, 52; vision of, 57; on the piercing, 304; revelation made to, 309, 395, 401
Burial, the, of Jesus, 341, 345

Cain, consolation of, 317
Caiphas, 208, 233
Calvary, the procession to, 209, 214, 232; a place for impatience, 283; hardest lesson of, 287; Bethlehem reproduced on, 308
Cana, miracle in, 30
Carmel, 23
Cartagena, 410
Catherine, St., of Bologna, vision of seven angels of, 58
Catherine, St., of Genoa, vision of sin of, 36, 215
Ceremonies, importance of, 122
Change, effects of, 241
Characteristics of the dolours, 41; the first, 42; the second, 43; the third, 45; the fourth, 46; the fifth, 47; the sixth, 48; the seventh, 49; the eighth, 50
Chastisements, supernatural, rare, 195
Children, made idols of, 10
Christians, foreigners in the world, 299
Church, the, unity of, 250; rubrics of, 310, 330
Circuminsession, the, 46
Circumstances, tyranny of, 138
Communion, preparation for, 322, 329; possible effect of one, 362
Compassion of our Lady, the, inseparable from the Passion, 5, 18, 181; becomes glory, 21; greatness of, 22; lies close to the Passion, 25; threw light on the Incarnation, 55; benefit of, to us, 56; during the sixth dolour,

319; during the seventh dolour, 368; divine purpose of, 379, 389; lessons of, 380; nature of, 392; a part of the Passion, 394; expiatory character in, 396; an example to the Church, 396; effects of, 400; a reparation of the Passion, 408; comparison of, with the Passion, 413; not co-extensive with the Passion, 414
Conception, the Immaculate, 25, 56, 85; effects of meditation on, 63; price of, 56, 417
Confidence, the only true worship, 25; in God, 371
Consolation, mother of, 23, 24; shallowness of human, 95; hard to refuse, 228; danger of human, 286; utter absence of, in the seventh dolour, 354
Contemplation, 123
Contemplatives, sinners most loved by, 141
Contradictions, 83; consequences of the Incarnation, 87
Contrition, 410
Converts, cause of failure of, 300
Co-redemptress, 7, 18, 59, 135, 381, 382; meaning of the word, 382, 388
Cord, a threefold, 359
Creature, one will of a, 283
Cross, the, the way of, 210, 236, 242, 244, 246, 347; our Lord laid on, 247; the lifting up of, 249; the taking down from, 272, 293, 306, 307; standing by, 285; adoration of, by our Lady, 345
———, an abiding, 241
Crosses, 20; recompense of sanctity, 98; how aggravated, 114; Jesus met with in, 235; how men bear their, 236; unusual quiet followed by unusual, 237; trials of, 239; succession of, 240
Crucifix, the, 245
Crucifixion, an invisible, 40
———, the, of our Lord, 247, 281; agony of, 248; the fountain of

all the dolours, 266; not to be understood without Mary, 291; sin of, 298, 397
Cruelty, common, 116

Darkness, the Divine, 169, 173; at the Crucifixion, 249, 254, 374; in the third and seventh dolours, 358
David, punishment of, 116; the Son of, 157; city of, 246
Dead, the, apparitions of, in Jerusalem, 340; presence of, 355
Death, the mystical, 92; a created punishment, 264; lessons about, 289; devotion to the dolours one of the best preparations for, 410; terrors of, 412
Deathbed, 117, 302; of our Lord, 289; our Lady's presence at, 291, 405
Decalogue, the, 109
Denys, St., the Areopagite, 228, 402
Denys the Carthusian, 171
Dereliction, the Divine, 262, 267, 274, 275, 367, 407
Descent of the Holy Ghost, 377
Desert, the, the Saints of, 104; wandering of Israel in, 108; a Carmelite, 178
Desolation of our Lady, 350, 374
Detachment, of our Lady, 187; from creatures, 287
Devotion to our Lady, effects of, 62; taught us by our Lord, 70
Diario di Maria, of Marchese, 56, 58
Dignity of our Lady, 21
Dimas, the leper boy, 107; the converted thief, 216, 223; sprinkled with the Precious Blood, 298
Direction, spiritual, grounds of, 91; desired in sickness, 145; necessity of, 238
Discretion, worldly, 300
Disinterestedness, importance of, 366

Dispositions of God about men, 112, 113; of our Lady in the first dolour, 88; of our Lady in the second dolour, 133; of our Lady in the third dolour, 187; of our Lady in the fourth dolour, 227; of our Lady in the fifth dolour, 278; of our Lady in the sixth dolour, 322; of our Lady in the seventh dolour, 361
Disputation, the, in the temple, 163, 165, 358
Dives, 260
Dolour, the first, 75; peculiarities of, 76; five distinct dolours of, 81; three graces of, 88; dispositions of our Lady in, 88, 90; sorrow of, 92; generous acceptance of, 93; lessons of, 95
——— the second, 104; St. Joseph, the instrument of, 113; peculiarities of, 114; harder than the first, 121; desolation of, 122; fear, an element of, 126; men's hatred of Jesus revealed in, 130; long continuance of, 132; dispositions of our Lady in, 133; lessons of, 141
——— the third, 152, 266, 271; pain of, 159; peculiarities of, 167; the greatest of all the dolours, 167, 352; desolation of, 167; our Lord the sole cause of, 175; anguish of, 176; fulness of, 181; dispositions of our Lady in, 187; source of a new love of our Lord in Mary, 185, 188; humility of our Lady in, 188; lessons of, 191; a shadow of the seventh, 167, 358
——— the fourth, 198, 209, 211; anguish of, 214; made more bitter by the desertion of the apostles, 220; and by the treason of Judas, 222; physical horrors in, 223; dispositions of our Lady in, 227; peculiarities of, 232; our Lady saw only the First Cause

in, 233; lessons of, 233; men, a part of, 234

Dolour, the fifth, 245, 353; the stripping, 246; profaneness of the soldiers, 249; increase of, by our Lord's speaking, 255; resignation of our Lady in, 263; our Lady's crucifixion, 266; peculiarities of, 267; a heroic trial of our Lady's faith, 268; efficaciousness of, 276; dispositions of our Lady in, 278; lessons of, 283

—— the sixth, 226, 293; sorrow of, 298; growth of our Lady's graces in, 302; Longinus an instrument of, 305; peculiarities of, 294; inward spirit of, 310; helplessness of our Lady in, 315; loneliness of, 318, 321, 355; dispositions of our Lady in, 322; lessons of, 326; perpetuity of, in the Church, 326.

—— the seventh, 168, 338; intensity of, 344; physical desolation of, 347; the consummation of the other dolours, 352; peculiarities of, 352; absence of all consolation in, 354; images of the sacred infancy in, 356; dispositions of our Lady in, 361; our Lady's exercise of faith in, 371; lessons of, 371

Dolours, the, of our Lady, unimaginable, 5; immensity of, 6, 8, 10; exceeded all martyrdoms, 9, 10; made greater by love, 9; proportioned to her greatness, 12; and to her enlightenment, 12; multitude of, 14; beyond the power of human endurance, 15; prevision of, 15; keenness of, 17; why permitted, 19; our Lady's merits increased by, 20; a treasure of the Church, 23; fountains of, 35; unity of, 28; characteristics of, 41; revealed to her at the Incarnation, 42; continuous, 43; joy amidst, 52; increased our Lady's joy, 54; devotion to, most pleasing to our Lord, 57, 407; a fountain of unworldliness, 68; without relief, 79; lifelong, 96; caused by Jesus, 101; not separate mysteries, 205; each a distinct sanctification of Mary, 205; terror in, 315; a divine work, 352; sanctified our Lady, 381; are divine mysteries, 390; comprised within the thirty-three years, 393; right way of regarding, 403; the deepest part of the Passion, 407; grandeurs of our Lady's holiness wrought in, 409; fruit of devotion to, 414

Dolours, the, devotion to, 57; four graces thereof, 57; has received the highest sanction of the Church, 58; spirit of the, 59; produces hatred of sin, 61; cultivated by missioners, 62; power of, 65; promises of our Lord to, 66; begun by our Lord, 66; a sign of predestination, 410; one of the best preparations for death, 410

Duty, 371

Easter, in Rome, 157
Eccentricity, an effect of sorrow, 336
Ecce homo, 34, 35, 208
Edens, 3, 126
Egypt, the flight into, 104, 106; natural beauty of, 110; spiritual desolation in, 122; the return from, 112, 132, 133; death of the first-born of, 160
Elect, the, work of, 383
Elevation, the, on the cross, 248, 284
Elias, 269
Embalming, the, 308, 310, 320, 323
Emmerich, Sister, 51
Engaddi, clusters of, 341

INDEX.

Epiphanius on the sojourn in Egypt, 112
Epiphany, the, 71
Esau, 250
Eve, 159, 378; the curse of, 272; the second, 341
Exaggeration of sorrow, 16
Example, Christ our, 17; Mary our, 19
Excess, the Passion an, 38; seeming, of the compassion, 415
Exile, sadness of, 125
Exodus, the, 109, 110, 143

Fainting, not to be attributed to our Lady, 36, 266
Faith, 370
Face of our Lord, 130; struck by the soldier, 14
Fall, the first of our Lord, 211
Familiarity, 67
Fathers, the, limbus of, 95
Fear, effects of, 127, 128; prominence of, in our Lady's dolours, 316
Feasts, ecclesiastical, 2; of the seven dolours, 58; the three great Hebrew, 153
Fervour, 67; sensible, 328
Finding, the, in the temple, 165
Flagellants, the, 57
Flight, the, into Egypt, 104; terrors of, 106, 129; dolour of, renewed in the fourth dolour, 215
Fountains, of the dolours, 28; the first fountain, 29; the second, 31; the third, 33; the fourth, 34; the fifth, 36; the sixth, 37; the seventh, 39
Frances of the Blessed Sacrament, the Ven. Mother, 302, *note*
Frenzy, popular, 216
Friend, a false, loss of, 280

Garments of our Lord, miracle of the, 250; lots cast for, 250, 253
Generation, the eternal, 274
Generosity of our Lady, 93, 94, 228

Gennesareth, 149
Gethsemane, 129, 181, 266, 285, 316; sufferings of, 34, 77; the agony in, 93
Gianius, historian of the Servites, 57
Gifts, of God, highest use of, 97
God, end of man, 3, 21; works of, 19; glory of, the true rest of man, 22; shut out from His own creation, 135; forbearance of, 149; ways of, inscrutable, 322; peace of, 326; faith in, 370
Golgotha, 315, 357
Gojos, Jeanne-Benigne, nun of the Visitation, 183, 184
Good Friday, 218, 270, 347
Gospel, how regarded by Catholics and heretics, 143, 299
Grace and glory, 21
Grace, operations of, 56, 91; continually given, 98; refinement of sorrow by, 237; all holiness correspondence with, 361; effects of correspondence with, 362; sense of the need of, 409
Graces, four, fruits of devotion to the dolours, 57, 410
Grandeurs of Mary, 63, 326
Grief, battling with, 120; indulgence in, 332, 374; discretion in, 374
Guillore on the effects of sickness, 144
Guilt, feeling of, how lost, 195

Habit, power of, 67
Hatred of sin, grace of, 61
Heart, the Immaculate, sorrows of, 6; perfections of, 29; beauty of, 110; unparalleled on earth, 353
—— the Sacred, piercing of, 297, 303; excesses of, 404
Hebrews, the garments of, during their wanderings, 250
Heliopolis, 110, 111, 126, 349
Hell, creation of, 176; in the centre of the earth, 275

Henoch, 269
Heresy, preference of, for the Old Testament to the New, 143; hatred of, 300; our Lady's hatred of, 301
Herod, 105, 128, 143, 160, 266; death of, 111
—— why rebuked by our Lord, 140
Holiness, reparation a necessary element in all, 331, 398; union with Jesus, the shortest definition of, 412
House, the holy, 199
Humility, 114; of our Lady in the third dolour, 188; the perfume of God, 189

Idea, the, of Mary in the Gospels, 177
Idolatry, evil nature of, 124
Ignorance, the mystical, 174
Imperfections, 187
Incarnation, the, law of, a law of suffering, 3, 20, 105; an impassible, 20, 64; many ends of, 385; consequences of, 87; not understood in heresy, 143; consent of Mary to, 183, 384; no succession in, 359; Mary, the minister of, 398, 399
Indulgence of self, 67
Infancy, the Sacred, perpetuated in the Blessed Sacrament, 310; imaged in the seventh dolour, 357; mysteries of, 389
Ingratitude, 38, 221
Innocent IV., 57
Innocents, the Holy, 3, 4, 105; lessons taught by, 87
Instincts, right, about our Lady, 177; of sanctity, 141; spiritual, 299
Institutions, reformatories, cause of failure in, 140
Instruments of the Passion, 38
Intercession of our Lady during the Passion, 225; spirit of, 369

Irreverence, apparent, of pious people, 148

Jacob, 40, 250; well of, 260
James, St., Bishop of Jerusalem, 39, *note*
Jane Mary of the Cross, 153
Jealousy, of God, 97
Jerusalem, loved of God, 86, 340; the departure from, 157; during the Passion, 340; doom of, 346
Jesus, beauty of, 1, 41, 418; found with Mary, 2; union of our Lady with, 31, 46; the sole love of Mary, 47; mysteries of, 64, 143, 390; silence of, on the Cross, 70; taught devotion to our Lady, 70; in the arms of Simeon, 73; rejected of men, 85; obedience of, 90; hated by men, 131; occupation of, in the third dolour, 162; three ways of losing, 194; never found among kinsfolk, 194; obtains our Lady's consent to the Passion, 207; falls under the cross, 211; attracted by sorrow, 235; on the cross, thirst of, 259; death of, 265, 294; beauty of, 269; effects of the presence of, 329; wrongs of, 331; His love of Mary, 394
Joanna of Jesus and Mary, 142
Job, querulousness of, 26; book of, 69, 180; patience of, 89, 228
John, St., the Baptist, 161
John, St., Saint of the Sacred Heart, 5; vision of, 57; the beloved disciple, 187; leads our Lady to meet her son, 209; at the Crucifixion, 247, 251, 268, 310; during the sixth dolour, 320
Josaphat, valley of, 346
Joseph, the son of Jacob, 40, 109
—— of Arimathea, 305, 311, 339
—— St., in the temple, 74; poverty of, 78; commanded to flee into Egypt, 105; flight of into Egypt, 106; shadow of the

INDEX. 427

Eternal Father, 106, 113, 156; return of, to the Holy Land, 111; holiness of, 113, 117; uncomplaining, 126; fatigue of, 133; had a revelation of the Passion, 153; sorrow of, at the loss of Jesus, 159; distress of, in the third dolour, 159; humility of, 183; death of, 204; office of, at the Crucifixion, 306; represented in the sixth dolour by Joseph of Arimathea, 320

Joy, in the dolours, 52; increase of, through the dolours, 54; makes God seem far off, 99; a prophecy of sorrow, 100

Judas, treason of, 207; a dolour to our Lady, 222, 224; graces of, 223

Justice, effects of original, in our Lady, 316; victims of God's, 367

Kindness, effects of, 107
Kindred, Jesus never found among, 194
Kings, the three, 70, 105, 200; represented by Nicodemus in the sixth dolour, 320
Knowledge, effect of, on grief, 12; by which sanctity knows, 84

Land, the holy, dear to our Lady, 85
Law, the, doctors of, 165
Laws, eternal, 89
Lazarus, 202, 277
Learning and believing, 120
Life, dangers of middle, 67; the tree of, 341
Lilies, the seven, 58
Limbus, 295, 358
Loneliness, a danger, 150; of Mary and Joseph in the third dolour, 159
Longinus, the soldier, 304, 305, 315; at the burial of our Lord, 339
Loss, the three days', 128, 158, 351, 358; the greatest of the dolours, 167, 181; anguish of, 184; a revelation to our Lady of the misery of sinners, 185; the three hours, a parallel to, 249; mystery of, 267; a shadow of the seventh dolour, 358; what our Lady learnt in, 403

Lost, the, lot of, 354
Love, no merit without, 52; the soul of religion, 142; of self, 148; the apostles', of our Lord, 187; conjugal, 313; all divine, self-denying, 372
Lukewarmness, effects of, 67
Lyons, the Poor of, 57

Machabees, mother of the, 33, 217
Magdalen, St. Mary, 10, 39, 49, 209, 234; at the crucifixion, 247, 251, 268; during the sixth dolour, 311
Magnificat, the, 74, 109, 156, 312, 356, 370
Mahometanism, desolation of, 124
Maldonatus, on the sojourn in Egypt, 112
Marchese, Diario di Maria of, 56, 58
Marriage, of Joseph and Mary, 113
Martyr, St. Peter, the Dominican, 58
Martyrdom, the, of our Lady, 10, 64, 117, 377; beauty of, 19; in soul and body, 36
Martyrs, the, sufferings of, 9; joy of, 53
Mary, not to be separated from Jesus, 1, 18, 401; sufferings of, 5; her worship of her Son, 10; enlightenment of, 13; death of, 16; dignity of, 20; mother of consolation, 23, 24; how redeemed, 25, 55; an emblematic revelation, 27; enables us to know more of God, 27; without sin, 27, 405; thirst of, for more

suffering, 31; love of, 32; present at the scourging, 34; permitted to see the horror of sin, 36, 37; pains of, 45; loneliness of, 49, 126, 317; repose of, 51, 182, 281, 316; devotion to, 62; grandeurs of, 63, 326; saw into the Sacred Heart, 65, 70, 75; commended to St. John, 70, 257, 271; first dolour of, 75; poverty of, 78; calmness of, 79; thirst of, for souls, 84; interior beauty of, 88, 278, 364; union of, with God, 94, 110; flies into Egypt, 106; heals Dimas, 107; sojourn of, in Egypt, 110; returns to Juda, 112; her love of Jesus, 29, 119, 131; an effect of her sanctity, 122; mourned for the heathen souls, 124; fears of, in Egypt, 126, 129; her love of men, 131; self-forgetfulness of, 134; power of the prayer of, 135; her love of sinners, 140, 184, 271; worship of, in the temple, 156; distress of, in the third dolour, 160; understood not the words of Jesus in the temple, 170; sanctifications of, 173; idea of, in the Gospels, 177; silence of, 178; science of, 182; detachment of, 187; simplicity of, 190; during the three years' ministry, 202; consents to the Passion, 206, 384; assists at the agony in the garden, 208; meets our Lord carrying His Cross, 210, 221; presence of, added to our Lord's sufferings, 213; distress of, at the desertion of the Apostles, 220; generosity of, 228; without a parallel, 230; at the foot of the cross, 249, 293, 318, 397; prays for the two thieves, 252; is deprived of all consolation, 254; commended to St. John, 257, 319; resignation of, at the foot of the cross, 263, 267, 272, 273; a creation apart, 266; effect of the seven words on, 270; pain of, because she could not die, 277; a divine vision, 279; peace of, 281; generosity of, 282; help of, in the hour of death, 289, 405; prayers of, for the two thieves, 295; silence of, at the taking down from the cross, 298; receives into her arms the dead Body of our Lord, 308; communions of, 312, 369; prostration of, in the sixth dolour, 318; submission of, to the Divine Will, 323; acts of reparation of, 324; greatness of the dolours of, 342; enters the sepulchre, 344; adoration of the cross by, 345; on the way of the cross, 348; exile of, 349; holiness of, 361, 363; correspondence of, with grace, 362; completeness of the sacrifice of, 366; spiritual detachment of, 367; intercession of, 369; compassion of, 379; above all saints, 383; fruits of the consent of, 384; rights of, to the title of co-redemptress, 386; co-operation of, 387, 405; share of, in the Passion, 393; presence of, at the Passion, 397; the minister of the Incarnation, 398; nearness of, to God, 402; no outward passion of, 414; inward passion of, 416

Mary of Egypt, 126

Mass, the first, 207; high, of the world's redemption, 292; hearing of, 329

Meekness, 225

Mendicancy, of our Lord, 163

Merits of our Lady, 12, 378; increase of, a cause of the dolours, 20

Methodius, St., on the joys of Mary, 66

Michael, St., fight of, against Satan, 54; stood by our Lord in His agony, 269; humility of, 324

Ministry, the three years', 44, 179,

200; like a new revelation to Mary, 202
Miriam, 109
Missioners, a special devotion of, 62
Mistake, a theological, 408

Nailing, the, to the cross, 247
Nails, the, 307
Nativity, the, 82, 265
Nature, grace and, 145
Nazareth, the sojourn in, 76, 79, 103, 105, 149, 167, 185, 197, 225, 251, 349; the silence in, 178; the hidden life in, 179
Nicodemus, 305, 306, 308, 311
Nile, the, 110, 111, 124, 142, 225
Novatus, on the words of our Lord to His Mother, 172
Nunc dimittis, the, 74

OBEDIENCE, of our Lady, 73; blessedness of, 90; of St. Joseph, 114; of our Lord to His Mother, 400, 407
Oblation of our Lord, in the temple, 72; in the Passion, 226; made by Mary, 406
Oblivion of self, the hardest lesson, 190
Obscurity, an effect of creatures', 287
Office, the divine, recitation of, 118
Omission, sins of, 354
Orphans, risks of, 136

PAIN, mystery of bodily, 8; pressure of, 47; excess of, death, 267
Palace, the ivory, 252
Parents, idolatry of, 10
Passion, the, continued in the apostles, 4; fully understood only by our Lord, 13; the dereliction in, 33; instruments of, 38, 344; foreseen by our Lady, 42; to be constantly kept in mind, 60; shadowed in the trials

of Job, 69; revealed to our Lady, 75, 92; ever present before our Lady, 77; beginning of, 206; cruelties of, 215; physical horrors of, 223, 259, 268, 418; the Divine Perfections eclipsed in, 268; unnecessary sufferings of, 391; sacrilege of, 397; the compassion of our Lady an intrinsic part of, 401
Penance of Adam, 246
Perfections, the Divine, eclipsed in the Passion, 268
Persecution, 101
Perseverance, grace of, 365; a prophesy of final, 410
Peter, St., on Tabor, 182; his love of our Lord, 187, 220; leaning on Mary, 357; greatness of the office of, 385
Pharisees, why rebuked by our Lord, 140
Pictures, untheological, of our Lady, 51
Piercing of the Sacred Heart, 108
Piety, effects of an ill-regulated, 373
Pilate, 35, 251, 269, 315
Please, the wish to, 192, 194
Poor, the, of Lyons, 57
Pope, none called by the name of Peter, 219
Popularity, 192
Positus in ruinam multorum, 84
Poverty, hardships of, 125
Prætorium, the, 357
Praise, inadequate, of our Lady, 363
Prayer, vocal, 122; of our Lady, 135; not the whole of spirituality, 148
Predestinate, the, procession of, 237; path of, 243
Predestination, devotion to the dolours a sign of, 410
Presentation, the, 72, 73
Priesthood, the, shadowed forth by our Lady in the sixth dolour, 310

Priests, the special mortification of, 373
Procession, the eternal, 274
Purgation, the mystical, 169
Purgatory, apparitions of souls in, 169
Purification, the feast of, 72

Queen, the, of heaven, 21; of the apostles, 38
Questions about the ways of God, 148
Quietness of our Lady, 283

Reason, use of, in our Lady, 36; in our Lord, 154
Redemption, how wrought, 23, 389; of our Lady, 25, 55; a seeming failure, 136
Regularity, advantages of, 144
Religion, what it is, 142
Reparation, 62; spirit of, 301, 304, 324, 331
Resignation, 4, 185, 331
Retribution, 291
Revelations concerning the Passion, 8; concerning the dolours, 15, 57, 158, 407; concerning the flight into Egypt, 143; concerning St. Joseph, 153; concerning the three days' loss, 167, 183, 184; concerning the Passion, 207; concerning the noonday sacrifice at the Passion, 249; concerning the dead Body of our Lord, 309; concerning our Lady's compassion, 395; concerning the bitterness of our Lady's grief, 400
Reverence, due to sinners, 140; familiarity and, 323
Rights of Jesus, 331
Robe, the seamless, 250
Rosary of the seven dolours, 58
Rubrics, the, 122
Running away from God, 136
Rupert, on the words of our Lord addressed to His Mother, 171

Sacrament, the Blessed, the support of our Lady, 11; not a stationary presence, 119; Procession of, in Transylvania, 124; unconsumed in our Lady during the Passion, 210; and from Communion to Communion afterwards, 376
Sacraments, worship of the, 326; grace of, 170
Sacrifice, how spoiled, 366
Sacrilege, pain caused by, 214; horrors of, 216, 296, 298, 301, 303; of the Passion, 397
Saint Amour, William of, 57
Saints, the, trials of, proportioned to their sanctity, 12; thirst of, for sufferings, 77; stigmata of, 84; variety of the graces of, 278; expiations of, 325; sorrow of, 335
Sanctification of our Lady, 173; epochs of, 203
Satisfaction, of Christ, 325; of our Lady, 406
Scapulars, 122
Scourging, the, 35, 269, 395
Sea, the Red, 109, 112
Search, the, after God, 194
Sebastian, St., 18
Self-forgetfulness, 190
Self-importance, 334
Selfishness, effects of, in sorrow, 334; tendency of spirituality to, 372
Self-will, 361
Senses, the, 36
Sensitiveness, to the interests of God, 134
Sentiment, mischief of, in religion, 18
Sentimentality, 223, 229, 285
Servites, the, of Mary, 57
Shakspeare, 113
Silence, the, on the Cross, 70, 253; in the holy house, 178; power of, 286; of our Lady at the taking down from the Cross, 298

INDEX. 431

Simeon, prophecy of, 15, 35. 42, 75, 120, 166; holiness of, 72; receives our Lord in his arms, 73; sword of, 82, 84, 213, 259, 266, 297, 360

Simon of Cyrene, 348

Simplicity, grace of, 190

Sin, horror of venial, 36; hatred of, a great grace, 61; misery of, 62; guilt of venial, 275

Sinners, our Lady's love of, 140, 184; best loved by contemplative saints, 141

Sinischalchi, Martirio del Cuore di Maria of, 58

Sojourn, the, in Egypt, 110; made bitter by fear, 126; a picture of the way in which our Lord is in the world, 141

Sophronius, St., on the joys of Mary, 66

Sorrow, human, exaggeration of, 16; unreality of, 17; characteristic of men, 25; of a mother who has lost her child, 28, 46, 115; caused by sin, 52; of mourners, 78; effects of, 85, 314, 333; universal, 95; a condition of true, 99; to be kept secret, 99, joy in, 100; hard to bear, 115; rushes on the sorrowful, 145; gives gentleness, 194; no sameness in, 213; Jesus attracted by, 235; blessedness of foreseen, 243; growth of, 279; a slow workman, 284; varieties of, 293; unselfishness, the proper grace of, 368; sense of unworthiness brought out by, 370; endurance of divine, 374

Souls, tepid, 39; lost, 39, 84; perils of, 139; thirst of our Lord for, 260; half crucified, 284; love of, 299

Spirit, peculiar, 91

Spirituality, defective, 148

Spirituality, steadiness in, 67; the feeling of many sorrows hindered by, 26; tendency of, to selfishness, 372

Stabat Mater, the, 58

Stammering, eloquent, 364

Stapleton, on the words of our Lord to His Mother, 171

Stripes, the, 40

Stripping, the, 246

Suarez, on the sojourn in Egypt, 112; on the words of our Lord to His Mother, 171

Suffering, a fruit of the Incarnation, 3; of all the martyrs less than those of our Lady, 8; the price of sanctity, 100; better than outward spiritual advantages, 144; graces of, gained by compassion, 146; how abused, 146; kept secret by saints, 147; preparation for, 211

Sympathy, 100; should be the measure of our sorrows, 147; danger of, 286; not to be sought, 335

Tabor, 23; St. Peter on, 182

Tears, infinite worth of our Lord's, 226

Temple, the, glory of, 71, 156; academy of, 165; humility of our Lady in, 188; trumpets of at the Crucifixion, 249

Temptations, exemption of our Lady from certain, 316

Tender-heartedness, spiritual dangers of, 333

Tenderness, spirit of, in the dolours, 61

Teresa, St., devotion of, to holy water, 122

Terror, an element in the dolours, 315

Thais, the penitent, 126

Thieves, the two, 252, 296, 298

Thirst, the, on the Cross, 259; increase of the fifth dolour by, 261

Thomas, St., the Apostle, 277

Thomas, St., on the divine maternity, 11

Thorns, crown of, 88; removed by Joseph of Arimathea, 306
Thrones, choir of, 282
Time, 169; use of, 373
Title, the, of the Cross, 251, 273
Titus, the Emperor, 340
Tomb, the, the procession to, 342; Jesus laid in, 343
Touch, the divine, 175
Transformation, deific, 118
Transylvania, 124
Trials, blessedness of, 99

Unfeelingness, no sanctity in, 26
Unhappiness, mystery of, 95; continuous, 97
Union of Jesus and Mary, 31, 46, 110, 246, 360; the Hypostatic, 155, 231, 262, 359, 360, 418; of our Lady's sorrows with those of our Lord, 231, 401
Unities, filial and maternal, 312
Unpunctuality, spiritual evils of, 242
Unreality, 336
Unselfishness, blessedness of, 145, 336; an effect of sorrow, 337; the proper grace of sorrow, 368

Veronica, St., 348
———, the blessed, of Binasco, 57, 144, 407, 408
Vision, the beatific, 279, 402; theology of, difficult, 13; ever present to our Lord, 52
Visitation, the, 82
Vocations, how treated by the world, 101

Vows, heroism of, 241

Waiting, risks of, 285
Way, the, of God with souls, 196; of God, not to be questioned, 147
Weakness, a cause of complaints, 180
Will, of God, 89; of Jesus in the agony, 94; of our Lady, 94; our Lady's submission to, of God, 215; sacrifice of our own, 372
World, the, shuns God, 136; thwarts God, 137; tyranny of, 139; our Lord would not pray for, 191; friendship of, 193; noise of, 288; axioms of, 300
Worldliness, corrected by meditation on the dolours, 68; curable, 195
"Woman," 257
Words, the seven, 35, 254, 270; marvels of, 255
Worship, spirit of, 327
Works, Divine, 387
Wounds, the five, 218

Year, the ecclesiastical, 2
Years, the eighteen, mysteries of, 200
Years, the thirty-three, 3, 20, 42, 54, 64, 70, 200, 212, 237, 256, 264, 271, 278, 311, 321, 323, 360, 389, 413; sorrow, the character of, 66
Yearnings of the patriarchs, 73; of our Lady, 187, 405

Zachary, 74

1886.

SELECTION

FROM

BURNS & OATES'

Catalogue

OF

PUBLICATIONS.

BURNS AND OATES.

LONDON:
GRANVILLE MANSIONS,
ORCHARD STREET, W.

NEW YORK:
CATHOLIC PUBLICATION
SOCIETY CO.,
BARCLAY STREET.

NEW WORKS.

Just Out.

The Chair of Peter; or, The Papacy Considered in its Institution, Development, and Organization, and in the Benefits which for over Eighteen Centuries it has conferred on Mankind. By JOHN NICHOLAS MURPHY. With several new chapters, and the statistics brought down to the present day. Popular edition, cloth, 720 pages, crown 8vo, 6s.

Literary and Biographical History; or, Bibliographical Dictionary of the English Catholics. From the Breach with Rome, in 1534, to the Present Time. By JOSEPH GILLOW. Vols. I. and II., price 15s. each. This work will consist of five vols., demy 8vo, price per vol., 15s.

The English Catholic Nonjurors of 1715: Being a Summary of the Register of their Estates, with Genealogical and other Notes, and an Appendix of Unpublished Documents in the Public Record Office. Edited by the late Very Rev. E. E. ESTCOURT, M.A., F.S.A., Canon of St. Chad's, Birmingham, and JOHN ORLEBAR PAYNE, M.A. One vol., demy 8vo, £1, 1s.

The War of Anti-Christ with the Church and Christian Civilization. A review of the rise and progress of Atheism; its use of Freemasonry and kindred secret societies, &c., &c.; and the Spoliation of the Propaganda. By the Right Rev. Mgr. GEORGE F. DILLON, D.D., Missionary Apostolic, Sydney. Imperial 8vo, cloth, 5s.

Life of St. Philip Benizi, of the Order of the Servants of Mary, 1233–1285. By Father PEREGRINE SOULIER, of the same Order. In one vol., 592 pp., crown 8vo, cloth, 8s.

Life of St. Charles Borromeo. From the Italian of JOHN PETER GUISSANO. With Preface by Cardinal MANNING. In Two Volumes, embellished with Portrait of the Saint. Cloth, 15s.

"The translation is a very readable one, and the style is simple and good.... We will therefore recommend the book to our readers as a most useful addition to English editions of 'Lives of the Saints.'"—*Month.*

The "Divine Office." From the French of L'ABBÉ BACQUEZ, of the Seminary of S. Sulpice, Paris. Edited by the Rev. Father TAUNTON, of the Congregation of the Oblates of S. Charles. With an Introduction, by H. E. the Cardinal Archbishop of Westminster. Cloth, 6s.

Studies of Family Life, a contribution to Social Science. By C. S. DEVAS (author of "Groundwork of Economics"). One vol., crown 8vo, 5s. (Ready during January.)

In the Press.

Leaves from St. Augustine. Edited by T. W. ALLIES. Crown 8vo, 6s.

SELECTION

FROM

BURNS AND OATES' CATALOGUE OF PUBLICATIONS.

ALLIES, T. W.
    See of St. Peter £0 4 6
    Formation of Christendom. Vols. I., II., III. . each   0 12 0
    Church and State as seen in the Formation of Christendom, 8vo, pp. 472, cloth 0 14 0

"It would be quite superfluous at this hour of day to recommend Mr. Allies' writings to English Catholics. Those of our readers who remember the article on his writings in the *Katholik*, know that he is esteemed in Germany as one of our foremost writers."— *Dublin Review.*

ALLNATT, C. F. B.
    Cathedra Petri; or, The Titles and Prerogatives of St. Peter, and of his See and Successors, as described by the Early Fathers, Ecclesiastical Writers, and Councils of the Church, with an Appendix, containing Notes on the History and Acts of the first four General Councils, and the Council of Sardica, in their relation to the Papal Supremacy. Compiled by C. F. B. Allnatt. Third and Enlarged Edition.
        Cloth 0 6 0
        Paper 0 5 0

"Invaluable to the controversialist and the theologian, and most useful for educated men inquiring after truth, or anxious to know the positive testimony of Christian antiquity in favour of Papal claims."—*Month.*

    Which is the True Church? Demy 8vo . . . 0 1 0

ALZOG.
    History of the Church. A Manual of Universal Church History, by the Rev. John Alzog, D.D., Professor of Theology at the University of Freiburg. Translated, with additions, from the ninth and last German edition by the Rev. F. J. Parbisch and the Rev. Thomas S. Byrne. With Chronological Tables and Ecclesiastico-Geographical Maps. 4 vols., demy 8vo   £1 10 0

ANNUS SANCTUS:
    Hymns of the Church for the Ecclesiastical Year. Translated from the Sacred Offices by various Authors, with Modern, Original, and other Hymns, and an Appendix of Earlier Versions. Selected and Arranged by ORBY SHIPLEY, M.A. In stiff boards .   0 3 6
    Also, a limited Edition in cloth, printed on large-sized, toned, and ribbed paper . . .   0 10 6

B. N.
    The Jesuits: their Foundation and History. 2 vols. crown 8vo, cloth, red edges 0 15 0

"The book is just what it professes to be—*a popular history*, drawn from well-known sources," &c.—*Month*, July 1879.

BOTTALLA, FATHER (S.J.)
    Papacy and Schism 0 2 6
    Reply to Renouf on Pope Honorius . . .   0 3 6

BRIDGETT, REV. T. E. (C.SS.R.)
    Watson's Sermons on the Sacraments . . .   0 7 6
    Discipline of Drink 0 3 6

"The historical information with which the book abounds gives evidence of deep research and patient study, and imparts a permanent interest to the volume, which will elevate it to a position of authority and importance enjoyed by few of its compeers."—*The Arrow*.

    Our Lady's Dowry; how England Won and Lost that Title. Second edition . . .   0 9 0

"This book is the ablest vindication of Catholic devotion to Our Lady, drawn from tradition, that we know of in the English language."—*Tablet*.

    Ritual of the New Testament: an Essay on the Principles and Origin of Catholic Ritual . . .   0 5 0
    Defender of the Faith: the Royal Title, its history and value 0 1 0

BRIDGETT, REV. T. E. (C.SS.R.), Edited by.
    Suppliant of the Holy Ghost: a Paraphrase of the 'Veni Sancte Spiritus.' Now first printed from a MS. of the seventeenth century composed by Rev. R. Johnson, with other unpublished treatises by the same author. Second edition. Cloth . .   0 1 6

CASWALL, FATHER.

Catholic Latin Instructor in the Principal Church Offices and Devotions, for the Use of Choirs, Convents, and Mission Schools, and for Self-Teaching. 1 vol., complete £0 3 6

Or Part I., containing Benediction, Mass, Serving at do., various Latin Prayers in ordinary use . . 0 1 6

(A Poem) May Pageant : A Tale of Tintern. Second edition 0 2 0

Words of Jesus (Verba Verbi). Cloth . . . 0 2 0

Poems 0 5 0

Lyra Catholica, containing all the Breviary and Missal Hymns, with others from various sources. 32mo, cloth, red edges 0 2 6

CISNEROS (GARCIAS).

Book of Spiritual Exercises and Directory for Canonical Hours 0 5 0

COLERIDGE, REV. H. J. (S.J.)

Life and Letters of St. Francis Xavier. (Quarterly Series.) 2 vols. Fourth edition 0 15 0
    Popular edition, 1 vol. 0 9 0

Life of our Life : the Harmony of the Gospels. Arranged with Introductory and Explanatory Chapters, Notes, and Indices. (Quarterly Series.) 2 vols. . 0 15 0

Public Life of Our Lord Jesus Christ. (Quarterly Series.) 8 vols. already published . . each 0 6 6

Vol. 1. The Ministry of St. John Baptist.
Vol. 2. The Preaching of the Beatitudes.
Vol. 3. The Sermon on the Mount (*to the end of the Lord's Prayer*).
Vol. 4. The Sermon on the Mount (*concluded*).
Vol. 5. The Training of the Apostles (Part I.)
Vol. 6. The Training of the Apostles (Part II.)
Vol. 7. The Training of the Apostles (Part III.)
Vol. 8. The Training of the Apostles (Part IV.)

⁎ Other Volumes in Preparation.

"It is needless to praise the matter of such a work, and the manner of its performance is admirable."—*Cork Examiner*.

"No Catholic can peruse the book without feeling how large is the measure of gratitude due to the richly-endowed intellect which has given a contribution so noble to our standard Catholic literature."—*Freeman*.

The Sermon on the Mount. Three vols. (the second, third, and fourth vols. of the above bound up separately, for convenience of purchasers. (Quarterly Series) 0 15 0

COLERIDGE, REV. H. J. (S.J.)—continued.

Life and Letters of St. Teresa. Vol. I. (Quarterly Series) £0 7 0

"Father Coleridge states that he is anxious to enlarge the knowledge of St. Teresa among English readers, as well on other grounds, as because a large number of English Catholic ladies in the days of persecution found a home in the communities of her Order abroad, established by their own countrywomen. He has made much use of the labours of Mr. David Lewis, whose translation of the Life of St. Teresa of Jesu, written by herself, was published eleven years ago."—*Tablet.*

Prisoners of the King, a Book of Thoughts on the Doctrine of Purgatory. New edition . . . 0 5 0

The Return of the King, Discourses on the Latter Days. (Quarterly Series) 0 7 6

"No one can read this book without having the horizon of his mind widened, and his sense deepened of the meaning to be attached to the words of our Lord, describing the last days of our present world."—*Catholic Times.*

The Works and Words of our Saviour, gathered from the Four Gospels. Cloth 0 7 6

"No English work that we know of is better calculated to beget in the mind a love of the Gospels, and a relish for further and deeper study of their beauties."—*Dublin Review.*

The Chronicle of St. Anthony of Padua, the "Eldest Son of St. Francis" 0 3 6

Dialogues of St. Gregory the Great. An old English Version 0 6 0

History of the Sacred Passion. By Palma. Third edition. Cloth 0 5 0

The Life of Mary Ward. By Mary Catherine Elizabeth Chambers, of the Institute of the Blessed Virgin. (Quarterly Series.) 2 vols., each 0 7 6

The Baptism of the King. Considerations on the Sacred Passion. (Quarterly Series) . . . 0 7 6

Preparation of the Incarnation (Holy Infancy Series, Vol. I.) 0 7 6

The Nine Months. The Life of our Lord in the Womb. (Holy Infancy Series, Vol. II. Vol. III. ready shortly) 0 7 6

COMPARISON BETWEEN THE HISTORY OF
the Church and the Prophecies of the Apocalypse . 0 2 0

DARRAS.
History of the Church. From the French. A General History of the Catholic Church from the commencement of the Christian Era until the Present Time. By M. l'Abbé J. E. Darras. With an Introduction and Notes by the Most Rev. M. J. Spalding, D.D., Archbishop of Baltimore. 4 vols. 4to . . . £2 8 0

DEHARBE (S.J.)
A History of Religion, or the Evidences for the Divinity of the Christian Religion, as furnished by its History from the Creation of the World to our own Times. Designed as a Help to Catechetical Instruction in Schools and Churches. Pp. 628 . . . . reduced to net 0 8 6

DUPONT, THE LIFE OF LÉON PAPIN, THE
Holy Man of Tours; being Vol. VIII. of the "Library of Religious Biography," edited by Edward Healy Thompson, M.A. This work is not a Translation, but has been composed, after a careful study of the Abbé Janvier's full and complete Life of the Holy Man, and that of M. Léon Aubineau. Cloth 0 6 0

"It is an original compilation, written in that well-known style of devout suggestiveness and literary excellence which characterise the writer's former volumes of religious biography."—*Dublin Review.*

FABER, VERY REV. FATHER.
All for Jesus 0 5 0
Bethlehem 0 7 0
Blessed Sacraments 0 7 6
Creator and Creature 0 6 0
Ethel's Book of the Angels 0 2 6
Foot of the Cross 0 6 0
Growth in Holiness 0 6 0
Hymns 0 6 0
Notes on Doctrinal and Spiritual Subjects, 2 vols. each 0 5 0
Poems 0 5 0
Precious Blood 0 5 0
Spiritual Conferences 0 6 0
Life and Letters of Frederick William Faber, D.D., Priest of the Oratory of St. Philip Neri. By John Edward Bowden of the same Congregation . . 0 6 0

FOLEY, HENRY (S.J.)
Records of the English Province of the Society of
Jesus. Vol. I., Series I. Demy 8vo, 720 pp. net £1 6 0
Vol. II., Series II., III. IV. Demy 8vo, 622 pp. net 1 6 0
Vol. III., Series V., VI., VII., VIII. Demy 8vo, over
850 pp. . . . . net 1 10 0
Vol. IV., Series IX., X., XI. Demy 8vo, 750 pp. net 1 6 0
Vol. V., Series XII. Demy 8vo, nearly 1100 pp., with
nine Photographs of Martyrs . . . . net 1 10 0
Vol. VI., Diary and Pilgrim-Book of the English College, Rome. The Diary from 1579 to 1773, with Biographical and Historical Notes. The Pilgrim-Book of the ancient English Hospice attached to the College from 1580 to 1656, with Historical Notes. Demy 8vo, pp. 796 . . . . . net 1 6 0
Vol. VII. Part the First: General Statistics of the Province; and Collectanea, giving Biographical Notices of its Members and of many Irish and Scotch Jesuits. With 20 Photographs . . . . . net 1 6 0
Vol. VII. Part the Second: Collectanea Completed; With Appendices. Catalogues of Assumed and Real Names; Annual Letters; Biographies and Miscellanea . . . . net 1 6 0

"As a biographical dictionary of English Jesuits, it deserves a place in every well-selected library, and, as a collection of marvellous occurrences, persecutions, martyrdoms, and evidences of the results of faith, amongst the books of all who belong to the Catholic Church."—*Genealogist*.

FRANCIS DE SALES, ST.: THE WORKS OF.
Translated into the English Language by the Rev.
H. B. Mackey, O.S.B. Vol. I. Letters to Persons
in the World. Cloth 0 6 0

"The letters must be read in order to comprehend the charm and sweetness of their style."—*Tablet*.
"The task of translation has been undertaken with a loving and scrupulous care, and is, on the whole, very successfully done."—*Dublin Review*.

Vol. II. On the Love of God. Founded on the
rare and practically unknown English Translation,
of which the title-page is as follows: A Treatise
of the Love of God, written in French by B. Francis
de Sales, Bishop of Geneva, and translated into
English by Miles Car, Priest of the English College
of Doway. 1630 . . . . 0 9 0
Vol. III. The Catholic Controversy. (In the Press.)
Devout Life 0 1 6

FRANCIS DE SALES, ST.: Works of—continued.

Manual of Practical Piety	£0	3	6
Spiritual Combat. A new and careful Translation. 18mo, cloth	0	3	0
The same, pocket size, cloth	0	1	0

GALLWEY, REV. PETER (S.J.)

Precious Pearl of Hope in the Mercy of God, The. Translated from the Italian. With Preface by the Rev. Father Gallwey. Cloth	0	4	6
Ritualism: Lecture I., Introductory	0	0	4
2. Is the Blessing of Heaven on Ritualism?	0	0	4
3. The Sanctity of the Ritualistic Clergy	0	0	4
4. Are Ritualists Protestants or Catholics? (extra size)	0	0	6
5. Ritualism and St. Peter's Mission as revealed in Holy Writ (double size)	0	0	8
6. Do Ritualists owe Obedience to their Directors? Do the Anglican Clergy hold the Place of Christ?	0	0	4
7. Ritualism and the Early Church. The Faith of St. Leo the Great	0	0	6
8. The Faith of the English Church Union, A.D. 1878; of Clewer, A.D. 1878; of the Council of Ephesus, A.D. 431	0	0	6
9. Anglican Orders. Part I.	0	0	4
10. Anglican Orders. Part II.	0	1	0
11. Anglican Orders. Part III.	0	0	8
12. Anglican Clergy in the Confessional	0	0	6
All the above bound in 2 vols. . . . net	0	8	0

GIBSON, REV. H.

Catechism Made Easy. Being an Explanation of the Christian Doctrine. 2 vols., cloth	0	7	6

"This work must be of priceless worth to any who are engaged in any form of catechetical instruction. It is the best book of the kind that we have seen in English."—*Irish Monthly.*

HERGENRÖTHER, DR.

Catholic Church and Christian State. On the Relation of the Church to the Civil Power. From the German. 2 vols., paper	1	1	0

HUMPHREY, REV. F.

The Divine Teacher: A Letter to a Friend. With a Preface in Reply to No. 3 of the English Church Defence Tracts, entitled "Papal Infallibility." Fifth edition. Cloth £0 2 6
    Sixth edition. Wrapper 0 1 0
Mary Magnifying God. May Sermons. Fifth edition . 0 2 6
Other Gospels; or, Lectures on St. Paul's Epistle to the Galatians. Crown 8vo, cloth . . . 0 4 0
The Written Word; or, Considerations on the Sacred Scriptures 0 5 0
Mr. Fitzjames Stephen and Cardinal Bellarmine . . 0 1 0
Suarez on the Religious State: A Digest of the Doctrine contained in his Treatise, "De Statû Religionis." 3 vols., pp. 1200. Cloth, roy. 8vo . . . 1 10 0

LIGUORI, ST. ALPHONSO.

New and Improved Translation of the Complete Works of St. Alphonso, edited by the late Bishop Coffin :—
Vol. I. The Christian Virtues, and the Means for Obtaining them. Cloth elegant 0 4 0
Or separately :—
    1. The Love of our Lord Jesus Christ . . . 0 1 4
    2. Treatise on Prayer. (*In the ordinary editions a great part of this work is omitted*) . . 0 1 4
    3. A Christian's Rule of Life 0 1 0
Vol. II. The Mysteries of the Faith—The Incarnation; containing Meditations and Devotions on the Birth and Infancy of Jesus Christ, &c., suited for Advent and Christmas 0 3 6
    Cheap edition 0 2 0
Vol. III. The Mysteries of the Faith—The Blessed Sacrament 0 3 6
    Cheap edition 0 2 0
Vol. IV. Eternal Truths—Preparation for Death . 0 3 6
    Cheap edition 0 2 0
Vol. V. Treatises on the Passion, containing "Jesus hath loved us," &c. 0 3 0
    Cheap edition 0 2 0
Vol. VI. Glories of Mary. New edition . . 0 3 6
With Frontispiece, cloth 0 4 6
    Also in better bindings.

MANNING, HIS EMINENCE CARDINAL.

Blessed Sacrament the Centre of Immutable Truth. A new and revised edition. Cloth 0 1 0
Confidence in God. Third edition 0 1 0
England and Christendom 0 10 6

MANNING, HIS EMINENCE CARDINAL—continued.

Eternal Priesthood. Cloth. Popular edition	£0	2	6
Four Great Evils of the Day. Fourth edition. Paper	0	2	6
Cloth	0	3	6
Fourfold Sovereignty of God. Second edition	0	2	6
Cloth	0	3	6
Glories of the Sacred Heart. Fourth edition	0	6	0
Grounds of Faith. Seventh edition. Cloth	0	1	6
Holy Gospel of our Lord Jesus Christ according to St. John. With a Preface by His Eminence	0	1	0
Independence of the Holy See	0	5	0
Internal Mission of the Holy Ghost. Fourth edition	0	8	6
Love of Jesus to Penitents. Seventh edition	0	1	6
Miscellanies. 2 vols.	0	15	0
Office of the Holy Ghost under the Gospel	0	1	0
Petri Privilegium	0	10	6
Praise, A Sermon on; with an Indulgenced Devotion	0	1	0
Sermons on Ecclesiastical Subjects. Vols. I., II., and III. each	0	6	0
Sin and its Consequences. Fifth edition	0	6	0
Temporal Mission of the Holy Ghost. Third edition	0	8	6
Temporal Power of the Pope. New edition	0	5	0
The Office of the Holy Ghost under the Gospel	0	1	0
True Story of the Vatican Council	0	5	0

MANNING, HIS EMINENCE CARDINAL, Edited by.

Life of the Curé of Ars. New edition, enlarged	0	4	0

MIVART, PROF. ST. GEORGE (M.D., F.R.S.).

Nature and Thought. Second edition	0	4	0

"The complete command of the subject, the wide grasp, the subtlety, the readiness of illustration, the grace of style, contrive to render this one of the most admirable books of its class."—*British Quarterly Review.*

A Philosophical Catechism. Fifth edition	0	1	0

"It should become the *vade mecum* of Catholic students."—*Tablet.*

MORRIS, REV. JOHN (S.J.)

Letter Books of Sir Amias Poulet, Keeper of Mary Queen of Scots. Demy 8vo	0	10	6
Troubles of our Catholic Forefathers, related by themselves. Second Series. 8vo, cloth	0	14	0
Third Series	0	14	0
The Life of Father John Gerard, S.J. Third edition, rewritten and enlarged	0	14	0
The Life and Martyrdom of St. Thomas Becket. Second and enlarged edition. In one volume, large post 8vo, cloth, pp. xxxvi., 632, price 12s. 6d.; or bound in two parts, cloth, price	0	13	0

NEWMAN, CARDINAL.

Annotated Translation of Athanasius. 2 vols. . each	£0	7	6
Apologia pro Vitâ suâ	0	6	0
Arians of the Fourth Century, The . . .	0	6	0
Callista : An Historical Tale. New edition . .	0	5	6
Difficulties of Anglicans. Two volumes—			
Vol. I. Twelve Lectures	0	7	6
Vol. II. Letters to Dr. Pusey and to the Duke of Norfolk	0	5	6
Discussions and Arguments	0	6	0
Doctrine of Justification	0	5	0
Dream of Gerontius. Twentieth edition, wrapper .	0	0	6
Cloth	0	1	0
Essay on Assent	0	7	6
Essay on the Development of Christian Doctrine .	0	6	0
Essays Critical and Historical. Two volumes, with Notes . . . . each	0	6	0
Essays on Miracles, Two. 1. Of Scripture. 2. Of Ecclesiastical History	0	6	0
Historical Sketches. Three volumes . . . each	0	6	0
Idea of a University. Lectures and Essays . .	0	7	0
Loss and Gain	0	5	6
Occasional Sermons	0	6	0
Parochial and Plain Sermons. Eight volumes . each	0	5	0
Present Position of Catholics in England. New edition	0	7	0
Sermons on Subjects of the Day	0	5	0
Sermons to Mixed Congregations	0	6	0
Theological Tracts	0	8	0
University Sermons	0	5	0
Verses on Various Occasions. New edition . .	0	5	6
Via Media. Two volumes, with Notes . . each	0	6	0
Complete set of his Eminence's Works, half bound, in 36 vols. . . . . net	14	0	0
Newman, Cardinal, with Notes on the Oxford Movement and its Men. By John Oldcastle. Third edition, illustrated. Cloth, crown 8vo . . .	0	2	6

NORTHCOTE, VERY REV. J. S. (D.D.)

Roma Sotterranea ; or, An Account of the Roman Catacombs. New edition. Re-written and greatly enlarged. This work is in three volumes, which may at present be had separately—

Vol. I. History	1	4	0

NORTHCOTE, VERY REV. J. S. (D.D.)—*continued.*
Vol. II. Christian Art £1 4 0
   III. Epitaphs of the Catacombs . . . 0 10 0
The Second and Third Volumes may also be had
   bound together in cloth 1 12 0
Visit to Louise Lateau. Written in conjunction with
   Dr. Lefebvre of Louvain 0 3 6
Visit to the Roman Catacombs: Being a popular
   abridgment of the larger work. . . . 0 4 0

QUARTERLY SERIES (Edited by the Managers of the "Month").
N.B.—*Those printed in Italics are out of print, but may be reprinted.*

Baptism of the King: Considerations on the Sacred
   Passion. By the Rev. H. J. Coleridge, S.J. . . 0 7 6
Christian Reformed in Mind and Manners, The. By
   Benedict Rogacci, of the Society of Jesus. The
   Translation edited by the Rev. H. J. Coleridge, S.J. 0 7 6
Chronicles of St. Antony of Padua, the "Eldest Son
   of St. Francis." Edited by the Rev. H. J. Coleridge, S.J. 0 3 6
Colombière, Life of the Ven. Claude de la . . . 0 5 0
Dialogues of St. Gregory the Great: an Old English
   Version. Edited by the Rev. H. J. Coleridge, S.J. . 0 6 0
English Carmelite, An. The Life of Catherine Burton,
   Mother Mary Xaveria of the Angels, of the English
   Teresian Convent at Antwerp. Collected from her
   own Writings, and other sources, by Father Thomas
   Hunter, S.J. 0 6 6
Gaston de Ségur. A Biography. Condensed from
   the French Memoir by the Marquis de Ségur, by
   F. J. M. A. Partridge 0 3 6
Gracious Life, A (1566-1618); being the Life of
   Madame Acarie (Blessed Mary of the Incarnation),
   of the Reformed Order of our Blessed Lady of
   Mount Carmel. By Emily Bowles 0 6 0
History of the Sacred Passion. By Father Luis de la
   Palma, of the Society of Jesus. Translated from
   the Spanish. With Preface by the Rev. H. J.
   Coleridge, S.J. Third edition . . . 0 5 0
*Ierne of Armorica: a Tale of the Time of Chlovis. By
   J. C. Bateman* 0 6 6

QUARTERLY SERIES—*continued.*

Life and Teaching of Jesus Christ, in Meditations for every Day in the Year. By P. N. Avancino, S.J. 2 vols.	£0 10	6
Life and Letters of St. Francis Xavier. By the Rev. H. J. Coleridge, S.J. 2 vols.	0 15	0
Cheap edition. 2 vols. in one	0 9	0
Life of Anne Catharine Emmerich. By Helen Ram. With Preface by the Rev. H. J. Coleridge, S.J.	0 5	0
Life of Christopher Columbus. By the Rev. A. G. Knight, S.J.	0 6	0
Life of Henrietta d'Osseville (in Religion, Mother Ste. Marie), Foundress of the Institute of the Faithful Virgin. Arranged and Edited by the Rev. John George M'Leod, S.J.	0 5	6
Life of Margaret Mostyn (Mother Margaret of Jesus), Religious of the Reformed Order of our Blessed Lady of Mount Carmel (1625–1679). By the Very Rev. Edmund Bedingfield, Canon of the Collegiate Church of St. Gomar, and Confessor to the English Teresians at Lierre. Edited from the Manuscripts preserved at Darlington, by the Rev. H. J. Coleridge, S.J.	0 6	0
Life of our Life: The Harmony of the Gospel, arranged with Introductory and Explanatory Chapters, Notes, and Indices. By the Rev. H. J. Coleridge, S.J. 2 vols.	0 15	0
Life of Pope Pius the Seventh. By Mary H. Allies	0 6	6
Life of St. Jane Frances Fremyot de Chantal. By Emily Bowles. With Preface by the Rev. H. J. Coleridge, S.J. Second edition	0 5	6
Life of the Blessed John Berchmans. Third edition. By the Rev. F. Goldie, S.J.	0 6	0
Life of the Blessed Peter Favre, First Companion of St. Ignatius Loyola. From the Italian of Father Boero. With Preface by the Rev. H. J. Coleridge, S.J.	0 6	0
Life of King Alfred the Great. By A. G. Knight. Book I. Early Promise; II. Adversity; III. Prosperity; IV. Close of Life. 1 vol. 8vo, pp. 325	0 6	0
Life of Mother Mary Teresa Ball. By Rev. H. J. Coleridge, S.J. With Portrait	0 6	6
Life and Letters of St. Teresa. Vol. I. By Rev. H. J. Coleridge, S.J.	0 7	6

QUARTERLY SERIES—continued.

Life of Mary Ward. By Mary Catherine Elizabeth Chambers, of the Institute of the Blessed Virgin. Edited by the Rev. H. J. Coleridge, S.J. 2 vols., each	£0	7	6
Nine Months. The Life of our Lord in the Womb. (Holy Infancy Series, Vol. II.)	0	7	6
Of Adoration in Spirit and Truth. By the Rev. J. E. Nieremberg. S.J. Old English translation. With a Preface by the Rev. P. Gallwey, S.J. A New Edition	0	6	6
Pious Affections towards God and the Saints. Meditations for every Day in the Year, and for the Principal Festivals. From the Latin of the Ven. Nicholas Lancicius, S.J. With Preface by George Porter, S.J.	0	7	6
Preparation of the Incarnation. By the Rev. H. J. Coleridge, S.J. (Holy Infancy Series, Vol. I.)	0	7	6
Prisoners of the Temple; or, Discrowned and Crowned. By M. O'C. Morris. With Preface by the Rev. H. J. Coleridge, S.J.	0	4	6
Public Life of our Lord Jesus Christ. By the Rev. H. J. Coleridge, S.J. 8 vols. . . . each Others in preparation.	0	6	6
Return of the King. Discourses on the Latter Days. By the Rev. H. J. Coleridge, S.J.	0	7	6
Story of St. Stanislaus Kostka. With Preface by the Rev. H. J. Coleridge, S.J.	0	3	6
Story of the Gospels, harmonised for meditation. By the Rev. H. J. Coleridge, S.J.	0	7	6
Sufferings of the Church in Brittany during the Great Revolution. By Edward Healy Thompson, M.A.	0	6	6
Suppression of the Society of Jesus in the Portuguese Dominions. From Documents hitherto unpublished. By the Rev. Alfred Weld, S.J.	0	7	6
[This volume forms the First Part of the General History of the Suppression of the Society.]			
Three Catholic Reformers of the Fifteenth Century. By Mary H. Allies	0	6	0
Thomas of Hereford, Life of St. By Fr. Lestrange	0	6	0
Tribunal of Conscience, The. By Father Gaspar Druzbicki, S.J.	0	3	6
Works and Words of our Saviour, gathered from the Four Gospels. By the Rev. H. J. Coleridge, S.J.	0	7	6

RAWES, THE LATE REV. Fr., Edited by.

The Library of the Holy Ghost:—

Vol. I. St. Thomas Aquinas on the Adorable Sacrament of the Altar. With Prayers and Thanksgivings for Holy Communion. Red cloth	0	5	0

Little Books of the Holy Ghost:—

Book 1. St. Thomas Aquinas on the Commandments, 32mo, 233 pp. Cloth gilt	0	2	0

RAWES, THE LATE REV. Fr., Edited by—*continued.*

Little Books of the Holy Ghost:—

Book 2. Little Handbook of the Archconfraternity of the Holy Ghost. Fourth edition, 111 pp.	£0	1	6
Gilt	0	1	2
Book 3. St. Thomas Aquinas on the Lord's Prayer. 139 pp.	0	1	0
Cloth gilt	0	1	3
Book 4. The Holy Ghost the Sanctifier. By Cardinal Manning. 213 pp. . . . 1s. 6d. and	0	2	0

RICHARDS, REV. WALTER J. B. (D.D.)

Manual of Scripture History. Being an Analysis of the Historical Books of the Old Testament. By the Rev W. J. B. Richards, D.D., Oblate of St. Charles; Inspector of Schools in the Diocese of Westminster.

Part I., 2 maps. Second edition .	0	1	0
Part II., „	0	1	0
Part III., „	0	1	0
Part IV.	0	1	0
Or, the Four Parts bound together. Cloth	0	4	0

"Happy indeed will those children and young persons be who acquire in their early days the inestimably precious knowledge which these books impart."—*Tablet.*

"The 'Manuals' we cordially recommend to schools and colleges in the preparation of the subject of Scripture History."—*Dublin Review.*

RYDER, REV. H. I. D.

Catholic Controversy: A Reply to Dr. Littledale's "Plain Reasons." Fifth edition	0	2	6

"Father Ryder, of the Birmingham Oratory, has now furnished in a small volume a masterly reply to this assailant from without. It will chiefly be useful as an antidote to Dr. Littledale's insidious misrepresentations of Catholic doctrine, and will, with God's blessing, do vast good amongst those for whom it is intended. The lighter charms of a brilliant and graceful style are added to the solid merits of this handbook of contemporary controversy."—*Irish Monthly.*

ULLATHORNE, BISHOP.

Endowments of Man, &c. New and revised edition	0	10	6
Groundwork of the Christian Virtues: A Course of Lectures	0	10	6

"We do not hesitate to say that by the publication of the discourses Dr. Ullathorne has conferred a boon, not only on the members of his own communion, but on all serious and thinking Englishmen. The treatment of the whole subject is masterly and exhaustive."—*Liverpool Daily Post.*

"A good and great book by a good and great man. This eloquent series of almost oracular utterances is a gift to men of all nations, all creeds, and all moral systems."—*The British Mail.*

www.ingramcontent.com/pod-product-compliance
Lightning Source LLC
Chambersburg PA
CBHW020738020526
44115CB00030B/162